I0345265

SHIʿISM IN KASHMIR

Islamic South Asia Series

Series Editor Ruby Lal, Emory University

Advisory Board
Iftikhar Dadi, Cornell University
Stephen F. Dale, Ohio State University
Rukhsana David, Kinnaird College for Women
Michael Fisher, Oberlin College
Marcus Fraser, Fitzwilliam Museum
Ebba Koch, University of Vienna
David Lewis, London School of Economics
Francis Robinson, Royal Holloway, University of London
Ron Sela, Indiana University Bloomington
Willem van Schendel, University of Amsterdam

Titles

Sexual and Gender Diversity in the Muslim World: History, Law and Vernacular Knowledge, Vanja Hamzic
The Architecture of a Deccan Sultanate: Courtly Practice and Royal Authority in Late Medieval India, Pushkar Sohoni
Sufi Shrines and the Pakistani State: The End of Religious Pluralism, Umber Bin Ibad
The Hindu Sufis of South Asia: Partition, Shrine Culture and the Sindhis in India, Michel Boivin
Islamic Sermons and Public Piety in Bangladesh: The Poetics of Popular Preaching, Max Stille
The Mosques of Colonial South Asia: A Social and Legal History of Muslim Worship, Sana Haroon
The Language of the Taj Mahal: Islam, Prayer and the Religion of Shah Jahan, Michael D. Calabria
Muslims under Sikh Rule in the Nineteenth Century, Robina Yasmin
Shi'ism in Kashmir: A History of Sunni-Shi'i Rivalry and Reconciliation, Sameer Hamdani

SHIʿISM IN KASHMIR

A History of Sunni-Shiʿi Rivalry and Reconciliation

Hakim Sameer Hamdani

I.B.TAURIS
LONDON • NEW YORK • OXFORD • NEW DELHI • SYDNEY

I.B. TAURIS
Bloomsbury Publishing Plc
50 Bedford Square, London, WC1B 3DP, UK
1385 Broadway, New York, NY 10018, USA
29 Earlsfort Terrace, Dublin 2, Ireland

BLOOMSBURY, I.B. TAURIS and the I.B. Tauris logo are trademarks of Bloomsbury Publishing Plc

First published in Great Britain 2023
This paperback edition published in 2024

For legal purposes the Acknowledgements on p. xi constitute an extension of this copyright page.

Series design by Adriana Brioso
Cover image: Women devotees at a shrine in Hasanabad on Shab-i Barat, Srinagar, 2016. Courtesy of Syed Shahriyar.

A catalogue record for this book is available from the British Library.

A catalog record for this book is available from the Library of Congress.

ISBN: PB: 978-0-7556-4394-3
ePDF: 978-0-7556-4395-0
eBook: 978-0-7556-4396-7

Series: Islamic South Asia

Typeset by Deanta Global Publishing Services, Chennai, India

To my daughter, Parirou, and the children of Kashmir,
may your world be full of nūr, omid, *and* khūshī

O Friend of the Believers, only guide to their salvation,
Muslims and Hindus, both your worshippers, your creation.
O One without a partner, our only sovereign, no sect could keep you to itself;
confined to a temple, limited to a sacred mosque.

Mullā Ḥakim ʿAbdullah (d. 1887, approx.),
Kashmiri *marṣiya:* ***Valī al- Mūminin*** (Friend of the Believers)

CONTENTS

List of Figures ix
Acknowledgments xi
Conventions xiii

INTRODUCTION 1
The Long Nineteenth Century 5
Sources and Structure 8

Chapter 1
NOT QUITE TAQIYYA: KASHMIRI SHIʿI AT THE START OF THE NINETEENTH CENTURY 11
The Fear of *Rāfz* 13
The Claim of Being First Muslims 17
Two Saints, Two Sects 20
Chaks: The *Pādshāhs* of Kashmir 27

Chapter 2
MAPPING EXISTENCE: IN SEARCH OF PATRONAGE AND PROTECTION 37
Navigating Shiʿiness under the Afghans 37
Tājiran-i Iran: Iranian Shawl Merchants in Kashmir 41
In the Court of Awadh Kings 48
Loss of Muslim Sovereignty 53

Chapter 3
SHIʿI IDENTITY, SUNNI SPACE, AND NON-MUSLIM RULE 59
Vocalizing a Community: Mourning and *Marṣiya* 59
The Ashura Procession and the Riots of 1830 66
The City Elders and a *Shahr-ashūb* 70
The Royal Physician and the Well-Wishing Merchant 77

Chapter 4
DISSENSIONS WITHIN THE *MŪMININ*: CHALLENGING THE ELITE 89
Controlling the Muharram Ceremonies 89
The Issue of *Khums* 93
The Last Riot: 1289 AH/1872 CE 97
Rival Families, Rival Grouping 107

Chapter 5
MOVING TOWARD A UNIFIED MUSLIM IDENTITY 119
At the Start of a New Century 119
Phyīr Circuit, the Annual Trade Journey to the Plains 126
Chaat-i haal, Papier-Maché, and a New Class of Shiʿi Merchants 132
Challenges of Modernity: Missionaries and Education 138
The *Anjuman*, A Murder Case and Call to Reform 141
Memorandum of the Kashmiri *Mussalmans* and a Muslim Ashura 151
Kashmiri Shiʿi and the Recent Past: Overview 156

Appendix I: Letter of Ḥakim ʿAẕim, written to Moulvi Sayyid Rajab ʿAli Shāh 161
Appendix II: Groans of the Muslims of Kashmir 164
Notes 167
Bibliography 203
Index 213

FIGURES

1 General map (courtesy: Hakim Ali Reza) xiv
1.1 *M'ārak, imāmbāda* at Zadibal prior to its dismantling, Srinagar, 2004 (courtesy: Mubashir Mir) 12
1.2 Shaykh Ḥamza Makhdūm, SPS Museum collection, Srinagar, 2022 (author) 21
1.3 Shaykh Ḥamza Makhdūm shrine-precinct, Srinagar, 2019 (courtesy: Mukhtar Ahmad) 35
2.1 Wall hanging commissioned for Imām Ḥusayn shrine (courtesy: The Metropolitan Museum of Art, New York) 47
2.2 Ruins of Mughal Mosque at Hasanabad, early twentieth century (courtesy: ASI, India) 56
3.1 Kashmiri *marṣiya biyāz* dated 1143 AH (1730 CE), Research Library, Srinagar (author) 61
3.2 Performance of *marṣiya* at a *majlis* at *M'ārak*, Srinagar, 2015 (courtesy: Imran Ali) 63
3.3 Srinagar city, nineteenth century with location of major sites and Shi'i neighborhoods (author) 68
3.4 Calligraphy written by Shāh Niyaẕ for William Moorcroft (courtesy: British Library) 76
3.5 Epistle of Ḥakim 'Aẕim to Moulvi Sayyid Rajab 'Ali (author) 79
3.6 Muharram procession in contemporary Kashmir, Srinagar, 2018 (courtesy: Hammad Ali) 85
4.1 Shrine of Sayyid Muhammad Madnī, Srinagar, 2019 (courtesy: Zubair Ahmad) 100
4.2 Kashmir, location of major towns and Shi'i-inhabited areas (author) 110
4.3 Moulvi Ḥaidar 'Ali Ansarī with the royal physician, Ḥakim Ḥasan 'Ali, early twentieth century, Srinagar (courtesy: Hakim Athar Hussain) 111
4.4 *Imāmbāda Hasanabad*, twentieth-century reconstruction, Srinagar, 2015 (author) 114
4.5 Members of the Mullā family, Srinagar, late 1890s (courtesy: Hakim Shaukat Ali Hamdani) 115
5.1 *Divān* of Ḥafiẓ Shirazī, copied by Mullā Muhammad Qāsim Hamdanī, 1796 (courtesy: Walter Art Museum, Maryland) 122
5.2 Quran codex, copied by Munshi Abū'l Ḥasan, 1851 (courtesy: Yasmin Ali) 123
5.3 Muharram procession in the interiors of Dal Lake, Srinagar, 2021 (courtesy: Sayed Shahriyar) 127

5.4 A papier-mâché *chaat-i haal* in nineteenth-century Srinagar (courtesy: British Library) 133
5.5 Āgā Sayyid Muhammad, early twentieth-century Budgam (courtesy: Zulfikar Ali) 141
5.6 Masjid-i Ḥājjī ʿAidī at Zadibal (courtesy: Zulfikar Ali) 144
5.7 A meeting of *Anjuman-i Imāmmia* presided by Nawab Fateh ʿAli Khān, Srinagar, 1922 (courtesy: Hakim Shaukat Ali Hamdani) 155

ACKNOWLEDGMENTS

Most, if not all, of the draft of this book was finalized during my fellowship with Aga Khan Program in Islamic Architecture (AKPIA) at MIT. Thanks are due to Nasser Rabbat for supporting my academic pursuits at the program. I would also like to thank all my colleagues at MIT, especially Nur Sobers-Khan and Matt Saba for their help in sourcing the vast collection of Aga Khan Documentation Center (AKDC). Also at Cambridge, I would like to thank Wheeler Thackston for his help with the translation of some of the dense Persian texts. Thanks are also due to Navina Haidar at the Met Museum, New York, Zahoor Ahmad Asmi at Research Library, Srinagar, Stephan Poop at the Institute for Iranian Studies, Austria, and Hakim Ali Reza at Politecnio di Milano.

I would like to acknowledge the help I received from Sayyid Mohsin Kashmiri and Moulvi Hakim Sajad with some of the Persian texts. Mohsin as one of the founding members of *Markaz Ihya-i Asar-i Bar-i Saghir* (MAAB) is at the forefront of mapping and documenting the cultural heritage of South Asian Shiʿi and has been kind enough to source and share some significant manuscripts related to the events recorded in this book. A special thanks is owed to a dear friend and colleague, Mehran Qureshi. Despite the time difference between Cambridge and Srinagar, he has always been there, helping in reading and translating passages which at times seemed undecipherable. The writing of this book has been enriched by his shared thoughts and, also, the initial editing.

At Srinagar, I would also like to thank Aga Sayyid Baqir, Amjad Ansari, Hakim Imtiyaz Hussein, Sheikh Muhammad Shafi, Saleem Beg, Imdad Saqi, Maqbool Sajid, Faizaan Bhat and Zulfikar Ali and all those who shared their memories of the past and hope for the future.

Working with I.B. Tauris has been a pleasure, and I would like to thank my editors Sophie Rudland and Yasmin Garcha for their patience and bearing with me despite all the delays on my part.

Lastly to my family, for all your unconditional support and patience, *shukriya*.

Cambridge, MA
2022

CONVENTIONS

Arabic and Persian transliterations follow a modified system based on the standard of the *International Journal of Middle East Studies* (IJMES). Kashmiri transliterations are largely based on the same convention. The use of diacritical mark for non-English words has been kept to a minimum and reserved for cases when no common transliteration in English language text is available. Also, for some names I have avoided the use of diacritical marks like Muhammad and not Muḥammad, Mahdi instead of Mahdī. Similar convention has been followed for public figures in the post-1947 period. The use of diacritical marks for name of places has been avoided.

This work includes translation of primary sources from Persian, Urdu, and Kashmiri. While I have taken some freedom with the translation, it has been my attempt throughout to remain true to the original context of the translated texts. Translations in the book which are sourced are acknowledged in the endnotes.

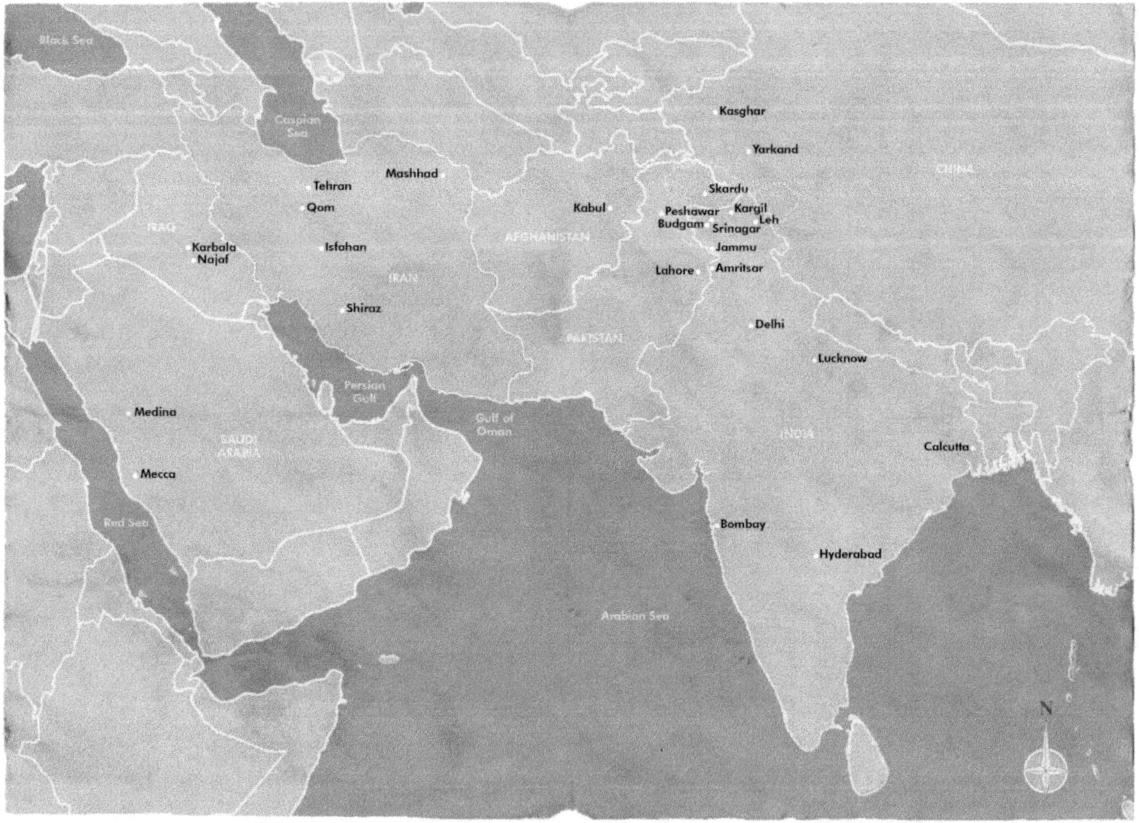

Fig 1 General map (courtesy: Hakim Ali Reza).

INTRODUCTION

In the vernacular traditions of Kashmir expressed primarily through oral narrations, we find that a report about an individual, society, or a historical event is often prefixed with a singular introductory word, *dapān*—it is said. In the *dapān* tradition, the narrator never claims to be the witness to the actual event, he is only vocalizing something that has been witnessed. *Dapān* not only absolves the narrator from the charge of fabrication, but it also seeks to satisfy the listener's demand for authenticity by indicating the presence of unnamed chain of narrators. Acting as a self-legitimizing, self-authenticating leitmotif, *dapān* maneuvers through the world of rumors, myths, and fables into a manufactured reality. And, while the *dapān* tradition originates in the realm of folklore, it can and does authenticate myths and legends that constitute both the memory of the past and often its remembered history. In the *dapān* traditions that originate within Kashmiri Sunni circles, it is said that in a forgotten past, the Kashmiri Shiʿi used to seek a Sunni youth, prick his body with the *yandir-i sitzhen* (tip of spindle),[1] draw blood, and kill. A similar claim about another such gory encounter between the Shiʿi and Sunnis of Kashmir finds mention in the travelogue of a European traveler, GT Vigne, who visited Kashmir in 1835:

> I was informed, they compelled a boy of the Suni persuasion to eat salt; then tantalized him with water; and when he was about to drink, they shot him to death with arrows, so that he might die like Husyn, in the desert of thirst. When Abdullah Khan heard of this, he ordered an attack to be made upon the Shiʿihs; their property was plundered, and their houses burned; and, collecting about one hundred and fifty (for there are very few in the city), he ordered their noses to be pierced, passed one string through them all, and thus linked together, he made them perambulate the bazaars.[2]

The testimony in Vigne's text relates to the Shiʿi-Sunni riots of 1216 AH/1801 CE, when the principal places of Shiʿi worship in Kashmir were destroyed on Ashura, one of the most revered days in the Shiʿi liturgical calendar. In Vigne's account of the riots, we see how a *dapān* tradition superimposes on the actual historical event to erase the lived reality of the past, in this case, the Shiʿi suffering at the hands of the rioters and the Sunni ruler, the Afghan *ṣubedar* (governor) ʿAbdullah Khān (1796–1805 CE).

Half a century earlier, Khwāja Muhammad A'ẕam Dedhmarī (d. 1179 AH/1765 CE) wrote his *Vāqi'āt-i Kashmīr*,[3] which can be argued to represent the summa of Kashmiri Sunni historiography, combining the narratives of a *tārīkh* (history) and a *taẕkira* (hagiography). Borrowing liberally from the polemical traditions found in earlier *taẕkiras*, especially those emanating from the circle of anti-Shi'i *Suhrawardī* master, Shaykh Ḥamza Makhdūm (d. 984 AH/1576 CE), Dedhmarī's text imagines a Sunni spiritual state which commences with the establishment of Muslim Sultanate (1320–1586) in this mountainous Himalayan land. For Dedhmarī, the original Muslim inhabitants of Kashmir are Sunnis, it is the Sunni *awliyā* (saints), *mashā'ikh* (religious scholars), and *salātin* (rulers), who transform Kashmir into a Muslim land; the arrival of the Shi'i is seen as a later development, a betrayal of the pure faith of Islam as represented by the Sunnis.

For future generations of Kashmiri Sunni historians, *Vāqi'āt-i Kashmīr* establishes the normative strictures relating to the origin and development of Muslim society in Kashmir. In foregrounding his discourse in a contested sectarian milieu, Dedhmarī portrays the Shi'is as outsiders who harmed the political and spiritual unity of the Muslim community. Though the contours of Dedhmarī's text are steeped in a Shi'i-Sunni rivalry, his own cultural background is more diverse. Hailing from the capital city of Srinagar, Dedhmarī was trained under leading *Naqshbandī* shaykhs of the city. The rise of the fortunes of the *Naqshbandīs* in Kashmir broadly coincides with the heydays of the Mughal rule (1586–1752) in the region. As a Sufi order, *Naqshbandī* influence was generated from scholarly circles in Srinagar, who during the course of the eighteenth and nineteenth century helped in establishing its reputation in the capital as a major Sufi order.[4] Though favored by Mughal emperors and their *ṣubedars* in Kashmir, the *Naqshbandīs* imbibed a narrow worldview which contrasted, and at times contested with the idea of Mughal cosmopolis in which people across ethnicities and religious persuasions who shared the Mughal sense of aesthetics were celebrated.

Dedhmarī's own training, though, is reflective of the cosmopolitan character of the city, under the Mughals. His *adab* (literature) training happened in the circles of the Shi'i poet, Mulla 'Abd al-Ḥakīm Sāṭiḥ (d. 1143 AH/1730 CE). The chronogram on the death of Sāṭiḥ compiled by Dedhmarī[5] is reflective of the fondness and respect that the historian must have felt for his old teacher and transcends the barriers of sectarian worldview that is so entrenched in the historiography of *Vaq'āt*.

Muslim presence in Kashmir dates from the thirteenth century, though the twelfth-century Sanskrit historian Kalhānā indicates that the first interaction between the court of Hindu kings of Kashmir and Muslim soldiers of hire might have taken place as early as the eleventh century during the rule of King Harsadeva (r. 1089–1101 CE).[6] Located in the northernmost part of South Asia at the intersection of transregional routes, Kashmir had historically forged cultural and political links through its northeastern border into Ladakh, Tibet, and China and on its west into Central Asia through present-day Afghanistan and down south into the Indian plains. While during the Ghaznavid invasion of North India (1001–27), Kashmir had briefly sealed the borders leading into the Indian plains, these restrictions were relaxed by the time of Harsadeva's rule.[7] In medieval Arabic sources, Muslim presence in Kashmir is indicated in the Shiʿi ḥadīth corpus of Muḥammad ibn Yaʿqūb al-Kulaynī (864–941 CE), who reports a meeting in Baghdad between the twelfth Shiʿi imam, al-Mahdī and Abū Said Hindī, a Kashmiri, who reportedly arrived in the city sometime after 264 AH/877 CE.[8] Also, in the semi-legendary accounts of *Kitāb ʿAjāib al Hind* (the Book of the Marvels of India),[9] the author Buzurg b. Shahriyar (d. 399 AH/1009 CE) describes the arrival in Kashmir of an Iraqi poet, sent from Baghdad at the request of the Hindu king of Kashmir. The poet provides the king with a translation of Islamic laws he had requested and secretly converts him to Islam.[10]

The earliest material evidence of Muslim presence in Kashmir is to be found in a series of Buddhist temples located in Alchi, Ladakh. These temples which are dated from the tenth to twelfth century represent Kashmiri craftsmanship in both the wooden ornamentation and the murals painted on the walls. Barry Flood in his seminal work on early cross cultural encounters between Hindu-Muslim in South Asia provides an insightful reading of the depiction of a male and a female figure in the Alchi temple murals wearing a specific kind of a dress matching in its style and design with *qaba*—a dress form common to Muslims of Central Asia and Eastern Iran[11]. Clearly, the paintings are indicative of a significant Muslim presence in Kashmir, which was responsible for carrying out this impressive program of iconography. The establishment of the Shāhmīrī Sultanate (1339–1561) marks the stabilization of Muslim rule in Kashmir which saw the development of a unique cultural synthesis incorporating elements from Sanskrit and Persianate worlds within an aesthetic grammar peculiar to Kashmir's geography. It was under the Shāhmīrīs that various Sufi orders originating in the Persianate world, *Kubrawī*, *Naqshbandī*, *Nūrbakhshī*, and *Suhrawardī*, were introduced into the socioreligious life of Kashmir. Representatives of an orthodox interpretation of Islam and proud of their Persianate origins, these Sufi orders established themselves in the capital city Srinagar and from their urban proximity to the court carried out their missionary activities. With their close ties to power, it was only natural that the Sufis would also get drawn into political conflict, as and when they happened, and would also seek political support in issues of religious contestations. In reaction to the cultural predilection of these non-native Sufi *silsilas* (order), around the first quarter of the fifteenth century, a local Kashmiri mystic order of the *Reshīs* evolved, which represented an assertion of Muslim-ness rooted in Kashmir's own experience of Islam, and predates the formal arrival of Sufi orders and their *khānaqāhs*.

In Kashmir, the Shiʿi-Sunni dispute originates within the politics of *khānaqāh* and the court and would result in the production of texts under the patronage of these Sufis that not only seek to establish the spiritual supremacy of a faction but also obscure the other as a heresy. The transfer of political authority from Shāhmīrīs (1339–1561), a Sunni dynasty, to the Chaks (1561–86) who adhered to the Shiʿi faith added to the play of tension and rivalry between competing Sufi orders, in which the *Nūrbakhshīs* came to represent the Shiʿi while the *Kubrawīs* and especially the *Suhrawardīs* represented the Sunnis.

By the time we arrive in the nineteenth century, works such as Dedhmarī's, *Vāqi'āt-i Kashmīr*, had effectively compartmentalized the Kashmiri Shi'i and Sunni as two distinct societies with an antagonistic past. At the start of the nineteenth century, it was from Dedhmarī's historiography that Kashmiri Sunni society inherited a textual understanding of who they were and how a Kashmiri Muslim society came into formation. While in his portrayal of Shi'i, Dedhmarī assumes a stringent polemical approach, Abu'l Qāsim Muhammad Aslam a near contemporary, who wrote a brief history of Kashmir under the title *Gowhar-i 'Ālam* (c.1776) adopts a more nuanced and conciliatory tone toward the Shi'i, while adhering to the underlying narrative of Sunni persecution under the Chak Sultans. Aslam address the Shi'i sect as *Firqa-i Imāmmia* (and *Firqa Ahl-i Bayt*)[12] unlike Dedhmarī who prefers the pejorative term: *rāfizī*[13]. Coming from the same socio-cultural milieu, can we posit this shift on a humanistic perspective that governed Aslam's vision of the past and his approach to sectarian diversity within the Muslim society of Kashmir as compared to Dedhmarī? Or was Aslam's attachment with the court of the Shi'i nawab of Awadh the mitigating reason behind this change is hard to decipher. Still, for the Kashmiri Sunni society, it was the Dedhmarī's *tārīkh* that framed the historical vision into the past. In comparison, Aslam's work given the lack of attention it attracted remained confined to obscurity, and is little known even today[14]. And in curating a narrative from the *dapān* traditions, Dedhmarī's achieved a construct of communities based on their sectarian associations, a construct in which the Shi'is remain a demonized people. In excluding the Shi'i from the body of Muslim society, Dedhmarī equates the experience of Kashmiri Sunnis with a manifestation of Islam. Like most medieval historians, Dedhmarī is not concerned with the people per se, his narrative is about the rulers, the courtiers, the religious scholars, saints, and occasionally the poets. In placing the Shi'i and Sunni ruling and religious class against each, and presenting the struggle as a sectarian issue, he manages to advance his narrative of a sectarian identity in which the good and righteousness is appropriated to the Sunni cause.

But then the question remains about the Shi'i, how did they perceive themselves? While the Sunni sectarian identity finds expression in *tārīkhs* and *taẕkiras*, Shi'i expressions of self-identity can only be traced in the literary genre of *marṣiya*, elegiac poems on the martyrdom of the third Shi'i imām, Ḥusayn b. 'Ali (d. 680). In these *marṣiya*'s, a vast majority of which date from late eighteenth century onwards, and are written in the local vernacular Kashmiri, as opposed to the court language, Persian, the poets address the Shi'i community of mourners as *mūminin*, the term used in Quran for believers. Simultaneously, the *mūmin* is presented as belonging to an oppressed community, the unnamed oppressor in the text being the Sunni. Much like what we see in Dedhmarī's narrative, the Shi'i' *marṣiya khwān* (elegy writer) also premises the Shi'i' identity on faith and a negative portrayal of the Sunnis as a rival community. The only significant departure in this imagination of the self lies in the Shi'i' acceptance of the Sunni community as belonging to the body of Muslim society, something we fail to see in *Vāqi'āt-i Kashmīr*.[15] Nevertheless, in both instances, we see that a Shi'i and a Sunni identity is articulated in opposition to one another, rather than on the basis of similarities within each group. Both the Shi'i and Sunni narratives establish a larger imaginary in which both the societies saw each other as a monolith other.

In its approach to the past, this work borrows heavily on the term "sectarian," which could be argued to be alien to the development of Muslim societies.[16] In Kashmir, there is no equivalence in the vernacular for sectarian. Even the use of *t'aṣubī* (lit. prejudiced), though part of the common speech, is itself a borrowed word via Persian and Urdu language and cannot be called a close parallel, as it is indicative of a sect-based prejudice against the others. The gradual increase in the use of *firqa-varanah* (interchangeably used for both sectarian and sectarianism) represents a modern usage, worked with great efficacy in news reporting and political commentaries. Regarding the usage of sectarian in the book, I have used it interchangeably, avoiding the modern tendency to fit in within a rigor of consistency of a particular meaning.[17] In sidestepping a categorical definitiveness which would preclude a fluidity of meaning, this study uses sectarian to negotiate the intersection of sect-centric groupism and sect-based religious identity, not sect-driven prejudices and othering.

A further observation needs to be added: while the contours of Shi'iism in medieval Kashmir, especially during the Sultanate period, are still not sufficiently explained,[18] in nineteenth-century Kashmir they were firmly located within the Twelver school—the *Ithnā 'Asharīyya*. Simultaneously, outside Kashmir, in the regions of Purig, Skardu-Baltistan communities of *Nizārī Ismā'īlīs* and the *Nūrbakhshīya's* continued to have adherents along with the Twelvers.

The Long Nineteenth Century

By the time we approach the nineteenth century, Kashmir marks a long period of divisions, contestations, and accord within its Muslim society as the region transitioned from a precolonial era to a subsequent period of colonial intervention. Significantly in nineteenth-century Kashmir, Muslims are a demographic majority, with the Shi'i as a small minority.[19] Within the Muslim society being a Shi'i or a Sunni was an important birth identity marker especially in the main urban center, Srinagar, where confessional identity was reflective of the way in which the city was organized and functioned. This period also marks the end of more than five hundred years of Muslim rule in Kashmir and the setting up of a non-native, non-Muslim rulership in the region first under the Lahore *darbār* (court) of the Sikh rulers (1820–46) and then under Hindu Dogra kings (1846–1947). Historically, by the time we arrive at the end of Muslim rule in Kashmir, Kashmiri Sunnis saw themselves as the "governing majority." As such this study covers a time period which essentially marks Kashmir's transition not only from Muslim political authority but also from a premodern, semifeudal society to modernity.

My study focuses on the reemergence and re-articulation of the Kashmiri Shiʿi' identity at the beginning of the nineteenth century and its development through and in the years and decades leading up to the early twentieth century. As a continually evolving process, I discuss the main characters, events, and spaces that led to the consolidation of this process in the background of an ever-changing dynamic of political and social history—and the resultant responses ranging from antagonism to accommodation and acceptance from the Sunni society.

The book builds an objective and factual inquiry into the dynamic—often contested but sometimes conflated—nature of intercommunity relations in nineteenth-century Kashmir which was then ruled by Sikh and later on by Dogra rulers on one hand and largely dominated by the Sunni religious orthodoxy on the other. In providing a detailed overview of the development of a Shiʿi' identity in this period and its operation within a Sunni-majority society, the book evaluates the enablers of this sectarian identity and examines the changing dynamics of intercommunity relationship within the Kashmiri Muslim community in the backdrop of a non-Muslim rulership and advancing days of European colonialism. Based on five chapters, the book avoids a narrow chronological format as it discusses the emergence of symbols of Kashmiri Shiʿiness which translated into formulation of a Shiʿi society, distinct and independent of the majority Sunni society. This book is not a chronological study of events during nineteenth-century Kashmir but rather focuses on the representation of symbols, rituals, and practices that articulated the Shiʿi' identity of Kashmiri Shiʿi society, and the perception and engagement of the native Sunni population with them.

The book begins with an overview of how, from being the last sovereign rulers of an independent Kashmir, Shiʿi were progressively disenfranchised under the non-native rule of the Dūranī kings. It follows by situating the experiences and tribulations of a Kashmiri Shiʿi society in the early part of the nineteenth century under an increasingly restrictive rule of the Dūranī kings of Kabul, often resulting in open persecution of the Shiʿi. The closing down of Muharram mourning ceremonies—a defining commemorative practice celebrating the community's Shiʿi-ness—and the burning down of two major *imāmbādas* in Srinagar city at Zadibal and Hasanabad are examined to analyze how the Shiʿi viewed and were viewed by the court of Dūranī and the elite within the native Sunni society.

I then go on to explain how the prevailing political environment in the early part of the nineteenth century resulted in transformation of Shiʿi society, which increasingly became reluctant to express their beliefs and practices in the public spaces largely managed by the Sunni intelligentsia and political class.

The sectarian divide within the Muslim community was also reflected in the narratives and historiographic traditions related to the history of Muslim origins in Kashmir as reported by the Sunnis. In examining these historiographical traditions inherited by Kashmiri Muslims in the nineteenth century, I demonstrate how these entrenched sectarian narratives defining the boundaries of a divided community are at variance with a common political ancestry shared by the two communities. The book explains how the otherness that was targeting the Shiʿi's helped them in reimagining themselves as a "community of persecuted," distinct and apart from the Sunnis. The adverse political conditions at home under the Dūranī's resulted in the establishment of a substantial Shiʿi Diaspora, outside Kashmir in the plains of South Asia—a Diaspora of not only artisans and merchants but also the religious class: the ulema, and the poets, who helped in establishing the credentials of Kashmiri Shiʿi scholarship in North India, especially in the Shiʿi-ruled state of Awadh. Maintaining their links with Kashmir, the Shiʿi Diaspora also helped in perpetuating the narrative of distinctness linked with Shiʿi society.

The collapse of Dūranī rule in 1820 and the transfer of authority to a Sikh and afterward Hindu rulers marked the end of Muslim rule in Kashmir. Coeval to the commencement of Dogra rule was the emergence of British colonial influence and thereafter interference in the affairs of the newly established princely state of Jammu and Kashmir. Responding to the need of the British power in South Asia to come across as impartial and unbiased toward various religious and sectarian groupings, the erstwhile Maharaja of Jammu and Kashmir adopted a policy of non-interference within the body politic of Kashmiri Muslims which was characterized by a long history of differences and disagreements between Shiʿi and Sunnis. Significantly, the *darbār* (court) of the Dogra rulers employed a number of Shiʿi, who used their position of influence to both guide the affairs of the Shiʿi community and safeguard their interests. The emerging public interface of a Shiʿi identity was challenged by the Sunni majority in two instances of riots that happened in the nineteenth century. The reconstruction of *Mʿārak*: the principal Shiʿi *imāmbāda* of Kashmir, after the riots of 1872, under semi-state patronage and the commencement of public mourning ceremonies there is contextualized as the community project which helped in giving visible shape to the Shiʿi aspirations for a separate and distinct identity celebrating their Shiʿi-ness. By examining the rebuilding of *Mʿārak*, the book explores the role of these courtiers comprising royal physicians, merchants, poets, and calligraphers as enablers of a Shiʿi identity. Co-opting the Shiʿi ulema in this process of identity formulation, the book demonstrates and explains the contours and the dynamics of the emergence of a grouping of community elites who through their patronage of community activities extended their own political and social leadership. I posit that the riots of 1872 and the coming of Dogra *darbār* to the aid of the Shiʿi community were watershed moments in the history of Shiʿi-Sunni relationship, which resulted in a significant downplay of polemical works targeting each other. Though this did not result in giving shape to an ecumenical movement between the two communities, it nevertheless helped in creating two distinct spheres of Muslim-ness in Kashmir operating in the same space yet in isolation from one another.

Continuing with the theme of patronage and community leadership, I explain how in the later part of the nineteenth century the Shiʿi religious leadership trained in the religious seminaries of Iraq had established themselves as leading community heads of Kashmiri Shiʿi. The consolidation of religious leadership of the ulema was followed by a conflict within the leadership body of Kashmiri Shiʿi. The split within the Shiʿi clergy, who in these dissensions and debates, also increasingly drew upon their transnational connections in Iraq, is studied as the main contributing factor to the emerging split within the community. The divisions and splits also got translated into an urban-rural and rich-poor divide, with the business families of Kashmir associating with a particular section of clergy and the poor craftsmen who worked for these businesses siding with the rival clerical party.

The approach of the twentieth century marks the gradual emergence of nationalistic concerns and the absorption of Kashmir into the anticolonial discourse emerging from mainland South Asia. In Kashmir, this also marked the emergence of a Muslim political consciousness against the ruling Hindu king. This is a subject which has drawn much interest in recent years, particularly following Chitralekha Zutshi and Mridu Rai's seminal work, which deals with the modern history of Kashmir with respect to the issues of Muslim religious identity and culture.[20] My study, however, engages with the dynamics of cultural and the spiritual identity of Kashmiri Shiʿi within the regional space occupied by the Dogra sovereignty and Sunni orthodoxy, something which remains untouched so far. Articulated by the community elites, I show how this "freedom" struggle against the Hindu rulers marks the emergence of a Shiʿi-Sunni ecumenical movement. Basically, political in its aspirations, this coming together of the Shiʿi and Sunnis does nevertheless mark a pattern which would continue through a greater part of the century. Sectarian conflicts and polemics targeting each other would be managed and attempts made to see that public spaces would function in a non-sectarian basis. These attempts, nevertheless, only succeeded to relegate differences to the realms of private interactions, not dismantle them.

Sources and Structure

Within the body of studies dedicated to Islam, works related to Shiʿi political history or material culture generally tend to be limited. Given the continued preoccupation and interest in events and changes happening in the Middle East, the historic heartland of Islam, studies on Shiʿism still broadly focus on the Arab and Iranian Muslims. And, when researchers do investigate Shiʿi history of South Asia, the bulk of focus tends to be on Shiʿism in the plains of North India. If, as Simon Wolfgang Fuchs in his formidable scholarship on Pakistani Shiʿi says, "Pakistani Punjab formed a veritable Shiʿi 'periphery,'"[21] Kashmiri Shiʿism remains a distant and obscure event, little explored or understood. This is in spite of the fact that one of the most consequential figures in contemporary Shiʿism, Ayatollah Ruhallah Khomeini (d. 1989), traced his ancestral roots to Kashmir.[22]

The book is primarily based on Persian, Kashmiri, and Urdu sources, unpublished manuscripts as well as published books, consisting of *tārīkh*, *taẕkira*, *marṣiya* literature, legal records, polemical tracts, pamphlets, newspapers, and archival sources from the local *darbār* as well as British colonial sources comprising government records and travelogues. Personal and family archives in the shape of letters and manuscripts have been accessed to frame an understanding of individuals who played an enabling role in events that are described in this book. The study also borrows from marginalia which serve as assembled bodies of family texts, especially in manuscripts preserved within family libraries for several generations till present day. The research also draws on the materiality linked with

Kashmiri Shiʿi to provide an insight into the cultural landscape linked with Shiʿi presence and aspirations. Exploring the linkages that connect the present with the recent past, this study also includes both oral traditions maintained within families who figure in this book, as well as the recollections of research informants. The cross-examining of the responses, which were collected through a series of nonstructured interviews, considers that personal recollections are also partially conditioned by a sense of nostalgia about the past. Though not an alternative to history, these collective memories are nevertheless used in charting out how Kashmiri Shiʿi view their immediate past.

This work does not seek to provide an exhaustive account of each event in the community of Kashmiri Shiʿi in the nineteenth century, but by engaging in an interlinked narrative it seeks to connect textual, literary, and oral history with material culture to describe the lived history of the community. Significantly, this study does reflect a preponderance of narratives and events originating from the capital city of Srinagar, reflecting the primacy of the city's mediatory presence in dictating not only the pulse but also the shifting contours of Shiʿi-Sunni engagements across the broader geography of Kashmir.

The first chapter traces the outline of Shiʿi history in Kashmir by revisiting available historiographical evidence and in doing so analyzes the differing textual accounts related to the inception of Islam in Kashmir. The chapter examines how at the start of the nineteenth century, Shiʿi and Sunni communities in Kashmir viewed their past in a contested narrative related not only to their point of origin in Kashmir but also to their memory of the Muslim rule in the region. In doing so, the chapter introduces us to the Persianate texts originating from Sunni sources, mostly serving as repositories of elite and mostly urban communities and how they sought to represent the Kashmiri Shiʿi as others.

The second chapter further develops the theme of Shiʿi identity in Kashmir by investigating the circumstances of Dūranī's rule in Kashmir and the resulting dichotomous relationship between the Shiʿi and the Sunni resulting in targeted violence against the Shiʿi. In addition to Persian texts which highlight the state of uncertainty facing the Shiʿi, I introduce the *marṣiya* as a source of vernacular literature located in the everyday life experience of the Shiʿi to highlight how the disorienting influences of these encounters helped in reinforcing their notion of a unique Shiʿi identity. I highlight the tentative attempts made by the Kashmiri Shiʿi community at re-articulating and expressing their spiritual and cultural identity, in a regional space largely controlled by Sunni orthodoxy. The chapter also focuses on the networks of trade and knowledge linking Kashmiri Shiʿi with the Iranian shawl merchants and the royal court at Awadh as a source of patronage while also exploring the material culture linked with this transfer.

Exploring the theme of a resurgent sectarian identity, Chapter 3 posits that integral to the articulation of a Shiʿi identity in Kashmir was the entire paraphernalia of various affective and performative practices associated with the commemoration of the martyrdom of Imām Ḥusayn and his family in Karbala. In addition, the materiality, not only associated with mourning Karbala but also linked to other practices and rituals of Islam, created a distinct habitus of Kashmiri

Shi'i Islam. This distinct set of spiritual and cultural practices was eventually mobilized by the intelligentsia of Kashmiri Shi'i Muslims for political ends as well. The most visible manifestation of this identity—a sectarian identity—was the reconstruction of *M'ārak*, the historic *imāmbāda* of Kashmir Shi'i. The fate of this construction, its patronage, and the ensuing Shi'i-Sunni riot resulting in its destruction form the central theme of this chapter. The process was further strengthened and intensified with the transfer of political authority to a Hindu Dogra dynasty by the British colonial administration in the middle of the nineteenth century. This chapter illustrates how the prevailing attitude on part of the powers that be naturally provided a space for the Shi'i Muslims to establish for themselves a spiritual and cultural identity distinct from the Sunnis. The Jammu and Kashmir of the nineteenth century and onward was a regional space where this identity was negotiated vis-à-vis the Hindu Dogra rule.

As the Shi'i of Kashmir saw the consolidation of their identity in the middle of the nineteenth century, it was soon followed by the emergence of divisions and rifts within the community. Primarily, the divisions were introduced via differences related to the control and maintenance of *M'ārak* and the mourning assemblies held there. Gradually, the differences expanded into all major functioning of the community activities, especially with regard to the collection and distribution of community monies. Chapter 4 looks at how the issue of dispensing of *khums* (religious tithe amounting fifth of the yearly savings) money led to a divide within the religious class. The chapter explores these dissensions within the Shi'i society and explores how these differences affected the worldview of the community to both Shi'i-Sunni relationship and responses to advancing European influences in Kashmiri society, especially in the field of education.

The onset of the twentieth century witnessed a birth of political consciousness in the Muslims of Kashmir. This was in response to the centuries of economic and political exploitation that the Kashmiri Muslims were subjected to by the likes of Afghan, Sikh, and eventually Dogra rulers. The chapter explores the nature of the Kashmiri Shi'i society at the start of the twentieth century, examining the factors and the individuals who served as the enablers of community identity. It examines the role of Christian missionaries in introducing modern education in the region and the responses from both the Sunni and Shi'i society. The chapter engages with the events and the individuals who were responsible for a coming together of Shi'i and Sunni Muslims of Kashmir, overlooking their mutual differences and disagreements in favor of working toward a unified Muslim identity vis-à-vis the Hindu rule. Consequently, the Shi'i of Kashmir, in seeking redressal to their century's long disenfranchisement, had joined hands with the Sunnis. Chapter 5 investigates the emergence of this ecumenical Muslim outlook, essentially political in its aims yet also seeking accommodation of sectarian differences. At the end of the chapter, I offer an overview of where Shi'i-Sunni relations in Kashmir stand today, as both communities find themselves drawn into transnational debates and divisions that originate outside of Kashmir. It concludes with how both the communities are navigating between strife and accommodation: originating from a sectarian outlook while trying to maintain an image of Muslim unity.

Chapter 1

Not Quite Taqiyya

Kashmiri Shi'i at the Start of the Nineteenth Century

In the summer of 1928, Ṣughrā Hemayun Mīrzā (d. 1958)[1] along with her husband, Barrister Sayyid Hemayun Mīrzā, arrived in Kashmir. The Mīrzās were traveling from Hyderabad, the princely state located in southern India, which much like the state of Jammu and Kashmir—though nominally not a part of the British colonial empire—was nevertheless a part of British political and colonial overreach. The visit to Kashmir was dictated by Sayyid Hemayun's illness, with a stay in the temperate Himalayan valley of Kashmir being advised by his doctor.[2]

After a stay of around four months in Kashmir, Ṣughrā Hemayun on returning to Hyderabad started writing her *safar nāma*—a travelogue about Kashmir in Urdu. Published two years after the visit, under the title of *Rahbar-i Kashmir* (Guide to Kashmir), this *safar nāma* provides the readers with not only an account of the Mīrzās' travel to Kashmir but also a brief historical description of some of the prominent monuments and landmarks in Kashmir. While we have multiple travelogues written about Kashmir by European visitors in the nineteenth and twentieth centuries,[3] *Rahbar* happens to be the only *safar nāma* that we know of, written about Kashmir by a Muslim woman of South Asian origin in the early twentieth century. In her description of the land, Ṣughrā also fills in with small but insightful details about her interactions with the natives, limited though these may be mostly to her social exchanges with the elite from the city of Srinagar. Still in their engagements with the Kashmiris, the Mīrzās form a link of commonality of being similar, which is missing from related meetings that are recorded in the European writings about Kashmir.[4]

An interesting description in the *safar nāma* relates to a visit of the Mīrzās' to the *ḥavelī* of a prominent Shi'i *jāgīrdār* (landlord), Sayyid Ḥusayn Shāh Jalālī (d. 1950) and their joint participation in the *majlis-i Chihlum* (The Assembly of the Fortieth) held at the *Imāmbāda* Zadibal. The narrative assumes a certain ekphrastic quality in its elaborate description of both the *imāmbāda* and the mourning performance taking place inside the building:

> In Srinagar there is a *moḥala* Zadibal where many Muslims live, and there are many Shi'i in this *moḥala*. The *majlis* happens here. Sayyid Shāh Jalālī is a big *jāgirdār* and *zamindār* and the father-in law[5] of his son is trader of pearls [. . .].

> All of us went to Jalālī Ṣahibs place [. . .]. After lunch we went to the *imāmbāda* which is near his house. The *majlis* starts at six in the morning and continues till six in the evening. The *majlis* is read in Kashmiri language and the *imāmbāda* is very large. There are buildings on all four sides, in the middle there is a lower ceiling supported on thirty-five columns, under which the *majlis* takes place [. . .]. The buildings on the four sides are two storied, the upper floor is in wood and has delicate wooden *jālīs* (screens). It is here (behind the *jālīs*) that women sit and listen to the *majlis*. The lower and the central floor is used by men. From morning till evening whoever desires, may come and be a part of the *majlis*. When men enter the *majlis* they remove their coats and turbans. All the men in the congregations were bareheaded. The *marṣiya khwānī* adopted here is distinct from that in the entire world [. . .]. In the end, Moulvi Imdād ʿAli Ṣahib of Lahore did *marṣiya khwānī* (recitation of elegies commemorating Ḥusayn b. Ali's martyrdom). He stood up and said that today, I will recite a *marṣiya* in Urdu, because Sayyid Hemayun Mīrzā Ṣahib who has arrived in Kashmir from Hyderabad is present with us in *majlis*.[6]

While the text regarding the *majlis* at Zadibal *Imāmbāda* is detailed and helps us in reimagining the entire environment—spatial as well as performative—of the event

Figure 1.1 *M'ārak, imāmbāda* at Zadibal prior to its dismantling, Srinagar, 2004 (courtesy: Mubashir Mir).

as practiced in the early twentieth century, it does nevertheless on the surface present the *majlis* as a common manifestation in the community life of Kashmiri Muslims, albeit Shiʿi Muslims. The *majlis* is important and the scale impressive, but in the *safar nāma* it stands situated in commonplace occurrences linked with the expression of faith in early twentieth-century Srinagar.[7] Additionally, measuring 22.86 m x 22.86m the *imāmbāda* in terms of its sheer size was the third largest monument within the sacred Muslim landscape of the city constructed in the native architectural idiom,[8] only outsized by the Jamia Masjid (117 m x 115.7 m) and ʿĀlī Masjid (61.2 m x 20.5 m). The scale of the building fits in with the desire of the author to engage with leading monuments in the city in a text whose primary appeal is as a guidebook for visitors.

Yet, the Zadibal *Imāmbāda* (Figure 1.1) more commonly referred to by its vernacular name, *Mʿārak*,[9] had a singularly chequered history, and the *majlis* witnessed by Mīrzā in the *imāmbāda* was of a much recent origin—dating from the second half of the nineteenth century. The affluence of the Shiʿi *jāgirdār*, Sayyid Husayn Shāh, and the prosperous conditions of the *imāmbāda* mark a gradual shift in the fortunes of the Kashmiri Shiʿi society that took place over the long and tempestuous nineteenth century. Significantly, both the *imāmbāda* and the *ḥavelī*, visited by the Mīrzās', embodied memories of a recent destruction resulting from the Shiʿi-Sunni riot that engulfed the city in 1872.[10]

The Fear of Rāfz

At the start of the nineteenth century, Kashmir formed a part of the kingdom of Dūranīs, who under Aḥmad Shāh Abdalī (r. 1747–72) had started an empire-building process from Kandahar before advancing over most of modern-day Afghanistan and then down into Mughal territories of South Asia. The Afghan conquest of Kashmir occurred in 1752, in the wake of Aḥmad Shāh's invasion of the Mughal territories and for most parts, Afghan rule (1752–1820) in Kashmir under Aḥmad Shāh and his successors failed to provide the level of prosperity that Kashmir had witnessed under the Mughals. Writing somewhere in the 1880s, Pīr Ḥasan Shāh Kuihāmī (d. 1898), a native historian, would make us understand that the acquisition of Kashmir by the Afghans was as much a result of unravelling of Mughal authority as due to local intrigues. In this play for personal power two Kashmiri Sunnis, Mīr Muqim Kanth and Khwāja Zahir Dedhmarī, who were a part of the court of the Mughal *ṣubedars* (governor), played a prominent part.[11]

The participation of Kashmiri elite in a political enterprise that resulted in a change in the political fortune of the land is a phenomenon that can be traced back toward the ending days of Mughal rule in Kashmir. It was a process in which the Kashmiri elite, especially those in Srinagar emerged as important power players with their ability to organize mobs and riots in the city for or against a contending *ṣubedar* or his *naīb (deputy)*.

And it was this new dynamic of power play, with its measurable role of local actors, in which successive Afghan officials operated in Kashmir, while at times turning hostile to the royal Afghan court at Kabul. And when a *ṣubedar* was served with a dismissal, he more than often refused to quit. It was in 1783, during the governorship of Āzād Khān (1783–5), that a European, George Forster, visited Kashmir and left us with the earliest impressions of life under Afghan rule. In his account, he provides us with information on foreign merchants (including Georgians) visiting Kashmir, where despite the oppressive nature of the court, they "were respected and even indulged."[12] The respect was also partially conditioned by the lucrative Kashmiri shawl trade which was a major source of income for the Afghans ruling Kashmir. According to Forster's informant, the total tax revenue generated from Kashmir amounted to twenty and thirty lakh rupees.[13] Yet, the overall condition of the people remained dismal, as can be seen in Forster's description:

> During my refidence {residence} in Kafhmire {Kashmir}, I often witneffed {witnessed} the harfh {harsh} treatment which the common people received at the hands of their mafters{masters}.[14]

About Azad's father, the previous *ṣubedar*, Hājjī Karīm Dād Khān (1777–83), he writes:

> was notorious for his wanton cruelties and insatiable avarice; often for trivial offences, throwing inhabitants, tyed {tied} by back in pairs, into the river, plundering their properties, and forcing their women of every defcription {description}.[15]

Sometime after Forster's visit, in 1786, Mīr Hazār Khān (1786–8) was appointed as the *ṣubedar* of Kashmir and embarked on a series of restrictive measures targeting the Shiʿis as well as the Pandits. In his *Kafiyat-i Intizām-i Mūlk-i Kashmir* (Conditions of Arrangement of the Country of Kashmir), Pandit Ram Joo Dhar makes a brief reference to some of the outrages committed by the *ṣubedar*. Written in 1882–3, this small work was composed when rulership in Kashmir had transferred to Hindu rulers, and as a member of the Hindu court, Ram Joo's text reflects Hindu sensibilities.[16] About Hazar Khān's rule, he writes:

> After the latter (Raḥmat al Lah Khān) was transferred in the year 1207 of Hijrah, Mīr Hazār Khān al Kouzī was appointed as the ruler of Kashmir. He kept company of one Khwāja ʿĪsā, a rich Muslim noble of the time, and on his behest and advice, became prejudiced towards Hindus and Shiʿites, and interfered in their religious practice. Many Hindus were therefore not allowed to tie sacred threads (*zunnār*) and apply *tilak* marks on their forehead. As a result, it became convenient for the Muslims to kill Hindus. False allegations were made against many well-known elites from Hindus and Shiʿites [. . .] Many of whom were consequentially drowned in the river Jehlum. The prejudice was so high in this time that a *jizya*[17] of rupees thousand was extracted from the Hindus.[18]

The events surrounding Mīr Hazar's rule are reflective of a degree of hostility that characterized the attitude of the Sunni religious elite, operating mostly from their urban base in Srinagar city, toward the Shiʿi. An elite which after the collapse of Mughal rule, rooted as it was in an imperial cosmopolitan character, came increasingly to reflect a narrow provincial outlook, orthodox, and at times with an activist thrust—targeting the others; Pandit and Shiʿi. Though the major preoccupation of a majority of Afghan *ṣubedars* in Kashmir was to maintain their rule and extract the greatest possible amount of revenue from the land, yet we find instances where individual *ṣubedars* got involved in a fanatical zeal to suppress any belief system other than that of the Sunnis. Of particular relevance are two separate incidents that took place in the early part of Afghan rule in Kashmir, which showcase how the Sunni elite viewed Shiʿi or Shiʿi-inspired public performances. During the rule of Lʿal Muhammad Khān (1765), a Sunni preacher, Ḥāfiz ʿAbdullah (d. 1765), who used to deliver sermons in the main mosque of the city, Jamia Masjid, was accused of being a *rāfizī* (rejectionist)—a claim that would indicate a certain degree of affinity with the Shiʿi belief. Consequently, ʿAbdullah was summoned for a confrontation of his heretical beliefs in the *Khānaqāh-i Naqshbandīya*, by the leading shaykh of the order, Khwāja Kamāl-al Dīn Naqshbandī (d. 1775). During the discussions, an enraged Khwāja stuck the unrepentant Ḥāfiz repeatedly on the head with his cane, resulting in death.[19] As an influential Sufi order, operating mostly within the folds of the educated religious elite of the city, the *Naqshbandīs* had emerged as a powerful voice of Sunni orthodoxy with marked anti-Shiʿi coloring. Significantly the first Shiʿi-Sunni riot in Srinagar during the Mughal rule of Kashmir (1586–1753) saw an active participation of Khwāja Khawand Maḥmūd (1563–1642), the Sufi shaykh who established the order in the city during the seventeenth century.[20]

Similarly, during the rule of Mīr Dad Khān (1786–8), another Sunni *waʿiẕ* of the city, Ḥāfiz Kamāl was accused of being a *rāfizī* and executed. The nineteenth-century Sunni historian Pīr Ghulām Ḥasan Shāh Khuihāmī relates the circumstances of Kamāl's execution in these words:

> A preacher in the city, Ḥāfiz Kamāl used to live in Malaratta area. During the time of Hājjī Karim Dad, as a result of giving sermons filled with *rāfz*, he was barred from preaching, (and) would at times offer sermons at his home. He would forbid people from visiting graves of saints (*awliyā-i Allah*) and giving offerings (*nazar-o niyaz*) at their shrines. Gradually he started abusing the Companions (of the Prophet). On the complaint of some pious individuals, Qāzī Ḥabib al Lah, based on the witness of countless persons proved his crime of cursing and disassociation from the Companions (*sabb o tabarrā*). He was mounted on a horse, paraded through the city and then smitten by a sword at Haft Chinar.[21]

Interestingly in both instances, we find prominent Sunni preachers of the city stand accused of bearing Shiʿi tendencies, before being executed on a similar and highly contentious charge of abusing the Companions of the Prophet. The accounts related to the execution, derived as they are from Sunni sources, maintain the authenticity of the accusations. Unfortunately, we do not have a Shi'i version of the events, only a saying in the local vernacular, Kashmiri, which commemorates Ḥāfiz Kamāl as a martyr, who spoke the truth while also alluding to a more gruesome death than what is recorded by Kuihāmī.[22]

> *Ḥāfizan wanuv poz, tes kadik aech*
> Transl: Ḥāfiz told the truth, they took out his eyes.

Much more than execution of individuals on motivated charges of blasphemy, it was the possibility of a full-blown Shi'i-Sunni riot that governed how the Kashmiri Shi'i society could express their religious and sectarian identity. An earlier riot had taken place during the *ṣubedarī* of Būland Khān (1762–4 CE), when the Shi'i of Zadibal were accused of using indecent language against Khwāja Ḥabib al Lah Nowsherī, a sixteenth-century Sunni Sufi. Consequently, the moḥala of Zadibal was burned, and many of its Shi'i residents were killed while among the survivors some had their ears and noses chopped and fines imposed on them by Būland Khān.[23] But to categorize the entirety of Afghan rule in Kashmir as a period of intercommunal and sectarian prejudices would be a wrong historical construct. Kashmir had witnessed the rule of the Shi'i Qizalbash, Amīr Khān Jawān Sher (1770–7), and an even longer rule of a *ṣubedar* of Hindu origin, Rajā Sūkh Jiwan Mal (1753–62). Both Amīr Khān and Sūkh Jiwan made an unsuccessful attempt at gaining independence from the court at Kabul. In the case of Amīr Khān, the final stand against the royal forces of Taimūr Shāh (r. 1772–93) resulted in betrayal by his most trusted officials—a consequence of the *ṣubedar*'s Shi'i beliefs. The memory of Amīr Khān's rule and the reasons for dissensions in his rank must have been still fresh when some six years later Forster recorded them from his native sources:

> Amir Khan, a Perfian {Persian}, one of the late governors of Kafhmire {Kashmir}, [. . .] is sfill fpoken {still spoken} of in terms of affection and regret; [. . .]. But in the hour of need, he was abandoned by the pufillanimous {pusillanimous} fickle Kafhmirians {Kashmirians}, who reconciled their conduct to the Perfian {Perisan}, by urging, that if he had remained in Kafhmire {Kashmir}, he would have converted them all to the faith of Ali and cut them off from the hope of salvation.[24]

Almost a century later, the Sunni historian Kuihāmī would paint Amīr Khān as a religious fanatic responsible for killing numerous Sunnis. This, according to Kuihāmī, was the reason behind a delegation of Sunni elders from the city under the leadership of Mullā Mājid approaching the Afghan king Taimūr Shāh at Kabul and requesting him to depose the Shi'i *ṣubedar*.[25] Much more than the *ṣubedar*, it was this leadership of the city, comprising religious and business elders who governed the nature of Shi'i-Sunni relationship and its public manifestations. At the start of the nineteenth century, these relations were strained to the extent that they resulted in executions and riots in the city. As a co-religionist, the Afghan court at Srinagar simply dispensed with the role of acting as an impartial arbitrator in these conflicts. And, under the patronage of the court, the Sunni elements of the city ensured strenuously that any public manifestation of Shiʿiness—*rāfz* in the words of Kuihāmī—would be erased.

The Claim of Being First Muslims

In the contested textual fabric of medieval *tazkirā* and *tārīkhs* through which Muslim writers in Kashmir have constructed their past, we find the mention of a Sufi, Bulbul Shāh (d. 1327), who is perceived as the saintly figure responsible for inaugurating Muslim faith in Kashmir. The earliest mention of Bulbul Shāh is to be found in an anonymous seventeenth-century political history of Kashmir, *Bahāristān-i Shāhī* (*c.* 1614), where the Sufi is introduced as a reticent mendicant living in Srinagar. A chance meeting between the Sufi and the Buddhist king of Kashmir, Rīnchanā (1320–3) convinces the latter to convert to Islam, thus marking a peaceful transition to Muslim rule in this northern Himalayan region. The event is remembered by the Shiʿi author of *Bahāristān-i Shāhī* in these words:

> The dervish told him that his name was Bulbul Qalandar, that his religion was Islam and that his community was that of Muslims. He disclosed to him that he was a member of the sect of Shāh Ne'matullah Walī. He mentioned some of the miracles performed by the prophet, the virtues and superior qualities of ʿAli, the imam, [. . .]. Now he subjected himself to the teachings of the religion of Mustafa (prophet), and the right principles of the truthful path of Murtaza (Ali) and embraced Islamic religion with sincerity and conviction.[26]

Following the author of *Bahāristān-i Shāhī* another seventeenth-century Shiʿi writer, Malik Ḥaidar, in his history *Tārīkh-i Kashmir* (*c.* 1620), also records the circumstances related to Rīnchanā's conversion, though the sectarian identification of Bulbul Shāh is not touched upon. While Bulbul Shāh figures prominently in later accounts, especially those written after the seventeenth century, we find no mention of him in earlier Sanskrit sources or even the oldest surviving Persian history of Sayyid ʿAli, *Tārīkh-i Kashmir* (*c.* 1579). In the highly Sunni-centric text of Sayyid ʿAli neither Bulbul Shāh, Rīnchanā nor even early Shāhmirī sultans find a reference.[27]

In their imagination of the past, Kashmir's Muslim historians have shown a marked predilection toward a narrative which links them to a singular moment in history, a moment which is then celebrated as the origin of Islam in the region. The conversion of Rīnchanā captures this moment. And in consecrating what is historically a highly ambiguous event in a specific sectarian milieu, later historiographic texts help in intertwining the narrative of arrival with that of sectarian identification, pride, and contestations.

In 1159 AH/1746 CE when Khwājā 'Aẕam Dedhmarī completed his *Tārīkh-i Kashmir*; the earlier works of Malik and *Bahāristān-i Shāhī* provide the textual links for him to posit his narrative of a Muslim beginning in Kashmir. A beginning in which Bulbul Shāh is remembered as "Chief of the Gnostics, Leader of the Saints, Promoter of Islam, Destroyer of the Idols, Heedful of the Truth."[28] Significantly, while the author of *Bahāristān-i Shāhī* makes repeated references to 'Ali, the first Shi'i imām, in his narration of the encounter between Bulbul Shāh and Rīnchanā, Dedhmarī carefully avoids any such mention, limiting himself to quoting the initial part of the original text about the "miracles of the Prophet."[29] By doing away with any hint of Shi'i-ness in visiting the beginning of Muslim rule in Kashmir, Dedhmarī systematically frames the foundation of Muslim rule in Kashmir as a Sunni enterprise. Later in the text, when he does visit the origin of Shi'ism in Kashmir he links it to intrigue and deceit. The historiography of *Tārīkh-i Kashmir* alternates between a chronology of events and a polemical worldview, weaving a narrative of how the body of Kashmiri Muslim society was laid open to dissensions by a charlatan and fabricators linked to Shi'ism.

For Dedhmarī, the disruption in the body politics of Kashmiri Muslims starts with the arrival of the *Nūrbakhshī* shaykh, Mīr Shams-al Dīn 'Irakī (d. 1525),[30] in the court of Sultan Ḥasan Shāh (r. 1472–84). 'Irakī arrived in Kashmir as the emissary of Sultan Husayn Bayqara (1470–1507 CE), the Timurid ruler of Herat. In the medieval Persianate world, the *Nūrbakhshī*'s had emerged as a messianic offshoot of the older *Kubrawī* order, with a distinct Shi'i coloring.[31] In Kashmir, the foundation of the *Kubrawī* order was coeval with the arrival of Mīr Sayyid 'Ali Hamdanī (d. 1384)—the first major transnational Sufi figure to visit Kashmir. Though the visit of Mīr Sayyid 'Ali proved inconsequential in its immediate aftermath, his son, Mīr Sayyid Muhammad Hamdanī (1372–1450), who retraced his father's footsteps into Kashmir, helped in consolidating both the image of the order and that of his father as enabler of Kashmir's Muslim identity. Sayyid 'Ali's *Tārīkh-i Kashmir* commences with a brief description of events leading up to Mīr Sayyid 'Ali Hamdanī's arrival in Kashmir. The contribution of Mīr Sayyid 'Ali to the conversion process is exemplified in the text by referring to him as the "founder of Islam."[32] For the historian, the benefits of Sayyid 'Ali Hamdanī's arrival in Kashmir are clear:

> In this country Islam advanced so much, that within the heart of its inhabitants no trace (scent) of infidelity or heresy remained. Due to his (Sayyid 'Ali Hamdanī) auspiciousness and abundant presence, this country became an unrivalled paradise.[33]

Coming back to Dedhmarī, we find that in a work which is broadly dedicated to honoring the memory of Muslim religious figures as pious, ascetic, and deeply spiritual individuals, events related to 'Irakī—given his Shi'i identity—are presented as political machinations devoid of any spiritual grace. Dedhmarī not only questions 'Irakī's link to the *Nūrbakhshīya* order but also refrains in his entire text from calling ʿIrakī by his full given name, Shams-al Dīn: The Sun of the Faith.[34] The full extent of Dedhmarī's hostility to ʿIrakī can be observed in these passages:

> It is a manifest truth that during Fateh Shāh and Malik Mūsā's rule, of the many strange and difficult events that took place, one was the arrival of Mīr Shams ʿIrakī [. . .].Shams ʿIrakī made spiritual connection with Bābā ʿAli Najār and slowly ever so slowly he was successful in entrapping ʿAli Najar in the glass of his misguided faith. [. . .]. Shams ʿIrakī had propagated his link to Sayyid Muhammad Nūrbaksh in order to deceive people. [. . .] ʿIrakī associated himself with him [Nūrbaksh], this is just a lie.
>
> He made relations with the officials of the Sultan and made people to propagate his "miracles". In this way many simple-minded people became a victim of his fraud [. . .].
>
> Malik Mūsā due to circumstances of fate became a disciple of Shams ʿIrakī, his [ʿIrakī's] shop became quite famous. [. . .] In this way Shiʿism spread widely and reached till Tibet.[35]

ʿIrakī's arrival in Kashmir coincides with emerging transformations in the Kashmiri Muslim society, in which Srinagar the main urban center represents an advancement of scripturalist orthodoxy operating from a network of Sufi operated *khānaqāhs*. The early Muslim rule in Kashmir was characterized by cultural experience rooted in syncretism. The arrival of the *Kubrawī*, especially under Mīr Muhammad Hamdanī had challenged this native Muslim culture both at the court and in the society at large. This had also resulted in an initial period of iconoclastic activities targeting the native non-Muslim population under Sultan Sikander (r.1389-1413). Nevertheless, by the time of ʿIrakī's arrival, we find that customs and rituals rooted in a cultural fusion of older Buddhist and Hindu societies and the expanding Muslim community continued to be a part of both the court culture linked with the Muslim sultans as well as the Muslim society at large. While Persian eclipsed Sanskrit as the court language and Persianate cultural influence became increasingly more visible, Kashmiri Muslim society continued to operate as an overlap of multiple practices, influences and outlooks.

Most of the textual information that we have of this period pertains to the upper classes linked to, and operating around the court. This results in a textual bias in which the information available to us centres on events and anecdotes related to the saints and preachers linked with the Sufi *khānaqāhs* These *khānaqāhs* operated as institutions of orthodoxy, and most of them were introduced from regions of Persianate influence. They also served as disseminators of Persian culture. Consequently, we find that most of the *tārīkh navis* and *tazkirā nigārs* who are providing us with information about medieval Muslim Kashmir are themselves intimately linked with these *khānaqāhs*.[36] Aside from the *khānaqāh*-based Sufis, we also find the presence of a loosely grouped order of native Muslim saints—the *Reshīs*. The *Reshīs* of Kashmir operate away from both court patronage and court culture and are representative of a folk tradition—a significant majority of the *Reshīs* were not only vegetarian but also celibate, linking them ideologically to pre-Muslim practices of Buddhist *Bikshus* and Hindu *Reshīs*. Additionally, the *Reshīs* adopted customs and the language that belonged to the common people—the local vernacular, not the Persianized customs and the Persian language that was being introduced at the court. In the verses of Shaykh Nūr-al Dīn (d. 1415 or 1438), the patron saint of the order, survive the earliest, extant critique of this new transformation being introduced into Kashmiri society in the name of Islam by the Sufis of the *khānaqāh*. For the most part, the *Reshīs* operated in a wider folk tradition of Islam linked with the Sunni population of Kashmir. Given the distance from court and court patronage, the *Reshīs* do not figure in the hagiographic accounts linked with *Nūrbakhshīyas*. As Shiʿi concentration in the medieval period was city-centric, an area studiously avoided by the *Reshīs*, it is safe to posit that during the period of *Nūrbakhshīya*'s ascendancy as the leading Sufi order of Kashmir, the path of the two did not cross. Both operated in self-contained zones, with minimal interactions.[37]

Two Saints, Two Sects

In an anecdote popular in Sunni circles and said to have taken place somewhere during the late nineteenth or early twentieth century, a Shiʿi *ʿālim*, a certain unnamed Āgā meets his Sunni counterpart, the Muftī Āzam (Chief Mufti). After an exchange of pleasantries, the two engage in what seems to be on the surface a polite conversation, though laced with hostile innuendos. The Shiʿi Āgā who is portrayed as the antagonist in the episode commences the dialogue by seeking the religious opinion of the Muftī[38]:

Āgā: It is known amongst us, that the *pul-i sirāt* (bridge of hereafter), which every individual has to cross on the Day of Judgement is extremely narrow, narrower than a thread and sharper than a sword. Do the Sunni's also hold a similar view?
Muftī: Yes, it is mentioned so in the books of Ḥadīth.
Āgā: Given the physical difficulty of the crossing, how would a lame (*lūngh*) pass over the bridge?
Muftī: By riding on the back of a mule (*tateh*).

What would appear to contemporary observers, even many Kashmiris, to be a farcical exchange between the two men of religion, reflects a case of lingering sectarian hostility that fashioned how the Shiʿi and Sunni viewed the past. The subtle reference to a lame and a mule marks a disrespectful allusion to two tradition-enabling figures among the Sunni and Shiʿi society of Kashmir: Shaykh Ḥamza Makhdūm (d. 984 AH/1576 CE) and Mīr Shams-al Dīn ʿIrakī. Where ʿIrakī is seen as the seminal figure who bought Kashmiri Shiʿi from the margins into the center of power and patronage, Shaykh Ḥamza would emerge as the inspirational figurehead of Sunni opposition to both the *Nūrbakhshīya* order and the rule of Shiʿi Chak sultans (Figure 1.2). Historically, Ḥamza emerges on Kashmir's political and

Figure 1.2 Shaykh Ḥamza Makhdūm, SPS Museum collection, Srinagar, 2022 (author).

spiritual landscape at a much later date after ʿIrakī's death, yet in folk traditions linked with both Shiʿi and Sunni societies, the two are seen as contemporaries with deep animus against each other. The disapproval which the two evoke in the memory of the other community is reflected in the scornful epithet we encountered in the conversation between the Muftī and the Āgā: lame for the Shaykh and mule for the Mīr. Though never explicitly consigned to a text, the offensive nature of these appellations of which the other community was aware, was enough to keep the Shiʿi and the Sunnis locked into an antagonist relation—sometimes taking the shape of riots and sometimes resulting in pithy exchanges as recorded at the start.

Of the various Sufis who arrived in Kashmir during the medieval period, ʿIrakī's marks the most successful career.[39] Arriving as a political emissary he, during the course of his two visits, achieved an unrivalled ascendancy in the court. The success was a gradual process with many setbacks on the way, including a brief exile to the inhospitable borderlands of Ladakh, yet a steely determination and a fanatical association to the *Nūrbakhshīya* order, paved his path to success. And on the way, while he succeeded in converting many among Kashmiri Sunnis, especially the *Kubrawī*'s to his order through persuasion, there was also a strong push back from Sunni religious elite. Initially, ʿIrakī succeeded in winning over both Baba ʿAli Najār[40] and Shaykh Ismāʿīl (d. 1510),[41] the two main *Kubrawī* shayks in the city. Later on during ʿIrakī's second visit to Kashmir, feeling slighted Ismāʿīl distanced himself from 'Irakī. Ismā'īl's son, Shaykh Fateh-al Lah, maintained a grudge against 'Irakī and was the prime instigator for getting 'Irakī's son, Shaykh Dāniyāl, executed at a later date.[42] Still within a short time after his second arrival in Kashmir, 'Irakī success at the court resulted in the initiation of some of the powerful clan of nobles, Dangars, Rainas, Maliks of Chadurah, and the Chaks, into Shi'i faith. While 'Irakī passed away before the Chaks ascended to the throne as sultans of Kashmir, yet in his own lifetime he received full patronage of the vizier Malik Mūsā Raina (1501–10)[43] with whose help he constructed a two-storied *khānaqāh* for himself at Zadibal. 'Ali reflects on 'Irakī's success at the court in these words:

> Shams 'Irakī saw a temple, which was properly oriented towards the *qibla* and had a door made on its eastern side, converting it into a mosque. Travellers used to offer *nimāz* in it. [. . .] He ('Irakī) made it his seat and made a vow to undertake a *chilla* (solitary penance) in it. Bābā 'Ali also came there (to visit 'Irakī). After that Malik Ghazī Chak also came and officials of the court also started visiting. When the general public came to know that officials of the state are going there, in their greed of this world they too started to go there. This news reached the Shaykh (Ismā'īl). During those days he was ill, and passed away. And the world became devoid of such people. People now started to turn towards him ('Irakī). Though the son of the Shaykh, Bābā Fateh-ul Lah was a learned man and presided over a *khānaqāh*, but few people would approach him and most of the people would go to Shams 'Irakī.[. . .] People from Hanjihal used to always be in difficulties due to non-payment of taxes, etc., that were due to them. Therefore ('Irakī) started making recommendations on their behalf, also endorsing soldiers seeking employment.[44]

Additionally, 'Irakī also revived the iconoclastic program in the region which had achieved a marked success during Sultan Sikandar's reign under the *Kubrawī* shaykh, Mīr Muhammad Hamdanī. The disdain that 'Irakī felt for the prevailing cultural practices of Kashmiri Muslims can be assessed in these words of his biographer:

> Such atheistic and idolatrous practices continue to be observed in the houses of scholars, theologians and leading personalities of this land (Kashmir). They observe all the festivals and feasts of infidels and polytheists. The family members of the elders and leading persons of this land, especially their womenfolk, do not do anything without the permission of the infidels and permission of astrologers. In fact, in all activities of daily life like eating, drinking, sleeping, rising from sleep, travel and rest, astronomers and polytheists have a role to play.[45]

In another instance, 'Irakī's biographer elaborates on one such "sinful practice", a practice which also helps us understand the syncretic nature of Muslim cultural practices in fifteenth-century Kashmir:

> On the occasion of the wedding feast, the Qadiís daughter, adorned as bride, was carried from the house of the Shaykh according to the customs [. . .] prevalent

> in this land from the ancient times. At Shaykh Shihab's house, the bridegroom mounted a horse [. . .] and moved towards the river flowing through the city in the town [. . .].
>
> The bride and the bridegroom, along with some women, dismounted their horses on the bank of the river [. . .] took a tumbler in his hand and filled it with water [. . .] lifted the tumbler poured water into the river from some height. After some time, the bridegroom took a sword in his hand and sliced the water from some height. The bride followed suit.[46]

The extent of ʿIrakī's proselytizing undertakings targeting the non-Muslims has been recorded by the sixteenth-century Sanskrit scholar Pandit Shūkā in his continuation of the *Rajatarangini*. Referring to ʿIrakī by a Sanskritized version of his name, Merashesha, he writes:

> Merashesha, the pupil of Shāhkāsima, was born in the country of Irāka; he knew all the sciences [. . .] According to Merashesha advice, Somachandra arrested men belonging to temples, confiscated lands of the Brahmanas and gave them to Merashesha's servants and thus pleased him.[47]

Though ʿIrakī comes across in both Shiʿi and Sunni accounts as an individual possessing a significant measure of charisma yet he was also a man of particular idiosyncrasies—a benevolent benefactor for his disciples, and also destitute people at large (as was the case with the residents of Hanjihal), he could also come across as an indifferent person especially in his dealing with non-Muslims. Well-read, and deeply welded to his Persianate culture, he both in his utterances and mannerisms displayed a particular disdain for anything Kashmiri. Presiding over a newly introduced Sufi order, ʿIrakī showed a remarkable lack of restraint in his dealing with the older established Sunni religious classes at the court.[48] The depth of ʿIrakī's dedication to the *Nūrbakhshīya* cause and the harshness of his conduct in dealing with rival Sufi orders is best exemplified by an incident involving a visiting Naqshbandī, Mullā Farhī. The mullā had in his possession a manuscript of *Silsilat al-Zahab*[49] the work of the famous Persian poet and Naqshbandī Sufi, Maulanā ʿAbd al-Raḥmān Jāmī (d. 1492). Given the adverse relations between Jāmī and his own shaykh, Shāh Qāsim Nūrbaksh, ʿIrakī had the entire volume consigned to flames in his kitchen much to the chagrin of Farhī, who also happened to be Jāmī's disciple[50].

More significantly, ʿIrakī showed none of the humility in his public dealings expected of a Sufi shaykh. A study of *Tuḥfatūl Aḥbāb* shows how in his dealing he embraced customs and mannerisms that are associated with royalty. It is worthwhile to note that among ʿIrakī's dedicated adherents, we find a majority of families and tribes such as the Chaks whose conversion from a nomadic to sedentary urban lifestyle was quite recent.

The man who would represent Sunni resentment and resistance to Shiʿism in Kashmir, Shaykh Ḥamza Makhdūm, was born in 1491 (or 1494), in a village of Tujar at a time when ʿIrakī was dominating the court life. During the course of his preaching, Makhdūm would attract some of the most preeminent Sunni *ulema* and preachers to his cause. And, they in their turn would propagate the life and legend of Shaykh Makhdūm Ḥamza through a series of hagiographic works; acting as his publicist within the circles of well-read classes in the city. These *taẕkira*'s[51], the largest in this genre dealing with any Kashmiri Muslim religious figure, would help in enshrining the image of Makhdūm as a miracle-performing, epoch-making figure who revived Sunnism in the region. While the image of ʿIrakī in the work of his biographer and partisans is of a shaykh well versed in all the rational and religious sciences, Makhdūm life as recorded by his devotees resembles a kaleidoscope of miracles—dazzling and audacious in their spiritual reach. In *Dastur-al Salikin* and *Virid-al Muridīn*, Bābā Dawud Khākī (1521–85), the principal *khalifā* of Makhdūm, records numerous such miracles, some to which he bears a witness, some of which he registers on the authority of Makhdūm. At various places in the text, we find that Makhdūm frequently obtained guidance from saintly figures, including through physical meetings with Jesus, Khizr, and Solomon. Living according to his biographers in a sectarian milieu, Makhdūm finds his guidance from the Prophet Muhammad himself. He is advised on the righteousness of the Sunni path by the *Khilāfah ar-Rāšidah*, the four Rightly Guided Caliphs. In one telling instance, we find insight into how deep the Shiʿi-Sunni fissure ran in circles associated with Makhdūm. One day Makhdūm is sitting with his circle of disciples when a seemingly pious person passed by. Makhdūm then informs the gathering that this man is a *rāfizī*. On being asked by Khākī how he came to know this, the shaykh replies that when I looked at his face, I found his resemblance to a pig.[52] The analogy of the unnamed Shiʿi with a ritually unclean animal (*najs*) not only manifests the portrayal of a negative stereotype but also seeks to dehumanize the community, which then becomes ingrained in Sunni historiography of the succeeding generations.

In the *taẕkira*'s of Khākī, and another of Makhdūm's disciple, Bābā Ḥaidar Tūlmūlī (d. *c.* 1590),[53] the awakening of Makhdūm is illustrated through illuminating spiritual experiences drawing the shaykh deeper and deeper into the folds of a Sunni identity, expressed in an anti-Shia rhetoric while seemingly grounded in a spiritual awakening.

Despite the acceptance Makhdūm found within the Sunni society, there was also a degree of hostility directed toward him, partly originating from the Shiʿi circles, to which he and his immediate disciples were deeply conscious and sensitive. In *Hidayat-al Mukhlisin,* Tūlmūlī writes:

> one day an individual remembered the pure name of Ḥazrat Makhdūm, at his home with contempt and loathing. (Hearing this) Ḥazrat Makhdūm's pure heart became disturbed (blurred). Instantly, from the sacred court of Allah the Most High, Ḥazrat Makhdūm received an order, "O! Makhdūm, how should I treat this opponent of yours?" Ḥazrat Makhdūm replied "As his punishment decrees". Immediately that person was dispatched to hell.[54]

Similarly, in Tūlmūlī's account, through his spiritual prowess and on the requests of his disciple, Shaykh Ḥamza Makhdūm effects the death of more than 5,000 individuals who contest his spiritual station—the religious or sectarian denomination of these condemned by the Makhdūm is not defined.[55] This would indicate that the aura of respectability and acceptance that the hagiographers from Makhdūm's circle want to impress upon their audience was not entirely widespread, even among contemporary Sunni society. In Qārī's *tazkira* we find instances where the text alternates between a desire to present a homogenizing account of the saint's spiritual status and popularity among the Sunni society, and events which highlight the opposition that Makhdūm faced from both the Sunni religious classes as well as laity[56].

An overview of the various hagiographic accounts emanating from the circle of Makhdūm's disciples portrays early sixteenth-century Kashmir as a tumultuous society deeply invested in faith conversion. It is a society in which Shaykh Ḥamza Makhdūm emerges as a person of an immense moral and spiritual character singularly reviving the Sunni faith. It also portrays, the Kashmiri Sunnis as a marginalized community living under an oppressive Shiʿi rule, a narrative that was then picked up by a later generation of Sunni historians in the eighteenth and nineteenth centuries. Instances of this victimhood, include the narrative of Makhdūm being exiled from Srinagar by the first Shiʿi sultan of Kashmir, Ghāzī Shāh (r. 1561–3) and an event said to have taken place during the reign of the second sultan in this dynasty, Ḥusayn Shāh (r. 1563–70), who tested the spirituality of the shaykh in what can be termed as a demeaning manner. Yet conversely, Tūlmūlī also argues that two of the leading wives of Ḥusayn Shāh were not only Sunnis but also *mūrids* of Sayyid Muhammad Zelālī, himself a disciple of Makhdūm. Again, while initially Tūlmūlī argues that Ḥusayn Shāh's misbehavior toward Makhdūm resulted in the sultan's immediate death, a bit later in the text he would lead us to believe that a chastised Ḥusayn Shāh repented, recovered and changed his behavior.[57]

In a strange paradox while we find numerous references to ʿIrakī, even though extremely hostile, in medieval texts authored by Sunni writers, not a single mention of Makhdūm is to be found in any Shiʿi work, whether a *tārīkh* or a *tazkirā*. Surprisingly a similar absence of a textual reference can also be observed in the work of a staunch Sunni historian like ʿAli, who would have been a senior contemporary of Makhdūm. ʿAli's work ends at Ḥusayn Shāh's reign, during which period, based on the work of Khākī and Tūlmūlī, the fame of Makhdūm was firmly established across Kashmir. Similarly, we find no mention of Makhdūm in any contemporary Sanskrit history. The historian Shūkā while mentioning various Muslim religious figures is silent about Makhdūm. Posit the inconspicuous presence of Makhdūm in this early textual evidence against this description of the shaykh offered by Khākī, and we get an interesting dichotomy:

> Many dignitaries, nobles, officials would visit the Honorable Sultan-al ʿArifin (King of those with Knowledge of God), but leave aside standing (in greeting) for anyone he would not bestow them with the least bit of favor or respect.

> Wherever Ḥazrat Makhdūm (May God's Mercy be on him) would take his presence, *jinns* would shake like the branches of willow and flee.[58]

Do then the works of Khākī and Tūlmūlī reveal a reworking of a historical figure? It is especially intriguing given that many of Makhdūm's disciples, including Khākī, were involved in negotiations with the Mughal emperor Akbar (r. 1556–1605), which finally resulted in the annexation of Kashmir and removal of the Chak sultans. Additionally, it is in Khākī's text that we come across the use of the honorific title *Sultan-al ʿArifīn*[59] for the Makhdūm. By establishing a claim to the rulership of a spiritual realm, the circle of Makhdūm effectively sought to challenge and circumvent the territorial sovereignty of the Shiʿi sultans. And, in his disdain for political classes, as reflected in Khākī's passage, Makhdūm dramatically contrasts his own ascetic, spiritual life with what is projected in these texts as the worldly, corrupt, and tyrannical court of the sultans. A court which for Khākī and Tūlmūlī is in a perpetual conflict with their shaykh, replicating the eternal drama of struggle between good and evil.[60] Aside from its core narrative of projecting an emblematic personality of Makhdūm through a series of mystical visions and miraculous occurrences, both the texts, that of Khākī and Tūlmūlī firmly locate this conflict between the shaykh and the sultans in a sectarian Shiʿi-Sunni milieu[61]. This dispute is not between any worldly court and the spiritual *darbār* of a shaykh, but between the explicit Shiʿi and Sunniness of these two spaces.

The semantics of these texts provide the basis for some of the most abiding prejudices marking Shiʿi-Sunni antagonism in Kashmir. These have in turn given rise to many colorful folklores projecting ʿIrakī and Makhdūm as arch-rivals, engaged in feats of spiritual contestations. It is safe to posit, given the level of emotions involved in these narratives, for Kashmiri Muslim society ʿIrakī and Makhdūm serve as markers of sectarian identification. Any attempt to construe a Muslim past in Kashmir involves self-positioning itself around how the two are viewed.[62] How entrenched these views had become as we arrive in the nineteenth century can be seen in the versified history of Kashmir, *Bāgh-i Suleimān* (*c.* 1294 AH /1877 CE) written by Mīr Saʿad ul-Lah Shāhabādī:

> In that age Mīr Shams of ʿIrak,
> came to Kashmir and established here the ways of hypocrisy
> He strengthened the citadel of Shiʿite creed,
> and created cracks in the faith of Sunnis.[63]

In the biographical works surrounding Makhdūm, his death in 984AH/1576CE comes across as a particularly inconspicuous event[64]. The text related to Makhdūms death, unlike what is written about his life, is strangely devoid of any display of miracles marking the event extraordinaire. Rather it is the congregational funeral, which is presented as a unique occasion, drawing a vast crowd comprising both scholars as well as the laity, the ruling classes, and the commoners in a popular homage to an exceptionally remarkable man. For his disciples, this display of popular vernation for the dead saint firmly establishes the historicity of the cult centered around Makhdūm[65]. Yet, as it happens where people contest, there is the actual event and then there are versions of the event more appealing to imagination especially when tailored to highlight competing visions. And it is again in the genre of the *dapan* tradition, that we find a colourful fable linked with Makhdūms death originating from the Shiʿi circle, which use the occasion to stereotype both the dead shaykh's animus toward the Shiʿi, as well as to showcase it as an event of divine retribution establishing the righteousness of the Shiʿi faith. In this legend, Makhdūm, driven by his hate against Iraki, decides to eliminate the Shiʿi neighbourhood of Zadibal by securing the help of jinns. He conjures a plan to transport the hillock of Koh-i Maran and have it dropped on the *khānaqāh* of ʿIraki at Zadibal eliminating both his rival and the Shiʿi community. ʿIraki gets to know of this plan and devises a scheme which seeks to disrupt the threat, involving an elderly Shiʿi couple who decide to confront the mechanization of Makhdūm and his jinns. The couple proceed to Koh-i Maran and succeed in their mission, and the hill while about to be transported falls on the jinn and Makhdūm resulting in their death. In its treatment of the subject, this oral legend mirrors contemporary textual traditions linked with the genre of *tazkiras*, locating itself in the fantastical and miracle happening world. Significantly, where Makhdūms disciples such as Tulmulī weave the narrative of a retributive death for the shaykhs Shiʿi opponents, the Shiʿi not only created a rival matching tradition, one grounded in Makhdūms own death but through it also sought to uncover the speciousness of the miracles claimed by Makhdūms disciples.

To a large extent these contrasting narratives capture the attitude of a majority of medieval native historians and hagiographers toward not only the ʿIrakī-Makhdūm tussle but also the rule of Chaks, and Kashmir's subsequent loss of sovereignty as an independent regional Sultanate.

Chaks: The Pādshāhs *of Kashmir*

Some five years after Akbar ascended the throne as emperor of Hindustan, in the court of Shāhmīrī sultans of Kashmir, ʿAli Khān Chak removed the crown from the head of his nephew and the titular sultan, Ḥabib Shāh (r. 1557–61)[66] and placed it on his brother, Ghāzī Chak.[67] The act marks the end of more than two centuries of Shāhmīrī rule (1339–1561) in Kashmir and their replacement by the short-lived Chak Sultanate (1561–86). Significantly, it also marks the transfer of authority from a dynasty adhering to the Sunni faith to one located within the Shiʿi belief system.[68] In his *Tārīkh*, ʿAli laments this transfer as a loss of Sunni temporal authority:

> After the passage of two hundred years the rule of (this) country passed from the hands of the offspring of Sultan Shams-al Dīn into the hands of the children of Langar Chak. ʿ*Ahl-i Tashi*ʿ (Shiʿi) again became custom (or came into prominence).[69]

This apparent Sunni-ness of the Shāhmīrī sultans is effectively posited against the Shiʿi-ness of the Chak rule. In the words of Dedhmarī:

> From the inauguration of Sultan Shams-al Dīn till the sultanate of Nazūk Shāh fourteen or fifteen pious stars sat in the lap of sultanate. They propagated and promulgated the religion of *Ahl-i Sunnat wal Jamat.* [. . .] In this way the family of Chaks gradually, who were the servants and foster brothers of this dynasty (i.e, the Shāhmīrī's), attained power and domination. Due to which the affairs of government (*sultanat*) and religion (*dīn*) and nation (*millat*) were interrupted.[70]

The portrayal of Chaks as servants of the Shāhmīrī, who usurped power from their former masters resonates with Sunni historians down the centuries—a late example is to be found in the *tārīkh* of Pīr Ḥasan Shāh Khuihāmī. This work, which was written in the last quarter of the nineteenth century, marks the culmination of Persian historiography in Kashmir, which significantly expands on the narrative of earlier historians. A narrative which again highlights the assumed lowly origin of the Chaks and then posits it with both their assumption of power and their faith: their Shiʿi identity.

By identifying the Shāhmīrī and Chaks with political fortunes of Kashmiri Sunni and Shiʿi society, the authors of these texts are also presupposing a fractured Muslim society in which the struggle for political power is transformed into a sectarian project. Yet, the details provided in these texts would lead us to a contrary reading. Also, as we saw in the writing of *Tuḥfatūl Aḥbāb* the lived history of sixteenth-century Kashmir is not as conscious of religion as writers in the eighteenth and nineteenth centuries would make us believe.

The rise of Chaks, rather than a sectarian venture as later generation of historiography would imply, is primarily a case of how a nomadic non-native group emerges from Kashmir's borderland and then over a period of century navigates itself into power, which is operating from an urban courtly setting. While there is no reason to question the sincerity of their conversion to Shiʿiism under ʿIrakī, yet the conversion must not be seen as a lone moment. Both ʿIrakī and Chaks struggled to achieve a position of preeminence in the court. As outsiders, both faced a certain disadvantage in the face of older established power centers: the politico-religious elite. The opposition ʿIrakī faced from the Bayhaqī Sayyids, Māgreys, and other nobles[71] at the court as well as from sections of *Kubrawī* order and the court *mullā*[72] is indicative of the level of this animosity. By allying themselves spiritually with ʿIrakī, the Chaks increased their visibility at the court through a charismatic though contentious Sufi shaykh who nonetheless commanded great attention. In a sole reference to the Chaks, ʿIrakī's biographer clearly mentions that the dynasty owed their property in the city to ʿIrakī's munificence.[73] For ʿIrakī, Chaks could not be the only means of advancing his own goal—primarily at achieving a wider circle of discipleship and court patronage. So more importantly, in addition to Chaks, he was also able to win Malik Mūsā Raina (d. 916 AH/1510 CE), a member of the old court elite predating Sultanate rule, who on assuming the office of vazir would offer the official patronage that ʿIrakī sought. Much more than the Chaks, it is Mūsā Raina who during his nine years of rule became the instrument of *Nūrbakhshī* shaykh's success[74] and also figures prominently in ʿIrakī's biography:

> The first amongst the nobles and rulers of the land of Kashmir to win Araki's special favour was Malik Mūsā Raina.[75]

Gradually through examples of personnel valor and marshaling of their resources, the Chaks were able to able to gain new adherents. While we have no idea of their actual number, most texts indicate that the initial progression of the Chaks was more of a tribe united under a compelling leader rather than that of an individual family. The advancement of the Chaks at the court also corresponds with a steady decline in both the power and the prestige of the Shāhmīrī sultans following the death of Sultan Ḥasan Shāh in 1472. With rival claimants[76] to the throne betting their chances on the support they could generate and more importantly sustain among the competing *amīrs*, the court politics of late fifteenth to early sixteenth-century Kashmir represents a quicksand of hopes realized and dreams quashed. And in this quest for power, it took little for former allies to turn into deadly opponents, where blood relations mattered as little as sectarian denominations of the participants. Additionally, it is from this period that we find Delhi's increasing interest in the affairs of Kashmir as the various constitutive parts of the Kashmiri court politics presented themselves at the Delhi court with a cry for support or refuge. Luckily, at the moment when Kashmir was at its weakest, the Lodhi sultans (1452–1526) of Delhi were more interested in expanding their territories southward into Jaunpur and Bihar than getting bogged down in a Himalayan region.

In the struggle for the throne between Muhammad Shāh and his uncle Fateh Shāh, we see Shiʿi *amīrs* attaching themselves to their political fortunes rather than forming sectarian groupings to advance the fortunes of faith. A similar political wisdom can be observed among Sunni *amīrs*, and in securing their personal fortunes both Shiʿi and Sunni *amīrs* would form mutual alliances, enter into matrimonial relations, and yet betray whosoever stood in their path of power. And it was within this ever-changing orbit of high stakes that Kājī Chak (d. 1544) emerged as a formidable warrior and a major player during Fateh Shāh's stint (1515–17) as sultan of Kashmir. Soon, Kājī attained the coveted post of vazir, under Muhammad Shāh, and continued in the post from 1517 to 1527, a long though tumultuous period. Much more than any other competing noble, Kājī exemplified a certain sense of "Kashmiri-ness"—a tie to the land. When the Mughal troops dispatched by Emperor Babur (r. 1526–30) invaded Kashmir, Kājī though dismissed and in exile, raised his forces and defeated the Mughal troops.

However, this was not to be either Kashmir's or Kājī's last encounter with the Mughals. After being forced out of the post of vazir once again due to court intrigue, we find Kājī returning from exile to lead Kashmiri troops in their fight against the Mughals who had occupied the city of Srinagar during 1531. The Chak ascendancy was however checked, when another Mughal army under Emperor Hemayun's (r. 1530–40, 1555–6) uncle, Mīrzā Ḥaidar Dughlat

(d. 1551), invaded Kashmir first in the name of Sultan Sa'id Khān in 1533, and then again in 1540 on behalf of Hemayun. While Dughlat's first offensive was marked by a quick retreat, the second attempt was marked by success The second half of Dughlat's (1540–51) ten-year rule in Kashmir, is marked by a determined effort to define the land by its confessional identity—as a Sunni land governed by Ḥanafī *mazhab*.[77] In his autobiography *Tārīkh-i Rashidī*, which was partly written in Kashmir, Dughlat provides us with an understanding of his resolve on this issue, writing:

> At the present time in Kashmir, the Sufis have legitimatised so many heresies, that they know nothing of what is lawful or unlawful. They consider that piety and purity consist in night-watching and abstinence in food; [. . .]. They blame and detest science and men of learning; consider the Holy Law second in importance to the True "Way," [. . .]. Thanks be to God that, at the present time, no one in Kashmir dares openly profess this faith; but all deny it, and give them-selves out as good Sunnis. They are aware of my severity towards them, and know that if any one of the sect appears, he will not escape the punishment of death.[78]

Similarly, 'Ali who along with his father was a partisan of Dughlat writes:

> Mīrzā Haider spread the tradition of *Ahl-i Sunnat wal Jamā't* everywhere and wiped out *Ahl-i Rāfizī* and disloyal (people). He got *Khānaqāh -i Shams 'Irakī* burnt and had his remains dug out of the grave and burnt.[79]

While briefly mentioning some of the atrocities linked to Dughlat's reign, including the gruesome details of his execution of a Shi'i *reshī*, Shanghlī Reshī, Dedhmarī also praises Dughlat for his promotion of Islam or rather the Sunni understanding and practice of Islam:

> He spread knowledge, trained ulema and honoured Islam and the people of Islam with great beneficence.[80]

In addition to seeing off the Chak threat to his rule and destroying the *khānaqāh*-shrine complex of 'Irakī at Zadibal, Dughlat was also responsible for and executing the *Nūrbakhshī* shaykh's son, Shaykh Dāniyāl. Not only was the *Nūrbakhshīyā* order banned, but Dughlat also indulged in killing of prominent elders associated with it. 'Ali would have us believe that all those targeted were Shi'i, the author of *Bahāristān* contests this by naming Sufis outside the *Nūrbakhshī* order, especially within the *Kubrawī*'s, as well as Sunni ulema belonging to the Shafī school who were either exiled or killed. In spite of his championing of the Ḥanafī orthodoxy, we know that at least one of the disciples of the Shaykh Ḥamza, Maulana Shams Pāl, engaged in debates with the Dughlat and his associates.[81]

Dughlat's fall and his death were a result of Kashmiri nobles uniting once again, in the face of his growing atrocities and more importantly his inability to assimilate within the native cultural ethos. It is again left to Dedhmarī to paint the demise of Dughlat in a sectarian milieu, writing:

> The news of this untimely death of Mīrzā (sounded) glad tiding of victory for his enemies. Especially the *'Ahl-i Tashi'* whom he had awarded just (*qarar-i waqeyi*) punishment, became very happy.[82]

Ten years after Dughlat's death, Ghāzī Chak (r. 1561–3) ascended the throne of Kashmir with virtually no opposition from the nobles, Shi'i or Sunni. A brief mutiny from within the Chak clan was easily quashed without much of a fight, again showing how the nature of conflicts was political rather than sectarian.[83] Prior to ascending the throne, as vizier, Ghāzī had been responsible for defeating a Mughal army sent by Akbar in 1561 to occupy Kashmir.

While 'Ali dismisses Ghāzī's reign in a little less than a line, Khwāja Isḥāq Qarī, another of Makhdūm's disciple, records a lengthy incident to show Ghāzī's apparent hostility to Sunnis, an enmity personified by his behavior toward Shaykh Ḥamza Makhdūm.[84] Whereas the sultan's father, Kazī Chak had been deeply involved in the conversion process, there is no evidence to suggest that Ghāzī Chak also followed a similar religious policy. Most of the sultan's time was spent in consolidating the outer territories of Kashmir, many of which had attained a semi-independent status and resisting the Mughals. Himself a soldier and an able administrator under the Mughal emperor Jahāngīr (r. 1605–27), the Kashmiri Shi'i noble Malik Ḥaidar notes Ghāzī's accomplishments and contributions to Kashmir in these words:

> During his region [*sic*], he conquered the whole of Khuistān-i Hind and brought Pakhlī and Bhimber under his control. [. . .] the type of victory achieved by Ghāzī Khān was never achieved by any of the great rulers (*Khawāqīn*) of the world.[85]

Though brave and well learned, Ghāzī Chak possessed an uncompromising nature—harsh to the extreme, combined with and a deep sense of justice. When his son and heir apparent, Ḥaidar Khān murdered his uncle, the sultan had Ḥaidar hanged in retaliation at 'Īdgāh, the main *maidan* of the city. Bought up in a tumultuous world of war, conflict, and intrigue, Ghāzī Chak governed with a strong hand, but with a marked lack of benevolence or sympathy. Where Dughlat had turned to confessional conformity to consolidate his rule, Ghāzī cultivated order and justice as the foundational basis of his Sultanate; but the sultan's retributive justice was devoid of mercy. The Shi'i author of *Bahāristān* while acknowledging Ghāzī's struggle at preserving Kashmir territorial sovereignty against repeated Mughal incursions of Akbar, castigates the sultan as a tyrant who relished in meting out harsh punishments. The Sanskrit historian Shūkā provides an interesting assessment of the first Chak sultan in these words:

> the great leader, the life of the world, the giver of good to the humble, the accomplished [. . .] the one versed in literature and the benefactor of the people

> [. . .]. The king robbed even the neighbors of those who committed a fault and he killed one hundred men every day. He imposed heavy fines for slight offences, and he robbed villages for the fault of one. He gave nothing to worthy men but bestowed his gifts on the unworthy.[86]

After abdicating the throne due to an advancing case of leprosy, Ghāzī Chak was succeeded by his brother Sultan Ḥusayn Shāh (1563–70). Among the rulers of the Chak dynasty, Ḥusayn Shāh is remembered as a just and cultured ruler; epitomized as *Khusraw-i ʿAādil.*[87] But unlike his brothers, Ḥusayn Shāh had to face revolts from his own family, favorites, and the wider circle of nobles. The nature of these conflicts was again political and not sectarian in nature. In, addition, Ḥusayn had to compete against renewed Mughal interest in the affairs of Kashmir. Having shaken off the restraints of both his regent, Bairam Khān (1556–60), as well the pull of the harem, a confident and increasingly independent-minded Emperor Akbar (r. 1556–1605) was overseeing a campaign of consolidating and expanding the Mughal territories. It was in the background of these events that the court of Ḥusayn Shāh became involved in an event, severely testing the court as well as the sultan. It also set a pattern where a section of the Sunni religious elite who had profited under the patronage of Dughlat start viewing the Chak rule as one rooted in Shiʿiism—dangerous for the survival and stability of the community of *Ahl-i Sunnat wal Jamat*. The hagiographers from Shaykh Makhdūm Ḥamza's circle celebrate this argument for a sectarian milieu.[88]

On the surface, the incident revolves around a confrontation between the Sunni *khatīb* (preacher: who reads *khutba* or sermon) of Srinagar's Jami Masjid, Qāzī Ḥabīb, and a nondescript Shiʿi soldier, Yūsuf Inder. Yūsuf was practicing his swordship outside the Jamai Masjid, when the qāzī arrived at the scene. An acrimonious exchange between the two resulted in Ḥabīb abusing the Shiʿi faith and Yūsuf retaliating against the qāzī. We may well visualize how this exchange between an ordinary soldier and the preacher at the main mosque of the city must have infuriated the qāzī who had in the past presided in the court of Dughlat overseeing a severe restrictive campaign against the Shiʿi. Enraged Ḥabīb stuck a blow at Yūsuf with his whip, but was in for another, more nasty surprise. The soldier in what the author of *Bahāristān* terms as "somewhat recklessly" stuck back at the qāzī with his sword, wounding him. Matters soon reached the court, where the *vazīr*, ʿAli Kokā got the sultan's permission to hold a trial under a council of Ḥanafī ulema presided over by Qāzī Mūsā, Mullā Fīrūz, and Mullā Yūsuf. The three unanimously issued a death decree against Yūsuf Inder who was swiftly executed. The injured party, Qāzī Ḥabīb, himself argued against the severity of the decision, as the death decree went against the principle of *ḳiṣāṣ*.[89] Of all medieval authors, only *Bahāristān* records the gruesome details of Yūsuf execution:

> The flesh of his body was cut into pieces which people carried as gift for their womenfolk, and many people drank his blood as *sharbat*.[90]

This particular extract, aside from the historical veracity of the details linked with the execution, does nevertheless suggest the level of public emotions involved in the incident, especially within the city. Unfortunately for the sultan the sentiments involved with the incident refused to die down. Questioning the justice and legitimacy of the death decree, Yūsuf's family along with some Shiʿi and apparently Sunni elite at the court made submission for a review of the entire case. As a result, both Mullā Fīrūz and Mullā Yūsuf were sentenced to death in accordance with the Shāfī law, the death decree being issued by a Shāfī'ite Qāzī Zain-al Dīn and a Ḥanafī jurist Qāzī ʿAbdul Ghafūr. The debate surrounding the case was presided over by Akbar's envoy to the Kashmiri court, Mīrzā Muqim,[91] and attended by "a large number of learned and scholarly men, dignitaries, theologians and the elite of the city."[92] While Qāzī Mūsā escaped death by fleeing from the city both Mullā Fīrūz and Mullā Yūsuf were executed. The judicial basis for the execution is summarized in *Bahāristān* in these words:

> It is said that the ruler of this domain, the sitting Qādī, and the executed person, all professed the creed of Imām Shāfiʿi. The *mullās* of *sunnat* and the *jamāʿat* were shown the letters with royal signets and they declared the decree sound. The decree pronounced that both the *mullās* on account of having issued false judgement and unjustifiable order [of execution] regarding the shedding of an innocent person's blood, should suffer retribution.[93]

The entire event, the execution of Yūsuf and the two *mullās*, shows a marked lack of political pragmatism on the part of Ḥusayn Shāh. By staying away from the deliberations, and handing over the issue to committees, the sultan may have thought he could impress his sincerity in a charged trail, but this was not to be so. ʿAli Kokā, the vazir, was looking to secure his own position at the expense of the sultan. His siding with the Qāzī in the initial trial may not have been based on any religious considerations, of helping a fellow Sunni, but the bungled nature of the trail and the ensuing tension between the court and a section of the Sunni ulema was to his help.

Ḥusayn Shāh neither stopped Yūsuf's execution initially nor that of the two *mullās* who in spite of their juridical indiscretion must have enjoyed support from both fellow Sunni ulema and the urban population of the city. The author of *Bahāristān* mentions that in the aftermath, many of the *mullās* migrated to Lahore and other parts of India, some returning back to Kashmir and office only after the intercession of their patrons at the court.[94] Coeval with the trials, the sultan's son passed away, and before long the sultan suffered from a stroke of paralysis. The trouble with his brother ʿAli Shāh resulted in a power struggle with competing groups of nobles supporting the sultan and his brother. Finally, Ḥusayn Shāh was deposed and his brother ʿAli Shāh (r. 1570–8) ascended the throne. After Ghāzī Chak's harsh and somber rule, Kashmir showed a revival of cultural undertakings under Ḥusayn and ʿAli Shāh. Poets and literary men from the wider Persianate world located to Kashmir's west arrived in Srinagar and were afforded court patronage. Poets like Mīr ʿAli, Mullā Nāmī, Bābā Ṭālib Isfhānī, and Mīrzā ʿAli originally hailing from Iran found court patronage and were well received by the sultans. We also find textual references to renewed building activities by the

Chaks, though barring a few ruins nothing survives from this period. A hospice, *Khānaqāh-i Naū*, constructed under the Chaks, for a leading Shiʿi divine of the time, Bābā Khalil-al Lah (d. 1591), at Nawa Kadal shows a significant departure from the traditional Kashmiri style of wooden architecture.[95] Surviving masonry at the site indicated that the building was based on Timurid architectural style, which had initially been introduced in the region during the mid-fifteenth century under Sultan Zain-al Ābidīn (r. 1420–70). The tradition of historiography, which forms a basis of our understanding of medieval Kashmir, is linked directly with the Chak period, the men who wrote them grew under the Chaks. The leading Indian calligrapher at the court of Akbar, Muhammad Ḥusayn Kashmirī, whose work was favorably compared with Mīr ʿAli Ḥarvī, had risen in the court of Chak sultans. On ʿAli Shāh's death, his son Yūsuf Shāh (r. 1579, 1580–6) ascended the throne, marking a break with the Chak tradition where the ruler was succeeded by his surviving brother and not son. This resulted in an open conflict between Yūsuf and his uncle Abdāl Chak, resulting in the latter's death. In the face of advancing Mughal aggression against Kashmir, Yūsuf proved to be a pragmatic, realizing early on that resistance against the Mughal Empire was futile. The sultan had inherited none of the fighting spirit that marked his ancestors' rise to power and throne. Immersed in the company of singers and women, he neither exhibited statecraft nor an understanding of how to marshal his resources when the need arose. Given his mis-governance, Yūsuf Shāh was deposed within two months of becoming sultan and replaced by Sayyid Mubārak (r. 1850), a Sunni noble who had ensured Yūsuf's ascent to the throne on the death of ʿAli Shāh. Fortune, however, favored Yūsuf and he soon regained the throne, returning back in 1581 to a warm public welcome in the capital, Srinagar. Bābā Dawud Khākī celebrated Yūsuf Shāh's return in an ode, *Qasideh-i Ghusuliya Yūsuf Shāh*':

> The Sultan of truth and glory, once again
> was bestowed with throne and destiny and crown and rich dominion
> God favored him, and in his share, he received
> a life and physical features harmonized by good character and beauty
> He is the friend of the Prophet and his family and companions
> He follows the righteous creed, this sultan of noble intentions[96]

Khākī's *qasideh* presents an intriguing text, with its complimentary praise of Yūsuf Shāh, given that in his *tazkira*, he paints the Chaks as opponents of Sunni faith. How do we then place the *qasideh* in the shifting complex dynamic of sixteenth-century Kashmir? What exactly does "righteous creed" (*mazhab-i maqbūl*) mean in Khākī's worldview? In most Sunni accounts, Khākī is said to have disassociated from court culture early on after joining the circle of Makhdūm. This aura of a worldly recluse does not fit in with the writing of a panegyric ode for a ruler. Can we then posit that Khākī was not as disinclined toward the court and court patronage as we are generally led to believe? Importantly, at the SPS Museum (Srinagar), we find a *vāthiqa-nāma* (legal document) pertaining to the shrine of Shaykh Ḥamza Makhdūm in the city. Written in Sharda (Sanskrit script) on birch bark, the *vāthiqa-nāma* is believed to have been issued by Yūsuf Shāh in favor of the shrine, implying court patronage of a shrine-complex which at least in the texts was highly inimical of both Chak rule and their Shiʿi belief. Unlike his *tazkira*'s, the *qasideh* of Khākī does not seek to enshrine the memory of "noble ruler" for some future generations—rather it seeks the ruler's audience, which "demands" the fulfillment of a worldly requirement and a worldly reward. The reward does not necessarily have to be for the writer himself, it can in Khākī's case be for the fraternity of *mūridīn* who saw him as their spiritual *pīr* or the shrine-complex of his shaykh.

Aside from his patronage of Makhdūm's shrine (Figure 1.3), Yūsuf Shāh was also responsible for abolishing the *jaziyā* tax on Kashmiri Pandits that had been imposed by Gāzī Chak. Liberal and cultured, the fickle-minded sultan betrayed his land when it needed him most. Rather than resisting Akbar, as his nobles and more importantly the people would have him, Yūsuf Shāh fled from Kashmir joining the Mughal camp in 1586. In the absence of their ruler, the Kashmiri nobles enthroned Yūsuf's son Yʿaqūb Shāh (r. 1586). The new sultan had earlier escaped from Akbar's court where he had been sent by his father as an envoy. Brave and strong-willed, Yʿaqūb Shāh fought the Mughal forces as the last sultan of Kashmir, continuing his struggle even after the Mughals had captured the capital, before finally submitting to Akbar on his visit to Kashmir in 1588. While the incorporation of Kashmir within the Mughal Empire was inevitable, given the vastly superior resources commanded by the latter, Yʿaqūb through his political indiscretion hastened this collapse. At a time when his *mūlk* was wavering under repeated Mughal attacks, the sultan opened an old quarrel with the Sunni preacher of the Jamia Masjid, Qāzī Musā. The qāzī who had escaped punishment in the

Figure 1.3 Shaykh Ḥamza Makhdūm shrine-precinct, Srinagar, 2019 (courtesy: Mukhtar Ahmad).

case of Yūsuf Inder had earned himself public goodwill due to his completion of the reconstruction of Jamia Masjid. The mosque's reconstruction had been left unattended by both the sultan and the various *amīrs*, engaged as they were in their political maneuvering. The qāzī must also not have forgotten his near execution at the hands of the Chaks. Retaining his animosity against the dynasty, we find Mūsā constantly working against the interests of sultan and *mūlk*, both during the reign of Yūsuf Shāh and Y'aqūb. On the advice of his Shi'i vizier, Mullā Aswad, Y'aqūb ordered the qāzī to recite the name of the first Shi'i imām, 'Ali b. Abī Ṭālib (d. 661), in the *khuṭba* (Friday sermon). This the qāzī refused to do. Based on his refusal and earlier acts Y'aqūb had the qāzī executed for disobedience, in spite of being advised against this by both Shi'i and Sunni councilors. The Sunni religious elite hailed the dead qāzī as a (*shahid*) martyr, and it is as such he is remembered among Kashmiri Sunnis today: Qāzī Mūsā *Shahid*. In the aftermath of the execution, a delegation of the city's leading Sunni religious scholars under Bābā Dawud Khākī and Shaykh Y'aqūb Sarfī proceeded to Delhi imploring Akbar to free them from the tyranny of the Shi'i sultans. The execution of the qāzī was presented as an undeniable proof of Chak intolerance and bigotry.

While Y'aqūb left the city to fight the invading Mughal army, a section of Kashmiri Sunni *amīrs* under the leadership of Zaffar Chak revolted against the sultan, and with a large body of soldiers and mob attacked Shi'i majority areas of the city, killing many and burning the shrine of Mīr Shams-al Dīn 'Irakī.[97] This is the first known instance of a Shi'i-Sunni riot in the city. With dissensions in his ranks, Y'aqūb engaged in a series of battles against the invading imperial Mughal army guided by Shaykh Y'aqūb Ṣarfī (d. 1595), the leading Sunni scholar of Kashmir, who had negotiated Kashmir's incorporation within the Mughal Empire with the emperor, Akbar.[98] Finally, the imperial Mughal army managed to enter Srinagar on October 14, 1586. The ceremonial *khuṭba* was read in the name of Akbar at Srinagar's principal mosque, Jamia Masjid, marking the end of both Chak rule and Kashmir's independence. The date of the Mughal conquest is derived from two conflicting Persian chronograms: *khush āmdīd* (welcome) and *zulm-i beḥad* (unlimited tyranny), reflecting the contentious views embedded in the texts disseminating from the community of educated elite of both the Sunni and Shi'i society. For Dedhmarī, the fall of the Chaks marks a sign of divine benevolence for an oppressed Sunni community.[99] A narrative which is uniformly echoed and "welcomed" by other Sunni historians. The end of the Chak Sultanate is seen as the vindication of the righteousness of Sunni faith. For their part, the Shi'i would symbolize loss with the betrayal of *qaūm*, *mūlk*, and *sultanat*.

Chapter 2

Mapping Existence

In Search of Patronage and Protection

Muslim rule in Kashmir ended in 1820 when the *ṣubah* (province) of Kashmir was annexed by the Sikhs under Maharaja Ranjit Singh. The event marked the end of five centuries of Muslim rule in Kashmir, marking a watershed moment in the life of the inhabitants, Muslims and Hindus alike. This event also provided a space for the Shiʿi Muslims to establish for themselves a spiritual and cultural identity distinct from the Sunnis. But the process was long drawn and contentious. The second chapter further develops the theme of Shiʿi identity in Kashmir by investigating the political, intellectual, and social activity within the Kashmiri Shiʿi society at the beginning of the nineteenth century leading up to the Sikh conquest. In exploring the period, I access the collective community memory embodied in a literary genre that became specifically associated with the Shiʿi society, the *marṣiya*. This chapter illustrates how due to the prevailing attitude on part of the Afghan rulers, many Kashmiri scholars migrated toward the Shiʿi kingdom of Awadh for patronage and security and in the process helped in establishing and mediating a transregional Shiʿi space of interaction based on the exchange of scholarly knowledge and financial patronage. Continuing with its focus on these transregional, transnational linkages the chapter also explores the connections and contributions of Iranian merchants based in Kashmir to the material culture of native Shiʿi society.

Navigating Shiʿiness under the Afghans

In his letter written to *Khān Bahadur* Moulvi Sayyid Rajab ʿAli Khān,[1] - a Shiʿi man of letters working with the British colonial administration in India, Mullā Ḥakim Muhammad ʿAẕim (d. 1269 AH/1852 CE), reminiscences about the restrictive environment in which Kashmiri Shiʿi found themselves during the Afghan rule of Kashmir in these words:

> In the era of *Sardār* ʿAbdullah Khān Afghan, who had sparked a fire in Zadibal from utmost hatred, fanatism and enmity for keeping up the anger, which ruined

> the believers daily in the publication from the mourning rites. They altered them every night clandestinely. And more so in the era of 'Abdullah Khān Afghan, in which 'Abdullah's mouth said more and more that in his days the remembrance of the Lord of Martyrs, peace be upon him, and the faith of the mourners, should be cancelled from the minds. Strangers prohibited crying when remembering Husain. It has gone so far now that we have to cry very much.[2]

Written around the middle of the nineteenth century, while serving as chief physician[3] of Maharaja Gulab Singh (r. 1846–57), the founder of the Hindu Dogra dynasty in Kashmir, 'Aẕim's letter specifically mentions the restriction imposed on the enactment of the Muharram rituals in Kashmir. It highlights the acts of the Afghan *subadar*, 'Abdullah Khān, in suppressing these ceremonies.[4] Interestingly, 'Aẕim's father, Mullā Ḥakim Muhammad Javad (d. around 1220 AH/1805 CE), had served as the personal physician of 'Abdullah Khān and would be accused by a later generation of Sunni historians of not only having worked against the Afghan *ṣubedar* but also harmed the Sunni population of the city due to his sectarian prejudice.[5]

The younger ḥakim's letter, on the other hand, was a remembrance of the events surrounding the Muharram of 1216 AH/1801 CE, when on the orders of the 'Abdullah Khān a medley of Afghan soldiers and city mob burned *Ma'rak*, the historical *imāmbāda* in the capital Srinagar. In the aftermath of the desecration, the frenzied mob spread out in the surrounding Shi'i-dominated moḥala of Zadibal engaging in acts of rape, loot, and a general massacre.[6] Kuihāmī in his description of ten major *tārāj* (massacres) against the Shi'i of Kashmir has listed the event as the *tārāj hashtam*—the eighth massacre.[7] The immediate provocation for the *tārāj* was an attempt by the Shi'i to open the closed gates of *Ma'rak* and engage in *marṣiya khwānī*[8]—the recital of elegies on the martyrdom of Ḥusayn b. 'Ali, which had been prohibited under successive Afghan *subadars* as also indicated in 'Aẕim's letter. In describing the event, Kuihāmī posits the causes of riots on Shi'i intemperance:

> The cause of the incident is that on the day of Ashura, the Shi'i clerics openly used abusive language against the Companions of the Prophet, and also showed blasphemy during chanting marṣiya. The news spread and caused commotion in the city. The Khāns of Kabul got enraged and they motivated the mischief monger and hooligans of the city to loot the Shi'is. Eventually, within no time a devastating fire of revenge devastated the community. Their property was ruined, and their modesty was ravaged without any scruple.[9]

For Kuihāmī, every Shi'i-Sunni riot is an unfortunate event. But, then, the argument if not the justification for Sunni excesses lies in the Shi'i intransigence—provocations testing Sunni sensibilities, invariably resulting in "the anger of the Sunnis breaks out after every thirty or forty years [. . .]."[10]

Another contemporary historian of Kuihāmī, Mullā Khalil Marjānpūrī, while also blaming the Shi'i of Zadibal, adds the moḥala of Hasanabad to the list of

Shiʿi-dominated areas in the city that were devastated and burned down in the riots.[11] An earlier attempt at reopening the doors of Zadibal *Imāmbāda* in 1203 AH/1788 CE during the rule of *ṣubedar* Juʿma Khān Alkozī had resulted in a severe backlash from the Afghans who ordered the demolition of both the *imāmbādas*.[12]

The determination of the Kashmiri Shiʿi to make the *imāmbāda* at Zadibal functional can be seen as a community attempt at reengaging with revered rituals in an equally revered public space carried out in the backdrop of perceived Shiʿi's strength at the *ṣubedar's* court: the *ṣubedar's* personal ḥakim, Mullā Javad, and his *peshkār*, Mīrzā Razā.[13] But, in reality, both the Shiʿi courtiers operated in a hostile court environment where their Shiʿiness was both manifest and a source of complaints against them. The degree of hostility can also be observed in the historiographies of Kuihāmī and Marjānpūrī, who perfunctorily blame the Shiʿi courtiers for the *ṣubedar's* debauchery and incompetence.[14] Nevertheless, the dichotomizing nature of Afghan rule as seen in the presence of Mullā Javad and Mīrzā Razā at the court is a clear indication that even in the case of what the Kashmiri Shiʿi perceived as a prejudiced *ṣubedar*,[15] pathways to royal service were not entirely closed for Shiʿi. Individual Afghan *ṣubedars* did certainly manage a court of sectarian elites, at times imposing a narrow-minded version of Sunnism, but this was primarily targeted against any manifestation of Shiʿiness in the public sphere—also, at times to extort money from wealthy Shiʿis as well as Hindus. The near-complete erasure of any performance of Muharram ceremonies during Afghan rule is a clear outcome of this sectarian prejudice.

Writing four years after the riots of 1801, a native poet, Ustād Muhammad Ja'far, in one of his *marṣiya* bemoans the condition of the Shiʿi community in these words:

> O! Men, four years have passed, since we crossed the threshold of *Mʿārak*,
> come let us pray for atonement, this phase might pass by,
> tell the mourners, the elegist, where can we cry?
> Alas! Where can we shed tears for Imām Ḥusayn?
> For should we but utter his name,
> death and mayhem become our fate.[16]

In a similar vein, a contemporary of Ustād, Khwāja Ḥassī Bhat also laments the difficulties and the danger that the Shiʿi community of Kashmir faced in commemorating the Muharram rituals:

> Who can bemoan the martyrdom of Imām Ḥusayn here?
> Alas! Those who dared are gone,
> their houses and *mātam sarāi* (imāmbāda) burnt.[17]

The verses of Khwāja Ḥassī and Ustād Ja'far serve as a graphical reminder of the destruction that took place during the rule of ʿAbdullah Khān and its continuing effects on the community. Given the restrictive political conditions, members of the community practiced mourning in secrecy but never gave up the observance of the ritual. This transformed the performance of the entire ritual from a public into a private commemoration, limited within the immediate families. Wherever possible, Shiʿi took to the construction of *tah-khāna* (basements) in their private houses, where they could discreetly recite *marṣiyas* during the month of Muharram, in the hope that any wailing sound made would escape notice.[18] Within Zadibal, a few old houses still survive, which retain the *tah-khāna* and the memory associated with them. The prevailing narrative for the Shiʿi community during the Afghan rule remains of silent mourning, best exemplified by another *marṣiya* writer in these verses:

> Those whose eyes cried in the path of religion (*dīn nich wa'tey*)
> tell them, may my life be your ransom,
> tell them to cry silently, for fear of discovery,
> O! Men for crying is followed here by mayhem.[19]

It is also noteworthy that the poet would compare mourning for Ḥusayn with acts performed in the path of religion: *dīn nich wa'tey*. Khwāja Ḥassī in one of his *marṣiya* has similarly epitomized grieving over Karbala with the *khānaqāh* of salvation.[20] Deliverance through the mourning of Ḥusayn remains a recurring theme in many of the *marṣiyas* from this period. In the *marṣiya* of Khwāja Muhammad Fazil, remembrance of the events of Karbala is presented as an assured path to deliverance in the afterlife.[21] An examination of the numerous surviving *marṣiyas* written during Afghan rule in Kashmir reveals how in accessing this commemorative text, the poets and through them the Shiʿi society of Kashmir were able to access the past and then select and summarize a worldview for the believers, of a suffering community which like the martyrs of Karbala had to endure.

Overall, the majority of *marṣiyas* written during the Afghan rule convey the feelings of impermanence of the human world, the greed, and the tyranny, emotions that mark the everlasting human conflict of good and evil. Yet the background for the poetic canvas remains the idea of the *Ahl-i Bayt* (Prophet's family) serving as the saviors of humanity, through their act of sacrifice. Given the importance of the sacrifice offered by the martyrs at Karbala, it also translates into a promise of "the other worldly reward" for acts of piety and faith. If the *marṣiyas* are evaluated within the prevailing sociopolitical conditions, one would see in them an assurance to the historically aggrieved and powerless Shiʿi community that their sufferings are a reflection of those at Karbala and the reward of faith lies in the hereafter. Within the cycle of sectarian violence targeted at the Shiʿi community under the Afghans, this otherworldly assurance also provided the audience with a reason on the basis of which to navigate within the turbulent world of death and destruction, so as not to lose hope. Consequently, in Kashmiri *marṣiyas* there is no celebration of the battle, no representation of heroic acts of valor but a personalized representation of grief and sorrow over the loss of a son, brother, husband, or companion and grief over indignities and sufferings that the women of Ḥusayn's household had to face after the battle. Once established, this theme would continue to resonate even when the Shiʿi society found the circumstances more favorable and secure, under the Sikh and Dogra rule.

While the riot of 1801 effectively ended any Shiʿi attempt at publicly rehabilitating the Muharram ceremonies even within Shiʿi majority areas, we do find a few isolated examples of patronage of community symbols even though on a much smaller scale. Though the Shiʿi ḥakim of the *ṣubedar*, Mullā Javad could not save the community from the enraged Afghan mobs, he did in the aftermath of the riot construct a smaller mosque and hammam at Hasanabad, within the wider precinct of the burned out *imāmbāda*. Nevertheless, such attempts were limited. More than Kashmiri Shiʿis, it was the influence of non-native Shiʿi merchants, notably those belonging to Iran, whose presence in Kashmir served as the source of patronage and political support for the Shiʿi society of Kashmir.

In his account of the riots of 1801, the historian Marjānpūrī makes a reference to an earlier episode of Shiʿi-Sunni disturbance, linked to a Kashmiri Sunni notable, Khwāja ʿĪsā, and an Iranian merchant, Āqā Raḥīm.[22]

Tājiran-i Iran: *Iranian Shawl Merchants in Kashmir*

In his description of Kashmir under Afghan rule, Forster remarks about the remarkable set of merchants from different nationalities based in Srinagar and engaged in transnational trade across the Himalayas in these words:

> In Kafhmire (Kashmir) are feen (seen) merchants and commercial agents of moft (most) of the principal cities of northern India, alfo (also) of Tartary, Perfia (Persia) and Turkey, who at the fame (same) time advance their fortunes, and enjoy the pleafures (pleasures) of a fine climate and the country.[23]

Based on accounts of visitors to Kashmir in the early part of the nineteenth century, mostly European (including that of Forster), the understanding that the Kashmiri shawl "trade was controlled by Iranian or Central Asian merchants"[24] seems correct. While Kashmir had witnessed a steady arrival of Sufis, preachers, artisans, and poets from Persianate land from the fifteenth century, it is only during the Afghan period we find textual as well as material evidence of merchants from Iran stationed in Kashmir.[25] Most, if not all, of these merchants were engaged in the highly lucrative shawl trade and would operate from the capital city, Srinagar. Forster also informs us that a part of the Afghan revenue collection in Kashmir was realized in shawls. Given the importance attached to the shawl trade and the revenue raised, foreign merchants involved in the shawl trade were well regarded and afforded a degree of immunity by the *ṣubedars*, irrespective of their communal or sectarian affiliations. And, once stationed in Srinagar, the Iranian traders did also engage with the local Shiʿi community at large. Vigne informs us that a colony of "Persian merchants, of whom there were two or three hundred," used to reside in Srinagar till the early 1830s.[26]

While we do not have the exact figure of the Shi'i population in Kashmir at the start of the nineteenth century, the presence of the community was predominantly located in the city of Srinagar. And, while they monopolized the papier-mâché craft, many Kashmiri Shi'i were also engaged in the shawl trade, as both *kār-khāndars* (manufacturers) and artisans: weavers and embroiders.

How deeply the fate of these non-native Iranian merchants was intertwined in the community life of Kashmir Shi'i can be understood in Marjānpūrī's narrative related to events surrounding Khwāja 'Īsā Dewanī and Āqā Rahīm. The account is given considerable space in Marjānpūrī's account.

The event is centered on Khwāja 'Īsā Dewanī, a Kashmiri acting as the agent for the Afghan *ṣubedars*. He seemed to have been particularly intimate with the *ṣubedar*, Mīr Hazār Khān (r. 1792–3) whose brief rule was extremely harsh on both Shi'i and the Hindu population of Kashmir.[27] From multiple accounts, including Marjānpūrī, we get an idea of 'Īsā operating as a shady agent of Mīr Hazār Khān, forwarding the *ṣubedar* with names of prominent figures within the Kashmiri Shi'i and Pandit community.[28] These then became a special target of the *ṣubedar* for financial extortion. While many supplicated Mīr Hazar with bribes, many more were killed including the pandit Dilā Ram Qulī who had served as *diwān* under previous Afghan *ṣubedars*.[29] For reasons which remain unrecorded, 'Issā played a pivotal role in the execution of a Shi'i merchant, Muhammad Taqī.[30] The removal of Mīr Hazar removed the main source of 'Īsā power and gave rise to a very bizarre incident in the city.

In the reports of Kashmiri Sunni sources, somewhere around 1208 AH/1793 CE, Āqā Rahīm invited 'Īsā over lunch at his *ḥavelī*, located at Qāzī Kadal (Q'adh Kadal) in the heart of the city.[31] Marjānpūrī refers to Rahīm as *sar-i halqah-i tājirān-i nāmdār* (head of the circle of famous merchants) and *bisyār sahib-i aitbar* (man of great trust). As the meet proceeds, the merchant leaves 'Īsā alone in the hammam, which he then asks his servants to heat up, the intention being apparently to suffocate 'Īsā to death, or in the words of Marjānpūrī burn him to death. In these dire circumstances, 'Īsā somehow not only manages to set himself free, breaking the glass panes of the window but then also succeeds to attract a huge mob, who in turn burn down the *ḥaveli* of the Āqā Rahīm. Marjānpūrī then proceeds from an anecdotal narrative to a personnel account of an unnamed witness. This witness forms the source for the remaining narration: about how after affecting his rescue, 'Īsā is paraded in a palanquin by a large attendant mob all the way to the city edge at 'Īdgāh. This vast open field also borders the nearby Shi'i *moḥala* of Zadibal, which bore the brunt of the mob's violence.[32] Located at the edge of the historic Srinagar and separated from the main populated areas of the city by Khushalsar Lake and the open fields of 'Īdgāh, Zadibal would remain the principal Shi'i majority quarter of the city. While there were small pockets of Shi'i population within the city, a majority of Srinagar's Shi'i population resided in Zadibal and in Hasanabad another Shi'i-dominated *moḥala* also separated from the main city by the vast public cemetery, Malkha. Outside Srinagar, Shi'i presence was virtually absent in any of the major towns of Kashmir, while a significant population was dispersed across the rural landscape of central and adjoining northern Kashmir.

The historian intersects the story of ʿĪsā at the very end with an amusing report about how the witness on being mistaken for a Shiʿi was saved from abuse and harm by an acquaintance.[33]

Regarding Āqā Rahīm, almost nothing is known about his origin, still, it is safe to posit that he was part of a merchant Diaspora of Iranian descent, based in Kashmir.[34] The Persian-origin prefix "Āqā" found limited favor among Kashmiri Shiʿi, we find its use only in the early twentieth century that too among certain Sayyid families. A wide network of Iranian merchants engaged in the Kashmiri shawl trade operated from Srinagar, till mid-nineteenth century. They remained an important part of the transregional trade network not only connecting Kashmir with the wider geography of South Asia but also drawing merchants into Yarkand, Kasghar, Persia, Turkey, and other cities of Central Asia.

Overall, the entire account of Marjānpūrī reflects a lack of sectarian bias or any sympathy for ʿĪsā, or the mob behavior. Aside from the actual circumstances of the event, is the intriguing case of how a Shiʿi merchant could imagine such an audacious move, even if his intent was to arrest ʿĪsā and not actually murder him.[35] The merchant's wealth cannot be the only reason—wealthy Shiʿi and Hindus had been widely prosecuted by ʿĪsā. While ʿĪsā may have lost the patronage of a *ṣubedar* who was personally invested in a sectarian conflict like Mīr Hazār, his standing at the *ṣubedars*' court was unchanged. This brings up the idea of Āqā Rahīm's origin. Did the merchant's non-Kashmiri origin provide him with a degree of impunity, which, combined with his standing as one of the leading merchants based in Kashmir allowed him the space to manoeuvre and undertake such a misplaced step? While Rahīm's *ḥavelī* was burned in the incident, no report mentions that he or his family came to any physical harm in the entire drama; unlike countless native Shiʿi who suffered in the riot. Also, it is worthwhile to note that Khwāja Īsā's rescue was due to an enraged city mob—not due to any effort of the Afghan soldiery. With connections in the local court and drawing on his privilege as member of a neighboring empire, it is possible that Rahīm used his influence to intervene in a situation which his Kashmiri co-religionist would have considered suicidal. Still, the protection offered by the court could not offset the sense of rage that this act of indiscretion provoked among the rioting Sunni mobs.[36]

The influence that transnational shawl merchants such as Rahīm wielded at the local court can also be understood in the backdrop of how significant the shawl trade was to Kashmiri economy. Though variously estimated, the figure of forty lakh rupees as the annual collection of revenue from Kashmir to the Kabul court seems fairly accurate[37]—a part of this revenue was realized in the shape of shawls.[38] Interestingly, the value of shawls produced in Kashmir during Afghan rule was estimated at thirty-five lakh rupees.[39] The reason behind the privileges that these foreign merchants enjoyed at the *ṣubedars* court in Kashmir has also been alluded to by Forster:

> In treating of the government of Kafhmire {Kashmir}, I omitted to mention, that it had not hitherto extended its apprehenfion {apprehension} to merchants,

> who, from the wealth which they introduced into the province, were refpetted {respected} and even indulged.[40]

In his letters, French traveler Victor Jacquemont, who arrived in Kashmir in 1831, reflects on both the presence of Iranian merchants in Kashmir and their network of travel and trade in these words:

> Merchants, it is true, go almost everywhere, from Cashmere to Tehran, and even to Meshed, they go through Lahore, Delhi, Bombay, Bushire, Shiraz, &c. &c..[41]

While the shawl itself was manufactured in Kashmir, the raw material used in it *pashm (or pashmina)* was (and still is) sourced from the high mountain plateau of Changthang in Tibet. In the early part of the nineteenth century, Iranian merchants played an important role in the pashmina trade between Kashmir and Tibet, with Jacquemont opining that the trade was controlled by the Iranians.[42] An earlier explorer and self-styled British diplomat, Willam Moorcroft also remarks about the transnational nature of merchants involved in the Kashmiri shawl trade during Afghan rule, including Iranian merchants:

> Kashmir was formerly resorted to for shawl goods by merchants from Turkey, both in Asia and Europe, by Armenians, Persians, Afghans, Uzbeks, and by traders from Hindustan and from Chinese Turkistan.[43]

In his work on Iranian *tujjārs*, Willem Floor writes about two Iranian brothers, "Mohammad Javad of Shiraz resided in Kashmir where he traded in Kashmir shawls, and Hajji Mohammad Hosayn, his brother, did the same in Baghdad."[44] He also mentions about another Iranian merchant, Ḥājjī ʿAli Rezā Tājir Dehdashtī, who was apparently well known in Kashmir as "for many years he lived in Kashmir and traded in Kashmir shawls."[45] At Hasanabad and Baba Mazar, two prominent Shiʿi cemeteries of Srinagar city, even today we can trace out inscriptions on isolated tombstones dating from Afghan rule in Kashmir establishing the Iranian connections of the deceased. These include a number of individuals from two Iranian cities, Isfahan and Mashad: Āqā Muhammad Taqī Isfahānī (d. 1188 AH/1755 CE), Ḥājjī Mīr Ṣāliḥ Isfahānī (d. 1188 AH/1755 CE), Āqā 'Adil b. Ṣadiq Isfahānī (d. 1181 AH/1767 CE), and Muhammad Qulī b. Imām Qulī Mashadī (d. 1193 AH/1779 CE), and Malik Ḥasan b. Muhammad Qulī Mashadī (d. 1213 AH/1794 CE).

These Iranian merchants, predominantly Shiʿi, were in a position to influence the affairs of the Shiʿi community of Kashmir both through their wealth and visible political role as witnessed in the case of Āqā Rahīm. Also, the ripple effects of their patronage could be felt across *kār-khānas* within the city, among local Shiʿi traders and artisans commissioned by the Iranians for sourcing shawls and other related products of decorative art practiced in Kashmir.

A fine example of this wider patronage and engagement between Iranian Shiʿi merchant community and Kashmiri Shiʿi society can be seen in a codex of

Quran copied in Kashmir in 1246 AH/1831 CE. While Kashmiri calligraphers had risen to prominence at Mughal court from the time of Akbar, this art form had experienced substantial expansion as we come nearer to the nineteenth century. In addition to a steady market for manuscripts of both religious and more secular nature that was to be found within Kashmir, we find that numerous nineteenth-century manuscripts of richly illuminated Quran from Kashmir dispersed across mainland India. Jacquemont in his letters speaks about Kashmir as a big center of production of manuscripts, with seven to eight hundred copyists in the region, primarily residing in the city of Srinagar.

The copyist of the 1831 codex has signed his name as Muhammad Ḥusayn. Interestingly the richly decorated cover of the codex names the patron of this work of art as, Muhammad Ismāʿīl *tājir-i Isfahan* (merchant of Isfahan). The Shiʿi origin of the codex and the patron can also be seen in the illuminated front piece of the manuscript where within two beautifully executed paisley motifs, the scribe has recorded the Shiʿi articles of faith and a ḥadīth on the authority of the fifth Shiʿi imām, Jaʿfar al Ṣādiq (d 765). One can safely posit that Ismāʿīl, the merchant from Isfahan, was a part of that large network of Iranian merchants based in Srinagar, involved in the shawl trade while also providing patronage to other professionals within the community, in this case, the copyist and the writer of the glosses as well the *naqāsh*—the artist who was responsible for some if not all of the illumination of the codex, ʿAziz Mughal. Like the copyist, ʿAziz has also signed his name, on the cover as *ʿamal-i ʿAziz Mughalū* (the hand of ʿAziz Mughal). The illumination or *naqāshi* (papier-mâché as it is known now) of the cover is an art form that has historically been associated with the Kashmiri Shiʿi community. The surname Mughal is still retained by a Shiʿi family of Srinagar, whose members have been historically practicing papier-mâché, though today the practice has almost died down in this family.[46]

In Jacquemont's letters, the Iranian merchants in Kashmir find a mention as belonging to a community of "small number of very rich and respectable Iranian merchants, mostly hajjis."[47] Referencing the merchants by the honorific title of *ḥājjī* for having made the *ḥājj* pilgrimage would indicate that these Iranian *tūjjārs* operated in a deeply religious milieu. This is something that has been documented by Floor in his work on the merchants of nineteenth-century Qajjar Iran, writing:

> More ever the merchants were very religiously minded. Many of them had made the pilgrimage to Mecca, which is shown by the frequent honorific "*ḥājjī*". In 1883, thirty of forty-three merchants in Tehran were *ḥājjīs*. In Shiraz almost every one of twenty-six merchants had made the pilgrimage, while in Isfahan we find the same phenomenon.[48]

The religiosity of these Iranian merchants was not only conditioned to expressions of personal piety—such as performance of the *ḥājj* ritual—but also manifested in engagements with the native Shiʿi community in Kashmir. While available archival material indicates that these arrangements were primarily conditioned to business transactions, involving patronage of Shiʿi owned and operated *kār-*

khānas and *kārīgars*, we do see that in the post-Afghan period they also resulted in the establishment of matrimonial relations between the merchant families of Iran and elite Shiʿi families of Kashmir. This resulted in funding and patronage of Shiʿi symbols by the Iranian merchants, especially in the city of Srinagar. The Iranian presence in Kashmir came about because of a lucrative trade opportunity: the Kashmiri shawl. Protracted residence in the Kashmir helped in deepening these ties further cemented by Persianate cultural values that were deeply ingrained in the urban center of Srinagar, especially among the Shiʿi society. Still, though the relation between the Iranian *tujjars* and the Kashmiri Shiʿis came about due to shared sectarian identities, they were not exclusionary. The Iranians operated under the watchful eyes of the Afghan *ṣubedar*, whose court was dominated by Kashmiri Sunni elites represented by the elders in both the religious and merchant community. The stability of their business demanded that the Iranian merchants engage with the Sunnis, especially the native Sunni merchants. The episode surrounding Āqā Rahīm does highlight the ephemeral nature of the immunity enjoyed by the Iranian merchants, in spite of their financial importance for the Afghan court.

The fluidity in relation between the Afghan court and any expression linked with Shiʿi imagery or symbolism can also be witnessed in the commissioning of a wall hanging for the shrine of Imām Ḥusayn at Karbala, by the Afghan *ṣubedar*, ʿAẕim Khān (1813–16). Besides serving as the *ṣubedar* of Kashmir, ʿAẕim belonged to the clan of the Barakzai's who at this time were becoming heavily involved in court politics, following the death of Taimur Shāh, the second Amīr of Afghanistan. The work commissioned by ʿAẕim Khān comprises a wall hanging in pashmina—the craft for which Kashmir was renowned. Presently located in the Metropolitan Art Museum, New York (Figure 2.1), the catalogue of the museum describes this work of art in these words:

> Of the vast and varied textile production of Kashmir, one of the finest, least common types of textile is the hanging with a design of an arch or niche. This example was woven using the typical kani shawl technique, which involved three different weaving structures: twill, tapestry, and double-interlocked weft. [. . .]. The millefleurs decoration on this pashmina hanging immediately brings to mind the shape of a mihrab niche, and the hanging may have been placed on a wall to indicate the direction of Mecca.[49]

The name of the *ṣubedar* and the dedication to Ḥusayn can be found in a golden cartouche in the upper section of the hanging with the legend, 'O Husain, Ordered by the most noble governor, Muhammad "Azim Khan," while in the bottom, virtually indistinguishable from the surroundings is the phrase "Blessing, O King of Najaf (*Shah-i Najaf*),"[50] invoking the blessing of first Shiʿi' imām, 'Ali, whose shrine is located in Najaf, Iraq.

The commissioning happened at a time when ʿAẕim Khān was involved in a struggle with both domestic opponents and the Sikh Empire of Ranjit Singh. While invoking Imām ʿAli can be seen as representative of a wider sentiment,

Figure 2.1 Wall hanging commissioned for Imām Ḥusayn shrine (courtesy: The Metropolitan Museum of Art, New York).

of veneration for the imām as a charismatic warrior, that was prevalent across sectarian boundaries in nineteenth-century North India, the public demonstration of devotion to Imām Ḥusayn, the martyr of Karbala appeals to the sentiments which are more rooted in Shiʿi memory and dedicatory practices. So, what could have been the reason for ʿAẕim's action? While one can see certainly link the wall hanging to the desire of the *ṣubedar* for conveying his dedication and loyalty to religious personages who figure prominently in the Sunni list of revered figures, yet the political and cultural context of the production suggests otherwise. This becomes all the more visible when we juxtapose the commissioning of the wall hanging with previous decrees of Afghan *ṣubedars*, banning commemorative mourning ceremonies linked with Imām Ḥusayn. With his commissioning of the wall hanging for the shrine of Ḥusayn, ʿAẕim Khān was in fact appealing to Shiʿi sensibilities of the Qizalbash contingent at his court, and not the Kashmiri Shiʿi. The Persian-origin Qizalbash had served the Dūrānī kingdom in prominent positions both in the administration as secretaries and in the army. In his rise to the throne of Amir of Afghanistan, Dūst Muhammed (r. 1826–39, 1843–63), ʿAẕim's stepbrother, would be supported by the Qizalbash contingent of the Afghan army.[51]

The twin riots of 1793 and 1801 though rooted in Shiʿi persecution also present us with two cases of Shiʿi assertiveness during Afghan rule. The assertiveness was, however, tempered by both the excesses of Afghan *ṣubedars* and more importantly the Sunni mob of the city—the *shawlbafs* (shawl weavers) of Marjānpūrī's account. The demise of Afghan authority in 1821 to the advancing Sikh troops of Maharaja Ranjit Singh removed the harassment of the state, now the Shi'i' had only to contend with the Sunni population of Kashmir, for the first time in five centuries, and under a non-Muslim rule.

In the Court of Awadh Kings

In 1805, while Kashmir was still under the Afghans and Iranian merchants were still arriving in Srinagar, an Iranian scholar, Āqā Aḥmad Bihbahānī arrived in India. Well trained in leading Shi'i seminaries of Iran and Iraq, Aḥmad Bihbahānī belonged to a prominent Shi'i ulema family with roots both in the Isfahan and the Shi'i shrine city of Karbala.[52] For a period of four years, Bihbahānī traveled across India from Bombay to Calcutta and then into North India. In his memoirs, *Mir'at al-Ahwal-i Jahān Nūmā,* he writes extensively about these travels and the people he came across. Arriving in Lucknow in 1222 AH/1807 CE, Bihbahānī while recording details about scholars and nobles residing in the city also writes about a Kashmiri *'alim* in the city:

> The exalted and high-titled Mullā Mohammad Muqim Kashmirī, who because of the oppression of his opponents, having fled from Kashmir has settled down in this city. He is an eminent scholar, very well-mannered and meek, and lives ensconced in his house.[53]

The "oppression of his opponents" is an oblique reference in the text to Shi'i persecution in Kashmir. Family records maintain that Mullā Muqim (d. 1235 AH/1819 AH)[54] left Kashmir sometime after the riots of 1801, a riot in which his family library was also burned down.[55] Muqim was accompanied in his journey by his grandson and student, Sayyid Ṣafdar Shāh (d. 1255 AH/1839 CE). Tracing his descent from the Razvī Sayyids of Ahmadpora, in north Kashmir, the family of Sayyid Ṣafdar would help in substantially expanding the Shi'i character of Awadh, especially through the work of Ṣafdar's eldest son, Sayyid 'Ali Shāh (d. 1269 AH/1852 CE). 'Ali Shāh was born in Lucknow in 1217 AH/1802 CE and spent more than twelve years in the *hawza 'ilmiya* (territory of learning) at the shrine cities of Iraq under leading Shi'i *mujtahids* (source of religious emulation) including Shaykh Murtaza Ansarī (d. 1281 AH/1864 CE), Shaykh Ḥasan Kāshf al-Ghiṭā' (d. 1848), and Shaykh Muhammad Mahdi Tabataba'i (1742–96). While some early Kashmiri Shi'i scholars at Awadh, including Mullā Muqim, were accused of adherence to the conservative Akhbārī school of Shi'i jurisprudence,[56] the nineteenth century marks the revival of the *Usulī* school in the Shi'i world—including in South Asia. Having learned under leading *Usulī* scholars of Iraq, Sayyid 'Ali on his return to Farukhabad would be instrumental in the spread of

Usulī school in Awadh, complementing the work of Awadh's own native Shiʿi' scholar, the *mujtahid* Sayyid Dildār ʿAli (d. 1820).[57]

The migration of Muqim and the Rizvī marks a steady arrival of Kashmiri Shiʿi in the Shiʿi kingdom of Awadh, both to escape religious persecution at home and to secure courtly patronage at a wealthy, munificent, and welcoming court. This migration happened in the backdrop of the loss of Imperial Mughal prestige and authority across the empire through the eighteenth century, resulting in two diametrically opposed possibilities for Kashmiri Shiʿi: a constrained existence in Kashmir under the Afghans or the possibility of migration to a nearby Shiʿi court where their scholarship would not only be welcomed but also promoted. In its immediate geography, the nearest possibility for Kashmiri Shiʿi was the Awadh and its twin cities of Faizabad and Lucknow.

Among the Kashmiri Shiʿi relocating to Awadh, we find a significantly large presence of individuals belonging to religious classes and the poets, the ulema, and *marṣiya khwāns*. The role of emigrant Kashmiri Shiʿi scholarship in advancing the Shiʿi faith within the boundaries of Awadh state can be discerned from two hagiographical accounts originating from Awadh: *Najūm al Samā* (*c.* 1286 AH/1869 CE) and *Tazkira-i Beybahā* (*c.* 1931). The Shi i scholars of Kashmir were accorded great respect in Awadh, most available contemporary sources are replete with references to their erudite scholarship, simplicity of behavior, and in more than one instance their status as enablers of miracles: *mʿujiza numā*.[58]

In his travelogue, Bihbahānī writes about another Kashmiri Shiʿi ulema family, that of Mullā ʿAli Padshāh (d. 1221 AH/1806 CE approx.), which had relocated to the capital city of Faizabad much earlier and played a pivotal role in the religious life of the Awadh kingdom. Bihbahānī speaks of Padshāh in highly laudatory words, writing:

> There also lived a number of literary men and scholars in that city. Among them, mention may be made of the exalted (*a'ali hazrat*), repository of learning (*fawazil'ul iktesab*) and highly distinguished Akhund Mullā Muhammad Javad, the eldest son of the sanctuary of divine bliss and forgiveness (*marhamat-wa-ghufran-panah*) the most learned and discerner of subtleties, Mullā ʿAli Badshāh Kashmiri, the founder of the Friday congregational prayer in the town of Faizabad.[59]

While Padshāh's arrival in Awadh is said to have taken place during the reign of Nawab Asaf-al Dawlah (r. 1775–97), Kashmiri Shiʿis presence in the region is almost coeval with the foundation of Awadh state. In 1744, the Mughal emperor Muhammad Shāh (r. 1719–48) appointed Abu'l Mansur Ṣafdar Jung (d. 1754) the second nawab vizier of Awadh as the *ṣubedar* of Kashmir, replacing Abū Barkat Khān, whose rule had seen widespread mis-governance and an insurgency that engulfed the city. Ṣadfar Jung deputed Jān Nisar Khān Sher Jung as his *naib* (deputy) to the region to restore order, especially in Srinagar which had seen the worst cases of rioting and looting targeting the Shiʿi population of Zadibal. After spending six months in Kashmir, Jān Nisar left the valley accompanied by many

Kashmiri Shi'is who in turn enlisted in Ṣafdar Jung's army. Those Kashmiri Shi'i who joined Ṣadfar Jung's army mostly belonged to the *moḥala* of Zadibal, adopted Mughal costumes and Persian language, and many settled down in Awadh.[60] In 1808, at the instance of Col. John Baille, a British Resident at Lucknow, Sayyid Ghūlam 'Ali Khān wrote his '*Imād-al Sadāt* (*c*. 1808), in which he provides us with an account of the Nawabs of Awadh and the Shi'i contingent in his army.[61]

Interestingly, while some Kashmiri scholars preferred to lead a quietist and retired public life in Awadh, most not only sought proximity to the court but also actively engaged in projects that sought to publicly demonstrate the Shi'i identity of the Awadh state. Mullā 'Ali Padshāh, whom Bihbahānī calls "the founder of the Friday congregational prayer," virtually single-handedly forced the issue of observance of Friday congregational prayers on Chief Minister Ḥasan Razā Khān and the emerging local religious leader Sayyid Dildār 'Ali.[62] Padshāh's arrival in Awadh had taken place in the aftermath of a severe bout of the targeted persecution of Shi'i's in Kashmir, under the Afghan *ṣubedar* Hājjī Karīm Dād Khān (1776–83). The *ṣubedar* confiscated many Shi'i properties, including the *jāgīr* of one of the oldest families of Kashmiri nobility: the Maliks of Chadurah dislocating them from their hereditary seat at Chadurah.[63] Arriving in the safety of Awadh, Kashmiri scholars such as Padshāh helped in disseminating and popularizing practices and rituals which in Kashmir remained forbidden, to a degree that even "the Sunni Raja of Nanpara kept Shi'i ulama, many of them from Kashmir, at his provincial seat to read elegies for the Imam Husayn."[64]

During Mughal rule, especially in the seventeenth and early eighteenth century, Kashmir had seen a broad arrival of poets (and scholars) from Iran, seeking patronage at the Mughal court. Given the Mughal fascination with Kashmir, many of these scholars and literati either visited the land regularly or even settled down in Srinagar. Marking this scholarly exchange, we find two of the *malik-al shu'arās* (poet laureate) in Mughal court buried in the *Mazār-i Shu'arā* (Cemetery of the Poets) in Srinagar: Ḥājjī Jān Muhammad Qudsī (d. 1646) and Abū Ṭālib Kalim Kashānī (d. 1651). This had not only resulted in widening the Persianate cultural influences in Kashmir, especially in the urban center of Srinagar, but also affected a scholarly exchange between Kashmiri Shi'i ulema and their Iranian counterparts. The Shi'i Mughal noble Nawab Ibrahim Khān, (d. 1709) who served as *ṣubedar* of Kashmir in four stints (1662–3, 1679–84, 1701–5, 1709), had set a committee of Shi'i scholars to write an encyclopedic polemic in defense of Shi'i faith: *Al-Biyāz Ibrahimī*. This work, which was compiled and drafted in Srinagar, involved both native Kashmiri scholars and those who were invited by the *ṣubedar* from Iran. The work not only seeks to defend the Shi'i position on issues of succession to the Prophet Muhammad but is also censorious of revered Sunni figures. While it seems that *Biyāz Ibrahimī* was never widely disseminated to the public, yet the memory of the work was enshrined in the memory of Kashmiri Shi'i scholars who would refer to it even as late as the nineteenth century. A major figure instrumental in getting this polemical work composed was Ibrahim Khān's Iranian teacher Āqā 'Ali Rizā Tajallī (d. 1674), who arrived in India during the reign of Emperor Shāh Jahān (r. 1628–58).[65]

The transnational links formed due to these scholarly exchanges between Kashmiri Shiʿi scholars and the Iranian religious elites helped in preparing a significant body of Kashmiris, who had trained and received *ijāza* (permission to transmit) from *mujtahids* of Iran (and Iraq) and, in turn, training aspiring scholars at home. Examples of these Kashmiri Shiʿi scholars studying under major Shiʿi ulema outside South Asia in the late seventeenth to early eighteenth century include, but are not limited to, Mullā Muhammad Murad b. Muhammad Ṣadiq (d. 1689 approx.) who received his *ijāza* from Shaykh Hūr ʿAāmlī (d. 1692), the author of *Vasail-i Shiʿi*, Mullā ʿAbd al-Ghanī b. Ṭālib Hamdanī (d. 1755), best known for *Jāmia al-Rizvī* (*c.* 1748), Persian translation of Abu'l Qāsim Najm-al Dīn Ḥillī's (d. 1277) major work on jurisprudence: *Sharah-al Islam*, from Mullā Ṣalih Māzandarānī, Mullā Muhammad Jaʿfar (d. 1737 approx.) from Mīrzā Muhammad b. Ḥusayn Shirvanī (d. 1686); Sayyid Ḥusayn Mūsāvī (d. 1757) who got his *ijāza* from Shaykh Yūsuf Bahranī (d. 1772), and Ismāʿīl b. Ḥusayn Māzandranī (d. 1759).[66] Additionally, there were scholars trained in Kashmir itself or those who studied under Iranian scholars who had settled down in the plains of South Asia such as Akhund Abu'l Qāsim Kashmirī (d. 1779), who studied under Shaykh Ḥasan the grandson of Shaykh Zain-al Dīn famous in the Shiʿi world as *Shahid-i Sanī*. Continuing these familial links of scholarly transmission between families in Kashmir and their Iranian teachers, we find Mullā ʿAbdūl Ḥakim Sāṭiḥ (d. 1730), the cousin of the author of *Jāmia al-Rizvī*, studied under Mullā Muhammad Saʿid Ashraf Māzandarānī (d. 1704–5), son of Ṣalih Mazandarānī. Outside Kashmir we find, in the imperial capital Delhi, Ḥakim Mīrzā Muhammad Kāmil Kashmirī (d. 1820), whose ancestors were from Kashmir, engaged in polemical exchanges with leading Sunni *ulema*, including the Shāh ʿAbd al-ʿ Aziz Dehlavī (d. 1824), whose *Tuhfa-i Isnā ʿAshariyya* had gained wide renown among Sunni circles of North India. Among Shiʿi circles, it is believed Kāmil was poisoned to death after he wrote *Nuzha-i Isnā ʿAshariyya* in refutation of the Dehlavi's *Tuhfa*.[67] Similarly, it is believed that Mullā Muqim also studied with Shaykh Hūr ʿAāmlī, though given the contradiction in the dates advanced for Muqim's death, this is not established. Members of the Majalisī-Mazandarānī-Beyhbanī family who visited or settled in India, during the eighteenth century, specially feature in the chain of transmission of many Kashmiri scholars, highlighting the connections forged between religious families in Kashmir and their Shiʿi teachers from Iran.

In the Kashmiri Shiʿi context it is important to remember that this scholarship emerged in absence of any institutionalized infrastructure in Kashmir to undertake religious studies: a *darsgāh*, *maktab*, and *madrasah*. Teaching was limited to home learning that too within a narrow network of mostly family-based associations. In such strained circumstances, the success of the Kashmiri religious elite to produce in continuity a significant body of scholars who also critically engaged in the areas of legal learning, ḥadīth sciences, and commentarial (*sharāh*) productions is all the more noteworthy. A scholarship which met a growing demand in the emerging Shiʿi state of Awadh, where it is only after the return of Sayyid Dildar Nasirābadī (popularly known as Ghufrān Maʿāb) that we find a traffic of aspiring Awadhī students toward the shrine cities of Iraq, seeking training in the *hawzas*.[68] In turn,

Sayyid Dildar would emerge as the progenitor of what would be termed among North Indian Shiʿi as the "*khandan-i ijtihad*"—an honorific title bestowed on his household, where many members in succeeding generations would emerge not only as respected ulemas but also certified *mujtahids*.[69]

Coming back to Kashmiri Shiʿi participation at Awadh, we find that two individuals of Kashmiri lineage also figured prominently in the administration, the viziers: Maulana Tafazul Ḥusayn Khān (d. 1800) and Ḥakim Mahdi Khān (d. 1837). Ḥakim Mahdi's rise in the Awadh court commenced with the reign of Nawab Saʿadat ʿAli Khān II (r. 1798–1814) who made him his vizir, from 1830 to 1832 and again in 1837. In his *Tārīkh-i Awadh*, Ḥakim Muhammad Najmūl Ghanī credits Ḥakim Mahdi with improving administrative affairs, reducing the extravagant court expenditure, establishing judiciary and police system across the state, and cultivating *kār-khānā's*.[70] A man of considerable personal wealth, Ḥakim Mahdi was also deeply involved in the welfare of Kashmiri Shiʿis. After a severe case of an earthquake in Kashmir in 1828, Mahdi provided financial aid for the reconstruction of devastated *moḥallas* of the city.[71] Similarly, he was responsible for rehabilitating Kashmiri Shiʿis in Awadh after the Shiʿi-Sunni riots of 1830. The vizier's partiality to individuals from Kashmir can also be observed in his patronage of Vasi ʿAli Khān, who also traced his roots to Kashmir and was appointed as *dārōghah* of the *Dīvān Khānā* by Mahdi.[72]

Despite his administrative reforms, the vizier faced stiff opposition from the very beginning from the British Resident at Lucknow. In 1824, when the bishop of Calcutta, Reginald Herber visited Lucknow as a part of his travels across North India he also visited Mahdi who had recently lost his job, primarily due to opposition from the resident and was living a retired life at his *ḥavelī* in Fatehgar. In spite of a colonial disdain for the oriental "character" which colors the bishop's narrative, Herber's opinion about the former vizier is complimentary:

> Hakeeme Mendee, a man of considerable talents, great hereditary opulence and influence, and to the full as honest and respectable in his public and private conduct as any Eastern Vizier can usually be expected to.[. . .] he now lives in great splendor at Futtehgur.[73]

On the other hand, we find Bihbahānī dismissive of the vizier, Maulana Tafazul Ḥusayn, who on account of his scholarly learning is still remembered as Khan ʿAllāma in South Asian Shiʿi circles. Tafazul served as the vizier to Nawab Asif-al Daula (r. 1775–97), and along with another scholar of Kashmiri descent, Moulvi ʿAbdūl Ḥakim also officiated as tutor to Asif-al Daula's eventual successor, Saʿadat ʿAli Khān II. Ghanī credits Saʿadat's accession to the throne to *ḥusn-i tadbir* (beautiful stratagem) of Tafazul Ḥusayn.[74] Aside from his involvement in court politics, Tafazul also undertook translation of various Latin works on logic, mathematics, and philosophy, while also imparting lessons on both Imāmī and Hanafī *fiqah* to students during his brief exile to Calcutta city.[75] Still Bihbahānī, while questioning the vizier's loyalty to the royal family, in one instance also belittles Tafazul's Kashmiri origin in these words:

> The (Nawab) Wazir[76] glanced at the gathering [. . .] While giving his mind to the proposal, he thought with himself that Tafazzul Husain Khan being a Kashmiri was a mine of frauds and deceits.[77]

Unlike Mahdi, we find no information regarding Tafazul's possible engagement with Kashmiri Shiʿi. This may partly be due to the fact that the vizier's family had migrated from Kashmir at an earlier date, settling down in Punjab. Though many Kashmiris, including a few families who became part of the Mughal administration in Delhi and Punjab, retained their links to Kashmir, it is important to remember that Tafazul's family was of Sunni origin. It is only after migrating from Kashmir that the family converted to Shiʿism. The vizier's link to Kashmiri Shiʿi if any would have been conditioned by their presence in the Awadh court, rather than based on older family links and connections dating back to Kashmir.

While Kashmiri Shiʿi continued to arrive in Awadh, back home Afghan rule in Kashmir was brought to an abrupt end in 1819, when the forces of Maharaja Ranjit Singh (r. 1801–39), defeated the forces of Afghan *ṣubedar*, Jabbār Khān[78] at Shopian—the first major town on the erstwhile Mughal Road connecting Kashmir to Lahore and further on Delhi. Arriving in Srinagar unopposed, the Sikh army raised their standards, including the saffron-colored *nishān* of the Khālsa in the city. This singular event marks the end of not only Afghan rule in Kashmir but also of Muslim authority and while a *ṣubedar*, Motī Ram was appointed for the newly conquered land, the political capital shifted to Lahore—the seat of the Punjab-based Sikh Empire of Ranjit Singh.

Loss of Muslim Sovereignty

Somewhere in between 1831 and 1834, a Kashmiri Pandit, Mohan Lal (d. 1855) accompanied the British explorer and diplomat, Sir Alexander Burnes, in his travels across Afghanistan-Turkistan-Iran, under the assumed name of Āgā Ḥasan Jān (or, Mīrzā Qulī Kashmīrī). In the Holy city of Mashad, Mohan met the Qajar crown prince, ʿAbbas Mīrzā (d. 1833), who was at that time involved in military enterprise against the Turkomans. The meeting between the two took place on the occasion of ʿĪd. Given the Persian prince's interest in military affairs, the conversation revolved around Maharaja Ranjit Singh's military prowess. Mohan Lal in "all frankness" apprised the prince about the superiority of the troops under Sher-i Panjab, as well as the grandeur of Ranjit's court, to which the prince to cover "his ground" replied rather amicably:

> but, if Ali, the Lion of God, favours us, we will yet plant our standard in Kashmir, and dress all our soldiers(??) in shawl pantaloons.[79]

The oblique reference to Kashmiri shawls by the ʿAbbas Mīrzā was occasioned by Lal's description of the opulence of Ranjit's court, where the "darbār tent was made of Kashmir shawl, and even the floor was composed of the same costly material."[80]

Interestingly, the lavishness of the Sikh *darbār*, especially the shawl tents, had also made a favorable impression on Lal's employer, Burnes, who in his memoirs also writes about one such tent which was provided to him by Ranjit Singh during his stay at Lahore:

> On taking leave of his Highness, we proceeded to our tents, which were a distinct suite from that we had yesterday occupied. They were made of Cashmeer shawls, and about fourteen feet square. Two of these were connected by tent walls of the same superb materials; while the intervening space was shaded by a lofty screen, supported on four massy poles, adorned with silver. The shawls of one tent were red; of the other, white. In each of them stood a camp bed, with curtains of Cashmeer shawls, which gave one an impression of a fairy abode more than an encampment in the jungles of the Punjab.[81]

In the nineteenth century, North India, in face of the ever-expanding power of the East India Company, Maharaja Ranjit Singh emerges as "the final independent indigenous sovereign."[82] Invested as Maharaja of Punjab in April 1801, by Bābā Sāhib Singh Bedī, a revered descendant of Guru Nanak (d. 1539), the first Sikh Guru, Ranjit's kingdom would embody the *Sarkār-i Khālsa jī* (Governance of Khālsa) a concept of sovereignty where Khālsa can be seen as "the body of Sikh collective or an individual member of the Khālsa," such as the maharaja himself.[83] Ranjit's capture of Lahore, which during the heyday of Mughal rule had also at times served as the capital for both the *ṣubah* of Punjab and Kashmir, was followed by expansion of his territories in the south, as well up north where he defeated various Pathan principalities before conquering Peshawar in 1818. The conquest of Kashmir a year later not only consolidated his territorial hold over the vast and fertile region between the Indus and Sutlej but also limited any Afghan involvement to the northerly frontier areas, away from Punjab, the heartland of Ranjit's empire.

The Sikh milieu would in many ways be fashioned by older cultural traditions of the Mughals juxtaposed with the peculiarities of Sikh religion.[84] As a substantial territory with a significant Muslim majority, which had witnessed uninterrupted Muslim rule from the early fourteenth century, Kashmir's incorporation in the *Sarkār-i Khālsa* evoked strong reactions among native Muslim historiographers, a reaction that is offset by the warm welcome afforded to Sikh conquest by the native Hindu society. In *Majmu'at ut-Tawārikh* (*c.* 1846), Pandit Birbal Kāchru[85] invokes the memory of Afghan *ṣubedars* as communal bigoted and unjust rulers who were replaced by a just mode of governance under the Sikhs. Birbal was himself connected to the Afghan court and his father, Pandit Daya Ram Kāchru spent a great deal of his time in Kabul where he served as the *munshi* of the vizier Wafādār Khan in the court of the third Durrānī king, Zamān Shāh (r. 1793–1801). A witness to the transfer of rule from the Afghans to the Sikhs, Kāchru reflects on what was assuredly a momentous change of his times, in these words:

> when due to the tyranny of Afghans there was much frenzy and evil [and] Kashmiris would moan and lament daily. [. . .] The Almighty opened on the

> inhabitants [of this land] his doors of mercy. The *sarishta* [constitution] of authority was removed from the hands of Afghans and given in the grip of Sikhs.[86]

For Kāchru the Sikh rule symbolizes a just, even if absolutist, mode of governance, which was also sympathetic to the Pandit grievances against previous Muslim rule. As opposed to Kāchru's rendition of events, Mullā Ḥamid-al Lah Shāhabādī (d. 1848) would see the Sikh rule as a continuation of evil that had chanced upon Kashmir under the Afghans, writing:

> As the evil of our deeds began to close in on us,
> The nation of Sikhs descended upon Kashmir.[87]

Interestingly, in introducing the shifting political fortunes of their time, both Kāchru and Shāhabādī are invoking the narrative of evil deeds: but for two opposing players. Meanwhile, for Ranjit Singh the acquisition of Kashmir added to the varied population of his domain, with the overwhelming Muslim character of Kashmir. Also, as a former Mughal and then Afghan *ṣubah*, the conquest also reflected the conqueror's glory, much more than a conquest of any other major town or city such as Multan or Peshawar. Yet, in spite of the cosmopolitan character of Ranjit's *darbār* at Lahore, Sikh rule in Kashmir commenced on a marked communal time. This is also reflected in the Persian chronogram of victory coined by the Sikh conquerors of Srinagar:

> *Wah-i Gūrūjī ka Khālsa,*
> *Wah-i Gūrūjī kī Fathah*
> (transl: Hail the *Khālsa* who belongs to the Lord God!
> Hail the Lord God to whom belongs the victory)

We can well imagine how grim the victory slogan might have sounded to the Muslim population of Kashmir, but far more disturbing was the decision of the Sikh rulers to ban *azān*, the Muslim call to prayers; close the main congregational mosque of Srinagar, Jamia Masjid and a threat to blow up one of the most revered monuments in the sacred geography of Muslim Kashmir—the Khānaqāh-i M'aulā.[88] Prominent mosques in the city constructed by the Mughals, *Masjid-i Naū* (Pather Masjid) and the Mullā Shāh Masjid were converted into granaries, while the open ground of the *'Īdgāh* was also confiscated. Similarly, a Shi'i mosque at Hasanabad constructed during the Mughal period which had been badly damaged was vandalized for the construction of a ghat at Basant Bagh near the royal citadel, Sherghari (Figure 2.2). This antagonistic relation between the Lahore *darbār* and the Muslim society of Kashmir would become a constant feature of Sikh rule in Kashmir. Unlike Hinduism, where killing a cow was seen as a mortal sin, the Sikhs did not have any prescribed notion of sacredness associated with the cow, yet in their dietary customs both beef and pork were avoided. Among Kashmir Muslims, especially in rural communities, beef consumption was

Figure 2.2 Ruins of Mughal Mosque at Hasanabad, early twentieth century (courtesy: ASI, India).

prevalent, especially on major festive occasions such as a wedding, while in the urban setting of the capital city, Srinagar, this was generally avoided. But the Sikhs not only banned consumption of beef but also made killing of a cow a capital crime, and offenders were publicly hanged. In certain cases, the offenders were burned, or the bodies of the deceased were dragged and paraded in the narrow lanes of the city.[89]

The old *jāgīrdār* Muslim families, some of them still retaining their *jāgīrs* from the Mughal era, had their lands confiscated, effectively ending the remaining sections of Muslim landed elites in Kashmir. Even the merchant class, which was engaged in the lucrative shawl trade, from which the Lahore darbār got most of its Kashmir-based revenue, was not safe from the communal character of the court. During the governorship of Diwān Chunī Lāl (1825–7), the fourth Sikh *ṣubedar* of Kashmir, members of a reputed merchant family of the city, Kawūsa, were publicly hanged and their corpses dragged in the city on charge of cow killing.[90] The event must have left a deep and scarring imprint on the minds of the urban Muslim aristocracy, and acted as a reminder of how past privileges of belonging to the governing majority had come to an end.

The banning of cow slaughter, and the threat to destroy a revered *khānaqāh* in the belief that it was built upon the ruins of an older Hindu temple, also highlight how Sikh rule in Kashmir came to identify not only with a plan for expanding the territorial might of the *Khālsa* but also with rectifying past Muslim "excesses" against the Kashmiri Hindus. Similarly, one can posit that in reviving the old, pre-Muslim name of the capital city, Srinagar, the Sikh rulers also made a symbolic gesture at undoing the Muslim past of the city—a past, in which the city had been simply known as *Shehar-i Kashmir* (The city of Kashmir).

Consequently, in Kashmir, during most part of the Sikh rule, we fail to see a glimpse of that nuanced, negotiated pragmatic tolerance and communal coexistence which had characterized Ranjit's own earlier conquest and subsequent rule in Lahore. But then in popular Sikh and Hindu narratives, the martyrdom of the ninth Sikh Guru, Tegh Bahādur (d. 1675), is seen as the fallout of the guru's decision to confront the Mughal emperor Aurangzeb (r. 1658–1707) for his persecution of Kashmiri Pandits. Did the memory of a past event linked with a revered memory also exacerbate the situation, thus defining the contours of power dynamics under the Sikhs in a communal milieu? One can only venture a guess.

Significantly, in seeking to secure the security and control of the land, the Sikhs tapped into the administrative and fiscal knowledge of the Kashmiri Pandits. A few Kashmiri Pandits had been intimately connected with the Afghan court: the Dhars, Bamzais, Kachrus, and so on, some even rising to the position of power in the Dūranī court at Kabul. Ranjit's conquest of Kashmir was facilitated by Raja Birbal Dhar, who in face of Ranjit's apparent reluctance to march into Kashmir, impressed upon the king the precarious situation of the Afghans in Kashmir.[91] The steady advancement of Pandits at the court would remain a constant feature throughout the rest of the nineteenth century and would in turn give rise to a relationship of mistrust, resentment, and protecting privileges between the Hindu and Muslim sections of Kashmiri society. And, in these early years of Sikh rule where the Sunni majority was being and feeling disenfranchised, the Shiʿi could not be blamed for sensing an opportunity in imagining they could break away from the chokehold of Sunni majoritarianism. Or, so they thought.

Chapter 3

SHIʿI IDENTITY, SUNNI SPACE, AND NON-MUSLIM RULE

This chapter looks at the tentative attempts made by the Kashmiri Shiʿi at re-articulating and expressing their spiritual and cultural identity in a regional space largely controlled by Sunni orthodoxy following the establishment of Sikh rule. In addition, the materiality, not only associated with mourning Karbala but also related to other practices and rituals of Islam, created a distinct habitus of Kashmiri Shiʿi Islam. Expanding on the theme of this resurgent sectarian identity, the chapter posits that integral to the articulation of a Shiʿi identity in Kashmir was the entire paraphernalia of various affective and performative practices associated with the commemoration of the martyrdom of Imām Ḥusayn and his family in Karbala. This distinct set of spiritual and cultural practices was eventually mobilized by the intelligentsia of Kashmiri Shiʿi Muslims for political ends as well. The most visible manifestation of this sectarian identity was the performance of the *marṣiya* and the reconstruction of *Mʿārak*, the historic *imāmbāda* of Kashmir. The fate of this construction, its patronage, and the ensuing Shiʿi-Sunni riot resulting in its destruction form the central theme of this chapter. The emergence of *Mʿārak* as a space for commencement of public mourning ceremonies in the mid-part of the nineteenth century is contextualized as the community project which helped in giving visible shape to the Shiʿi aspirations for a separate and distinct identity celebrating their Shiʿi-ness.

Vocalizing a Community: Mourning and Marṣiya

The nineteenth century marks a flourishing manuscript culture in Kashmir, whose consumption was limited not only to non-native collectors but also in demand with a local market, albeit a limited market. This calligraphic outpouring was majorly responsible for the production of Quranic codices—like the one commissioned earlier by the Isfahanī merchants mentioned earlier. Additionally, works on literature, history, religion, sciences, and other prevailing knowledge traditions were also produced, mostly for the local market.

A greater part of this manuscript production is located in the Srinagar Research Library, comprising texts written in Persian, Arabic, Sanskrit as well as the local vernacular, Kashmiri. Within the collection, a large number of the manuscripts belong to the eighteenth and nineteenth centuries, including three *biyāz* (literally plain white paper): a collection of Kashmiri *marṣiyas.*

Written on fine glossy burnished paper: *kashur kākaz* (Kashmiri paper), for which Kashmir was famous, the manuscripts themselves are mostly devoid of any ornamentation or decoration, aside from the leather covers which are occasionally embossed. This is in sharp contrast to the Quranic codices produced in the same period, with floral and geometrical decorations in multiple colors representing a high point of the Kashmiri style of book illumination. Also, while many of the *biyāz* come from a single scribe, numerous *biyāz* are assembled copies, comprising multiple authorships bound within a single cover at a much later date. More importantly, a *marṣiya biyāz* in Kashmir is never dedicated to the work of a single poet, rather it exists as a collection of works in the genre, which are either popular among the public or which appeal to the sensibilities of the patron who commissioned the production. This is also a reason why many copyists fail to record the name of the poet, whose *marṣiya* forms a part of the collection.

Aside from these three *biyāz* composed in eighteenth-century Kashmir, more than a hundred handwritten manuscripts from the nineteenth century have so far been identified in private collections within the Kashmiri Shi'i society.[1] The production of such a large number of manuscripts, unparalleled in any other genre of Kashmiri literature, religious or secular, is indicative of the widespread popularity of the *marṣiya* tradition within the Shi'i of Kashmir.

Of the three mentioned manuscripts in possession of the Research Library, two were completed before the start of the nineteenth century (Figure 3.1). In contrast, outside the *marṣiya* genre, the oldest extant manuscript of any Kashmiri poetical work can be dated only up to the mid-nineteenth century. This includes the collection of Bābā Kamāl (*c.* 1251 AH/1836CE), recording of the verses of Shaykh Nūr-al Dīn (d. 1415 CE or 1438 CE), the founder of the *Reshī* order of Sufis in Kashmir.

The oldest of the three *biyāz* dates from the latter part of Mughal rule in Kashmir and was compiled in stages, with the last date recorded as 1161 AH/1748 CE. This manuscript is also signed by the scribe Sayyid Mustafa Shāh at two different places.[2] In its entirety, the *biyāz* comprises two sections, an early part dating to the first decade of the eighteenth century, which was then added upon by Mustafa. Spread over 231 folios (28 x 11.5 cm) the portion of the *biyāz* written by Mustafa was compiled in a period of twenty-three years. In his section, Mustafa marks the *biyāz* at different places with the year marks: 1138 AH/1725 CE, 1143 AH/1730 CE, 1146 AH/1733 CE, 1148 AH/1735 CE, 1149 AH/1736 CE, 1157 AH/1744 CE, and the last dated year 1161 AH/1748 CE, three years before Kashmir passed into Afghan control.

More importantly, Mustafa also mentions many of the poets whose work he has copied in the *biyāz*. Given the absence of any other manuscript on Kashmiri literature predating this *biyāz*, Mustafa's brief notes on the poets assume an added significance in so far as they inform us about the people who were associated with composing in the vernacular Kashmiri, rather than the language of the court and the elites, Persian. Interestingly, in giving the *nisbat* of many of these poets,

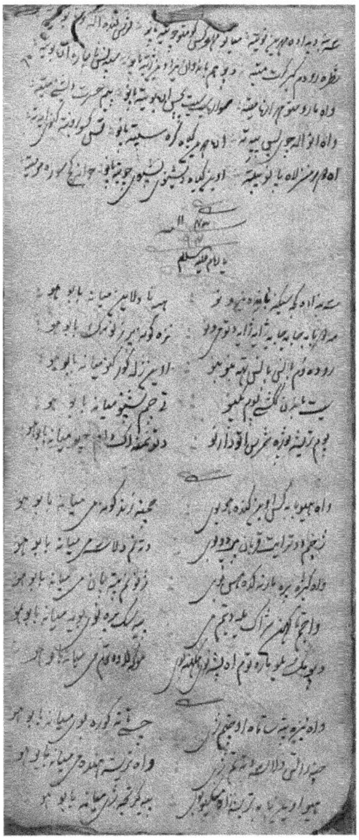

Figure 3.1 Kashmiri *marṣiya biyāz* dated 1143 AH (1730 CE), Research Library, Srinagar (author).

Mustafa also reveals the non-Kashmiri origin of some of the individuals involved with this literary genre. A majority of the poets who find a mention in the *biyāz*, including Mullā Aḥmad Neshapurī (Neshapur, Iran), Āqā Mahmūd Ardebelī (Ardebil, Iran), Khwāja Muhammad 'Ali Tabrezī (Tabriz, Iran), Mirzā Aḥmad 'Ali Tusī (Tuss, Iran), Mīr Saif, son of Mullā Khalil Niynī (Niyan, Iran), are directly linked by the scribe through their *nisbat* to Iran. Though none of the surnames mentioned by Mustafa survive in contemporary Kashmiri Shi'i society, it is safe to posit that these poets were descendants of those numerous men of letters arriving from Iran seeking the patronage of the Mughal court, especially in the seventeenth century. Many of the émigré poets settled down in Kashmir, making it their home and in turn became indigenized, some it seems only in a generation, given the names Mustafa has recorded in his *biyaz*.

The second *biyāz* written by Sayyid 'Abbas Shāh broadly follows the same physical dimensions as of Mustafa comprising 227 folios (28.5 x 14.5 cm). The manuscript was still under compilation in the year 1209 AH/1794 CE,[3] we do not know when it was finally completed. As opposed to Mustafa, 'Abbas Shāh is very sparse on biographical notes regarding the poets whose works he collected and in the entire *biyāz* we come across just three names: Sayyid Ṣaliḥ (of Ahmadpora),

Mullā Raḥman, and Ḥassī Bhat. The third *biyāz* was also composed during the Afghan rule by an unknown scribe, and the years 1183 AH/1769 CE and 1188 AH/1774 CE are mentioned on the margins. More importantly, it mentions some poets who were alive at the time of the compiling of the *biyāz*. These include Mīr Muhammad ʿAbbas, Mirzā Jaza-al Lah, Qāzī Aḥmad ʿAli, Ustād Raḥman, Mīr Sharif-al Dīn Rizvī, and Mullā Muhammad Askrī; latter's Persian *marṣiya* is the first work that finds mention in the *biyāz*. The scribe also lists elegies of two other poets, Ḥassī Bhat and Mīr Sharif-al Dīn Rizvī, both of whom were dead when the *biyāz* was composed.

Another *biyāz* from a slightly later date, written in the last years of Afghan rule in Kashmir, was compiled in 1235 AH/1819 CE and is part of a private collection.[4] Taken all together, these manuscripts of Kashmiri *marṣiya* from the eighteenth and early nineteenth centuries highlight the centrality of *marṣiya* as both a literary genre and a normative practice through which Kashmiri Shiʿi's sought to protect and promote their confessional identity. The decision of the various Afghan *ṣubedars* to ban this practice and the resolve of the Kashmiri Shiʿi society to engage in it, in spite of the threats and dangers associated, mark the importance of this practice. Interestingly, the form of the *marṣiya*, both its textual written base as seen in the *biyaz* manuscript and its vocalization in communal gatherings (*majlis*), seeks to resemble and replicate the phenomenon of recitation and memorization which were at the foundation of Muslim pedagogy, in both literal and general methodological senses.

An examination of the Kashmiri *marṣiya* also indicates that after a prolonged hiatus in its development, this genre took on a new form in the early part of the nineteenth century, coeval with the establishment of Sikh rule. Unlike the short *marṣiyas* that were in vogue during the eighteenth century, the *marṣiyas* from Sikh rule are significantly longer. The Kashmiri *marṣiya* as it evolved in this period can be seen as a poetic rendition of an elaborate, highly scholastic prose comprising hundred or more verses, which unfortunately loses almost all of its poetic spirit in any attempt at translation.

A major innovation that took place in the Kashmiri *marṣiya* under the Sikh rule was fixing four basic *maqām* (station) in the structure of the *marṣiya* and linking them to a central unifying theme which would serve as the *unwān* (title) under which a poet would compose his work. The *maqāms* include three stations of praise: of Allah (*hamd*), Prophet Muhammad (*n'aat*), Imām Ali (*madah*), and a final *maqām* of *dard* (grief) which is the elegy proper. Given the introduction of *maqām* and the corresponding increase in its volume, the *marṣiya* was no longer limited by the basic elegiac format of its origin, simply to bemoan a loss. This extended format gave the poets plenty of opportunities to source the vast corpus of Shiʿi religious literature and simultaneously contextualize it in their work so as to educate the community about their heritage, both in terms of the faith and its related history. By the mid-part of the nineteenth century, Kashmiri *marṣiya* would evolve into an unrivaled medium of sermonizing and with the wide audiences it attracted; it became one of the widest dissimulators of religious teachings. As the appeal of *marṣiya* was primarily located in its performance, a collective recitation

Figure 3.2 Performance of *marṣiya* at a *majlis* at *Mʿārak*, Srinagar, 2015 (courtesy: Imran Ali).

by the assembled congregation, managed by the vocalization of the text by the principal reciter, the *ẕākir*, and his troupe of assistants, the *pashkhawan*, and the use of the local vernacular, Kashmiri, made it easier for the audience to commit to memory (Figure 3.2). The importance of the reciter, the *ẕākir*, for the performance of the *marṣiya*, as well as the success of the *majlis* in the *imāmbāda*, is established in these verses:

> *Ẕākir:* candle of this assembly,
> and mourners: light of the *Mʿārak;*
> his existence on fire, wick of a candle,
> and the diffused smell of camphor.
> His breath: smoke, sigh of a burnt heart
> and yet, the mourners circle him like moths;
> he, thoughtless of being consumed,
> annihilate, smear yourself with ashes, O *Ẕākir.*[5]

The man who would provide the initial impetus for this literary innovation was a Sunni convert to Shiʿism, Qāzī Aḥmad ʿAli (alive in 1774). In eighteenth-century Kashmir, the post of *qāzī* was limited to Sunni. But like other similar titles of religious office—*mufti*, *mullā*, *moulvi*, or *akhund*—*qāzī* was mostly used as a surname rather than necessarily signifying a man who was issuing a religious decree (*fatwa*). Not much has been recorded in Shiʿi sources about Qāzī

'Ali, but we know that another *marṣiya* writer from the eighteenth century, Qāzī Aḥmad Dīn, also converted to Shi'iism. Shi'i sources maintain that Aḥmad Dīn was the serving Sunni *qāzī* of Varmul (Baramulla), a small but significant town in north Kashmir, devoid of any Shi'i presence. After his conversion, Aḥmad Dīn migrated from Varmul to Ahmadpora, a settlement in north Kashmir which had sustained itself as a center for Shi'i scholarship in the eighteenth century under the Rizvī Sayyids. As a member of the Sunni religious community, Aḥmad Dīn's conversion would not have been favorably seen by the Sunnis of Varmul, making the migration a necessity rather than a choice. We know that Aḥmad Dīn was actively writing *marṣiyas* around 1780s, so we may speculate that his conversion must have also happened during the Afghan rule. Interestingly, like Aḥmad Dīn, Qāzī 'Ali also hailed from Varmul, before migrating to Gund Khwaja Qāsim, a village some 13 kilometers to the west of Srinagar. This village was established in mid-eighteenth century by Khwāja Qāsim, a *ẕākir*, whose family would emerge as one of the leading *ẕākir* dynasty of Kashmir. Was there any relation between the conversion of the two *qāzī*, both hailing from the same area, Varmul, we have no way of assessing. But it is intriguing that even in a period when Shi'i existed as a marginalized community, we find reports of conversion to Shi'ism of individuals hailing from Sunni religious elite class. Similarly, the conversion of another marṣiya writer, Ḥassī Bhat, who was born in a Hindu family in the *moḥala* of Rainawari in the capital, Srinagar, underlies how even under adverse social and political conditions of the late eighteenth to early nineteenth century, conversion to Shi'iism was taking place. Coming to the eighteenth century we find another prominent *marṣiya* writer, Khwāja Muhammad Dāim (1766–1838 approx.), who also converted from Sunnism. Significantly, these processes of conversion were not backed by a proselytizing campaign orchestrated by members of the Shi'i society, but in most cases were conditioned by an individual's predisposition, which in Shi'i traditions is seen as a mark of divine intervention and blessing.[6] In these oral traditions maintained among Kashmiri Shi'i, Dāim's[7] conversion mirrors an experience from the Prophet Muhammad's own life in which the angels split his chest, which is metaphorically understood as a sign of spiritual purification. Among Kashmiri *marṣiya nighārs*, Dāim is equally celebrated for his Kashmiri *manqabat* (devotional poem) in praise of Imām 'Ali. While the tradition of composing *manqabat* in the vernacular was well established among Kashmiri Sunni,[8] especially within the Sufi circles, Dāim's work is the earliest extant example in this literary genre associated with the Shi'i of Kashmir. In this instance, we also see how Dāim's Sunni background helps in introducing an established Sunni literary genre to a Shi'i audience. The *manqabat* despite its simplicity remains an integral part of many *majlis* recitals in contemporary Kashmir, a popularity which is largely based on its melodious refrain: *'Ali ḥal-i mūshkil, 'Ali bū 'Ali* ('Ali, the disperser of difficulties, 'Ali say 'Ali):

> Read the praise of the Almighty, eulogize 'Ali
> 'Ali, the disperser of difficulties, 'Ali say 'Ali.
> The friend of Allah, 'Ali say 'Ali,

the Prophet's legate, ʿAli say ʿAli.
Neither was heaven or the throne, nor the pen or the tablet,
neither the foundation of the Universe, nor Adam- yet absent;
ʿAli is the beginning, His manifest desire,
ʿAli, the disperser of difficulties, ʿAli say ʿAli.[9]

In the immediate aftermath of Dāim's composition, we also find the reappropriation of a popular *nashid* (devotional chant): *Ḥasbī Rabbī Jalla-llāh* (Sufficient is for me my *Rabb*; Allah is Great) in Shiʿi folk culture of Kashmir. In this nineteenth-century reworking of the *nashid*, the original Arabo-Persian text was expanded in the colloquial to incorporate verses highlighting Shiʿi devotion to the Prophet and the twelve Imāms:

Sufficient is for me my *Rabb*; Allah is Great,
there is none in my heart besides Allah;
and, the light of Mohammed, peace be upon him,
Truly, there is no God but Allah.
At the gate of heaven, stands the tree of *Ṭūbā*,[10]
with a single root and branches twelve.[11]
The first branch: Ḥazrat Shāh,[12]
I seek the intercession of that Pādshāh;
Nourish all, Yā Allah.[13]

Coming back to the Shiʿi accounts of these *marṣiya nighārs*, we see how the narrative of their conversion is posited as the main motivational reason behind their composition of *marṣiyas*, in turn sustaining the popular legend which looks upon this literary genre as being divinely inspired.[14] While Kashmiri Sunni *tazkiras* originating from Sufi circles are replete with instances of miracles and supernatural experiences (*kramāt)* of the saints, it is only in folk traditions linked with the life of *marṣiya* writers in the nineteenth and twentieth century that we find a similar manifestation. Gradually these legends would expand into a miracle narrative surrounding not only the lives of *marṣiya nighār* but also prominent ulema, *zākirs*, before expanding into elaborate stories of communal miracle manifestation linked with the Muharram assemblies.

As a performative practice, for most of the Afghan rule it was in the small, isolated Shiʿi settlements of rural Kashmir, such as Gund Hassi Bhat, Ahmadpora, Gund Khwaja Qāsim, Magam, that the practice and tradition of Kashmiri *marṣiya* was kept alive by the *marṣiya nigars* (poets), the *zākirs* (reciters), and their limited audience. The development and possibly the first enactment of the new *maqām*-based *marṣiya* took place in these Shiʿi villages of north Kashmir. A contemporary of Qāzī Aḥmad ʿAli, Khwāja Ḥusayn Mīr (d. 1820s approx.) expanded on the initial experiment of Qāzī Aḥmad and also introduced it to the Shiʿi audience of the city. And it was in the city Srinagar that this new form of *marṣiya* was publicly witnessed and performed by the assembled mourners in the Muharram of 1246 AH/1830 CE.

The Ashura Procession and the Riots of 1830

While compilation of a *marṣiya* was an internal Shiʿi process, any public congregation was sure to test sectarian sensibilities and limitations as had been defined under the Afghans. The resolve to test these boundaries and the ensuing Sunni backlash resulted in the infamous Shiʿi-Sunni riot of 1830, an event which happened nearly a decade into the Sikh rule. The historian Marjānpūrī records the details of the riots, which occurred on Ashura, the tenth of Muharram, in these words:

> On the Day of Ashura, the Shiʿi undertook two-three unusual (acts), kept on doing *marṣiya khawani* and *sina-kubī* (beating of chest). And along with them were Shiʿi's of Punjab and Hindustan, who were employees of the *nāzims* (governors) *jargha* (assembly). They with great boldness paraded a *tābūt* (coffin) from Zadibal to Hasanabad. And the writer of these lines saw it with his own eyes near the gates of Shaykh Baha-al Dīn Ganj Baksh, and for some time remained standing there, and the Sunni with envy and grief saw this beating chest (the procession) proceeded from there. And the writer of these lines had not yet reached his home that people in group upon group started attacking the Shiʿi [. . .] That day many people (Sunnis) had assembled at *Ziarat-i Ḥazrat Makhdūm*, first they beat the bearers (of the *tābūt*) and (those) standing by, then they invaded the *moḥala* and houses of Shiʿi and started burning them down, dishonored women, till no one was left safe from this attack, and on such great day (Ashura), they attacked the Shiʿi and in some houses small, small, children were killed and burnt in fire and at many places the Holy Quran was burnt, and so many people were killed, that it is a cause for torment in the world and hereafter. And on this day the Shiʿi's were scattered as dust, and during this attack the *nāzim* remained a mere spectator and could not do anything.[15]

Marjānpūrī's account is the first reference that we have of Kashmiri Shiʿi's taking out a mourning procession on the occasion of Ashura. Though some twentieth-century Shiʿi writers assume that this tradition must have been originated under the Chaks, yet we have no record of such an occurrence.[16]

Unlike Marjānpūrī, the historian Kuihāmī provides an altogether different reason for the riots. In his account of the event which he refers to as the *tārāj-i nayum* (the ninth desolation), Khuihāmī sees a Shiʿi community, emboldened by the transfer of authority to the Sikhs, transgressing on past practices related to the distribution of *pezh* (candlewick of the bulrushes), which was used traditionally in Kashmir for weaving mats. The best *pezh*, used to grow in Khusal Sar, a lake near Zadibal and from traditions dating back to eighteenth century, the produce would be equally divided between the Sunni Jamia Masjid of the city and the Shiʿi *imāmbāda* at Zadibal. As the lake was located near the *imāmbāda*, the responsibility for collecting the *pezh* was with the Shiʿi custodian of the *imāmbāda*. In Kuihāmī's account, the Shiʿi kept delaying in the matter, in the hope of usurping the share of the masjid. Consequently, in the days leading up to Ashura, the elders of the Sunni community after mutual discussion approached the governor, who authorized the Sunnis to enter the *imāmbāda* and remove their share. While proceeding to do this on the Day of Ashura, the Sunnis were assailed by the Shiʿi, who abused them. Significantly, without naming the Sunni audience of this event, Kuihāmī asserts that the Shiʿis were involved in mourning, parading the *tābūt*, and reviling revered Sunni figures. On their return to the Jamia Masjid, the Sunni delegation narrated the whole event to the assembled audience, which resulted in the enraged Sunni mobs despoiling the wealth and honor of the Shiʿi. In Kuihāmī's account the Shiʿi mourning ceremonies though a contributing factor, are nevertheless not the main reason for the riots. Rather it is the Shiʿi refusal to honor a past practice, which is the main cause. An examination of both Marjānpūrī and Kuihāmī's account brings to the fore how both the authors perceive the Shiʿi indiscretion as being representative of the change in the political landscape of the land, as an opportunity to assert their presence. Primarily, the opportunity is pivoted on a Shiʿi understanding of Sikh rule as emblematic of the Sunni loss of power and authority. While the Shiʿi version of the events, based on oral tradition would be given a textual form at a much later date, they don't question the main sequence of events, only the intentions. The Sunni insistence on distributing the *pezh*, on Ashura, the most revered and solemn occasion in the Shi'a religious calendar is seen as a deliberate provocation; intended to do harm. In both Marjānpūrī and Kuihāmī's version, we again see how the entire event unfolds within the city; this is true of most if not all Shiʿi-Sunni riots in Kashmir which originate from the capital, Srinagar. Sometimes, though not often, events in the city had their ripple effects in the countryside but given the physical distance between the two communities in rural Kashmir, and the time involved in the spread of the news, such occurrences were rare.

Regarding the actual chronology of the events as narrated by the two Sunni writers, unfortunately it is hard to establish whether the mourning procession precedes the confrontation at the *imāmbāda* or did it take place later. Also, the setting of the event is of particular importance, while the *imāmbāda* at Zadibal is a part of the Shiʿi sacred space located in a Shiʿi-dominated *moḥala*, the area in and around the shrine of Shaykh Baha-al Dīn is a part of the Sunni geography of the city. The area forms the physical as well as a visual gateway to the shrine of Shaykh Ḥamza Makhdūm, and a Shiʿi procession right at its doorsteps would certainly be seen by the Sunnis as an affront to their Sunni identity, represented as it was in the cult of Makhdūm (Figure 3.3). Where in Kuihāmī's account it is the intransigence of Kashmiri Shiʿi which bears the responsibility for the clash, Marjānpūrī indicates toward the nonlocal factors: the presence of Punjabis and Hindustani Shiʿi courtiers. In Marjānpūrī's account, we again see how the local Shiʿi society seeks and is supported by members of a non-Kashmiri Shiʿi community with a powerful presence at the court. Unfortunately, in his works, Marjānpūrī identifies only one of these nonlocal Shiʿi players, slightly later in the text, unrelated to the riots.[17]

The riots also find a mention in the memoirs of Vigne who visited Kashmir in 1835, some five years after the event. Based on reports, which are partial to

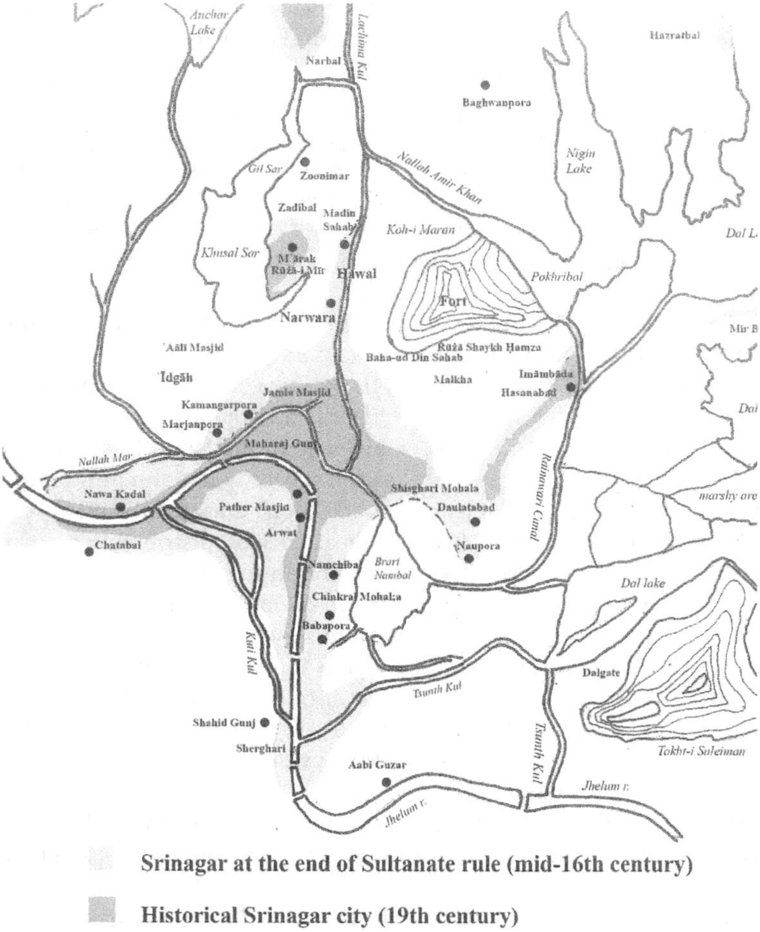

Figure 3.3 Srinagar city, nineteenth century with location of major sites and Shi'i neighborhoods (author).

the Sunnis in terms of both the historical differences between the two sects and the actual reason for the riot, it is safe to summarize that Vigne's informants were Sunnis. As such, much more than Kuihāmī's report written as it was in the last of the nineteenth century, Vigne's account is closer to how the Sunnis viewed the event immediately in the following years. Vigne writes:

> In the time of the governor Bama Singh, the Shi'is again attempted to celebrate the Moharem. Mukudum Saheb, a Sunni, who lived four hundred years ago, was always followed by a great number of disciples. Amongst them was a Persian Shi'ih, Syud Shams-ud Dyn (the sun of faith), who disguised his real faith, and

whilst he always paid marked respect to his master, he employed his time and abilities in making secret converts to the Shiʿih tenets. In consequence of this, his name is much celebrated by the Shiʿihs, who, in celebrating the Moharem, purposely spat in the direction of Mukudum Shah's tomb. The enraged Sunni fell on them and killed fifteen of them, plundered their property; and the Persian merchants, of whom there were two or three hundred, retreated from Kashmir, and have never since then resided there.[18]

In addition to the reason for the riots, Vigne's description also provides us with an interesting glimpse into nineteenth-century Sunni worldview. In this Sunni understanding of the past the Shiʿi-Sunni dispute is firmly established in the narrative of the Makhdūm-ʿIrakī confrontation. For the Sunni community, the two are the central protagonist of a historical dispute. This narrative is not situated in a historical understanding of the past but is based on legends which are passed on to Vigne by his informants. In this reworking of the past, ʿIrakī is made a disciple of Makhdūm, whom he nevertheless cheats. Also, an examination of the story, indicates, that at least in the minds of Vigne's storytellers, Persian origin is equated with being a Shiʿi This is a major departure from texts surviving from the seventeenth century, where Persian ethnicity and Shiʿi'ness are never defined as being identical to one another and reflects upon a contemporary nineteenth-century worldview reflecting on the preponderance of Shiʿi Iranian merchants in the city[19].

Coming back to the riots, the reason as recorded by Vigne, is broadly in conformity with Marjānpūrī's eyewitness account. And, while the insult to Makhdūm, real or imagined, seems to be an addition of Vigne's witnesses, the clash in both the descriptions takes place near the open ground leading to the shrine of Makhdūm. By holding congregational *majlis* and engaging in *marṣiya* at the recently reconstructed Zadibal *Imāmbāda*, the Shiʿi of Srinagar were breaking away with a past tradition, of secret assemblies limited to the immediate family. But an attempt to take out a daytime mourning procession from Zadibal to Hasanbad, and in doing so seek passage through one of the most contested sites in the city linked to Shiʿi-Sunni division, the Shi'a were asserting their ownership on an important public space of the city. This was not simply an act of transformation seeking a fair share of the way the city operated, benign in its origin, but a radical challenge to how these spaces had operated during the Afghan rule, and their Sunni ownership. While the Ashura procession can be seen as an attempt by the Shiʿis to physically connect two significant Shiʿi-dominated suburbs of the city through a public display of mourning; in doing so, the city's spatial layout demanded that this passage could only happen through the Sunni heart of the city. Significantly, prior to the riots of 1830, we see a steady movement of Shiʿi scholarly families, from far-off and isolated villages in rural Kashmir into the city, who in turn helped in enriching the intellectual life of the city, and though newcomers were rapidly observed in the Shiʿi social hierarchy of the city. For this migrant community, the establishment of Sikh rule, with its disinterest in any Shiʿi-Sunni conflict was the impetus for this sedentariness and urban culture. Was the Shiʿi assertiveness in the city also linked to the presence of the newcomers who had yet to understand the sectarian undercurrents of the city life, seems plausible but is difficult to establish in the absence of any supporting narrative. Also, it is possible that the Shiʿi's attempted to duplicate a similar Sunni event, the annual procession from *Khānaqāh-i Mʿaulā* in Srinagar to Char-i Sharif in central Kashmir. This procession, covering a total distance of around 32 kilometers, would take place over a period of two days,[20] and connected two Sufi orders: the Persianate origin *Kubrawīs* with their base in *Khānaqāh-i Mʿaulā* in the heart of Srinagar and the shrine of Shaykh Nūr-al Dīn, the founder of Kashmiri Sufi order of the *Reshī's* located at Char. Though we have no record of when or how this annual procession started, by the nineteenth century it seems to have been a well-established tradition in the city's religious cycle of celebrations and festivities.

The violent Sunni reaction was a response to Shiʿi attempt at seeking an equal partnership in the functioning of the city, rather than targeted against any perceived Shiʿi act of irreverence toward a saintly Sunni figure. Both Marjānpūrī and Kuihāmī are aware of this crucial factor, and in their narratives, they link the riots with what they perceive as misguided Shiʿi understanding of changed political circumstances. Following the disturbances in the city, it is again in the genre of *marṣiya* that the Shiʿi feeling of helplessness gets registered:

> O Master[21]! you are our guardian
> fortify our souls,
> for our wings are clipped, flights aborted.
> .....
> Secure us under your wings,
> we are devoted to you, do not abandon us
> O you with a phoenix wing.
>
> We are caught in the talons of a tyrant,
> like an innocent dove in a hawk's,
> there's no refuge for us except you,
> redeem us, O Master![22]

The City Elders and a Shahr-ashūb

But then, how real was this loss of Sunni power that Marjānpūrī and Kuihāmī allude to? The closing of Jamia Masjid, the threat to *Khānaqāh-i Mʿaulā*, and the ban on the *azan*[23] clearly point to how the prominent Sunni symbols of religious identity were targeted at the street level and in the day-to-day functioning of the city at the commencement of Sikh rule. The brutal execution of Khwāja Madin Kawūsa and his family, and the inability of the Sunni elders to intervene in the matter, points to this loss of power.[24] When Marjānpūrī begins his narrative of Sikh rule in Kashmir, he equally makes a point about how under the Sikhs, *jāgīrs* of Muslim landowners were confiscated under "a single stroke of the pen."[25] The loss of estates must have certainly affected the Sunni landed elites and those who depended upon them. Marjānpūrī writes about the family of Khwāja Isḥāq Diwānī which had fallen upon bad times,[26] but the economic dispossession of the Sunni elites was not a uniform occurrence. Two earlier European contemporaries of Vigne, who visited Kashmir during the Sikh rule, William Moorcroft (arrived: 1822, d. 1825) and Victor Jacquemont (arrived 1831, d. 1832) while speaking about the miserable condition of the Muslim working classes, also write about Sunni elites who were not only well established but also well respected in the Sikh court. A branch of the Naqshbandī family, who had at one time served as hereditary rulers of Tashkent, migrated to Mughal Empire, before settling down in Kashmir, during the Afghan rule. At the time of Moorcroft's visit, the family was headed by Khwāja Shāh Niyaẕ Naqshbandī (d.1829), a recognized shaykh in the Naqshbandī Sufi order, with extensive trade and spiritual connections across Central Asia. Shāh Niyaẕ, represented a transnational Kashmiri link based on trade and in certain cases faith, in which Kashmiri Sunni merchants could be found in cities not only in the mainland India but also in geographical and cultural locations as diverse as Leh, Iskardu, Lhasa, Yarkand, Bokhara, Kabul, and Kasghar.

Since the beginning of the sixteenth century, the *Naqshbandī* Sufis had played a prominent role in the governance, trade, and administration of *alti-Shahr*: the six cities of Kashgar.[27] It would be safe to speculate upon the faith and trade-based connections of *Naqshbandīs* of Kashmir with the *Naqshbandīs* of nineteenth-century Kasghar and Bukhara. These connections worked in favor of individual Sufi-merchants such as Shāh Niyaẕ and mostly remained undisturbed even after the conquest of Kashmir by the Sikhs.

At the start of Sikh rule, Khwāja Shāh Niyaẕ Naqshbandī like the rest of Kashmiri Sunni *jāgīrdars* had also lost his vast estates in Kashmir. Consequently, he migrated to Ladakh, where he was well received by the *khalun*, the chief minister at the Leh court. It was at Leh that he met Moorcroft and befriended him at the court and "deployed his regional influence to negotiate safe passage and living arrangements from Kashgar to Khoqand and Bukhara for the Company mission."[28] The overwhelming faith and reverence among the Sunnis of Central Asia for the *Naqshbandī* order,[29] both among the rulers and common masses, made the task easier.

And, in return, Shāh Niyaẕ asked and received help from Moorcroft[30] in restoring his *jāgīr* in Kashmir.[31] Continuing with the tradition of assisting European visitors to Kashmir, members of Shāh Niyaẕ's family remained in high standing with the court at Srinagar, besides exercising their immense spiritual and economic connections across Central Asia. And it was these individuals, Sunni elders in Srinagar, who acted as informants to visitors such as Vigne about contemporary events in Kashmir, including the riots of 1830.

It was also during the Sikh rule that a native Kashmiri who is seen as one of the last great Persian poets of Kashmir, Mullā Mahdi Mujrim (d. 1273 AH/1857 CE), wrote his *shahar-ashūb* "the cities misfortune." *Shahar-ashūb* is defined "as a cry of lament on the decay of a city" and emerged as a poetic form that attained a certain popularity with the decline of Imperial Mughal prestige in India. One could call it a South Asian specialty, a unique genre in Urdu poetry, but then it is neither limited to Urdu or South Asia.[32] According to Hammad Rind, *shahr-ashūb* originally meant "someone who brings ruin to a city (usually, owing to their extraordinary beauty)" and a genre of poetry in praise of such a beauty in Persian literature.[33]

An acclaimed court panegyric who served both under the Sikh and later Dogras, Mujrim's life is an interesting example of how a poet maneuvered his way around the shifting political landscape of nineteenth-century Kashmir for patronage. Born and raised a Shi'i, Kuihāmī in his work on the poets of Kashmir mentions that Mujrim converted to Sunnism and married his daughters in prominent Sunni families. Though later Shi'i writers would contest the story of Mujrim's conversion, in the poet's surviving *diwān* no trace of a Shi'i-inspired subject, or imagery is to be found.[34] Yet, the *diwān* does include verses in praise of both Sunni and Hindu subjects, indicating that Mujrim was conscious about his audience, those whom he actively sought to appease.

The immediate context of the *shahar-ashūb* is the mutiny by Sikh soldiers against the *ṣubedar* Behma Singh Ardelī in 1831. Thus, the composition of this work which happened a year after the riots marks a period of decay in the urban fabric of the city—a decay that started under the Afghan rule. About the recent riots, Mujrim ominously chooses to remain silent. The *shahar-ashūb* itself starts on a note of complaint:

> The corrupt of this city trade in pleasant appearances
> The traders of the age trade in damages and penalties
> All the merchants that I see in this town
> Know of only one profit in this market: loss![35]

Aside from the cry of pain and anguish, the *shahar-ashūb* also names some of the leading elites of the city, both Sunnis and Hindus, albeit for some of the individuals, Mujrim adopts a slightly derisive tone. While the Hindus mentioned by Mujrim were courtiers in the employment of Sikh court, the Sunni nobility comprises of the business community—the merchants and the traders of the city[36]. This shift from the older aristocracy of the landowners (*jāgīrdārs*) is itself reflective of a long-drawn process starting in the eighteenth century, during the closing years of Mughal rule in Kashmir, when community leadership of the Kashmiri Sunnis became located in the business class. With the lackadaisical Afghan interest in the patronage of community works, aside from repair or renovation of a select few Sunni religious sites, it was the wealth of these traders and merchants which was the source of community projects, patronage, and power projection.[37]

Coming back to the issue of the limits of Sunni dominance of the city life, Kuihāmī's account does indicate that the Jamia Masjid was in use. It simply serves no practical purpose in preparing mats for furnishing a mosque which is closed. Likewise, the decision of the Sunni elite to approach the Sikh *ṣubedar* for the release of their share of the mats again supports the contention that the Jamia was in use, and earlier restrictions had been relaxed if not totally removed.[38]

Significantly, the riots of 1830 is the first Shi'i-Sunni conflict in which the rioters could not count upon any support from the court. In the absence of official backing, the mob would have put its faith in the community elders for supporting them. As we have seen, in the past communal or sectarian confrontations, it was invariably members of the Sunni community leadership who were responsible for inflaming the passions of the masses in such episodes while also co-opting the administration.

The tragic loss in the riots must certainly have tempered any Shi'i hope of asserting their identity in the public space. In Shi'i accounts more than 800 members of the community, men and women alike, were killed during the riot, a number which Vigne's Sunni informants reduce considerably.[39] The *ṣubedar*, Sardar Bhima Singh Ardalī (1830–1) remained mostly unresponsive to the happenings in the city.[40] In the face of the indifference of the Sikh rulers, Ḥakim Mahdi Khān, the vizier at Awadh, provided the Shi'i of Kashmir with financial relief for the reconstruction of the burned *imāmbāda* at Zadibal.[41] The event also resulted in a renewed Shi'i migration to Awadh, with a few settling down in Amritsar in Punjab. At Faizabad, the capital of Awadh, Ḥakim Mahdi set up a weaving factory for Shi'i shawl weavers who had fled from Kashmir, but unlike Amritsar, this factory does not seem to have made much progress. Mahdi got himself not only involved in the financial rehabilitation of the migrant Shi'i' but also set up special schools for the Kashmiris, with a fixed stipend for the students. Often, the vizier would visit these schools and sit with the students, examining their progress, and maintaining a healthy interest in the progress of the émigré community.[42] These enclaves of Kashmiri Diaspora in the Awadh and Punjab maintained their cultural links with Kashmir, a major institution that sustained these links was that of *majlis* and the recital of Kashmiri *marṣiya*. Until the third quarter of the nineteenth century we find *biyāz* of Kashmiri *marṣiya* being produced in Faizabad, Lucknow, Lahore, Amritsar, Peshawar, and even far off Calcutta. Simultaneously, the poets also assigned the right of recital to different *zakirs* among the Diaspora community.[43] In the case of Awadh with its cosmopolitan *nawabi* culture we find that in addition to Shi'i, Kashmiri Pandits living in Lucknow also participated in the Muharram *majlis*. The ancestors of the Kunzrū-Mushran family had migrated from Kashmir to Awadh somewhere in the late eighteenth to early nineteenth century fleeing the Afghan oppression of Hindus in Kashmir. During their escape, some children of the family are said to have been killed by the Afghans. In Lucknow, the family settled down in Kashmiri Moḥala—a predominantly Kashmiri Hindu neighborhood which also housed some Kashmiri Shi'i after their relocation to Awadh.[44] Besides holding Muharram *majalis* in their *havelis* at Kashmiri Moḥala and Rani Katra, the member of the Kunzrū-Mushran clan would also recite an Urdu *nūḥa* (lament) said to be written by an ancestor. This *nūḥa* which recalls the pain of Bībī Rabāb,[45] wife of Imām Ḥusayn, on the killing of her infant son at Karbala, is said to additionally echo the loss of Hindu children in Kashmir:

> With an arrow has been killed the of child of Rabāb,
> the child who was a fragment of the heart of Rabāb.[46]

Coming back to Mahdi's *shahar-ashūb*, intriguingly it does not mention a single Shi'i, which would lead one to assume that the Shi'i lacked any such presence among the city elders. This view finds some support in Marjānpūrī's narrative, which pointedly speaks about non-Kashmiri presence as an enabling factor in the Ashura procession. Though the Shi'i community both in the city and in the countryside was dispersed and decentralized into self-contained *moḥala*, yet individual Shi'a traders were as much a part of the city's functioning and wealth as their Sunni counterparts.

Moorcroft, who sought and received help from Shāh Niyaẕ[47] at Leh, was accompanied by Mīrzā Najaf 'Ali[48] in his journey, and Najaf like Moorcroft has left us with his own impressions of their travels across Punjab, Ladakh, Kashmir, and Central Asia. Speaking about Ladakh, the starting point of the Kashmiri shawl industry,[49] Mīrzā Najaf writes:

> The *saudagars* (merchants) of Kashmir residing in Ladakh like Khwāja Muhsin 'Ali[50], and Muhammad Razā Shāwl, are the companion and confidant to the *khalun*, and have bought land (in Leh) [. . .] and are of Shi'i faith, and Mīr Akbar Shāh and Rasul Joo and Naqī Joo and Khwāja Yūsuf 'Ali are all Shi'i. And Aḥmad Joo and Ghafar Joo are Sunnis, and Imam Muhammad Heratī is of Shi'i faith.[51]

Najaf 'Ali's information is proof of the cultural, commercial, and political capabilities that the Kashmiri Shi'i merchants enjoyed in protecting, promoting, and organizing their business at the start of the eighteenth century. This ability to position themselves in a transnational arena of operation outside the boundaries of Kashmir is a testament to the overall Kashmir spirit of enterprise and endurance, which was not limited to any sect. The strength of this Trans-Himalayan trade both in the east and west of Kashmir can be understood by the fact that during the early part of the nineteenth century there were 150 Kashmiris based in Lhasa and around 300 in Yarkand. When, in the summer of 1823,[52] Moorcroft left Srinagar for the purpose of visiting Bukhara, the collection of people and ethnicities in the city must have presented a sunny colorful spectacle, which Moorcroft captures in these words:

> the greatest variety of nations that ever marched together, enrolling English, Hindustanis, Gorkhas, Tibetans, Persians, Kashmiris, Kurds and Turks, in its ranks.[53]

The influence of Kashmiri traders can be understood by the fact that they managed to frustrate Moorcroft's plan to visit Yarkand, while also putting him in a tough situation at Leh. According to Moorcroft, in his audience with the *khalun* at Leh, the Ladakhi minister told him:

> the Kashmiris had endeavored to prejudice him against us, and to prevail upon him to prevent our coming to Le.[54]

Though Moorcroft seems unaware of Shiʿi origin of Naqī Joo as well as that of his other opponents in the Kashmiri merchant community at Leh, we do get a sense of sectarian disquiet at the Leh court, with its origin in the divisions in Kashmir. When Moorcroft approached Shāh Niyaẕ for help, he was told by the shaykh:

> that the persons most adverse to our reception were the Kashmir traders, who apprehended we should interfere with their shawl wool traffic, and would, therefore, oppose every possible impediment to our journey: he had incurred great disgrace with them, he said, on our account, as they accused him of having invited us to Ladakh: he had been consulted by the Khalun.[55]

The possibility that a revered Sufi shaykh such as Shāh Niyaẕ could find himself accused of misconduct, by merchants from Kashmir can only be understood in the Shiʿi origin of these business elders. For them, Shāh Niyaẕ's eminence as a *Naqshbandī* shaykh was a reason for distrust, rather than reverence. This is especially true when we see how some of the major Shiʿi-Sunni riots in Srinagar during the seventeenth and eighteenth century, involved active participation of *Naqshbandī* elders.[56] Of the major Sunni Sufi orders operating in nineteenth-century Kashmir, the *Kubrawī, Suhrawardī, Qādrī;* the *Naqshbandīs* were marked by a strong *sharia*-mindedness, framing a religious outlook in which the Shiʿis were seen as heretics, outside the boundaries of Muslim faith and community. Also, as we come nearer to the nineteenth century, we find that most of the educated religious classes of the city were either members of the order or had trained under shaykhs belonging to this order, thus imbibing a sharp sectarian outlook linked with the *Naqshbandīs.*[57] Still, even in his self-imposed exile at Leh, the influence of Shāh Niyaẕ across the Central Asian region would have made active opposition to him detrimental to the business interests of the Shiʿi merchants. So, from their position of power, the merchants rather chose to attack Shāh Niyaẕ for advocating the interests of a European seen as the agent of British colonial influence (Figure 3.4). Much more than the *Naqshbandī* shaykh,[58] it was the Kashmiri merchants who proved more astute in their reading of the changing political circumstances, especially about the advancing colonial threat across South Asia. They rightly perceived Moorcroft as an agent of the East India Company, whose main aim was furthering the British political and financial interest, rather than being simply an interested visitor. A perturbed *khalun* in his interview with the *munshi*[59] of Moorcroft voiced the concerns raised by the Kashmiris:

> he had been told it was the practice of the English to appear at first in the guise of merchants, merely to gain a footing in the country, and that, having affected this, they speedily brought it under their authority.[60]

This awareness was also a result of their wider interest of Kashmiri merchants in happenings in mainland India, as opposed to Shāh Niyaẕ whose attention was fixed on Central Asia.[61]

Figure 3.4 Calligraphy written by Shāh Niyaẕ for William Moorcroft (courtesy: British Library).

In their opposition to Moorcroft, the Shi'i merchants at Leh also managed to seek and elicit the support of Kashmiri Sunni merchants at Yarkand. The coming together of the Kashmiri merchants, outside of the boundaries of their native land, highlights how the merchant community acted to protect their shared "Kashmiri interests" in the face of a real or perceived threat. Significantly, it also highlights how binaries of division related to sectarian origin, could and were set aside, in securing a common financial interest. In doing so the Shi'i and Sunni merchants were self-identifying with a broader Kashmiri identity transcending the barriers and the limits of confessional identification linked to sectarian boundaries. At Yarkand, according to Moorcroft's informant, the Kashmiri, Naqī Joo represented before a joint council of Chinese and native Yarkandi officials his opposition to Moorcroft's plan to visit the city.[62] Moorcroft also provides us with interesting information about the presence of "chief Kashmiri merchants at Yarkand," who were in correspondence with their Kashmiri counterparts in Leh.[63] This group of unidentified chief merchants would be found across cities in Central Asia and Tibet, and in later writings, we find the reference to a Kashmiri trader serving as *Aksakal* (Turkoman: white beard)[64]—a member of the high guild of merchants at Yarkand as well as in other cities.[65] Similarly, when he visited Yarkand, during the early years of the twentieth century, the Hungarian-born British explorer and archaeologist Auriel Stein[66] (d. 1943) wrote about a significant Kashmiri presence in the city built on earlier business contacts:

> and a sprinkling of Muhammadan Kashmiris, of whom there is quite a settled colony here. [. . .] The colonies of Kashmiris, Gilgitis, Badakhshanis, and people from other parts of the Indian frontier regions are large.[67]

While the Moorcroft affair showcases the fluidity of identities created by an intersection of mercantile power dynamics and outsider threats, it also serves as a powerful indicator of Shiʿi presence in the power structure, albeit the financial power. The episode also highlights how Shiʿi traders managed to straddle neutral spaces, for furthering their interests and in doing so also engage in a working relationship with their Sunni counterparts. What was still missing in the overall picture was a substantial Shiʿi presence in the court which could help to protect community interest in the face of adversity, such as the riots of 1830.

The Royal Physician and the Well-Wishing Merchant

Following the riots, the Shiʿi community proceeded to rebuild the *imāmbāda* at Zadibal with funds made available by the Awadh vizier, Ḥakim Mahdi Khān. We have no idea about when the work was completed; textual evidence indicates that in 1841 the new building was already in need of repairs.[68] The act of reconstruction, following a devastating loss, can be seen as a part of a sustained effort by the community elders to revive the institution of *Mʿārak* as a focal point of Shi'a identity in Kashmir.[69] After being closed during most of the Afghan rule, the rehabilitation of *Mʿārak* coincides broadly with the Sikh rule in the region and was a gradual process primarily dependent upon the collective community efforts originating in the city. Such activities would also draw upon the links of patronage connecting Kashmiri Shiʿi to both non-native Iranian traders based in the city and Kashmiri Shiʿi Diaspora located at Leh, Awadh, Calcutta, and other parts of South Asia. The vizier Ḥakim Mahdi was also regularly sending a sum of money as *khums* to Kashmir, a part of which also percolated into community affairs such as rebuilding and upkeep of the *Mʿārak*.[70] The reconstruction of *Mʿārak*[71] in 1830 was overseen by an Iranian merchant, Ḥājjī Baqir, who had married into the family of the Mʿārakdars, the hereditary *mutwalī* (custodians) of *Mʿārak*.[72]

Though, as I have shown earlier, Kashmiri Shiʿi community retained a high level of religious scholarship, yet the *Mʿārak* was used singularly for the performance of Muharram ceremonies alone: the *majalis*, involving recital of *marṣiyas*. Performing of *nimaz* (prayers) was limited to smaller *moḥala* mosques of which only a few were to be found in the city, while entire Shiʿi villages lacked this facility. Also, in most cases, the prayers would be offered individually and not in the congregation. This was as much a reflection of prevailing societal tensions, especially in mixed Shiʿi-Sunni areas as of the Shiʿi belief in suspending congregational prayers in the absence (*ghaibyat*) of the twelfth imām, Muhammad al-Mahdi (b. 255 AH/879 CE).[73] Sermonizing in public spaces such as *Mʿārak* or even the *moḥala* mosques was unheard of; imparting religious education was done at the homes of religious scholars: the *mullās*, the *molvis*, the *sayyids*, and the *akhunds*, and would draw a limited audience mostly derived from the affluent and religious circles.[74] Though the writer of *Kūhal-al Jawahir* (*c.* 1264 AH/1847 CE), Sayyid ʿAli ibn Razā, mentions that his father, Sayyid Mīr Razā (d. 1830), was killed in the riots of 1830 while giving a sermon at Zadibal *imāmbāda*, the circumstances indicate that this was an isolated event associated with this particular Muharram rather than a part of established practice.[75]

It was during the governorship of Shaykh Ghūlam Mohyi-al Dīn (1841–5)[76] that we find the first mention of an individual from the Kashmiri Shiʿi community, rising to a position of prominence in the court. A Sunni Muslim from the plains of Punjab, Mohyi-al Dīn and following him his son, Shaykh Imām-al Dīn (1845–6), would serve as the last two governors of Kashmir for the Lahore *darbār*. A crucial element of Mohyi-al Dīn's tenure as *ṣubedar* of Kashmir was his reinstatement of Kashmiri Muslims at the court, as well as resuming *jāgīrs* to them. In his *Ākhbārāt's*,[77] written between 1847 and 1877, Mīrzā Saif-al Dīn writes about how after the demise of Sikh rule in Kashmir in 1847, Maharaja Gulab Singh (r. 1847–57), the Hindu ruler of Kashmir, sought to reorganize the sericulture industry in his kingdom. Early on in his reign, in a conversation with his trusted Kashmiri Hindu adviser, Raj Kāk Dhar, the maharaja opined that the industry was better served if it was overseen from Jammu. At this point, Dhar interjects to advise the maharaja that it would be better if the production was handed over to the maharaja's chief physician, Ḥakim ʿAẕim (1803–52). He then goes on to inform the maharaja[78] about how during Shaykh Mohyi-al Dīn's rule, the *ṣubedar* had also selected the ḥakim for the position, as he had found no one else as *mʿūtabar* (reliable), *danā* (prudent), and *fahmida* (intelligent) as ʿAẕim.[79] In another instance, Saif-al Dīn writes about the complete faith vested in ʿAẕim by Mohyi-al Dīn who gave the ḥakim full authority in matters of government, especially in the affairs of the newly conquered territory of Gilgit.[80] Based on Dhar's advice, Gulab Singh appoints ʿAẕim to oversee the industry,[81] though in Saif-al Dīn's account, the ḥakim tries his best to sidestep from the responsibility but to no avail.[82] Saif-al Dīn also writes that among the Kashmiri *jāgīrdārs* serving the Sikh Empire, the names of Pandit Raj Kāk Dhar, Khwājāghan-i Naqshbandī, Sayyid Yasin Shāh, Ḥakim ʿAẕim, Diwān Dina Nath, and the descendants of Khwājā Munwar Shāh and Valī Joo were enlisted in a special *diwān* at Lahore,[83] and when Gulab Singh assumed control of the country in 1947, these individuals were allowed to retain their land.[84] Son of Mullā Ḥakim Javad, the court physician, whom we had encountered earlier in the account of *ṣubedar* ʿAbdullah Khān, ʿAẕim's progress at the Sikh and later Dogra court was to prove highly consequential in negotiating the contours of Shiʿi identity in Kashmir.[85] He would also emerge as one of the prime movers and enabler of emerging social hierarchies in nineteenth-century Kashmiri Shiʿi society. On his death, Gulab Singh appointed ʿAẕim's eldest son, Ḥakim ʿAbdul Raḥim as chief physician and in charge of the sericulture industry, marking a continuation of the family influence and presence in the court.[86]

The life of ʿAẕim, spanning a greater part of the nineteenth century, marks a period of transformation in the life and behavior of the Shi'a community of Kashmir. It represents a transition from an age of marked quietism under the

Afghan to that of gradual celebration of a sectarian identity under the Sikh and Dogra kings. The ḥakim was also an eyewitness to the riots of 1830 and must have been aware of lingering tensions, especially in the city. Starting his life under Maharaja Ranjit Singh, ʿAẕim initially joined the royal court at Lahore rather than attaching himself to the provincial court of the *ṣubedar* at Srinagar. While we have no idea of when, and in what capacity he joined the Lahore *darbār*, but based on a manuscript[87] copied by ʿAẕim at Lahore in 1248 AH/1832 CE, it is certain that at least in the aftermath of the 1830 riots, he was in the capital city of the Sikh Empire.[88] In his letter to Maulvi Sayyid Rajab ʿAli Naqvī, ʿAẕim alludes to how he was using the literary genre of *marṣiya* to commemorate both the martyrdom of Imām Ḥusayn and in doing so also consolidate the commemoration as a symbol of Shiʿi identity (Figure 3.5). Written in highly ornate Persian prevalent across much of nineteenth-century South Asia, this epistle, which we touched upon earlier also, highlights the importance that ʿAẕim attached to the performance of the *marṣiya* as a Shiʿi symbol of deliverance as well as his own standing as a man of letters in these words:

> Having sent that for such a long time at an adverse fate, I necessarily intended to bring out the shining pearls of its sad contents, which I had spun together in new ways, and arrange it on the lines of a Kashmiri *marṣiya*, so that your Lordship's beautiful grace receives a jewel tear, the price of which gives plenty of recompense

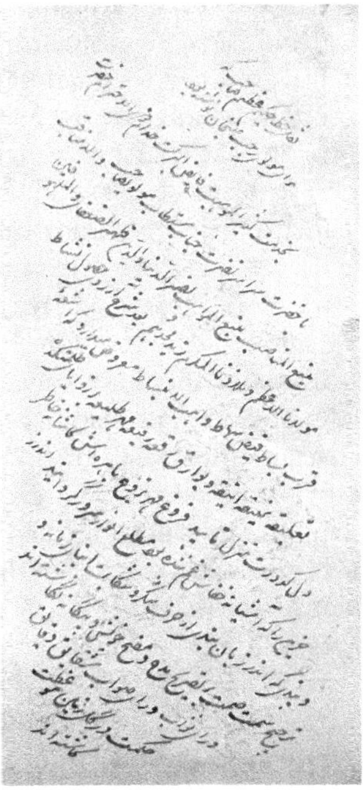

Figure 3.5 Epistle of Ḥakim ʿAẕim to Moulvi Sayyid Rajab ʿAli (author).

> to each of those who ask for help. With this precious pearl in the crown, (your) glorious crest will be remembered in the plain of the Last Judgment. [. . .] and they try to dishonour and reproach those who commemorate. But they know that their sad predominance deserves an enormous price for their abovementioned piety [. . .]. It has gone so far now that we have to cry very much.[89]

The ḥakim would be joined by two of his cousins, Munshi Shāh Muhammad (d. 1863) and Munshi Muhammad Yūsuf (1797–1884),[90] in composing *marṣiyas*. Both ʿAẕim and his cousins Shāh Muhammad and Muhammad Yūsuf would be trained in this literary genre by the *marṣiya khwān*, Khwāja Ḥasan Mīr. A modest farmer from the village of Habak, Ḥasan Mīr's meeting with ʿAẕim is represented in folklore as a serendipitous act; ʿAẕim's participation in this genre helped in furthering the literary quality and imagery of this genre.[91] Aẕim's oeuvre which includes twenty-four *marṣiya* is also reflective of the efforts he made into popularizing the high craft of *maqām*-based *marṣiya* for public recitation.[92] And as *marṣiya khawani* became the leitmotif of Shiʿi identity in Kashmir, we find that in the next generations, the family of ʿAẕim would produce thirteen *marṣiya* writers who participated in this genre while continuing their association with the court as physicians, calligraphers, teachers, and administrators.[93] And, in contemporary Kashmiri Shiʿi society, the memory of ʿAẕim for which he is remembered is that of a *marṣiya* writer, not a courtier.

Simultaneously with the reopening of *Mʿārak* before the riots of 1830, the ḥakim had also secured the consent of a learned Shiʿi scholar, Mullā Fazl ʿAli Ansarī[94] (d. 1263 AH/1846 CE) and had convinced him to relocate to the city from his ancestral seat in the Tantraypora near Ahmadpora, in northwest Kashmir.[95] During the eighteenth century we find that outside of Srinagar, Ahmadpora had emerged as the nucleus of Shiʿi scholarship, primarily centered on the Rizvī Sayyids.[96] Where many Shiʿi scholars of the city[97] had sought proximity and patronage at the Mughal court as poets, artisans-calligraphers, and miniature painters, the Rizvī Sayyids had remained singularly committed to religious studies, and any poetical disposition was limited to writing religious elegies—the *marṣiyas* for Imām Ḥusayn. Also, as we saw earlier many of the Rizvī scholars who migrated to Awadh after the establishment of the Shiʿi kingdom, used their new court connections to create lines of scholarly transmission as well as financial patronage between Kashmiri Shiʿi society and the Awadh court.[98]

Some accounts link both Ḥakim ʿAẕim and Mullā Fazl to the *madrassa* (school) of Mullā Muhammad Muqim which operated from Muqim's residence at Zadibal, offering training to a small select group, but this is by no means certain.[99] Nonetheless, the relocation of Mullā Fazl to Nawa Kadal in the heart of the city would be the first step in establishing the Ansarī family in the role of religious leadership of Kashmiri Shiʿi. In *Matlaʿ-i Anwār*, Sayyid Murtazā Husayn refers to Mullā Mahdi Khatāʾi, a student of Muqim, who had settled down in Lahore and drew a significant circle of students in the city.[100] The most prominent disciple of Mahdi Khatāʾi,[101] who would exert his influence on Shiʿi society of Punjab, was Maulvi Sayyid Rajab ʿAli Naqvī (1806–69).[102] We have already come across Maulvi

Rajab ʿAli, in the epistle written to him by Ḥakim ʿAẕim. A second-generation student from the school of Mullā Muqim, Rajab ʿAli would be intimately linked with ʿAẕim as well as Fazl, who as we have seen were a part of Muqim's circle. In the tumulus nineteenth-century South Asia, with a waning Mughal court at Delhi, Rajab would remain loyal to the British during the Great Rebellion of 1857. In return for his loyalty, he was richly rewarded by the British, with *jāgīrs* as well as a lofty-sounding title of *Aristūjāh* (Aristotle of the Age). Rajab's introduction to the Kashmiri court occurred somewhere around 1847, during the proceedings leading to the sale of Kashmir to the future Dogra Maharaja of Kashmir, Gulab Singh.[103] Based in Punjab, as the confidant of Sir Henry Lawrence (d. 1857), architect of the Kashmir sale, Rajab ʿAli had worked for a Shiʿi revival in Punjab, also setting up a press at Ludhiana, *Majmʿa-ul Bahrayn*, which was instrumental in printing lithograph editions of Shiʿi works.[104] In his letter, ʿAẕim expresses his gratitude to Rajab for sending him a copy of a book, which had been circulated widely among the Indian audience by Rajab ʿAli.

It was at Lahore that Rajab ʿAli along with the Nawab ʿAli Rizā Qizalbāsh (d. 1865) helped in laying the footprints of Shiʿi identity in the city.[105] Under ʿAli Rizā's son, Nawab Nawazish ʿAli a distinct set of spiritual and cultural practices associated with the commemoration of the martyrdom of Imām Ḥusayn and his family in Karbala came into formation in the city of Lahore. In addition to native Shiʿi population of the city, and the associates of the Qizalbāsh clan, Kashmiri Shiʿi who had taken residence in the city in the aftermath of the 1830 riot also participated in these rituals.[106] Aside from their contribution in Punjab, we find the Qizalbāsh nawabs taking an active interest in the affairs of the Kashmiri Shiʿi community. While we have no textual evidence to prove how this link came into being, it is safe to posit Rajab ʿAli as a prime mover in the formation of this transregional, sectarian link given his own standing with the Kashmiri Shiʿi elite. Both ʿAli Rizā and Rajab ʿAli were a part of the entourage that accompanied Henry Lawrence on his visit to Kashmir in 1846.[107]

Rajab's association with ʿAẕim must have encouraged the ḥakim to explore possibilities of mirroring a similar Shiʿi revival in Kashmir. The invitation to Mullā Fazl, a classmate from Muqim's circle, to preside over the religious needs of the Shiʿi society in the capital can be seen as a step in this direction. Pertinently, Rajab ʿAli's nephew also briefly studied under Mullā ʿAbdullah Ansarī (d. 1878), Fazl ʿAli's grandson, highlighting the continuing links of knowledge transmission among Shiʿi scholarly families who owed their intellectual training directly or through an intermediary link to the *madrassa* of Mullā Muqim. Likewise, we find the family of Muqim's grandson, Sayyid Ṣafdar Shāh, playing a central role in the development of Shiʿi intellectual traditions in Awadh, highlighting the significance of Muqims school in the revival of Shiʿi intellectual traditions not only in Kashmir but also across major centers of North Indian Shiʿism, in Punjab and Awadh. This is especially true of Ṣafdar's son, the Iraq-trained mujtahid, Sayyid ʿAli Shāh (d. 1853), and grandson Sayyid Abuʾl Hasan *Abū Ṣāhib* (1844–95) who laid the foundation of *Sultan al-Madāris (1894)*.[108] Over the years *Sultan al-Madāris* would emerge as the principal seat of Shiʿi learning not only in Awadh but across South Asia. The pressing desire to see the establishment of a Shiʿi seat of religious knowledge in the city, for men like ʿAẕim, can also be observed from the text of a letter he wrote to Fazl ʿAli's grandson, Mullā Ṣādiq ʿAli (d. 1878).[109] An accomplished cleric like his grandfather, Ṣādiq was also the leading Shiʿi scholar of *ʿilm al-Kalām* (science of discourse) in nineteenth-century Kashmir.[110] In the letter, ʿAẕim discusses the obligations of a believer based on the famous Prophetic tradition, known as the *Ḥadīth Saʿah*,[111] which relates that an individual is free from a religious obligation, of which he is unaware. Some other theological issues touched upon in the letter include the principle of *ihtiyāt* (precaution), a practice that was common among South Asian Shiʿi scholars in the nineteenth century, who would practice caution, rather than opting for *ijtihād* (independent reasoning), "in acts whose legitimacy remained unknown to the jurist due to lack of evidence."[112] Read in the context of Kashmiri Shiʿi society, the letter expresses not only a deep concern for the direction of the religious life of the community but also seeks to establish remedial practices that would ensure observance of religious obligations in a manner that was in conformity with the principles of jurisprudence. Given the geographical distance between Kashmir and the *hawza's* in Iran and Iraq, ʿAẕim saw the scholars of the Ansari dynasty as the natural choice of circumventing the near-impossible possibility of approaching the *hawzas* in the shrine cities for direction in the day-to-day life of the community.

At Gulab Singh's court, in addition to ʿAẕim, we see the presence of one of the last Iranian shawl merchants in Kashmir, Ḥājjī ʿAbid. Not much is known about ʿAbid's origin, but in a document related to the custodianship of *Mʿārak*, his name is mentioned as the person responsible for efforts at reestablishing *Mʿārak* in the aftermath of the riots of 1830.[113] Somewhere in between 1841–5, during the rule of Mohyi-al Dīn, he carried out repairs and minor additions to the *imāmbāda*, from his own funds.[114] Arriving in Kashmir in the fall of 1850, Mrs. Harvey, a European traveler, met Ḥājjī ʿAbid at his showroom in Srinagar and with a degree of astonishment wrote about the merchant's European connection:

> His name is "Hājee Abid". He is the best of his fraternity and receives orders from the London house! [. . .] He is a great man, and wears the colour green, a token of his sanctity and great position. He sits down on a chair in the presence of a gentleman, as he is entitled to that privilege. When I went to see his shawls, he insisted upon my drinking a cup of tea and eating some sweetmeats. The former was served in small Yarkand cups, and the latter on China saucers.[115]

While Harvey indicates the Ḥājjī ʿAbid as a Kashmiri, referring to the merchant's house as "good for a Kashmirian one; the rooms he occupied were painted and carpeted,"[116] Saif-al Dīn clearly indicates ʿAbid's non-native status by stating that the merchant was presently stationed in Kashmir.[117] Mahdah Shāh Deykah in his *Raʿyis Nāma-i Kashmir* mentions ʿAbid as a native of Mashad[118].

The author of the *Ākhbārāt* also writes about ʿAbid's favored status in Gulab Singh's court. In one instance, Saif-al Dīn mentions an episode about a shawl merchant, Muhammad Saudaghar who had been assigned a task in the department of *dagh-i shawl* (stamp on shawl), which oversaw the stamping and collecting of taxes on shawls. An inquiry in the functioning of the department revealed Saudaghar's embezzlement. This discovery led to Muhammad Saudaghar's imprisonment, while his duty was then transferred to ʿAbid, who executed the job promptly.[119] Far more consequential than Ḥājjī ʿAbid, in furthering the interests of the Kashmiri Shiʿi society at court and in the city was the presence of a native Shiʿi merchant, Mīrzā Muhammad ʿAli, son of one of the leading merchants of the city Mīrzā Rasūl.[120] Like his Iranian contemporary, Ḥājjī ʿAbid, Muhammad ʿAli had also participated in the repairs to the *imāmbāda* in Zadibal, somewhere around 1857–8.[121] For Muhammad ʿAli, the author of *Ākhbārāt* uses the epithet of *khairkhwah* (well-wisher) in his text wherever he mentions the shawl merchant's name.[122] While the reason for the epithet is not mentioned in the text, it does indicate the Shiʿi merchant's privileged status at the court. Very early in Gulab Singh's reign, we find Muhammad ʿAli sharing the responsibility for organizing the feast of *Aukut* with Ḥakim ʿAẕim. The festival of *Aukut*[123] was introduced by Gulab Singh, and in the very first mention of the celebrations linked with it in the *Ākhbārāt*, the two Shiʿi's at the court, the chief physician and the shawl merchant, are asked to oversee the preparation to feast at Bagh-i Dilawar Khan, for their Shiʿi co-religionist.[124] The decision to allow two Shi'a courtiers to oversee the arrangement for organizing the feast for their community was a mark of favor by the maharaja, and this contrasts vividly with his decision to have similar arrangements for the Sunnis to be overseen by a Hindu courtier.[125] On another occasion, Saif-al Dīn records that the *Aukut* arrangements for the Muslims were supervised by a team of Sunni Muslims comprising Moulvi Mustafa ʿAli, Moulvi Farzand ʿAli, Kummandan Amīr Khān, and the Shiʿi physician, ʿAẕim.[126] As with most nineteenth-century Kashmiri Sunni historians, Saif-al Dīn always uses the terms Muslims and Sunnis interchangeably, yet in this instance the text speaks of only a Hindu and a Muslim event, held on either side of the royal citadel, Sherghari, indicating that Muslim as a category is used in its broadest sense to include both the Shiʿi and Sunni. This is the first known instance in nineteenth-century Kashmir, where in public space; the Shiʿi and Sunni are seen as comprising a single religious grouping and seated together for a celebration. That this happens under the direction of non-Muslim ruler is equally noteworthy, as is the fact that this entire episode unfolds in a display essentially featuring a shared meal. The breaking of a sectarian taboo; of sitting together in the same open space and sharing food between communities who had rioted in the past could be seen as marking a paradigm shift in intra-Muslim relations, but it was not so. Writing in the early part of the 1890s when Gulab Singh's grandson, Maharaja Pratap Singh (1885–1925) was presiding over the event, the colonial administrator, Walter Lawrence speaks about separate Shiʿi and Sunni gathering on *Aukut*.[127]

Still, the episode during Gulab Singh's life is of particular interest as it not only highlights the desire of the maharaja to appease the sensibilities of his majority Sunni Muslim subjects—a gesture of goodwill on the occasion of state celebrations—but also shows how for the Hindu ruler, the Shiʿi's and Sunni's were essentialized as belonging to a single community: the Muslims. It was now left for the Sunni and Shi'i elites to internalize this image of being one but that would still take time.

While we have few details of Muhammad 'Ali's connection outside Kashmir, barring a reference to his *kothi* in Calcutta, there are indications that his mercantile links were wider and operated in other princely courts. In a condolence letter written by Munshi Tālib 'Ali (d. 1891), a Shi'i scholar from Srinagar to the Shi'i Nawab of Khairpur, Mīr Murad 'Ali Khan (d. 1894) on the death of his two children, there is a reference to Muhammad 'Ali acting as a messenger of Murad 'Ali.[128] Similarly, the author of *Aftāb-i 'Aālam Tāb* (*c.* 1873), a contemporary of Muhammad 'Ali writes about how the Kashmiri merchant provided him with details about leading Persian poets of Kashmir along with specimens of their compositions.[129]

Coming back to the account of Saif-al Dīn, we find a crucial detail about the role of Mīrzā Muhammad 'Ali in establishing Shi'i symbols in the city. Saif-al Dīn writes about a request made to Gulab Singh by Muhammad 'Ali during the Muharram of 1850, a request to take out the Ashura procession in the city. The maharaja however refused the permission, after consulting with Pandit Raj Kāk Dhar, fearing that a Shi'i procession in the city could lead to riots.[130] For the Kashmiri Shi'i, especially those in the city, the desire to take out the Ashura procession highlights the centrality of the Muharram commemoration and *M'ārak* in defining their Shi'i-ness, in this instance articulated through a request by the maharaja's *khair khwah*, at a time when the Dogra rule was hardly three years old in the region. In *Ra'yis Nāma-i Kashmir*, we are told that every Thursday night, Muhammad 'Ali would host *majlis* of *marṣiya khwānī* in his house, attended by both the poor and the rich. The Sunni poet also remembers the merchant as the one who kept the religion of Shi'i alive through his patronage[131].

In narrating the events of the Muharram of 1855, Saif-al Dīn informs us about the *vakīl* (representative) of Rajā 'Ali Shāh, grandson of Rajā Aḥmad of Skardu, arriving in the court to report about the Muharram ceremony that would take place at the Zadibal *imāmbāda* on the first ten days of the month. Apprehending the possibility of disturbances, the *kotwal* (chief police officer) of the city, Lala Bola Nath, asks the Rajā to set up a quarter near the *imāmbāda* during the ceremonies.[132] Saif-al Dīn's text clearly indicates the continuing unease in the *darbār* about the possible repercussions of Shi'i commemoration on the peace of the city.

Years later, the exact date is not recorded; Mīrzā Muhammad 'Ali would eventually receive the permission to take out a small procession on Ashura from his residence at Namchibal in the heart of Srinagar, to *M'ārak*. This Ashura procession would start at the break of dawn from Muhammad 'Ali's house and culminate at *M'ārak* in the early morning, much before the city woke up. On the way, it would also briefly stop in Kamangarpora, a Shi'i-majority *moḥala*, located midway between Namchibal and Zadibal. Unlike the *Ashura* of 1830, the somber and restrained procession taken out by Muhammad 'Ali, accompanied as it was by a dozen or so mourners, whispering the first part of the Muslim *shahādah*—testimony of faith: *lā 'ilāha 'illā-llāhu* (There is no God but Allah); avoiding any distinct Shi'i symbol of mourning such as wailing, beating chest or reciting *marṣiyas*, found

Figure 3.6 Muharram procession in contemporary Kashmir, Srinagar, 2018 (courtesy: Hammad Ali).

acceptance in the ritual landscape of the city.[133] Given the obscurity surrounding it, the procession while fulfilling a manifest Shi'a need to commemorate Ashura also emerged as a nonevent for the Sunnis living along the route (Figure 3.6). The hushed early morning procession: the absence of a Sunni audience viewing it also blurred the reality of the experience—in what was not seen was not recognized and what was not recognized did not exist. And, once the procession had reached its designated space safely, for the Shiʿi's it would be followed by a daylong elaborate *majilis* at *Mʿārak* with the performance of *marṣiyas*. Additionally, at *Mʿārak,* the predominantly male audience would be joined by women, who would watch and participate in the ritual from the wooden screened galleries (*dalān*) of the first floor, looking down into the main assembly below, participating yet remaining unseen. In the spatial layout of *Mʿārak*, based as it was on a modification of the plan of the Jamia Masjid at Srinagar, the stepped galleries on the side provided an amphitheater perspective on the main central assembly located beneath a double-height covered roof (*pukhār*) in what would otherwise be an open courtyard.[134] The shared participation, even if visually and physically segregated, of men and women mourners, nourished and testified to the image of a Shiʿi collective in a Shiʿi space, commemorating a Shi memory, in one voice: the recital of a *marṣiya*. This coming together of the genders and participating in a collective recital was a singular Shi'a innovation in the nineteenth-century urbanized setting of Kashmir, operating within the boundaries of gender segregation and *pardah* (women veiling), especially in public spaces. It would also give birth to Sunni myths and misrepresentation about the assembly, in which the Shiʿi's are seen as participating in some unnamed depraved rituals during their *majilis* at *Mʿārak*, especially on the night of Ashura, a particularly painful moment in Shiʿi remembrance of Imām Ḥusyan's martyrdom-the grief and loss of his household, especially women.

The practice of Ashura, once it got established in the 1850s, again highlights how the Shiʿi society negotiated their presence in the ritual landscape of the city by managing the event of Ashura in two ways, a scaled-down hurried movement through the heart of a predominately Sunni city and an elaborate commemoration within the Shiʿi space of Zadibal. While Sunni historians are silent about how the Sunnis viewed this new introduction in the cycle of city life, narratives based on anecdotes, dehumanizing both the event and the Shi'a as a people, made themselves a part of popular Sunni folklore. Drawing blood of innocent Sunni children on Ashura by the Shiʿi is a frequent trope in these Sunni folk traditions. Also, the narrative that the Shi'a during their *marṣiya*, slander revered Sunni figures. Where such stories repeated, elaborated, and embellished from one oral narrative to the next, did manage to maintain the image of Shiʿis as being "others," it is also possible that the fabrication of these stories served a more practical and benign purpose. These myths helped in maintaining a social distance between the two communities, limiting interaction among the masses—interactions which could turn hostile and lead to disputes and riots. Engagements between the two communities were then left to the community elders, to be managed and negotiated as they deemed fit, under the watchful eyes of a Hindu court.

The reputation of the main organizer behind the event, Mīrzā Muhammad ʿAli, not only as a wealthy trader with connections to the court but as a respected philanthropist helping the destitute of the city irrespective of their sectarian or communal background, also tempered any possible backlash from the Sunni elites.[135] But the crucial element in the entire event was the authorization of the procession by the maharaja who was deeply involved in both maintaining his control over the country and ensuring its stability. And at a time when the Sunni elite were reestablishing and repositioning themselves in the court, an open defiance of the ruler would have proven detrimental to their personal interests and to those of the Sunni community at large.

The organizing of the Ashura procession, the opening of the *Mʿārak* and performance of *marṣiya majilis*, speaks about a successful realization of Srinagar-centered Shiʿi project. This bold assertion of a sectarian identity after decades of quietism is also reflected in some of the *marṣiyas* written during the Dogra rule. In his *marṣiya*, *Khamūshī* (Silence), written somewhere around the late 1850s, Mullā Ḥakim ʿAbdullah (d. 1887 approx.), the nephew of Ḥakim ʿAẕim, gives voice to this newfound confidence in verses which contrasts vividly with what had been written earlier by poets like Ustād Jaʿfar and Khwāja Ḥassī Bhat:

> How can a *muḥib*[136] ever choose to remain silent,
> while remembering the immodesty of the Kufis.[137]

On the surface, the Shiʿi of the city realized a cherished dream enunciating a distinct Shiʿi identity in public spaces and navigating it successfully against any antagonism from the Sunnis. While at the start of the nineteenth century, it was the experience of religious persecution and vulnerability which had provided the Shiʿi society with strong group cohesion, the same was replaced now by community members acting as participants in performances transforming once proscribed rituals into a normative practice. In the process, the community elite, the courtiers, the traders, and the religious scholars had managed to foreground a sense of Shiʿi identity in the religious imagery centered on Muharram, *marṣiya*, and *Mʿārak*. In nineteenth-century preindustrial Kashmiri society, where a majority of people both Shiʿi and Sunnis were illiterate and survived as artisans, craftsmen, or agriculturalists, the consolidation of a sectarian identity under a feudal-mercantile elite also helped this small, select, and literate group to secure the sectarian loyalties of the common masses, toiling in the workshops and on the lands of their Shi'a employees. The elite saw and projected themselves as the benefactors and protectors of the community. But as the hope of secure existence became a reality, the unity of the Shiʿi society started unraveling in the face of internal dissensions and divisions related to the dynamics of class, power, and exploitation. For the Shiʿi, the challenge was now from within, who represented them and what that representation meant for the different sections of the Kashmiri Shiʿi society.

Chapter 4

DISSENSIONS WITHIN THE *MŪMININ*

CHALLENGING THE ELITE

As the Shiʿi of Kashmir saw the consolidation of their identity in the middle of the nineteenth century, it was soon followed by the emergence of divisions and rifts within the community. Primarily, the divisions were introduced via differences related to the control and maintenance of *Mʿārak* and the mourning assemblies held there. Gradually the differences expanded into all major functioning of the community activities, especially with regard to the collection and distribution of community monies. The chapter looks at how the issue of dispensing of *khums* money led to a divide within the religious class. By the later part of the nineteenth century, the religious leadership trained in the seminaries of Iraq had established themselves as community heads. The disagreement within the Shiʿi clergy, who in these dissensions and debates, increasingly drew upon their transnational connections in Iraq, is studied as the main contributing factor to the emerging split within the community. The divisions and splits got primarily translated into an urban-rural and rich-poor divide, with the merchant families of Kashmir associating with a particular section of clergy and the poor craftsmen that worked for these businesses siding with a rival clerical party. The chapter explores these dissensions within the Shiʿi society and explores how these differences affected the worldview of the community. The chapter also explores the circumstances behind the riot of 1872, the last major Shiʿi-Sunni conflagration in the nineteenth century, locating the reason in personal resentments and competition among merchants acting as community benefactors.

Controlling the Muharram Ceremonies

In the letter of Ḥakim ʿAẕim to Moulvi Rajab which we addressed before, there is an interesting reference to Sayyid Ibrahim Qazwinī,[1] an Iranian religious scholar who arrived in Kashmir in 1850.[2] While during the seventeenth century, under the Mughals, Kashmir had remained a favored land for Iranian scholars arriving in the Indian sub-continent, such scholarly links had ceased once the Mughal Empire started unraveling in the eighteenth century. The last time Kashmiri Shiʿi had hosted a prominent Shiʿi scholar from Iran was when Mullā Muhammad Said Ashraf (d. 1704),[3] son of the renowned Safavid Shiʿi' *alim*, Mullā Ṣāliḥ Mazandaranī (d.1704), arrived in Kashmir in the seventeenth century during the reign of Emperor Aurangzeb (r. 1658–1707). Though during the first half of the nineteenth century some educated Iranians did seek employment as munshis in British expeditions and embassies traveling into Central Asia, originating from British India and passing through Kashmir, such ventures would not interest a religious scholar.[4]

The only sustained Iranian presence we see in the nineteenth century is that of the shawl merchants. The association of the Iranian merchant, Ḥājjī ʿAbid with the Kashmiri court, is indicative of this lingering Iranian presence in Kashmir. Wealthy Shiʿi merchants and traders would enlist the help of a religious scholar to help maintain and distribute the *khums* money to be taxed from their earnings. For the Shiʿi, *khums* is an obligatory tax to be paid by the believer, calculated as one-fifth of a person's annual savings, and split equally into two shares; half to be distributed among destitute sayyid families (*saham-i sadat*) and the other half known as *mal-i Imām* (the Imām's share) to be forwarded to a living *mujtahid* which in nineteenth-century Kashmir would mean sending it to the shrine cities, the *ʿatabat-i ʿaliyat* (sublime thresholds) in Iraq; seat of principal *mujtahids* in the Shiʿi world.[5] In Kashmir, the issue of *khums* distribution had a complex history, and in the past, there had been disputes involving the monies dispersal, disputes which lingered on into nineteenth-century Kashmir.[6]

The arrival of Sayyid Ibrahim also finds a mention in the *Akhbarat*, where Saif-al Dīn specifically mentions that the Iranian *ʿalim* accompanied Ḥājjī ʿAbid, indicating that the introduction was done by the Iranian *sudagar*.[7] In his entry for September 1850, Saif-al Dīn refers to the *ʿalim* as, Mullā Ibrahim, a *mujtahid* (an authoritative interpreter of law for the Shiʿi) of the community of *Shiʿi* and *Rāfizī*.[8] The presentation of the scholar by a wealthy patron of the Kashmiri Shiʿis, who had personally undertaken the repairs to *Mʿārak*, must have also helped in creating a favorable reception for Sayyid Ibrahim among them. By enlisting an Iranian *ʿalim*, ʿAbid was not only co-opting a compatriot for facilitating his financial outreach to Kashmiri Shiʿis, but also strengthening the principal Shiʿi institution of Kashmir, the *Mʿārak*. As I have shown earlier, the courtier Ḥakim ʿAẕim had also, with a similar intention, initiated the relocation of Mullā Fazl Ansarī to the city. Until Sayyid Ibrahim's arrival the *imāmbāda* at Zadibal had remained a ritual space, solely dedicated to the performance of *marṣiya* in Muharram. On his arrival, Sayyid Ibrahim used *Mʿārak* not only for holding congregational prayers (*nimaz-ijamat*) but also as a platform for preaching, by delivering sermons in the *imāmbāda* after prayers. This was unheard of in the Shiʿi society of Kashmir. Undertaking congregational prayers was still a highly contested topic for Shiʿi, especially those living under a non-Muslim rule, and aside from one failed attempt to engage in *waʿiẕ khanī* (sermonizing) in the Moharram of 1830, Kashmiri Shiʿi had not participated in these practices. Even, Mullā Fazal Ansarī, though associated with the functioning of the *Mʿārak*, had not openly preached in the *imāmbāda*. In the accounts of Saif-al Dīn, Sayyid Ibrahim's actions at the *imāmbāda* are termed as *khilāf-i ma'mūl-i qadim*—against established old precedents. Saif-al Dīn then goes on to add that the practices initiated by Ibrahim were taken up with great fervor by the Shiʿi rabble of Zadibal, the *shawlbaf* (shawl weavers). He ends the episode by detailing out how the maharaja, fearing a Shiʿi-Sunni unrest because of Ibrahim's action, initiated an inquiry which was conducted by Raj Kāk Dhar and consequently Sayyid Ibrahim was banished from Srinagar to Lahore.[9] The text of Saif-al Dīn while laying the blame on Sayyid Ibrahim for breaking from past traditions locates the reasons for his banishment in a fear of possible Shiʿi-Sunni unrest. Yet nowhere in the text does he indicate that this misgiving, given the circumstances, originated from the Sunni circles. Rather, the fear of trouble is shown to emanate in the minds of the maharaja who then asks his confidante, the Hindu vizier to investigate the matter. And the reason for the misapprehension is posited on the popularity of Ibrahim with the poorest section of the Shiʿi society—the underpaid, hard-worked shawl weavers. Given that the Shiʿi elite had been steadfast in building up the symbols of their sectarian identity, why they were not equally receptive of Ibrahim's program remains unexplained. Writing in the 1970s, the author of *Shiyan-i Kashmir*, locates the reasons for Ibrahim's exile in the internal dynamics of Shiʿi society, and tries to mediate the role played by the maharaja's Shiʿi physician, Ḥakim ʿAẕim:

> In his (Ḥakim ʿAẕim's) time, an eminent Iranian religious scholar, Sayyid Ibrahim arrived in Srinagar. He established himself at Zadibal and started imparting religious education to the Shiʿi. He would establish daily congregational prayers and deliver sermons. People would attend the prayers and his sermons in great multitude. During those days the industry of shawl weaving was at its peak in Srinagar. [. . .] Shiʿi weavers would leave the factories during the prayer time for (attending) the sermons, causing disruption for the factory owners, but they were helpless (to intervene). [. . .] Finally, they persuaded others to join them and a Shiʿi delegation approached Ḥakim ʿAẕim and told him wrong and unfounded tales about Sayyid Ibrahim. [. . .] They took an oath that the Sayyid's preaching went against the laws of Islam and if he is not made to leave the country, there is fear of divisions and riots. Placing trust in their oath and statements, he [ʿAẕim] had Sayyid Ibrahim banished from Kashmir immediately.[10]

The extract in *Shiyan-i Kashmir*, based on oral and textual traditions preserved in ʿAẕim's family, provides the missing links in Saif-al Dīn's account and highlights how Ibrahim's banishment was caused by internal Shiʿi dissensions in which the agency of the royal court was involved through the maharaja's trusted physician. The event also provides a brief but tantalizing glimpse into how intra-community conflict had started to emerge within the Kashmiri Shiʿi society, almost immediately after the community had succeeded in reviving symbols of its sectarian identity. Though the author of *Shiyan-i Kashmir*, whose description is sympathetic to Sayyid Ibrahim, concludes by portraying ʿAẕim's regret on becoming acquainted with truth, there are other texts which depict a negative image of the Iranian *alim*.[11] Even in his letter, which was written nearer to the actual event, ʿAẕim presents

Ibrahim as the leader of a misguided group bent upon obscuring the memory of Imām Ḥusayn and his martyrdom from Kashmir:

> But they have given priority to a group (that is) all faults, the disciples of Sayyid Ibrahim, who hides in confusion about religion, over all adversaries. They have taken the ball of precedence from Āzar the Idol-maker. They have made the market of remembering His Excellence the Lord of Martyrs, may he be lauded and praised, a dead market for *marsiyas*, and spoiled the belief of the people.[12]

ʿAẕim's letter clearly indicates that some of Sayyid Ibrahim's utterances were critical of religious practices prevalent among Kashmiri Shiʿi, specifically those related to *marṣiya khwānī*. Ibrahim's disappointment was reserved for what he felt was the excessive fervor exhibited by the Kashmiri Shiʿi toward observance of *marṣiya khwānī*, as opposed to more basic requirements of faith, like the enactment of *nimāz-i jamat* (congregational prayers). On his departure from Kashmir, Sayyid Ibrahim offered a severe rebuke of the Kashmiri Shiʿi by remarking:

> *Shii'yān-i Kashmīr Ḥusayn rā mī dānand magar khudā rā namī shināsad*
> (transl: The Shiʿi of Kashmir are aware of the name of Ḥusayn but not of God)[13]

While Sayyid Ibrahim's departure resolved the immediate dispute, a year later in 1851 we find ʿAẕim involved in another and more serious controversy—involving the maintenance and custodian ship of *Mʿārak*. Historically, a branch of Mīr Shams-al Dīn ʿIraki's family, based in Zadibal, had served as the *mutwalī*[14] (custodians) for both the shrine of ʿIraki as well as the *imāmbāda*, which were located in close proximity of one other. The close relationship between the family and *Mʿārak* was also reflected in their *nisbat*—Mʿārakdars, which had emerged as the more popular surname for members of this family. In the immediate aftermath of the fiasco surrounding Sayyid Ibrahim, an attempt was made to organize the management of the *Mʿārak* in a manner, reflecting the opinion of the community elite and dispossessing the Mʿārakdars of their hereditary role in the functioning of the *imāmbāda*. While we have no understanding of the role the Mʿārakdar family played in the earlier event surrounding Sayyid Ibrahim's arrival in Kashmir, His ability to pray and preach at *Mʿārak* could not have been possible without the acquiescence of the *mutwalī* of the *imāmbāda*—the Mʿārakdars. Additionally, through matrimonial ties, the Mʿārakdars were linked to the circuit of Iranian *saudagars* based in Srinagar, a circuit of which Ḥājjī ʿAbid was a prominent member.

In his verdict on the issue of custodianship of *Mʿārak*, Ḥakim ʿAẕim supports the contention of the Mʿārakdar family and their hereditary role as responsible for undertaking various services in the *imāmbāda*, writing in his decree:

> since old times, the *Mʿārakdarī* (looking after *Mʿārak*) of *Mʿārak -i Zadibal* (the *imāmbāda*) from generation to generation has been the responsibility of the descendants of the *marhum-o magfur* (the forgiven on him Allah's mercy is

> bestowed) Mīr Muhammad Razā, may he be forgiven, for carrying the service of burning lights (*chirag-i sozī*), etc. In the said *M ʿārak*, the descendants of the above mentioned have fulfilled their responsibility with competence. For the moment, they are retained in their old authority [. . .] no one has the authority, on his own without the permission of the descendants of the fore mentioned to appoint someone else to this responsibility.[15]

Though on the surface, Azim's verdict seems to be an unambiguous endorsement of the authority of the Mʿārakdars, even figuratively linking the *M ʿārak*, *M ʿārakdarī* and the Mʿārakdars, he avoids the use of a more legally binding term-*mutwalī*. The role of Mʿārakdars is defined in their ability to carry out various services linked with the *imāmbāda*, of which strangely the only one defined in the text is the task of *chirag-i sozī*. But the authority of a *mutwalī* is more absolute.[16] The position and role of the *mutwalī*, clearly defined in *sharia*, includes appointing and dismissing a prayer leader, authority for overseeing and managing religious ceremonies in the *imāmbāda* including performance of *marṣiya* and *wa ʿiẕ kahanī*, and so on. And, as a hereditary *mutwalī*, the Mʿārakdars would have enjoyed absolute freedom in exercising their authority—but the verdict of ʿAẕim while recognizing their right in the functioning of *M ʿārak*, sidesteps their role as *mutwalī*.[17] Though in his verdict, ʿAẕim managed to patch the emerging differences in the community, the calm was to prove illusory, and with the royal physician's death in 1852 would erupt into a major rift splitting the Shiʿi of Kashmir into two opposing parties, disrupting the image of a homogenous, essentialized community. Where the tensions in the functioning of *M ʿārak* originated in the episode of Sayyid Ibrahim, there was another underlying difference that positioned the Mʿārakdars against the Shiʿi aristocracy of the city—the disposal of *khums* money.

The Issue of Khums

The Mʿārakdars as descendants of Mīr Shams-al Dīn ʿIraki, claimed descent from the seventh Shiʿi imām, Mūsā al-Kazim (d. 799) and as such had a rightful claim on the share of the Sayyids in the *khums* money. But, to do so they or any other Sayyid family had to prove their genealogy as *sahīh al-sanad sa ʾādāts* (Sayyids with authentic attested geologies). Among Kashmir Shiʿi the two main groups within Sayyid families are those claiming descent from the Imām Mūsā-al Kazim and his son, Imām ʿAli b. Mūsā Razā (d. 818). The descendants of the seventh imām are collectively known as Mūsāvī and those descending from Imām Razā are named Rizvī. In addition, there are families who trace their ancestry to the fourth Shiʿi imām, Zain-al Ābidīn (d. 713), these include the Hamdanī,[18] the Madnī,[19] and the Zaidī Sayyids, though their number is insignificant as compared to the first group.

Following the demise of Afghan rule in Kashmir, a significant amount of *khums* money arrived in the region from Awadh bequeathed by Ḥakim Mahdi Khān. The money was apparently sent on a yearly basis to be distributed among the Sayyid families, the recipient for the distribution, a respected ʿ*alim* from the Rizvī family,

Sayyid Ṣafdar Shāh (d. 1255 AH/1839 CE). Ṣafdar Shāh had migrated from his ancestral seat in Haigam to Srinagar to study with his maternal grandfather, Mullā Muqim. When Muqim arrived in Awadh, Sayyid Ṣafdar accompanied him on his travels and the links between the Sayyid and the future vizier of the Awadh, Mahdi Khān, date from this time. On Muqim's death, Ṣafdar settled down at Nabdipora in Zadibal succeeding his grandfather in the intellectual leadership of the community. Meanwhile Ṣafdar's son, Sayyid ʿAli[20] after completing his religious education in Iraq, settled down in Awadh becoming a part of the religious circle in the Shiʿi-ruled kingdom. The author of *Risala-i Saif al Ṣaram*, a tract written in Kabul by Sayyid Muhammad Bāqir about the state of Kashmiri Sayyids, extolls Ṣafdar as "*sultan-al sadat al fazil-i kamil-o kamail*" (the sultan of Sayyids, the eminent, the effective, and the perfect). Notwithstanding his stature as the leading Shiʿi religious scholar of Kashmir, Ṣafdar's distribution of the *khums* did alienate a section of the Sayyid families in Kashmir, mostly belonging to the Mūsāvī branch. The resentment they showed must have weighed heavily on the Sayyid, for he soon stopped accepting any *khums* money for distribution in Kashmir. Ṣafdar's policy in distributing the money was based on his predilection to adopt *iḥtiyaṭ* (precaution in religious affairs) in the matter, the distribution was seen by the Mūsāvī Sayyids as an assault on their privileges by an individual belonging to the Rizvī family. Aside from the financial loss, the controversy also socially stigmatized the Mūsāvī Sayyids, as their claim to being Sayyid was seen as lacking authenticity. In nineteenth-century Kashmiri society, where social hierarchies were primarily based on an individual's family decent, the Sayyids as descendants of the Prophet (*Āl-i Rasūl*) occupied the highest social standing. For the Mūsāvī sayyid, the social loss far outweighed the financial loss. While in Shiʿi regions outside Kashmir, such as Awadh, Sayyid families claiming a share from the *khums* "risked their honor by claiming the 'share of the Sayyids' (*sahm-i sādat*) even though they were not particularly indigent,"[21] this was not the case in Kashmir, where at least in the nineteenth century no stigma was associated with it.

Unintentionally, Ṣafdar's action saw the Rizvī and Mūsāvī Sayyids, on opposite sides of a bitter fight for distribution of the *khums* money. With the impasse over the *khums* unresolved, the task of distributing the *khums* was taken up briefly by Mullā Fazl Ansarī, before the money stopped arriving altogether due to Ḥakim Mahdi's death in 1837.

Soon after, Ṣafdar who was already in his old age, left for Lucknow to join his son, and passed away far from home. The precedent established by Safdar in the distribution of *khums*, resulting in the alienation of the Mūsāvī Sayyids was also followed by Fazl ʿAli, though with some modifications. Nevertheless, it resulted in a situation where the interests of Ansarī and the Rizvī family coincided, to the disadvantage of the Mūsāvī Sayyids. And, as the principal Mūsāvī family in Srinagar city, the Mʿārakdars found themselves increasingly alone, and on the opposite side of this power dynamics, with their hold on *Mʿārak* being challenged.

Following Fazl ʿAli's death in 1263 AH/1846 CE, his son Akhūnd Mullā Javad (d. 1281 AH/1864 CE) emerged as the leading Shiʿi *alim* in the city. Javad's succession to his father, also marks the first stage of a successful "transmission of scholarly eminence,"[22] within the Ansarīs after the family's migration to the city. It can be argued that the Shiʿi elite of the city in coalescing around the personality of Mullā Fazl ʿAli had already laid the ground for marking the Ansarīs as the preeminent religious family of the community, but this cannot be the only reason. In his leadership role, Akhūnd Javad also benefitted from the assistance of his nephew Mullā Muhammad Ṣādiq[23] (d. 1296–98 AH/1878–80 CE), the fame of whose scholarly contribution was acknowledged in Shiʿi religious circles of Awadh. But more than his father or his other siblings,[24] it was Akhūnd Javad,[25] and the personal charisma linked with him, which sustained the imagination and the loyalties of the Kashmiri Shiʿi. And, in turn, Javad would transfer and institutionalize this charisma into the body of the Ansarī family. Writing about Javad, the author of *Shiyan-i Kashmir* lists Akhūnd's achievements and the reverence people had for him in these words:

> In knowledge and excellence, piety and austerity he was one of his age. He had attained the highest stations of spirituality and knowledge of God (*maʿarifat*) [...]. The respect and esteem which people held for him can be gauged by the fact that anyone who would invite him would prepare separate utensils for his eating and drinking.[26]

As a leader of the community, Akhūnd Javad imbibed qualities that evoked all those attributes which mark a charismatic leader, "a following deference, devotion and awe toward himself as the source of authority. A leader who can have this effect upon a group is charismatic for that group."[27] The relatively peaceful atmosphere in the city, the consolidation of Shiʿi symbols in the city and their public display, coupled with the presence of a powerful Shiʿi vizier in the court created a unique convergence of opportunities and circumstances favoring around the akhūnd. In addition, while financial patronage from Awadh and Iranian merchants had dried down, the same was replaced by Kashmiri merchants like Mīrzā Muhammad ʿAli, which helped the *ulema* of the Ansarī family to expand their circuit of patronage and community services. These circumstances not only contributed to the persona of the akhūnd, but also consolidated the role of Ansarīs as the eminent clerical family of Shiʿi Kashmir.

Coinciding with Akhūnd Javad's role, we find several Rizvī families migrating toward Srinagar city, settling down in Zadibal. A convergence of interest between the procedure adopted by Akhūnd Javad in distributing the *khums* money and the benefits that the Rizvīs derived from such a division, may have given an impetus to this migration—a need to be closer to the source of their financial munificence. It also made the two natural allies. And the Rizvī Sayyids with their scholarly disposition and deep connections outside Kashmir at Awadh, Lahore, and even further afield Kabul, helped in sustaining a sympathetic campaign for the Ansarīs. The degree to which this issue occupied the minds of Kashmiri Shiʿi can be understood by the fact that in the last decade of the nineteenth century, four works; *Risāla-i Sayf al Sāram, Al S'ādah fi Sayādat al S'ādāt, Dāfi ul Mughāltah* and *Risālah i Hidāyat al Dhalīl ilā Siwā' al Sabīl* were compiled on the subject by members of Kashmiri Shiʿi Diaspora, of which the first three works were compiled by Rizvī Sayyids in Kabul, Lahore, and Awadh. The geographical outreach of the Rizvī Sayyids of Kashmir can also be seen in a letter written by Kashmiri pilgrim, Sayyid Qāsim, who found himself in the shrine city of Mashad. In his letter to the custodians of the shrine, dated Muharram of 1307 AH (1889 CE) the pilgrim petitions for assistance from the shrine money:

> This is the petition of one among the *sa'ādāt*, Ḥājjī Sayyid Qāsim Rizvī Kashmiri, a scholar. In the blessed presence it is submitted that the petitioner is from among the residents of *vilayat* of Kashmir and it has been year since he offered salutations at the sanctified shrine of his blessed ancestor. It will take me six months to travel back to Kashmir. I am a foreigner and of old age, and I seek permission from my grandfather. My family awaits me. I am of the Sādaat of Rizvī and a scholar; I request assistance from the blessed presence for travel and other expenditure from my grandfather. So that with his prayers I hope to be with my family once again.[28]

The letter also highlights how accessing the munificence of the shrine, was not something that the Sayyid Qāsim felt would make him lose his face. He is equally very forthcoming is his self-description as a scholar. The wording of the actual request makes an interesting read, Qāsim as a descendant of Imām Razā is seeking assistance from his "grandfather," not a charity. This assertiveness was also felt in Kashmir, in the demand of Rizvī and Mūsāvī sayyids, for getting their legal and rightful share of the *khums* money.

Coming back to *M'ārak*, we find that somewhere in the later part of the 1850s, repairs to the *imāmbāda* were again undertaken by Mīrzā Muhammad ʿAli. In the repair and reconstruction work, Muhammad ʿAli was assisted by another Kashmiri Shiʿi merchant residing in Zadibal, Ḥājjī Khwāja Ṣafdar Bābā (who passed away in or before the early 1880s). Much more then Muhammad ʿAli, who at times would display an independent position, Ṣafdar Bābā's devotion to Javad was unquestionable. And it was somewhere around the early 1850s, that Ṣafdar Bābā sent a large amount of *khums* money to Akhūnd Javad for distribution.[29]

In *Risāla-i Sayf al Sāram*, the incident related to the *khums* of Safdar Bābā is presented as a larger event in which in addition to Safdar Bābā; Mīrzā Muhammad ʿAli, Mīrzā Rasul and other Kashmiri merchants participate. We also find mention of Kashmiri merchants who at that time were residing outside Kashmir, in the city of Peshawar. All the merchants allocate their *khums* for distribution to Akhūnd Javad.[30] The Peshawar connection is especially important, as many Kashmiris had settled down in the city, which had emerged as a major entrepôt for trade on the roads linking Kashmir to Kabul, Iran, and even Punjab. The Shiʿi presence in the city dates to early nineteenth century when Peshawar came under Ranjit Singh's control, and oral traditions indicate that many of the traders in the *Bāzar i Abreshūn Farūsh* (market of the Silk Sellers) were of Kashmiri Shiʿi origin.[31] The author of *Risāla-i Sayf al Sāram* specifically mentions traders in Peshawar who would send a part of their *khums* money to Srinagar for dispersal among the Kashmiri Shiʿi, including Ḥājjī Ṭayyib Khān, Ḥājjī Malik Rehmān, Ḥājjī ʿAli Akbar, Ḥājjī Karim, Ḥājjī Būzurg Āgā, and Ḥājjī ʿAidī. A large number of these Kashmiri merchants in Peshawar, is indicative of their presence and prestige in the *Bāzar i Abreshūn Farūsh,* which they are said to have regulated in the nineteenth century.[32] Returning to the issue of *khums,* we find that the merchants displayed great caution about the proper disposal of the money; both Mīrzā Rasul and Ḥājjī Ṭayyib Khān refused to give a share to their sons-in-law, and Malik Rehmān to his brother-in-law, from the *khums* money.[33]

On receipt of the *khums* from the Kashmir traders, Javad adopted a unique system of dispersal, dividing the share of the sayyids into two portions, a majority share comprising two-thirds of the total money which he proceeded to distribute among those deemed as *sayyid-al sanad* (Sayyids with established authentic genealogy) and a remaining share dispersed among those considered as *mashkook sadat*—Sayyid families who could not provide satisfying documents to support their claim of ancestry.[34] In a letter written by Akhūnd Javad in reply to objections raised by a young Kashmiri seminarian, studying in Najaf, he explains the reason for the practice and names three sayyid families who received a lesser share: *saadat-i khanqahi, saadat-i Bemina, saadat-i Amīr Shams-al Dīn.* The seminarian, Āgā Sayyid Mahdi (d. 1309 AH/1892 CE), himself a Mūsāvī Sayyid, in his reply, asserts the rights of his fellow sayyids to an equal share in the *khums.* This brief exchange of letters between the two is indicative of a gradual entrenchment of individuals, clerics, and families on the issue.[35]

From the viewpoint of Sayyid Mahdi, the practice formulated by Akhūnd Javad resulted in a large part of the money getting dispersed among Rizvī families, while a majority of the Mūsāvī families had to contend with a minority share. As would be expected, the affected party—the Musvīs took issue with this system of distribution, alienating them from the Ansarīs and those associated with them. Despite this, the possibility of an immediate fissure in the community was prevented by a series of unlinked events that shattered the peace in the city and the Shiʿi sense of safety, making the community see itself again as an endangered minority.

The Last Riot: 1289 AH*/1872* CE

Eight years after the death of Akhūnd Mullā Javad, far away from Kashmir in continental Europe an act of war would set in motion a series of events which would culminate in the last major Shiʿi-Sunni confrontation in Kashmir. Earlier in 1857, Maharaja Gulab Singh died and was succeeded by his son Ranbir Singh (r. 1857–85) as the ruler. At the same time, the sub-continent was shaken by the Great Rebellion against the East India Company in 1857, which resulted in the British crown directly taking over the governance of India after quelling the rebellion. During the rebellion, Ranbir Singh remained loyal to the British, while the Shiʿi kingdom of Awadh joined the cause of the rebels. Along with numerous other families in Awadh, Kashmiri Shiʿi who had migrated to the region also perished in the conflict. In the aftermath of the revolt, some of these Kashmiris fled to Punjab to escape British persecution in Awadh.[36] Punjab had a substantial colony of Kashmiris residing in the cities of Lahore and Amritsar, who had migrated from Kashmir during the early part of the nineteenth century to escape poverty and excessive taxation under the Sikhs.[37] This original immigrant community of Kashmiri Diaspora in Punjab included members of the Shiʿi community, a majority of whom had left after the riot of 1830 and settled in the plains, mostly working as weavers.[38]

Back in Kashmir the mainstay of the urban economy, the shawl industry came under severe stress in the aftermath of the Franco-Prussian war of 1871. Arriving in Kashmir in 1862, a few years after Ranbir's accession to the throne, Frederic Drew who left his job in England to enter the services of Kashmir *darbār* describes the importance of shawl industry to the life and economy of Srinagar:

> A large proportion of the town inhabitants are shawl-weavers, whose handicraft has made Kashmir to be familiarly known over the whole both of India and Europe. [. . .] The other ornamental arts of Srinagar are silver-work and papier maché paintings.[39]

And it was France that had been responsible for introducing the Kashmiri shawl fashion to Europe, where

> The Kashmiri shawl was a symbol of the French bourgeois status from the Restoration (1815-48) through the Second Empire (1852-70).[40]

The loss of France in the war[41] led to a decline in the French demand for the shawls, but a reading of *Akhbarat* would indicate that the distress of the shawl weavers in Kashmir had started much earlier, in the 1860s.[42] The decline in the market, combined with excessive tax demand from the court affected both the shawl merchants and the weavers[43] working in the *kār-khānas* of the merchants. When Richard Temple, a colonial administrator, visited Kashmir in the spring of 1871, the maharaja voiced his concerns about how the war in Europe was affecting the shawl trade:

> lamenting the injury it had done to the shawl trade of Kashmir. He said he had only prevented hundreds of shawl-makers and weavers from deserting the land by giving them State assistance for their temporary support.[44]

Interestingly in Temple's account, we find mention of some of the leading Sunni merchants of the city, linked with the shawl trade, merchants who would play a major role in the city life defining the contours of the Srinagar's social and religious landscape in the late nineteenth century.[45] The person who figures prominently in Temple's journals was a man who would be held responsible for instigating the riot of 1872, Khwāja Mohyi-al Dīn Gandrū of Srinagar. On an earlier visit to Kashmir in 1859, Temple met Mohyi-al Dīn at his house near Khanyar,[46] and describes his visit in these words:

We went to see the house of Ghulam Muhayyu'd din, a Kashmiri merchant, who had a house in Calcutta, and had recently come to visit his home. The principal room was rather pretty, and he gave us a capital breakfast in the Kashmiri fashion.[47]

Somewhere around the third quarter of the nineteenth century, Mohyi-al Dīn had been responsible for the manufacture of a shawl map of the city at his *kār-khāna* (workshop) in the heart of the city. The shawl was commissioned specially for Maharaja Ranbir Singh, again showcasing the merchant's closeness and familiarity with the Dogra court.

In addition to Mohyi-al Dīn, Temple met some other city-based merchants–all Sunnis, including, Khwāja Mukhtār Shāh ʿAshaʿi,[48] Khwāja Saif-al Lah and ʿAbdu'l Ghafār Shāh Naqshbandī[49]—a descendant of Shāh Niyaz̲, the *Naqshbandī* shaykh. On the surface, Temple's journal helps in establishing the rising prominence of Sunni merchants in the commerce of the city witnessed in their interactions with colonial administrators such as Temple, who at the time of his visit to Kashmir was serving as the Foreign Secretary for the British administration in India. It is from this period we also, see the presence of merchants such as Mukhtār Shāh in the court. Deeply involved in the maintenance and upkeep of leading Sunni shrines of the city, merchants such as Mukhtār Shāh, Mohyi-al Dīn and members of the Naqshbandī family represented the Sunni elite of the city along with other merchants such as Khwāja Sana-al Lah Shawl[50] about whom it is said that he had trade houses in Punjab, Calcutta and Mumbai.[51]

Yet, the city still retained a significant number of the Shiʿi shawl merchants whose *kār-khānas* included both Shiʿi and Sunni weavers. These include the *kār-khānas* of Mīrzā Muhammad ʿAli, Khwāja Ṣafdar Bābā, various members of the Jalālī family,[52] and other *kār-khāndars*, some of whom were recent migrants to the city. The *Gazetteer of Kashmir*, written by Charles Ellison Bates, a British administrator on deputation to Kashmir in 1873, provides some interesting figures about the relative economic situation of the Shiʿi and Sunni communities. Within the overall Muslim population of the city, Shiʿi comprised a meager 7 percent while their number in the entire Kashmir valley stood at less than 4 percent. Similarly, though Shiʿi merchants owned a great number of the shawl *kār-khānas* in the city, of the thirty thousand weavers, Shiʿi numbered only a thousand workers.[53] The ascendancy of Shiʿi elite class in the city can also be seen among the landed aristocracy, out of the five Muslim *jāgīrdārs*, three were from the Shiʿi community.[54] The relative prosperous condition of the Shiʿis is visited in the Gazetteer, which speaks about the community as

found chiefly at Zadibal, about two koss to the north of Srinagar, at Nandapor and Hassanabad, near to the city lake. Though so few in number, the men of this sect form the most active, industrious, and well-to-do portion of the Mohamedan community. The finest papier-mache workers and shawl makers in Srinagar are Shiʿihs, and some of the wealthiest men in the city belong to sect.[55]

The depression in the shawl market resulted in the foreclosure of some of the *kār-khānas*, with many owners preferring to cut losses rather than sustain the poorly paid weavers whose labor formed the foundation of their mercantile wealth. The relation between Shiʿi owners and their Sunni workers was of recent origin, dating from the 1840s, not an established tradition which joined the weavers and the owners in a relation of trust. In the closing of the *kār-khānas*, the Sunni workers saw the Shiʿi owners as not only representative of an exploitative *kār-khāna* system but also belonging to a rival religious community. An economic depression, leading to unemployment of the main worker force of the city gradually reopened the old rifts in the Muslim society as tensions between the Shiʿi merchants and the Sunni weavers mounted.[56] The tension between the two groups came to a head in the riot which targeted Shiʿi merchants and *kār-khāna* owners, riots whose principal instigator was a rival Sunni merchant, Khwāja Mohyi-al Dīn Gandrū.

The riot started on the occasion of the *ʿurs* at a prominent fifteenth-century religious site, the mosque-shrine precinct of Madin Ṣāhab which was claimed and revered by both the communities (Figure 4.1). This small complex was in a predominantly Shiʿi moḥala, in close vicinity to the main Shiʿi center of Zadibal. The Shiʿi had constructed a small mosque adjacent to the older, historical mosque built by Sayyid Muhammad Madnī in 1444.[57] The construction of the mosque and offering prayers in the building was part of the ongoing process of revival and reemergence of Shiʿi presence in the urban landscape of the city, removing the visual and physical anonymization that had been characteristic of the community life previously under the Afghan rule. The construction itself was overseen by Mīrzā Muhammad ʿAli. Hearing about this Shiʿi construction, Mohyi-al Dīn objected to building on what he saw as a Sunni territory. Though a well-meaning

Figure 4.1 Shrine of Sayyid Muhammad Madnī, Srinagar, 2019 (courtesy: Zubair Ahmad).

philanthropist, Muhammad ʿAli's personality was marked by a temperament at times arrogant and disdainful of the consequences. The poet, Deykah, in his description of Muhammad ʿAli's father, Mīrzā Rasūl writes about the merchants' considerable pride and arrogance, which was ostensibly famous in the city[58]. Probably, the son had inherited not only his father's immense wealth but also some of his less seemly traits, which in this instance proved to be the doom of the Kashmiri Shiʿi. Earlier, in the 1283 AH/1866 CE Muhammad ʿAli had broken away from the company of fellow Shiʿi elites and constructed a rival *imāmbāda* in the city at Hasanabad, simply because his request favoring a particular *zakir* at Mʿārak had been turned down.[59] In this instance too, Muhammad ʿAli not only refused to pay any heed to Mohyi-al Dīn's objection but also delayed his reply to the Sunni merchant's letter by twelve days. This inordinate delay was rightly perceived by Mohyi-al Dīn as a personal insult- a breach of etiquette, showing Muhammad ʿAli's disdain for a newcomer who was projecting himself as the representative of Sunni community. A day before the ʿ*urs*, Mohyi-al Dīn visited the shrine and asked the Shiʿi to stop the construction work on the mosque, also forcefully forbidding them from performing *marṣiya* at the site. In doing so, Mohyi-al Dīn was portraying a role far bigger than his mercantile wealth or patronage of Sunni shrines afforded him—he was essentially acting as the arbitrator and enforcer of the public spaces and the cultural boundaries in the city. The Shiʿi refusal was similarly posited on their wealth and positioning in the city, especially in the court, still substantial. Yet, the khwāja had the ability to enflame the Sunni masses and incite a mob, and that he did.

On the day of the ʿ*urs*, a large crowd of Sunnis, mostly the recently retrenched *shawlbafs* assembled near the mosque and after a heated argument with the Shiʿi razed the adjacent and yet to be completed Shiʿi structure to the ground. On the surface, the act marks the Sunni assertion of their ownership and control of the mosque precinct, including the vast open land adjoining it, on which the Shiʿi structure had come up. Overnight the news of the skirmish; of the existence of a Shiʿi mosque and its destruction spread in the city and on the following day a large Sunni mob assembled near the shrine of Shaykh Ḥamza Makhdūm. Mohyi-al Dīn was seen near the crowd and left the shrine only after the assembled crowd proceeded *en masse* toward the Shiʿi areas of the city.

The crowd first proceeded toward Rajouri Kadal—the seat of the *Mīrwaʿiẓ-i Kalān* (the elder Mīrwaʿiẓ). The post of Mīrwaʿiẓ (chief preacher of Sunnis) was institutionalized during the nineteenth century in the family of Ṣiddiq Bābā (d. 1155 AH/1742 CE), a respected Sunni cleric who had arrived in the city from the Tral, a small town in south Kashmir.[60] After their relocation to the city, the family split into two rival branches in the mid-nineteenth century, the *Mīrwaʿiẓ-i Kalān* with their seat at Jamia Masjid and the *Mīrwaʿiẓ-i Hamdanīya*, who operated from *Khānaqāh-i Mʿaulā*. The early twentieth-century Sunni historian Mufti Muhammad Shāh Saʿādat refers to Moulvi Yaḥya Shāh (1251 AH/1835 CE–1308 AH/1890 CE) of the *Mīrwaʿiẓ-i Kalān* as the *Mīrwaʿiẓ-i Awilin*—the first *mīrwaʿiẓ* of Kashmir.[61] Newcomers to the city, in their early years in the city, the family of *Mīrwaʿiẓ-i Kalān* was imbibed with a parochial vision deeply laced with sectarianism. And as they presided over the religious life of the cities Sunni majority, they failed to negotiate with the emerging ecumenical trends in the Muslim society.

Returning back to the riots, we find that on reaching Rajouri Kadal, Rasūl Shāh (1271 AH/1854 CE–1327 AH/1909 CE) the young son of *Mīrwaʿiẕ* Yaḥya, extolling the mob to attack the *rāfizī*- the Shiʿis. Rallying to the cry "*dīn-i Muhammad tchu barkarar, rafizan patichey kafiran laar*" ([transl: The religion of Muhammad is alive, after the rāfizī (Shiʿi) we will throw out the *kāfirs* [Hindus]), the mob first ransacked the nearby locality of Kamangarpora which housed some of the richest Shiʿi merchants of the city before fanning out toward Zadibal, Madin Ṣāhab and other pockets of Shiʿi presence in the city. Meanwhile, the governor of Kashmir, Vazir Pannu was made aware of the happenings in the city and marched toward Cawdara with a light escort, hoping to intimidate the mob with official presence and stop their march toward Zadibal. But, on reaching the site, the *vazir* was surrounded by an incensed, impassioned crowd which overwhelmed his guards, and in a moment of fear, Pannu told the mob "*phounk dū*"—a colloquial expression in Urdu meaning "take them out." This was taken by the assembled crowd as an official sanction to loot, and they marched into Shiʿi *moḥala* of the city burning Zadibal and Madin Ṣāhab. At Zadibal, the first target was again *Mʿārak* the *imāmbāda*. While the destruction of Shiʿi properties was widespread and indiscriminate, Shiʿi *kār-khāna* owners and merchants became a special target of the rioters. In his autobiography, Munshi Muhammad Isḥāq (d. 1969), recollects the loss his family suffered during the riots based on the writings of his father, Munshi Ḥasan ʿAli (d. 1343 AH/1924 CE),[62] in these words:

> My ancestors were from Shaukpora (Zazbugh) in Budgam district [. . .] Due to change of fortune they had to leave their village and settled down in the *mohalla* of Nowpora (in the city)[63]. During those time the shawl industry was lucrative. They too adopted this profession [. . .].
>
> During the time of my great grandfather ʿAli Muhammad Karbalaī, a deadly Shiʿi-Sunni conflict took place. In 1873[64] our ancestral residential houses and shawl *kār-khānas* were burnt down, but due to the efforts of our Sunni Muslim neighbors no loss of life took place.[65]

The Gazetteer published a year after the riot provides the perspective of an "impartial European viewer" on the happenings in these words:

> The disturbances then raged for more than a week, and for some time defied the efforts of the governor who called in the aid of the troops, whole districts were reduced to smouldering heaps of ruins; and business was for some time entirely suspended, a great portion of the city being deserted. The Shiahs fled in every direction, some seeking safety on the adjacent mountains, while others remained in the city in secret lurking places. Many of the women and children of the Shiahs found asylum from the hands of their infuriated co-religionists

> in the houses of Hindu portion of the community. When order was at length restored the ringleaders of the riot were seized and imprisoned, besides hundred or thousands, it is said, of the poorer inhabitants.[66]

The construction of a mosque by the Shiʿi is represented as the immediate provocation for the riot by Kuihāmī, who then goes on to write how innocent Sunnis were caught up in the retribution, some jailed and some fined by the government, including Mohyi-al Dīn. In Kuihāmī's narrative Mohyi-al Dīn is presented as a blameless bystander, wrongly framed in the riots and unjustly targeted by the government. It is the Shiʿi in the court who use their money and influence to get an unfair verdict against the Sunni merchant, who is consequently fined an amount of fifty thousand rupees *in lieu* of imprisonment.[67]

Yet, in the testimonies presented in the court, Mohyi-al Dīn hardly comes across as an innocent and uninvolved witness to the frenzy, rather he is the instigator and the prime mover. Mohyi-al Dīn's position as a benefactor of the Sunnis of the city was based on his patronage of major Sunni religious symbols, involving repairs and maintenance of shrines and mosques in the city, especially the shrine of Shaykh Ḥamza.[68] This was unlike other Sunni elders such as Khwāja Sana-al Lah Shawl or Shaykh Muqim whose patronage was not limited to religious enterprises alone but had also manifested into civic projects benefitting the residents of the city. During a particularly bad case of famine Sana, al Lah and Muqim had operated public kitchens (*langars*) across the city, benefitting the needy of all communities.[69] The Shiʿi merchant, Mīrzā Muhammad ʿAli also in addition to his support of Shiʿi specific projects, was part of this ecumenically shaped munificence. From the testimonies presented in the case, including Mohyi-al Dīn's own, he emerges as a man firmly grounded in Sunni sectarianism.[70] As a pattern of this predilection for sectarianism we find him intervening in a land dispute involving a Shiʿi cleric of Hasanabad, Sayyid Zamān Shāh (d. 1887) and the plaintiff who happened to be Sunni- essentially reshaping a personal property dispute into a broader sectarian conflict.[71] The riots of 1872, pervasively underpin how even under a non-Muslim rule, individuals could maneuver a city into conflict based on their money, power, and the influence among the masses.

The Shiʿi' losses in the riots were heavy, Mʿārak was again burned down to ground, and more than 600 houses destroyed in the city. In his *marṣiya*, '*Musiqī*' (Music) written sometime after the riots, Munshi Muhammad Yūsuf captures the pain and the anguish of the Shiʿi society and their sense of loss:

> Oh! Death, my heart lies skewered over coals;
>
> how those bookless (people) burnt down Quran[72]

Among those financially damaged on the Shiʿi side, the most prominent was Mīrzā Muhammad ʿAli. The rioters had specifically targeted his *kār-khānas* and business establishment in the city, including those in a *bāgh* he had created near Nowpora on the famous Mar canal (*Nallah Mar*).[73] Sometime soon after he left for Calcutta, before finally proceeding to Karbala. In his later years, spent in Karbala, Muhammad ʿAli is remembered as distributing water and food to pilgrims in the shrine city free of cost. His final act of charity, in the city associated with the most popular Shiʿi imām, guaranteed that in Kashmir, his memory as a benefactor of Shiʿism would endure for posterity. Kashmiri pilgrims returning from Iraq in the nineteenth century, carried back reports of his continuing charity, and the narrative that on his death Muhammad ʿAli was buried near the *kashaf khāna* (entrance portal for the keeping the shoes) of the shrine itself. In these anecdotal accounts anyone visiting the shrine of Imām Ḥusayn, on removing his shoes in the *kashaf khāna* and before crossing the sacred threshold, would offer the first *fathiya* (prayer for the deceased) at the grave of this Kashmiri shawl merchant. The Jalālī family, who also owned major *kar khānas* were also targeted in the riots, and the *haveli* of Sayyid ʿAbdullah Shāh Jalālī which was also located near the Madin Ṣāhab shrine burned. Given the improvement in communication, the riots spread to neighboring Shiʿi populated villages, targeting both the rich and the poor in the community.[74]

Once the order was restored in the city, the aggrieved Shiʿi' were given permission by the court to seek, search and take back their property wherever they found it. While the visuals of the order appear extremely arbitrary, for the poorer members of the Shiʿi community, the artisans, and the laborers this was an opportunity to reclaim what they had lost: a copper *samovar*, a heavy woolen blanket, and a piece of silver jewelry. In addition to the fines imposed on Mohyi-al Dīn, Sunni religious figures whose names figured in the riots were also punished; the young Rasul Shāh was forbidden from delivering sermons in the city and Moulvi Nāṣir-al Dīn (d. 1876) who was working in the *darbār* as qāzī dismissed from his job. The maharaja's government also awarded a compensation of three lakh rupees to the Shiʿi, a part of the amount raised as fines from Sunnis.[75] While the main culprits in the riots escaped with fines or lighter punishment, it was the poor Sunnis, the *shawlbafs* and the workers who faced the brunt of punishment. Bates in his *Gazetteer* hints toward the arbitrary nature of the arrests, with the poor left to bear the consequences:

The apprehensions appear to have been made in the most indiscriminate fashion.[76]

While the suppression of the riots, was overseen by the administration of the maharaja, the event did draw British attention, especially the native government's efforts at rehabilitation and the trial proceedings. In a letter written on September 15, 1872, by the Assistant Secretary, Government of Punjab, to his immediate superior, the incident is reported as

> on the 16th instant a serious riot occurred in the city, between the Sunni and Shiʿih sects of Mahomedeans [. . .] pending the expected receipt of full details from the local authorities, I regret however that whether from a jealous reluctance to impart such particulars to me as alleged merely because the investigations into the matter are still proceeding, these authorities have failed up to this date to supply me with anything deserving to regarded as a detailed account of the affair.[77]

The riots, the first instance of a major large-scale public disorder in Kashmir after the Dogras assumed control of this region, belied the image on which Dogra rule had been built. For the British, the princely state of Jammu & Kashmir was to serve as a dependable buffer protecting the interests of the empire in face of the Russian advances in Central Asia. In the second half of the nineteenth century, Kashmir was the staging ground for some of the British expeditions and embassies into Central Asia, especially into Yarkand and Kasghar. These expeditions formed a part of the "Gate Game," the tussle for paramountcy in the vast Asia heartland spread from Iran all the way to Kasghar. The "jealous reluctance" of the Kashmir *darbār* to share information with the British political agent was as much governed by a desire to hide the embarrassment of failing to maintain order in the capital city as to protect symbols of authority of the native court. This projection of a stable state, in control of the situation can also be seen in the interim report forwarded to the Assistant Secretary by Bābū Nilambar Mukerjee[78] who was serving as the city judge for Srinagar:

> The real cause of the riot is to be traced to the well-known religious ill feelings between the two sects of Islam, which neither the advance of modern civilization nor the strictest government in the world has succeeded in eradicating and which bursts forth as on the last occasion and lead to the most inhuman acts of fanaticism.[79]

By locating the reasons for the riots in "Muslim fanaticism," Nilambar not only absolves the administration of any serious lapse but also feeds on the British fear and misgivings about the "uncivilized" Muslims instigators of the Great Rebellion of 1857. The insular Muslims, Shiʿi and Sunni, bereft of the advantages of Western education and culture (unlike Nilambar) are to blame for their own ills. In a rather perfunctory manner, Nilambar writes about the mutual transgression that the two communities had engaged in:

> both the sects having in spite of all precautionary measures adopted by the authorities, brought themselves within the hearing of the abusive religious expressions used by one sect against others while engaged in congregational prayers to ward off the present cholera scrouge the Shiahs anathematizing Abu Bakar, Omar and Osman and the Sunnis Ali.[80]

Again, while justifying the administration, Nilambar in addition to the Shiʿi also blames Sunni for reviling a religious figure, ʿAli, who though highly considered among the Shiʿi as their first imām, is equally respected and revered in the Sunni faith tradition as one of the Rightly Guided Caliphs (*Khulafāʾar-Rāšidūn*). Did such an anathema really happen or was the city judge imagining it for a report to be forwarded to the British authorities, is an open guess. The judges' initial findings, assigning blame to both the parties equally, manifest how native courts were trying to appropriate the colonial narrative of "appearing impartial and just," in settling disputes. In his report, Nilambar also mentions that trials in the case have started, and he is being assisted by twelve individuals drawn from Hindu, Sunni, and Shiʿi communities.

Multiple accounts, native as well of Europeans, also speak about how the beleaguered Shiʿi, especially in the city found refuge with their Hindu neighbors. In a particular instance, the Hindu historian, Pandit Hargopal Kaul Khasta writes about a pandit courtier, Mahanand Jeo Dhar whose house was burned by the rioters, because he had given refuge to some Shiʿi families.[81] The aid that the Shiʿi received from the *darbār* and the Pandit community, the trial and conviction of Sunni elders, and the ensuing disquiet among the Sunni elite of the city finds expression in a satirical work, *Shiʿi Nāma* of Khwāja Sa'ad al-Dīn:

> Flames took over their dwellings, as if the lightening set ablaze their houses
> Every Shiʿi in those days was rendered homeless
> ....
> Every hypocrite Pandit was friends with the Shiʿi
> And the helpless true believer was the captive of these two serpents
> ....
> Every helpless Shiʿi came after the Sunnis
> Like a hunter's hound ready to pounce on their neck
> ....
> If a brave Shiʿi ever got hold of a dagger, he raises his hand in mourning
> For his hands can't reach for anything[82]

For the Kashmiri Shiʿi, the rebuilding of destroyed homes, individual and community lives became the immediate priority. Families who had fled returned to the city. From the relief given by the government a substantial amount, twenty-five thousand rupees was earmarked for the reconstruction of the *imāmbāda* at Zadibal.[83] A smaller amount of four thousand rupees was earmarked for repairing the *imāmbāda* at Hasanabad,[84] which had also been damaged in the riot. Architecturally, the reconstructed *Mʿārak* with its forest of wooden columns was an interesting synthesis of Kashmiri vernacular architecture, motifs, and features inspired by Mughals to the region. Of particular significance was the rich papier-mâché ceilings of the building, which represent the oldest extant example of this decorative technique used in illuminating a building's interior.[85] The papier-mâché craft was and is still largely monopolized by Shiʿi artisans. The work on the ceiling was a manifestation of their dedication to the sacred site. While none of the names of the artisans who worked on the ceiling have survived, oral traditions within the Shiʿi community maintain that the artisans involved in the project worked on a voluntary basis. These traditions also speak about Shiʿi women, donating their jewelry for the reconstruction. At a time when people must have been occupied in building their own devastated homes and lives, the contribution of the artisans, the women, and people at large, both from the city and outside, showcases how deeply community emotions were invested in *Mʿārak* as the symbol of Kashmiri Shiʿiness. Work on the reconstruction of *Mʿārak* was completed in 1289 AH/1872 CE. When the *marṣiya* writer Munshi Mustafa ʿAli (d. 1896) was asked to write the chronogram for the new construction, he compiled a verse which captures the hope for a city free of prejudice and hate:

> This mourning house of the sorrowful martyr (Ḥusayn);
> set ablaze by the rouge with the fire of hate.
> First snuff out this toxic fire;
> then ask for the auspicious date of building it anew.[86]

Rival Families, Rival Grouping

On *Badun* 8 in the year 1945 *Bikrami* of the Hindu calendar (corresponding to September 8, 1888 CE), the court of Bābū Rishambar Mukerjee,[87] the chief judge of Kashmir, gave its final verdict in a dispute between two rival Shiʿi claimants, *Firqa-i Qadim* (Old Group) and *Firqa-i Jadid* (New Group) involving the ownership of *Mʿārak*.

Commenting about the rifts and groupism that emerged in the Kashmiri Shiʿi society in the nineteenth century, the political activist and reformist, Munshi Isḥāq writes:

> During this time the leadership of *Firqa-i Qadim* was in the hands of Jalālī family and the Mullā family of Babapora. *Firqa-i Jadid* was represented by the Dangar family of Zadibal, the Khwāja family of Kamangarpora and my ancestor late Muhammad ʿAli Karbalai.[88]

Following the destruction of *Mʿārak* in the riot of 1872, the Mʿārakdar family had been sidelined in the reconstruction process. The work on the building was initially overseen by Mīrzā Muhammad ʿAli, aided by leading members of the Shiʿi community living in Zadibal; Āqā Aḥmad ʿAli, Malik ʿAli (dead before 1303 AH/1885 CE) and Karim Khān.[89] After Muhammed ʿAli left Kashmir, two members of the Jalālī family, Sayyid ʿAbdullah Shāh (d. 1309 AH/1891 CE) and Sayyid Ṣafdar Shāh took over the work of reconstruction of the *imāmbāda* along with Malik ʿAli and Āqā Aḥmad. This involved completing the roof, which had been left unfinished and constructing the main entrance portal (*dīdh*) to the *imāmbāda*. In addition to local donations, the Kashmiri Shiʿi also received financial aid from the wider South Asian Shiʿi community; a Bombay-based merchant, Ḥājjī ʿAta-al Lah Bombaywalā donated nine hundred rupees for the construction of the *dīdh*. Simultaneously, the people overseeing the construction; Mīrzā Muhammad ʿAli, Sayyid Abdullah Shāh, and Sayed Ṣafdar Shāh had the right of the custodianship (*mutawalli*) transferred to themselves.[90] Despite the Mʿārakdars protestations against this takeover, the matter remained unresolved, with both claimants operating from the same venue.

Meanwhile, the seminarian, Sayyid Mahdi who had contested the issue of *khums* with Akhūnd Mullā Javad Ansarī earlier, returned to Kashmir in 1297 AH/1879 CE after completing his studies in Najaf, Iraq. Despite the recent riots, the Kashmir that Sayyid Mahdi returned was a much-changed place, in which as a community the Shiʿi found themselves greatly empowered in their functioning and exchanges with the Sunni majority, especially in Srinagar. And as we saw previously, an elite urban plutocracy comprising the courtiers, merchants and the religious classes had established themselves as both the representee and spokesman of the community—the core of what would be retrospectively termed as the *Firqa-i Qadim*. Acting as the benefactors of the community interest, they in their personal dealings as *jāgīrdārs* and *kār-khāndars* were also enablers of an oppressive social and caste system. Nineteenth-century Kashmiri Shiʿi society was divided into "*sov*" (upper class) and *pous* (lower class),[91] a class formation based on caste differences rather than occupational stratification.[92] Uniquely positioned as possessors of knowledge, wealth, and access to court, members of the self-constituted upper class also maintained their elite power through matrimonial alliances. Given the relatively small size of the Shiʿi society, the boundaries between the two, though not hermitically sealed, were nevertheless virtually unsurmountable for the vast majority of what was termed as the *pous*.

As opposed to the existing elite structure prevailing in Kashmir, Sayyid Mahdi's upbringing had been conditioned by personal struggle with hardship and poverty. This could be one of the many reasons why he had engaged earlier in a terse exchange of letters with a more senior cleric on the issue of *khums*.

Coming back to Srinagar, we find that on his return, Sayyid Mahdi was invited by the Mʿārakdars to preside over the newly refurbished *Mʿārak*. This involved the revival of the practice of congregational prayers and offering sermons—an event which had taken place earlier during Sayyid Ibrahim's brief stay in Kashmir. Yet, Mahdi's sermons drastically differed from those which had stepped Ibrahim into trouble—he did not limit himself to theological issues alone but forcefully questioned the existing power structure in Kashmiri society as being oppressive and inhumane. In doing so Mahdi set himself on a collision course with those who controlled the pulse of the Shiʿi society in Kashmir. The retribution was swift. Sayyid Mahdi's entry to *Mʿārak* was barred and when the Mʿārakdars tried to intervene, their access to the *imāmbāda* was also restricted.[93] The management of the *imāmbāda* was taken over by Sayyid ʿAbdullah, assisted by his cousin Sayyid Ṣafdar.[94] Simultaneously, they contested with the Mʿārakdars over the management of the shrine of Mīr Shams-al Dīn ʿIraki, the ancestor of the Mʿārakdar dynasty. The lack of support for the Mʿārakdars within the Shiʿi elite on the two issues, management of the *Mʿārak* and the custodianship of the ʿIraki shrine, highlights how removed they were from the power center of Shiʿi community life in the city: the *Firqa-i Qadim*.[95]

Meanwhile, the new custodians of *Mʿārak*, approached Ḥakim Mahdi (d. 1309 AH/1891 CE) to seek Sayyid Mahdi's banishment from Kashmir.[96] Ḥakim Mahdi was the nephew of Ḥakim ʿAzam, and as royal physician, quite close to the ruler, Ranbir Singh. But, possibly remembering the fallout from the earlier affair involving Sayyid Ibrahim, the ḥakim desisted from intervening in the case of Sayyid Mahdi. Failing to enlist the royal physician to their cause, the custodians approached the *darbār* directly, denouncing Mahdi as a spy for the British, whose aim was to disrupt the affairs of Kashmir. The maharaja's *darbār* in spite of working under the overall suzerainty of the British colonial administration as the paramount power in India was equally conscious of protecting the symbols and privileges of the native court. Earlier in 1873, Ranbir Singh had rejected a British proposal to appoint a British Resident at Srinagar. A Kashmiri subject accused of working as a spy for the British government was a serious charge, sufficient to ensure the accused's banishment from Kashmir territories. As a result of these maneuvers, Sayyid Mahdi was called before the *darbār* to explain the charges before the maharaja himself. Oral traditions within the Shiʿi community maintain that at the court, Sayyid Mahdi not only managed to dispel the accusations against himself but also impressed the maharaja with his simplicity and strength of character. The maharaja is said to have told his Shiʿi physician, Mahdi, "this man cannot be a spy, he is a simple god-fearing person, he should be left alone."[97]

The failure to get the court to censure Sayyid Mahdi did not deter his adversaries from their opposition to the cleric. The resolve of Mahdi on the other hand, not to bow down to the opposition and seek an amicable compromise, marked him with the Shiʿi poor and working classes as their hero. And once he had taken upon the mantle of acting as the spokesman of the powerless, the message of Mahdi was as much dictated by his personal convictions as by the aspirations of those he chose to represent. While the divide among Kashmiri Sunnis during the same period, between the followers of *Mīrwaʿiẕ-i Kalān* and *Mīrwaʿiẕ -i Hamdanī* had a theological underpinning,[98] the conflict within the Shiʿi community was a manifestation of class struggle. In this group contestation *Firqa-i Qadim*, represented the Shiʿi elite and those associated with them, while *Firqa-i Jadid* represented the followers of Sayyid Mahdi and the countless poor in the city and across villages. The high-sounding title of *Firqa-i Qadim* neatly obfuscates a very basic fact, that this *firqa* was not a very old entrenched grouping as its supporters wanted to project, rather it came into formation around the mid-nineteenth century, coeval with the establishment of Dogra rule. The elite of the *Firqa-i Qadim* represented a coming together of individuals and families based on kinship, wealth, and social prestige. While the main enablers of the group were organized in the limited geography of the city, it nevertheless claimed adherents from a similar social class across major Shiʿi settlements and villages outside of Srinagar (Figure 4.2).

Arriving in Kashmir soon after the riot of 1872, Sayyid Mahdi was deeply impressed by the suffering and the devastation due to the Shiʿi- Sunni conflict, from which the poor Shiʿis were yet to recover. The communal politics of the city, and the conflicting interests of the elite, helped to perpetuate an atmosphere of hate and antagonism, which no one had attempted to break: Shiʿi or Sunni. The fragmented situation, both in the city and outside it, can be understood by Lawrence's observation on the deeply divided spatial practices of Kashmiri Muslim society:

> There is only one ziarat in Kashmir, that of Alam Sahib, in the Narwara Mohalla of Srinagar, where Shiʿihs and Sunnis meet. Elsewhere their places of religion

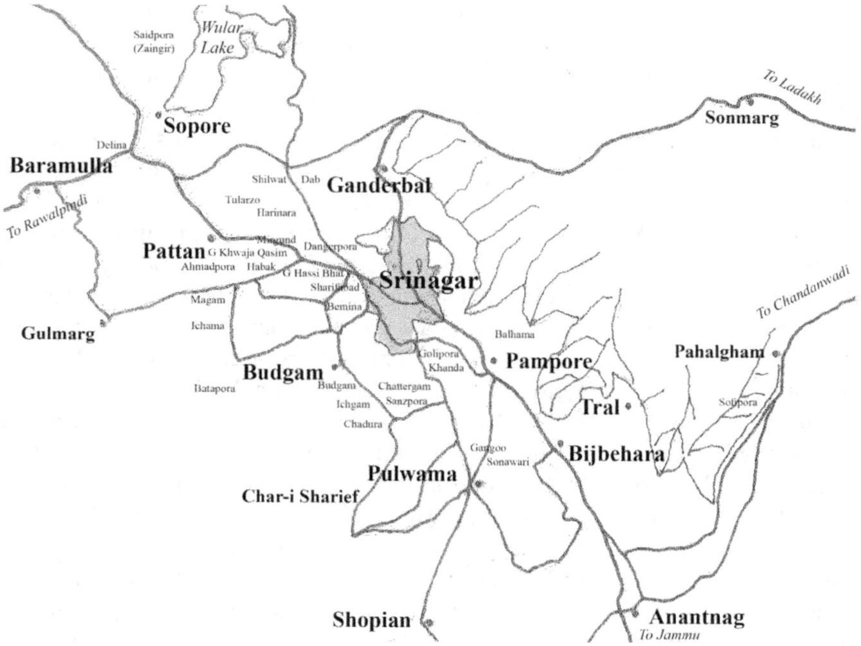

Figure 4.2 Kashmir, location of major towns and Shiʿi-inhabited areas (author).

> are wholly distinct. Zadi Bal and Hassanabad in Srinagar, and Saidpura and Ahmadpura in the Kamraj district, contain the chief shrines of the Shiahs, but no Sunni would ever go to these places.[99]

In an attempt at bridging the sectarian divide in the city, Sayyid Mahdi sought to navigate through the broken sacred landscape of Muslim Kashmir. He was the first major Shiʿi cleric who offered his obeisance at two prominent Sunni shrines of Kashmir, Dastgir Ṣāhab shrine at Khanyar, Srinagar, and the shrine of Shaykh Nūr-al Dīn at Budgam. The image of a Shiʿi cleric all too easy to be recognized based on his clothing, the black turban and an equally black cloak must have made an interesting visual spectacle for a Sunni audience. How were these visits received, is difficult to establish, especially as Sunni sources fail to register this event. But, within the descendants of Sayyid Mahdi, these occasional visits are viewed as enablers of a change in community relation, resulting in a softening of sectarian boundaries between the Shiʿi and Sunnis.[100]

While Sayyid Mahdi may have charted the Shiʿi-Sunni divide with some measure of success, within the Shiʿi society he came under increasing pressure. Somewhere in early 1880s, Moulvi Ḥaidar ʿAli Ansarī (d.1915), the nephew of Akhūnd Mullā Javad Ansarī returned to Kashmir from Najaf following the death of his uncle Mullā Ṣadiq Ansarī in 1880 CE (Figure 4.3). Like Sayyid Mahdi, Moulvi Ḥaidar ʿAli had also studied in Najaf under leading *mujtahids* of the Shiʿi world,[101]

Figure 4.3 Moulvi Ḥaidar ʿAli Ansarī with the royal physician, Ḥakim Ḥasan ʿAli, early twentieth century, Srinagar (courtesy: Hakim Athar Hussain).

especially Ayatollah Mīrzā Sayyid Muhammad al-Ḥasan Shirazī (d. 1895), the Iranian *mujtahid* who played a leading role in the Tobacco Revolution of Iran. The future Iranian *marja*, Ayatollah Shaykh Muhammad Nainī (d. 1936) was a contemporary of Ḥaidar, and in Najaf both attended the school of Shirazī. Nainī is remembered for his support of the Constitutional Revolution of Iran and for his attempts to bridge the gap between religion and European influenced, "modern sciences." Like Nainī, Moulvi Ḥaidar would also be supportive of integrating European educational systems and traditional Muslim values.

It was on Shirazī's advice that Ḥaidar returned to Kashmir to guide the religious affairs of Kashmiri Shiʿi, who had taken Shirazī as the *marja-i taqlid* (source of religious emulation). On reaching Srinagar, Ḥaidar ʿAli was asked by the custodians of *Mʿārak* to use the *imāmbāda* as his seat and offer sermons from there. Unlike Sayyid Mahdi, Moulvi Ḥaidar did not seek to establish congregational prayers in the *imāmbāda*. Nevertheless, he was the first cleric from the Ansarī family who on various religious occasions offered sermons in the *imāmbāda*. In projecting Ḥaidar as the legitimate, preeminent Shiʿi cleric of Kashmir, the constituents of *Firqa-i Qadim* set the cleric on a path of confrontation with Sayyid Mahdi. The first break between the two Najaf-trained clerics commenced on the issue of *khums*. A series of letters exchanged between the two, published later as a tract by Ḥaidar, reveal the level of divergence between their positions. Though on the surface both sides maintain a level of respect and decency in addressing each other, it is glaring how Ḥaidar in his replies restrains from addressing Mahdi as a Sayyid.[102] Additionally, while in his reply Moulvi Ḥaidar goes to great lengths to describe his practice on the issue of *khums* distribution, the spirit of his reply refuses to acknowledge the seminary trainings of Mahdi as a fellow cleric. These two omissions become all the more obvious when we observe how throughout the last ten years of his life, in the 1880s, a series of books and tracts written outside Kashmir targeted both Sayyid Mahdi's claim to a religious scholarship, as an individual who had received an *ijaza* as well his ancestry—of belonging to sayyid family with authentic genealogy. The affair turned murkier, when Sayyid Mahdi was accused of having claimed to be a *mujtahid*. In the transnational network linking Kashmiri ulema with their seniors in Iraq, the role of the Kashmiri cleric had always been of a *vakīl* (representative), who would seek guidance and also remit some of the *khums* money to the shrine city. In assuming an independent position of a *mujtahid*, Sayyid Mahdi sought to operate outside the established traditions governing this relationship, where the Kashmiri ulema of nineteenth century always assumed a subservient role to the *mujtahids* in the shrine cities of Iraq. In many of the tracts written during this period by scholars sympathetic to the Ansarī's, Sayyid Mahdis projection as a *mujtahid* is met with great derision and often ridicule.[103] Additionally, these texts indicate that Mahdi's supporters promoted his image as the first Kashmiri *mujtahid*, and his rivals in their writings take great pain in establishing the line of Kashmiri scholarship in preceding generations to refute this claim. The writer of *Majālis-al Abrar*, Ḥājjī Sayyid Ḥasan Rizvī (d. 1928), himself a respected Shiʿi cleric from Zadibal, without naming Mahdi, questions his scholarly claims and decries how unaware Shiʿi are caught in the guile of a person who has taken to wearing an *ʿamāma* (turban),[104] and fashion a rosary in his hand.[105] Historically, aside from the acrimonious nature of these exchanges, the monographs, and tracts written on the intra-Shiʿi divide in the last quarter of the nineteenth century have helped in preserving the memory of many Kashmiri Shiʿi scholars, who would otherwise have been lost to obscurity.

Much more than his contested genealogy, it was this scholarly claim which provided the members of *Firqa-i Qadim* the propaganda material with which to launch a campaign against Sayyid Mahdi, both inside Kashmir and outside the valley. Presenting Sayyid Mahdi as a pretender who was a threat to community interests, fatwas against him were obtained from leading Shiʿi *mujtahids* in Iraq, including Ayatollah Mīrzā Ḥusayn Nūrī Tabrisī (d.1320).[106] Some other issues of jurisprudence in which Mahdi differed from Ḥaidar, include the conditions for sighting of the crescent of moon as well as the stipulations for a person who could officiate a marriage contract. Mahdi also targeted the rich backers of Ḥaidar directly,[107] pointing to their negligence in performing the Ḥājj ritual. This argument also resonated with his own supporters, who saw those opposing Mahdi as immersed in their worldly affairs, while exhibiting a marked laxity in fulfilling the obligations of the religion. Much more than the financial expenses of the journey, it was the rigors of a long journey which disheartened people from embarking on the pilgrimage, and this was common to both Kashmiri Shiʿi and Sunni Muslims.[108] While the date is not known, but somewhere around the same time, in mid-1880s, Mahdi led a *qāfila* (caravan) of Kashmiri Shiʿi on the

Ḥājj pilgrimage.[109] This is the first known instance that I have come across, in the nineteenth century of an organized pilgrimage to Arabia, and remained a regular feature among the supporters of *Firqa-i Qadim*.

The rulings from senior *mujtahids* in Iraq against Sayyid Mahdi, though serving the cause of *Firqa-i Qadim* failed to quell the popularity of Mahdi among his large number of supporters, an overwhelming majority of whom were illiterate.[110] To a large extent the books, tracts, and the fatwas issued against Sayyid Mahdi, were produced, and consumed by those who were opposed to him. In the end, this vast textual production was an exercise in self-gratification and record-keeping alone, which failed to sway those whose support for Mahdi was based on the egalitarian and ecumenical nature of the cleric's message. A prolific producer of texts himself, some of Mahdi's own writing which he wrote to establish his scholarly hold on a diverse range of subjects from jurisprudence to societal issues further deepened the dissensions within the community.[111] Within his lifetime, Mahdi came to be referred by the exalted title of *Sarkār* Āgā Sayyid Mahdi. In native Kashmiri Shiʿi society, the honorific *sarkār*, was not only a sign of respect, but also a title generally reserved for *mujtahids*.

Despite being vilified by his opponents within and outside Kashmir, the social forces at play- the mercantile wealth and the resentment among the underpaid worker and peasant classes, galvanized a momentum for Mahdi, which he purposefully channelized into creating public spaces and institutions for propagating his message. These included a network series of small-sized mosques, easy to construct and operate. Based on the level of popular support, Mahdi felt confident enough to take on his opponents and make a claim before the *darbār* for custodianship of *Mʿārak*. Somewhere in the 1890s supporters of Mahdi were able to physically restrain Sayyid ʿAbdullah Shāh Jalālī from organizing a *majlis* at Ahmadpora, north of Srinagar. Despite his prestige as the leader of *Firqa-i Qadim*, it was only through the agency of his son-in-law, the royal physician, Ḥakim Ḥasan ʿAli that ʿAbdullah could proceed with the *majlis* with the help of soldiers deputed by the court.[112]

The rift and the maneuvering to control community symbols, especially *Mʿārak*, highlights how the community elite, those representing the *Firqa-i Qadim*, through a network of matrimonial linkages evolved into a cohesive group, seeking to maintain their shared interest and privileges. This involved three different centers of power working in cohesion—the courtiers, the ulema, and the traders.

The importance of these relations and how they weighed on the collective community life is also established through proceedings in Bābū Rishambar's court. In an earlier session held in the *darbār*, representatives of Āgā Sayyid Mahdi had remained silent when Ranbir Singh advised that the matter should be resolved through division of the two main *imāmbādas* in the city, *Mʿārak* and Imāmbāda Hasanbad, between the two competing parties (Figure 4.4). As a part of this proposal, the party of Sayyid Mahdi- *Firqa-i Jadid* is offered the relatively smaller (and less historical) Imāmbāda at Hasanabad and asked to surrender their claim to *Mʿārak*. While on the surface this seems a judicious offer for the newly formed group, accepting it would have meant that the Mʿārakdars who were supporting

Figure 4.4 *Imāmbāda Hasanabad,* twentieth-century reconstruction, Srinagar, 2015 (author).

Sayyid Mahdi would essentially surrender their traditional seat of operation. The reluctance to accept this compromise makes the presiding judge, Rishambar, question the representative of *Firqa-i Jadid*, Sayyid Najaf Shāh M'ārakdaar. In his reply, Najaf Shāh excuses himself by detailing out the circumstance in the *darbār*, where the maharaja was accompanied by his physician, Ḥakim Mahdi. Najaf asserts that his silence was conditioned by the fear that the physician would convince the maharaja against the position of *Firqa-i Jadid* in case they entered a discussion.

The royal physician, Mahdi, belonged to the Mullā family (Figure 4.5), of which Isḥāq speaks in his description of *Firqa-i Qadim*. Mahdi's third wife was the daughter of Mullā 'Abdullah Ansarī (d. 1887), another renowned Shi'i cleric from the Ansarī family. 'Abdullah' s other sons-in-law included his nephew, Moulvi Ḥaidar 'Ali, Sayyid Javad Shāh Rizvī, and a cousin of Mahdi, Ḥakim Nur-al Lah. Besides intermarriage within the two branches of the Mullā family, the Ḥakim and the Munshi, the family would also enter marriage alliances with the Wa'iẕ family and Munshi family of Chinkral Moḥala and the Sayyids of Shamswari.[113]

The main participants in the dispute between the two *firqas*, the Jalālī family also built upon their marriage alliances to consolidate their position. Sayyid 'Abdullah Shāh popularly known as *Ablī Pādshāh* ('Abdullah the great king) on account of his immense wealth, and Ṣafdar Shāh were both grandsons of Sayyid Valī Shāh Jalālī, who is remembered in Jalālī family traditions as a pious religious scholar.[114] The house of Sayyid Valī at Madin Ṣāhab was also burned during the riots of

Figure 4.5 Members of the Mullā family, Srinagar, late 1890s (courtesy: Hakim Shaukat Ali Hamdani).

1872. Subsequently, one of his sons, Sayyid Najaf Shāh, migrated to Doonipora in Zadibal. Najaf's son, Sayyid Ṣafdar was married to Mīrzā Muhammad ʿAli's daughter, and followed his father-in-law's footsteps as a shawl merchant, marking a break from the family tradition of scholarly engagement.[115] He also benefitted from the prestige of his father-in-law as a community elder and benefactor. Safdar's cousin, ʿAbdullah Shāh had also married into the family of a prominent merchant family from Srinagar whose other surviving daughter was married to Ḥakim Bāqir, cousin of the royal physician, Ḥakim Mahdi. Sayyid ʿAbdullah's eldest daughter in turn married Mahdi's son, Ḥakim Ḥasan ʿAli, who after his father's death would rise to the position of influence in the court as the royal physician to Maharaja Pratap Singh.[116]

The convergence of matrimonial linkages can also be found in the case of Ḥājjī Ṣafdar Bābā, who was married to the sister of Malik ʿAli. Malik ʿAli traced his origins to the *Malikan-i Chadura*, a family of old Kashmiri nobility, who had lost all of their landed property during the Afghan rule. After marrying into the family, Ṣafdar Bābā convinced ʿAli and his brother to relocate to Srinagar, where they joined him in the lucrative shawl business. Malik ʿAli is also mentioned by the *Firqa-i Qadim* in the court documents relating to *Mʿārak* as one of the custodians who figured in its reconstruction. Continuing with the interlinkages formed through matrimonial alliances we find that Malik ʿAli's daughter was in turn married to Ṣafdar's son, Qāsim Bābā. On Javad's death she would remarry into the Mullā family. Qāsim's son, Javad Bābā would be adopted by another member of the Malik family, Malik Asad-ul Lah (d. early 1920's)—a leading merchant who patronized many community projects in the twentieth century. Another branch of the Malik family entered marriage links with the Jalālī family, the Rizvī family of Kathi Maidan, and the Rizvīs of Naulor, a small village outside Srinagar.[117]

Similarly, among Mīrzā Muhammad ʿAli's children, we find that in addition to Sayyid Ṣafdar, his other sons-in-law included Sayyid Naqī Rizvī, a prominent shawl merchant with business house in Calcutta, while another of his daughter is said to be married into the Ansarī family, though the exact details are not clear. Sayyid Naqī's daughter in turn would be married to Āgā Sayyid Ḥusayn Rizvī, who would become the first Kashmiri Muslim minister in the Dogra court. Early in his childhood, Sayyid Ḥusayn was adopted by his maternal family, the Qizalbash.[118] The Qizalbash family was a relative newcomer to Kashmir, the first member of the family to settle down in Kashmir, Āgā Rahīm. The family's formal association with the Dogra court starts in the ending years of Gulab Singh's rule, when in 1856, Āgā Ḥakim Bāqir who was accompanying a British officer from Punjab, was introduced to the maharaja.[119] During Ranbir Singh's reign, Bāqir was entrusted with the job of translating books on medicine from Latin and Arabic into Persian and Dogrī and rose to the post of Chief Physician. The Qizalbash also used his familial connections with the head of Qizalbash clan in Lahore, Nawab Nawazish ʿAli Khān (d. 1898)[120] for the benefit of Kashmiri Shiʿi. During the riots of 1872, Āgā Bāqir along with Ḥakim Mahdi had been successful in securing the aid of the *darbār* for helping the besieged Shiʿi community. Bāqir was able to secure additional financial aid from Nawazish ʿAli which was then distributed through the agency of Ansarī family.[121] In Kashmir, the first native family to enter in matrimonial relation with Qazilbash were the Jalālī's, both Bāqir and his son Ḥakim ʿAli Naqī married in the Jalālī family.

Similarly, in the Ansarī family, the patriarch of the family in the late nineteenth century, Moulvi Ḥaidar ʿAli had nine children, two of the daughters were married in the Mullā family, while a daughter was married into the Mīrzā family of Daulatabad and the Munshi's of Chinkral Moḥala. Among his sons, we find two were married into the Qizalbash family, while another was married into a branch of the Mullā family, the Munshis. The family line would continue with Moulvi Javad whose first wife was from the Qizalbash family, while he later married into the Ghāzī family of Namchibal.[122]

One major disadvantage that the elders in the *Firqa-i Jadid* faced was the inability to replicate this network of marriage alliances. Till the beginning of the twentieth century, the Mʿārakdars would only marry within their own family.[123] The absence of any major marriage alliance severely hampered their ability to maneuver for community leadership—and this inability also served as a contributing factor in their loss of control over *Mʿārak*. Similar was the case in the family of Āgā Sayyid Mahdi, where till the twentieth century the family would intermarry within their cousins.[124] While there are many reasons for marrying within the family, including a Prophetic injunction to do so, as well as the notion of preserving a Sayyid bloodline; a major reason behind the practice related to inheritance and disposition of family property. In marrying within the family, the Mʿārakdars and many other families which followed this custom sought to prevent the daughters" share from leaving the family. Importantly, among Kashmiri Shiʿi families, especially in the city, family inheritance was generally guided by *sharia*, allowing daughters to inherit a third of the property as the legal share. As opposed to it, most Sunni families followed "*urf*" the customary law, in which the daughter's share in land was retained by the family.[125]

Though by the end of the nineteenth century the membership in *Firqa-i Jadid* would match, if not outnumber their rival group, yet through their control of *Mʿārak*, members of *Firqa-i Qadim* were seen as the representatives of the community. It was in 1315 AH/1897 CE that Āgā Sayyid Muhammad, Sayyid Mahdi's son and successor would construct a major *imāmbāda* outside Srinagar, at Budgam in central Kashmir. Soon in the mid-part of the twentieth century they would take a rival Ashura procession in Srinagar, expanding their power and influence on the city, marking rival territories of operation within the splintered Shiʿi space of the city.

Chapter 5

MOVING TOWARD A UNIFIED MUSLIM IDENTITY

The long-drawn nineteenth century represents a unique moment in the history of Kashmiri Shiʿi society, when Shiʿi identity served as a tool for promoting individual and collective group interest as well as the mobilization of the people around shared rituals and sacred performative spaces and paths. On the surface the Shiʿi, especially in the capital city Srinagar, had realized a cherished dream: *Mʿārak*, the locus of the community's collective memory was rebuilt, *marṣiya* were publicly performed and for the first time Muharram procession was observed through routes which were predominantly Sunni. In enunciating a distinct Shiʿi identity publicly and negotiating it successfully against any antagonism from the Sunnis, the Shiʿi eschewed restrain in favor of public commemoration. The management of this public commemoration in turn gave impetus to the evolution of a community leadership which as we saw gradually erupted into inter-Shiʿi factionalism.

The onset of the twentieth century witnessed a rising awareness of the challenges posed by British colonialism and allied Christian missionaries' activities, primarily through the introduction of modern education and health services. The state of Kashmiri Shiʿi society at the dawn of the new century and its responses to issues of modern education, social justice, and political empowerment are the key themes explored in this chapter.

The chapter also explores the birth of political consciousness in the Muslims of Kashmir and how early twentieth century witnessed a coming together of Shiʿi and Sunni Muslims of Kashmir, overlooking their mutual differences and disagreements in favor of working toward a unified Muslim identity vis-à-vis the Hindu rule. But the process of a Muslim collective while representing a momentous change could not override ingrained inter-sectarian prejudices. The chapter examines the processes through which the celebration of a collective identification and political mobilization took place.

At the Start of a New Century

In Kashmir following the establishment of the Hindu Dogra kingdom, the position of Kashmiri Shiʿi showed a marked improvement and as I detailed out in the previous chapter manifested into a discernible social, cultural, and visual image of the community, exemplified by the reestablishment of Mʿārak and the performance of *marṣiya khwānī*. The marked improvement of the affairs of the community is also noted by Lawrence, who speaks about the Shiʿi' as

> a most respectable community, and in Srinagar many of them are men of good position. They are true to one another, and are kind and helpful to poor members. [. . .] In the city the Shiahs are chiefly shawl-weavers, and they practically monopolize the papier-mache industry. The Shiahs are famous physicians. A little experience enables one to tell a Shiah at once. They tie their turbans in a peculiar way, and trim their whiskers differently from the Sunnis.[1]

The early Dogra maharajas had inherited an appreciation for an urbane Persianate culture from the Lahore darbār of Ranjit Singh. In Srinagar, they patronized not only Kashmiri Pandits but also members of the Muslim gentry. This included not only the ḥakim but also the poets, calligraphers, and teachers. Both Gulab Singh and his successor, Ranbir Singh, offered patronage to Persian poets, some of whom were also Shiʿi. The poets Mīrzā Lām ʿih (d. around 1850s) and Mullā Mahdi (d. 1895) were associated with the court and respected by the courtiers. In Gulab Singh's court, Lām ʿih also occasionally aided his distant cousin Ḥakim ʿAbdu'l Raḥmān, the eldest son of Ḥakim ʿAẕim, in administrative affairs.[2] Mahdi had also served as the tutor to Pratap Singh, the last Dogra ruler of Kashmir, who received some Persian education.[3] Similarly, when the Bengali Bābū Nilambar Mukerjee[4] was recruited as Chief Judge of Kashmir on the advice of the Chief Minister Divan Kripa Ram, Ḥakim Ḥabib-al Lah (d. 1904) was officiated to teach him Persian.[5]

The Shiʿi influence in the court was primarily governed by the presence of ḥakim, the physicians. The first family to represent this courtly presence was the Mullās of Babapora, they were soon joined at the court by the Qizalbash family and later by a family of ḥakims hailing from Nandpora,[6] an isolated ward located on the outskirts of the city, near the Nigeen Lake. Significantly also during the last quarter of the nineteenth century and the first decade of the twentieth century, two Shiʿi royal physicians, Ḥakim Naqī Qizalbash[7] (d.1914) and Ḥakim Ḥasan ʿAli (d. 1334 AH/1914 CE), died under mysterious circumstances in the court, leading to the rumor that both had been murdered because of their political affiliations with the rival factions within the court.[8] Following Ranbir Singh's death, the royal court was deeply divided between Maharaja Pratap Singh (r. 1885–1925) and his ambitious brother, Raja Amar Singh (d. 1909).[9] Pratap Singh's powers were to be greatly curtailed due to the maneuvering of his brother, and after his forced abdication in 1889, shifted to a ruling council in which the British Resident and Amar Singh played a leading role.[10] In the troubled relationship between Pratap Singh and his brother, Ḥasan ʿAli and before him his father, Ḥakim Mahdi, had acted as partisans of Amar Singh. In a family diary[11] written by Mahdi's grandson, Ḥakim ʿAli Razā, on Pratap Singh's accession to the throne, Mahdi is said to have been removed from his job as the royal physician.[12] The death of two royal physicians, in questionable circumstances within a year of one another, does lend a certain credence to the theory of political murder, as recalled in their family traditions. Did the Shiʿi hakims act in unison at the court as partisans of Amar Singh which resulted in their death or were the causes located somewhere else, in personal rivalries among courtiers, is hard to establish in the absence of any direct evidence. Still, given the contours of the court, and its Hindu character, the actual role of a non-Hindu, non-Dogra courtier in any political maneuvering would have been limited.[13]

In addition to the poets and the ḥakims, some of the leading calligraphers in the city also hailed from the Shiʿi society. One of the oldest calligraphic families in the city belonged to the Akhūnds of Zadibal, and it was in the nineteenth century that one of the members from the family Akhūnd Muhammad ʿAli migrated to Bombay and achieved some fame in the city as a calligrapher.[14] Aside from the Akhūnds, the Munshis of Babapora and Chinkral Moḥala also produced many renowned calligraphers, some of whom were patronized by the Dogra darbār. The oldest surviving work from a member of the Munshi family is an illuminated *divān* of Ḥafiẓ Shirazī, copied by Mullā Muhammad Qāsim Hamdanī in 1201 AH/1796 CE (Figure 5.1). The manuscript which includes forty-eight paintings is an important source for understanding the development of Kashmiri painting under the Afghans.[15] A poet who also wrote on religious subjects, Qāsim was a part of the scholarly migration from Kashmir to Awadh but returned to Kashmir somewhere in the nineteenth century.[16] Aside from Qāsim, another major figure from the munshi family who would enjoy great acclaim as a calligrapher, poet, and teacher of Persian, Munshi Mustafa ʿAli (d. 1896), would train some of the leading calligraphers of nineteenth-century Kashmir. Apart from his own son, Munshi Ḥasan ʿAli, Mullā Mahdi, Munshi Aḥmad ʿAli Ghazī, Munshi Ṭalib, Munshi Ḥaidar, Ḥakim Ḥabib-al Lah, Moulvi Mustafa, Mīrzā Ṭālib, and Mīrzā Ḥaidar, also took classes with Mustafa, in poetry as well in the art of calligraphy. A renowned *marṣiya* writer, who also taught Persian in the State School, Mustafa's students also included some leading Pandit courtiers including those from the Dhar family.[17] Mustafa's son, Munshi Ḥasan ʿAli (d. 1933) would succeed his father as the Head Persian teacher at the State School, which had been set up in the heart of the city at Bāgh-i Dilāwar Khān.[18] An accomplished calligrapher like his father, Ḥasan would design the Persian inscription on the medal[19] which was distributed among native Indian chiefs and rajas to mark the Delhi Darbār of 1903.[20] Aḥmad ʿAli Ghazī was another Shiʿi calligrapher who acquired wide acclaim for his penmanship and briefly relocated to Lahore, where he also taught a small circle of students.[21] It was during his sojourns in the plains of the sub-continent, that he joined a publishing house, and calligraphed the first lithographic edition of Maulana Altāf Ḥusayn Halī's (d.1914) epic, *Mūsāddasi-Madd o-Jazri-Islam* (The Ebb and Tide of Islam) in 1879. Though Ghazī returned to Kashmir, many Shiʿi calligraphers from Kashmir would permanently settle down in the plains, especially under the Shiʿi nawabs of Rampur, and *tālukdars* such as Raja of Mahmudabad, finding employment as calligraphers copying manuscripts on literature, religious works or Quran codex.[22] While there was a limited local market for consumption of handwritten manuscripts in Kashmir, the arrival of meticulously prepared large-sized lithographed books

Figure 5.1 *Divān* of Ḥafiẓ Shirazī, copied by Mullā Muhammad Qāsim Hamdanī, 1796 (courtesy: Walter Art Museum, Maryland).

served as a novelty that adversely impacted the craft of calligraphers. A survey of some of the leading private libraries among Kashmiri Shiʿi families highlights this transformation,[23] with most of the handwritten manuscripts from the second half of the nineteenth century limited to works of Kashmiri *marṣiyas*, the *biyaz*, or Quran codex. With shrinking local market, many calligraphers ventured outside, some like Ghazī, also finding employment as a copyist with publishing houses. Other prominent calligraphers who achieved fame in the nineteenth century include Munshi Abū'l Ḥasan and his sons Munshi Muhammad Taqī and Muhamad ʿAli of Chinkral Moḥala. In 1278 AH/1851 CE, Abū'l Ḥasan finalized a codex of Quran commissioned by the courtier, Ḥakim ʿAẕim.[24] Completed in two years' time (Figure 5.2), this illuminated manuscript is one the finest example of the art of book illumination associated with Kashmir and recalls some of main the decorative features of the codex commissioned by Muhammad Ismāʿīl, the Isfahanī merchant in 1831. Outside Srinagar, we find several calligraphers engaged in the production of manuscripts dealing with religious sciences or particularly the *marṣiya biyaz*. These include Sayyid Ḥusayn Rizvī, Sayyid Ibrahim Rizvī, Sayyid Mahdi Rizvī,

Figure 5.2 Quran codex, copied by Munshi Abū'l Ḥasan, 1851 (courtesy: Yasmin Ali).

Sayyid Rasūl Shāh, Sayyid ʿAbbas Shāh, Zakir Khwāja Aḥmad ʿAli, Asad Mīr, and Akhund Ṣafdar Mīr.[25]

While the art of calligraphy could be picked by studying with an accomplished master, the necessary lessons in penmanship along with elementary schooling were usually undertaken at the *moḥala maktab*. Traditional education in the city remained operational on two scales, a basic *maktab* level knowledge made available by the *akhunds* and the *pirs*, and a high knowledge which remained the preserve of a few scholarly families in the city. In the *maktab* an individual would, in addition to the Quran and the ritual knowledge of the faith, also be trained in the basics of mathematics. In certain instances these introductory classes included lessons from the Persian poet Shaykh Sʿadī's (d. 1292), *Gulistān, Būstān* and *Pand Nāma* popularly known as *Karimā*. This basic learning provided in a *moḥala maktab* or at home by a tutor constituted the essential of education for the Shiʿi gentry both in the city and in villages. Depending on an individual's interest, taste, and understanding the *maktab* education could be curated to delve into a deeper appreciation of Persian literature. Somewhere in the last quarter of the nineteenth century, the cleric, Ḥājjī Sayyid Ḥasan Rizvī wrote the *Manzūm-Usūl-i Dīn* in Kashmiri, which describes the basic, essentials of the faith. This work, in addition to *Uṣūl al-Dīn* (principles of religion), *Furūʿ al-Dīn* (ancillaries of religion) also included a section on *Shikāyat-i namaz* (doubts relating to prayers), in an easy-to-memorize prose, enjoying great popularity among *maktab* going students.

The high knowledge, however, remained confined within a few families in the city, the Mullās, Ansarīs, Shaykhs (from the Mullā Muqim family), and many of the scholarly Sayyid families. In rural Kashmir, it broadly remained the preserve of the Rizvī and Mūsāvī families, aside from the family of the elegy writer Mīrzā Abu'l Qāsim[26] (d. in the second quarter of the nineteenth century) and his maternal uncle, Khwāja Muhammad Bāqir Gundī. The high knowledge was based on the historical, literary, religious, and medical traditions of the Persianate world, and manuscripts surviving in the libraries of the families mentioned include medicinal works of Avicenna, work on grammar by Sa'ad al-Dīn al Taftāzanī, *Sullam al-'Ulūm* a major work on logic written by Muḥib Allah al-Biharī (d. 1707),[27] and religious works including those of Shaykh Ṭūsī, 'Allāma Ḥillī, Mullā Majlisī, works of Shi'i philosophers including Mīr Bāqir Dāmād, Mullā Muḥsin Kāshānī, Mullā Ṣadrā, and other similar works. In most cases, home doubled as the school, lessons were studied with father, uncle, or a grandfather. Though in the eighteenth and early nineteenth century, transnational scholarly exchanges had strongly featured among Kashmiri Shi'i scholarly families linking them with leading scholars of Iran and Iraq, we find that relatively few families participated in this scholarly exchange as we approach toward the end of the nineteenth century. The most notable exception being the Ansarī family, and the descendants of Mullā Muqim commonly known as the Shaykh family. A possible reason for this could be the large-scale migration of ulema families from Kashmir toward Awadh in the early to mid-nineteenth century who then became a part of the discourse and cultural life of South Asian mainland, though many retained a degree of association with Kashmir till early twentieth century. The relocation of a branch of Jalālī and Rizvī family from Kashmir to the shrine cities of Iraq in the early nineteenth century is representative of this phenomenon.[28] Simultaneously, we also find evidence of individuals, studying with Sunni teachers, outside of Kashmir, especially those who were teaching in colleges that had been set up by the British in Lahore. The royal physician and *marṣiya* writer, Ḥakim Ḥasan 'Ali in a letter to Nawab Fateḥ 'Ali Qizalbash Khān (d. 1923) of Lahore,[29] mentions his intention to participate in private classes on a reading of Mullā Ṣadrā, and logic with the renowned Sunni teacher (and later Principal of the Oriental College, Lahore), Mufti 'Abdullah Tonki (d. 1920).[30] Earlier Ḥasan's cousin, the poet Ḥakim Ḥabib-al Lah would during his stay at Lahore take lessons with Sunni teachers of *adab* (literature). Still, such cross-sectarian scholarly exchanges were limited in terms of both their occurrence to a narrow audience and the settings of geographies outside of Kashmir. A similar occurrence within Kashmir during the nineteenth century or even early twentieth century is unheard of. Curiously, we know of Hindus who studied under Shi'i teachers, receiving their training in Persian *adab* with the poet-calligrapher Munshi Mustafa 'Ali and his son Munshi Ḥasan 'Ali.[31]

Within Kashmir, the *maktab* of the nineteenth century, in both the urban and the rural setting, remained a highly gendered space, with no access for any girl students. Acquiring and perpetuating knowledge was a male privilege, women remained confined to household activities, their public appearance conditioned by observance of the *pardah*. Shāhzada Begam (d.1983) belonged to the Munshi family of Bābapora, her father and grandfather were both Head Persian teachers at the State School, yet she remained illiterate.[32] In her travelogue, Ṣughrā Hemayun Mīrzā, similarly points out that the wife of the *jāgīrdār* and community elder, Sayyid Ḥusayn Shāh Jalālī is illiterate.[33] In rare instances of women literacy, we find education was limited to acquiring a reading knowledge of Quran. The only exception with some material evidence, is of Fatima Begam, Mullā Muqim's daughter who is reported as not only being educated, but a scholar. In the Shakyh family library, a complete codex of Quran exists which is assumed to have been copied by her somewhere in the nineteenth century.[34]

During my study, I came across numerous instances where people would recollect how in their childhood, entire *tāngah* (horse-drawn carriage) would be draped in white cloth for maintaining the *pardah* of women in travel. Though such observances were mostly limited to the elite, in the city as well as the villages, it does reflect on the level of gender stratification in the society and the concern for privacy. Similarly at home, the male space for meeting, gathering, and discussions, the *divan khāna*, would be off bound for women of the house limiting them to the knowledge of cooking, childcare, and household chores. It is only during the twentieth century that we find basic education being provided to women. In many instances these literate women would later serve as the first teachers in their families, teaching the letters and basic rituals of the faith, *wazu*, *nimaz*, and *roza* to children. Rarely do we find instances when a woman would teach to the wider community. The only recorded case of a woman teaching in the nineteenth century is of again of Fatima Begam, who used to offer lessons to girls. In the twentieth century, there are more reports of women teaching the Quran and the rituals of players. Fizā Begam, wife of Sayyid Ḥaidar Rizvī of Kathmaidan, Zadibal used to offer limited lessons to the girls in the area, mostly drawn from her extended family. Among the Ansarīs, Sakina Begam, daughter of Moulvi Ḥaidar ʿAli, taught the young children in the family. Similarly, Farzana Begam, wife of the revered ʿ*alim*, Ḥājjī Sayyid Ḥasan Rizvī is said to have taught at home to girls from her immediate family, but this is by no means established.[35] The only known case of a *maktab* for girls, was that of Sughra Begam, daughter of Ḥakim ʿAbdullah, who some years after her marriage to Malik Ghulām Ḥasan of Zadibal started teaching girl students.[36] It is possible that many such stories were repeated across the geographical spread of Kashmiri Shiʿi society in the early twentieth century, but they remain uncharted and unmapped[37]. Significantly, all the women mentioned earlier operated in an exceptional family circumstance: Fizā Begam was a widow, Sughra Begam and Farzana Begam were both issueless, while Sakina Begam had separated from her husband. The disruption in their matrimonial life can be posited as a possible reason, for providing them with the prospect to operate within a scholarly space that was otherwise the privilege of men.

Coming to the Dogra rule we find that in the nineteenth century, various members of the Ansarī family including, Mullā Ṣadiq I, Akund Mullā Javad, Moulvi ʿAbdullah II, Moulvi Ḥaidar ʿAli, Mullā Ṣadiq II, and Mullā Muhammad ʿAbbās would offer classes, but these were limited to the elite of the city. The operation of the Christian missionaries in the city during Ranbir Singh's rule, with its focus on Western education was a severe challenge to the traditional and limited means of educating, both among the Shi'i and Sunni community. The challenges and the responses marked the transition of Kashmiri Muslim society to modern times.

Much more than the religious scholars it was the *pirs*, who would maintain a daily contact with the community. The *pirs*, a majority of who belonged to Sayyid families, a few of whom were religious scholars of some standing, were the one that men and women would approach for a *tāwīz* (*amulets*), used for protection, to ward off an evil eye, for health, wealth, for a marriage, or any material or spiritual need that would arise. They would be also the first recourse for seeking remedy from an ailment, reciting Quranic verses over the ill. It was the *pirs* would also officiate on ceremonies related to marriage and death, especially in rural Kashmir.

Phyīr *Circuit, the Annual Trade Journey to the Plains*

Away from the court, it was the merchants who not only financed community projects but employed many in the Shi'i society. Unlike the Sunnis, the Shi'i society was highly urbanized, half the Shi'i population was in Srinagar alone.[38] Given the non-agrarian base of the city's economy and the widespread illiteracy, the major source of employment in the city was in the craft sector. For reasons that remain largely unexplained, the Shi'i community had not been able to develop a community of *tāifdar*-those engaged in trades which would have offered employment in an urban setting, these include jobs such as butcher, baker, carpenter, and milkman. Similarly, in the craft sector, the Shi'i presence was limited to shawl and papier-mâché, Shi'i engagement as, silver or goldsmiths, ironsmiths, paper makers, lapidarists was unheard of. The argument that is generally posited for the lack of Shi'i presence in many of these trades is the absence of a secure environment in which to engage in a commercial activity on a day-to-day basis.[39] The sectarian conflicts in the city, which erupted periodically lend strong support to this hypothesis, but it is difficult to posit when the Shi'i isolation from the bazar life became a permanent feature of the city life. The bazar—its market economy—was driven by processes of interaction. After facing repeated riots, the mood among the Shi'i was to minimize any interaction with the Sunni majority. In the aftermath of the riots of 1830, many Shi'is living in the moḥalas of Malkah-Shampora, Hasanabad, and Zadibal fled into the interiors of the Dal Lake, self-isolating themselves from the city at large and evolving a unique lifestyle centered on the waters of the lake (Figure 5.3). This forced movement away from the city also resulted in a loss of skills available to the community at large.

In 1873, out of the nearly 30,000 shawl weavers, a thousand were Shi'i, yet these thousand weavers constituted around 6.5 percent of the total estimated Shi'i population of Kashmir,[40] and 14 percent of the urban population of Kashmiri Shi'i. Most of the shawl *kār-khāna* were in Srinagar, or in south Kashmir which had a negligible Shi'i presence. Discounting the negligible presence of rural Shi'i

Figure 5.3 Muharram procession in the interiors of Dal Lake, Srinagar, 2021 (courtesy: Sayed Shahriyar).

population in the shawl trade, we could approximate that nearly fifteen percent of the Shiʿi in the city were employed as weavers. Yet for the most part, the *shawlbafs* existed as semi-free workers, dependent on the mercy of the *kār-khāna* owners and squeezed by the excessive taxation of the *darbār*.[41] In many of the European accounts of the region, written during the Dogra rule, we find repeated mention of the impoverished state of the Kashmiri *shawlbafs*:

> The shawl-weavers get miserable wages, and are allowed neither to leave Kashmir nor change their employment, so that they are nearly in the position of slave.[42]

In 1865, the *shawlbafs of* Srinagar had taken to the streets, protesting against the Maharaja's in-charge for the shawl department *(dārōghah-i daag shawl)*, Raj Kāk Dhar. The protestors were charged by the soldiers and in the ensuing stampede, twenty-eight weavers were killed, the first major causality of a confrontation between the Hindu rulers and his Muslim majority subjects. While the industry had survived, the riots of 1871 and the effects of the Franco-German war had adversely affected the Shiʿi *kār-khānadars.*

Within the traditional Shiʿi merchant families, after Mīrzā Muhammad ʿAli, no one from the community of Shiʿi shawl merchants and *kār-khānadars* achieved a similar position of intimacy at the court. Following Muhammad ʿAli's departure from Kashmir, his family's fortunes diminished considerably. While the big Shiʿi *kār-khāna* owners belonging to the Jalālī, Bābā, and Malik families continued to operate, by the end of the nineteenth century they were no longer major players on the shawl circuit, which was increasingly being dominated by Sunni merchants.

Before the riots of 1870, we find that aside from the traditional *kār-khāna* owners, trading in shawls had given rise to a new group of prosperous traders in the city, many of them recent arrivals to the city. Somewhere in the 1860s, Ḥājjī Sayyid Naqī Shāh (d. 1926) belonging to a family of religious scholars, left his hereditary profession, and started to trade in Shi'i villages, peddling in cotton, linen, and silken *pūzh* (women headscarves). The family had arrived in Srinagar in the early 1840s, settling down in Zadibal, before constructing a house in the area in 1848.[43] The Sikh rule as I have shown earlier marks the first major movement of Shi'i families from rural centers of Shi'i population to the capital city of Srinagar during the nineteenth century. Most families such as the Rizvīs settled down in Zadibal, some, albeit very few, including the Ansarīs preferred to establish themselves in the heart of the city in areas of mixed population, which in addition to Sunnis also had considerable Hindu presence[44]. Returning to Sayyid Naqī, we find him diversifying into the more profitable shawl business, somewhere during the 1860s. While, not a *kār-khāna* owner himself, Naqī represented the increasing class of traders who would act as the middleman in the shawl business, working with *kār-khāna* owners as well as artisans—the embroiders, without a formal establishment of their own. With an expanding business, Naqī was joined by his nephew, Ḥājjī Sayyid Aḥmad Shāh (d. 1949) who on the advice of his uncle settled down in Zadibal. Among Naqī's sons, while the eldest Sayyid Ḥasan was educated in religious sciences by Moulvi Ḥaidar 'Ali Ansarī, another son, Sayyid Ḥaidar would continue in the shawl trade, and be the first in the family who went on- *phyīr*.

Phyīr came to be associated with the annual winter journey, that mid-ranking Kashmiri traders would take into various cities of the Indian plains to sell various shawl products. During their three-to-four-month journey into the plains, these traders would sell and earn enough to maintain their families and workers for the year. The operation of the *phyīr* during the pleasant winter months made the journey tolerable for the Kashmiris, who were otherwise unaccustomed to the heat of the Indian plains. Most of the Shi'i traders engaged in the *phyīr*, would plan their journey in a manner that their return would coincide with the *Navrouz*,[45] the major festival of Kashmiri Shi'is occurring in spring. The *phyīr* was not a Shi'i phenomenon, Sunni traders also participated in this trade journey. For those engaged in this trade circuit, the clientele included both European colonial officials and native aristocracy comprising the landowning families (*jāgīrdārs*) and more importantly members of the new Indian bourgeois class, the rich bank merchants, the western educated natives serving in the colonial administration. Calcutta, the capital of the British colonial administration in India, remained the main center of the *phyīr*, though some traders also operated in Bombay.

The margins of profit in the *phyīr* were substantial, depending upon the skillset of the trader. Thus, Sayyid Aḥmad would part ways with his maternal uncle, Sayyid Naqī Shāh, set up a separate business along with his brothers Sayyid Muhammad and Sayyid Razā, with Muhammad embarking on the *phyīr* to Calcutta.[46] Both

Sayyid Naqī and Sayyid Aḥmad would buy considerable amount of land in Zadibal, build new houses, and when in the early twentieth century, the government opened *Numaish*: The Exhibition Bazar, they would also set separate shops in the bazar.

Aside from the Rizvīs, other Shiʿi families from Srinagar who were major players in *phyīr*, included that of the Mīrs[47] and the Ghazīs also living in Zadibal. From Hasanabad, one of the first Shiʿi trader who figured on the *phyīr* circuit during the early part of the twentieth century, was Ḥājjī ʿAli Muhammad. In the years leading up to partition of South Asia, many individuals from Srinagar joined the annual *phyīr*, a tradition which continues to this day among both Kashmiri Shiʿi and Sunni community.

At Calcutta, the presence of Shiʿi traders operating in the *phyīr* circuit was preceded by a few Kashmiri Shiʿi families who owned their own *kothis* in the city, serving as their residence as well as showroom. In addition to Mīrzā Muhammad ʿAli, we know of Mīrzā Ḥusayn ʿAli, Sayyid Naqī Rizvī and Ḥājjī Ṣafdar Bābā[48] who had their own *kothis* in the city selling shawl products. The *phyīr* traders, living in rented accommodation, would sell their merchandise at the house of their prospective clients. Over the years individuals engaged in the *phyīr* created a new network of relations with their patrons in the city, at times returning to the city with advance orders from their client families. Sayyid Ḥusayn Rizvī (d. 1989), Naqī's grandson is said to have been the supplier of pashmina to the Tagore family, most famously the poet-philosopher Rabindranath Tagore (d. 1941).[49] The annual movement of people from Kashmir into mainland South Asia also resulted in the introduction of customs and rituals which originated among Shiʿi communities of Calcutta and Lucknow. In *Khulasat al-Azkar*, the Iranian scholar Mullā Muḥsin Fayd Kashanī (d. 1681) provides an assortment of Shiʿi rites, prayers, and supplications. One of the practices mentioned in the *Khulāsat al-Adhkār* is of *sageh-i akhuvvat*[50] or as it is commonly known in Kashmir *sageh baradarī*; a brotherhood established between a group of two or more individuals. It was the Kashmiri traders engaged in *phyīr* who introduced this ritual in Kashmir which became popular in the Zadibal and Hasanabad, the moḥalas which served as the nucleus of *phyīr* trade among the Kashmiri Shiʿis. By the second half of the twentieth century, the practice spread to rural Kashmir, and we also hear of instances where it was introduced among women, functioning as a bond of sisterhood. It was also during this time that the ritual of *shabī*—a ritual coffin, taken out in a procession to commemorate Imām ʿAli's martyrdom was introduced in the mourning ceremonies of the Kashmiri Shiʿi community. All the main initiators of this novelty, Ḥājjī Asghar Mīr, Sayyid Safdar Rizvī, and Sayyid Rasūl Rizvī were associated with the *phyīr* trade, and in the oral traditions of the community the practice is believed to have imitated rituals prevalent among the Shiʿi of Calcutta and Lucknow.[51]

The mobility and integration of Shiʿi traders and merchants in geographically distant locales and cultures were not limited to the plains of South Asia or the mountain borderland of Ladakh-Skardu-Baltistan alone. As opposed to the trader's journeying into the Indian plains, Sayyid Tūrab Shāh Madnī (d. 1364 AH/1944 CE), a merchant from Narbal in Srinagar, operated on the Trans-Himalayan trade circuit, taking annual trade caravans into Yarkand (in present-day Xinjiang). His brother-in-law, Sayyid 'Ali Shāh, was the last Shi'i merchant who traveled into Yarkand right up till 1947, owned a house in the city, even marrying into a Yarkandi family. In, 1911 the city of Yarkand housed three to four hundred families from Baltistan, Gilgit, Chitral, and Kashmir, many of them settled for three to four generations in the city.[52] While prominent Sunni business house of Shāhdads, Tibet Baqals, and others continued their operation into Yarkand, Shi'i presence in the area became limited to the family of Tūrab Shāh and 'Ali Shāh. Earlier, 'Ali Shāh's father Sayyid Aḥmad and grandfather, had also participated in the Trans-Himalayan trade, and according to family traditions died in Yarkand.[53] In official colonial accounts we find some isolated reports on Tūrab Shāhs operation in the Yarkand area. During 1914–16, Tūrab Shāh approached the British Resident at Srinagar for help in resolving two unpaid debts from Chinese subjects of Yarkand. Earlier appeals to authorities in Yarkand, including the *Amban* of Yarkand (Imperial Qing Resident of the six cities of Altishahr)[54] for resolving the issue proved unsuccessful, highlighting some of the difficulties for Kashmiri traders doing business in the region.[55] After the fall of the short-lived Second East Turkistan Republic to China in 1949, the family returned to Kashmir. Unlike Tūrab Shāh, most Kashmiri Shi'i engaged in the Trans-Himalayan trade, limited their activities to Ladakh, focusing on Baltistan and Skardu, the Shi'i populated area of this Himalayan borderland. While some like Munshi 'Aziz Bhat (d. 1948), a Kashmiri-origin trader, settled down permanently in the area, others combined business interests with missionary activities. Leaving his job as a *patwarī* (revenue officer), 'Aziz Bhat would successfully set up his own business house, Munshi 'Aziz Bhat & Sons, constructing a caravanserai at Kargil, on the banks of river Suru. This caravanserai, second in Kargil, was the first private *sarai* on the Indian side of the Trans-Himalayan trade network and formed an important staging post for traders traveling to Leh, the capital city of Ladakh or proceeding toward Skardu.[56] Though Kashmiri Shi'i interests in the Trans-Himalayan trade across the Karakorum mountains faded significantly in the second half of the nineteenth century, with most of the business centered around cities in the Indian plains, yet some connections linking the Shi'is of Kashmir with their co-religionist in Ladakh continued. Occasionally, these links also resulted in continued ventures of business for the Kashmiri Shi'i.

During the early part of the nineteenth century, after the riots of 1830, Mullā Muqim's elder brother Mullā Mahdi had migrated to Baltistan.[57] He settled down at Kharmang, a small principality which also formed the first stage of rest on the route between Kargil and Skardu. Accompanied by a Kashmir sayyid, Sayyid Akbar Shāh, the two helped in introducing many Kashmiri customs to the area. Mahdi was also responsible for constructing small *imāmbādas* in the region, known as *ḥusaniyā*. The success of his work in the region can be judged in how a century later, European explorers arriving in the region would speak about the inhabitants of Kharmang as being "remarkable for their zeal as Shi'i Mahummadans."[58] Drawing upon the links of discipleship, later generations of ulemas from Muqim's family also maintained their religious connections to the area, additionally participating in trade centered on this Himalayan region.[59]

Similarly, the ruler of Kharamang, Rajā J'afar Khān, also formed friendly relations with the munshi family of Babapora, after Munshi Muhammad 'Ali (d. 1902) was appointed under Ranbir Singh as head of the *shafā- khāna* (dispensary) at Skardu. Earlier during the *ṣubedarī* of Shaykh Ghūlam Mohyi-al Dīn, Muhammad 'Ali's father Munshi Yūsuf(d. 1883) and uncle Mullā 'Aziz-al Lah had also been deputed to Skardu after its conquest by the Sikh army in 1841. During his stay in Skardu, 'Aziz-al Lah copied a popular collection of Shi'i prayer manuals, *Zad-al Mad* in the fort of Skardu.[60] One of the sons of the *'alim* Sayyid Zamān Shāh (the first *mutwalī* of imāmbāda at Hassanabad), Sayyid Muhammad Taqī also settled down in Skardu combining his missionary work in the area with trade in the Trans-Himalayan region. His son Sayyid Muhammad left for Nanital to work as a civil contractor for the British colonial administration.

Similarly, during the last quarter of the nineteenth century, Sayyid Fazal Shāh (d. 1354 AH/1935 CE) a Mūsāvī Sayyid from Anderkote in north Kashmir, migrated to Skardu, settling down in lower Skardu. A polymath, Fazal Shāh worked in Skardu as a cleric, a physician, and a poet, who composed verses not only in Persian as well as in his native Kashmiri but also in Balti, the language of Baltistan.[61] While individuals like Mullā Mahdi, Sayyid Fazal, and Mullā 'Aziz-al Lah represented the movement of Shi'i gentry—the ḥakims and the ulema from Kashmir toward Ladakh—we also come across craftsmen, laborers, and farmers who fled to the region in the aftermath of riots that plagued Kashmir. Working as barbers, weavers, goldsmiths, and farmers, members of the Thākr, Mīr, and Rathir families arrived in the village of Zanga in Skardu somewhere after 1830 permanently settling in the region.[62]

The continuing penetration of Kashmiri Shi'i clerics into Ladakh can also be seen in the twentieth century, when the trader, Tūrab Shāh enlisted the help of Sayyid Rasūl Rizvī (d. 1960) a Najaf-trained Kashmiri seminarian, to help him in distributing his religious dues from the *khums* money. While advising the trader, Rasūl also used the opportunity to widely preach in Ladakh, before marrying and settling down in the village of Chushoot near Leh. Kashmir's connection with Baltistan was also strengthened by a political event which resulted in forced dislocation of families from the region toward Srinagar. In 1891, the rulers of Nagar and Hunza in the Gilgit-Baltistan region revolted against the Dogra rule. Assisted by the British, the Dogras managed to reconquer the area, and Azur Khān the raja of Hunza was sent to Srinagar as a prisoner. After Azur's death in 1922, his surviving family members and retainers remained in Srinagar maintaining their native customs, language as well as links to their homeland. Gradually, the members of this small community, known as Bota Rajā, also established matrimonial links with Kashmiri Shi'i community, especially after 1947 when land routes between Kashmir and the Skardu–Gilgit region were shut, sealing the community from its native land. Following Azur Khān's defeat, he was succeeded by Mīr Zafar Zahid Khān (d. 1905) as the Mir of Nagar though given his ill health the region was managed by his son, Sir Sikander Khān (d. 1940) who eventually succeeded his father as the Mīr of Nagar in 1905. Maintaining their link with Kashmir, we find that Sikander, who in Dogra records is described as "a strict Shiah," took a second wife, the daughter of a Kashmiri Shiʿi *ʿalim*.[63]

Chaat-i haal, *Papier-Maché, and a New Class of Shiʿi Merchants*

Though a large number of Kashmiri Shiʿis were engaged in the shawl trade, papier-mâché had also emerged as a significant contributor to the community economy. Most writers in the nineteenth century associate the craft exclusively with the Shiʿi community of Kashmir, practiced within the city alone, which had greatly suffered from European market preferences, about which Lawrence writes:

> Papier-maché has perhaps suffered more than any other industry from the taste of foreign purchasers.[64]

As opposed to the shawl industry with large-scale *kār-khāna*, given its limited market papier-mâché mostly survived as a household practice in the neighborhood. The workshop or the *chaat-i hal* (lit: apprentices place), would simply be the living room or the attic floor of the house of the master craftsman(*vasta*), where the artist and his apprentices would work. The apprentices (*chaat*) would help in preparing the mineral and vegetable colors, prepare the paint surface, the artwork itself was the domain of the master—the *vasta*. One of the renowned papier-mâché artists from the nineteenth century was Sayyid Tūrab (d. around 1894) about whom Sufi says "there were artists in the past, who carried the art of papier-mâché to the highest pitch of excellence, [. . .], and the last one was Sayyid Tūrab who died over fifty years ago."[65]Though the craft flourished in the moḥalas of Hasanabad, Kamangarpora, and Zadibal, barring a few names we have no memory of the masters who were associated with this craft in the nineteenth century. In *Risāla-i Sayf al Ṣāram*, Sayyid Bāqir names some of the descendants of Bāqir Joo (deceased in 1880s), a *naqash* (papier-mâché arist) from Kamangarpora whose family continued in the craft.[66] Additionally, unlike most other craft practices in the region which operated as hereditary occupations, while a son could, and at times did inherit his father's *chaat-i haal*, there was no way of ensuring that a *vasta* would be succeeded in his craft by a son, the stroke of the brushwork could be practiced but not inherited (Figure 5.4). Products prepared in the *chaat-i haal* would be sold to traders to display in their showrooms, most of which were located on the Jhelum riverfront in *kothis*. Shiʿi presence along the riverfront was limited to two small sections near Nawa Kadal and Arwat at Fateh Kadal, but we have no account of Shiʿi merchant owning a *kothi* in either of these two areas. The first major Shiʿi owned *kothi* on the riverfront was only set up in the early twentieth century, when an Afghan trader of pearls, Ḥājjī Jaʿfar Khān settled down in the city and bought a *kothi* at Zaina Kadal from the family of Khwāja Mohyi-al Dīn Gandrū.[67] The river which passed through the center of the city served as the principal transportation spine as well as the public interface of the city. Major shrines, mosques, temples, and residences were located on the

Figure 5.4 A papier-mâché *chaat-i haal* in nineteenth-century Srinagar (courtesy: British Library).

riverfront, including the residences of the city merchants—the *kothis* which also served as the business establishment for these merchants. With an increasing inflow of Europeans into the region, vacationing in the valley to escape the summer heat of the plains, the traditional *diwān- khāna* (living room) of the *kothis* were reinvented as the "showroom" where the crafts of the region were put on display. J. Duguid, who arrived in Kashmir during the summer of 1870, describes in some detail the interaction in these *kothis* between prospective European buyers and the Kashmiri traders.

> Passing down the city you receive the salaams of the shawl and other merchants whose places you have visited and temptations resisted [. . .]. Shawl merchants, nearly all Muhammedans, cash cheques on the principal cities of India [. . .].
>
> Their show-rooms, principally on the river banks with balconies of lattice- work, during summer open, and in winter closed with paper, are posts of vantage from which they watch their British customers proceeding along the river. The merchant, his head man, sons or brothers, rush down to meet you as they see your boat approach escort you to the show-room, and as soon as you have entered it call for "cha," the name for tea brought by the Portuguese, and thus spread through the Asiatic world; it comes from Ladakh. A row of arm-chairs is placed for European visitors [. . .].

> We have gone through the merchant's stock, purchased some trifling articles, and rise to leave. His "Cha" we have declined, but he insists on our taking a basketful of almonds and raisins, sweetmeats, sugar candy, or preserves.[68]

More than half a century later, Duguid's experience with the traders and merchants of Srinagar is mirrored in the accounts of the socialite and actress, Yvonne Fitzroy(d. 1971), who served as Private Secretary to the Marchioness of Reading. Yvonne who accompanied the Marchioness and her husband the Viceroy, Lord Reading during their state visit to Kashmir in October 1921,[69] writes about a similar encounter during her stay in Srinagar:

> Once I was entertained to a Persian breakfast by the leading papier-mâché manufactures, and never before have I eaten so much or felt so sick! There were, I think, twenty-four courses, all fearfully and wonderfully made.[70]

Similarly, W Wakefield, a British doctor, who arrived in Srinagar five years after Duguid speaks about the spectacle of city life carried on the riverfront. This includes the Maharaja promenading on the river along with his *darbār* and European guests to showcase his latest acquisition,[71] a steam boat gifted by Queen Victoria (r. 1837–1901), to European visitors eagerly sought by the native merchants from their *kothi* "overlooking the river."[72] Most of the *kothis* along the riverfront were owned by Sunni merchants,[73] a majority of which, especially those dealing in Kashmiri Art were located at Fateh Kadal (Third Bridge). The major showrooms operating from the *kothis* of Fateh Kadal which dealt with the Europeans included, *Samad Shāh, Ḥabib Shāh, Bahar Shāh & Sons,*[74] *Ḥabib Joo & Sons, Ganymede, Subḥana & Sons, Kabir Joo & Sons, Lasso & Sons, Khizr Mohammad, Ṣidik Joo& Sons, Aḥmad Allah, Ghulām Ḥusayn, A Peer,* and *Ghulām Mohyi-al Dīn & Sons,*[75] all of which were Sunni owned. And it was in their showroom that the papier-mâché artefacts of the Shi'i *vasta*, would be displayed, the sale negotiated by a mechanism simply known as "on approval." Under the system of operation, the Shi'i *vasta* would receive the money for his goods, only after they were sold to a buyer. As a part of this transaction, the Sunni showroom owner's commission, which comprised the profit he made from the actual sale as opposed to the rate that was previously fixed with the *vasta*, could and did vary depending on his selling skills. And these skills did vary with individuals and circumstances. When a young American visiting Srinagar, ignored the advice of a British explorer on procurement of precious stone, the piqued Britisher advised a Kashmiri merchant selling stone to try his luck with the naïve American. The merchant managed to sell to the American, cut color glass made in Paris as sapphires, for an incredible amount of eight hundred rupees, the actual price being less than a hundred!

With an increase in the volume of Europeans visiting Kashmir, especially after the setting up of British Residency in Kashmir, we find a corresponding increase in the commercial activity taking place in Srinagar. In a period, of less than half a century, fortunes were made as new business establishments rose to prominence on the entrepreneurial strength of a single generation. Unlike many other cities of the Indian plains, Srinagar did not possess an organized bazar. Rather than a row of shops on a major street or important urban avenue,[76] as seen in some of the cities of medieval India, Srinagar had evolved a unique urban morphology centered around the river Jhelum and a series of water canals: Nallah Mar, Tsunth Kul, Shāh Kul, Katti Kul, Lachma Kul, and the Nowpaora-Khawja Yarbal channel. Major supplies in the city would arrive on the Jhelum in boats: the *dunga* and *behak* before disembarking on the many ghats of the city. From the ghats these supplies would be manually transported through narrow *gullies* and *kuchas* to the residences and workshops. The only shop to be found would invariably be located at the rear of the *moḥala*, catering to the immediate needs of the residents; the shop of the *pujj* (butcher), *kandur* (baker), an occasional tailor shop, and the quintessential *wani dukan* selling everything from salt to cloth. The absence of the much fetishized "Oriental Bazar," from the landscape of the city, did leave a vivid impression on the Europeans arriving in the region during the early years of Dogra rule:

> There is no respectable quarter, not a single good street; scarcely even a single respectable bazaar, considering the size of the place. And what is true of Srinagar is more than true of all the smaller towns.[77]

By the early 1900s the few shops had expanded into a row of shops on some of the major streets of the city.[78] In addition, two of the seven bridges on the Jhelum had shops on them, as also some of the smaller bridges on the Nallah Mar canal, offering a unique if limited shopping experience. It was only around 1865, that the city got its first organized market, New Bazar (popularly known as Maharaj Gunj), in the heart of the city near Shaykh Moḥala.[79] The bazar, approached from stone steps leading up from the river, was designed as "a great square building with open courtyards in it, the building itself consisting of innumerable little houses in which the ground floor is usually devoted to manufacturing."[80] Nevertheless, it was Fateh Kadal with its *kothis* opening onto the river, that remained the real center of craft trade in the city. During the late 1920s, the Bund would be developed upriver near the British Residency and would serve as an exclusive European promenade, housing the banks, stores, and firms dealing in Kashmir craft owned by Europeans, non-native Parsis and some of the Kashmiri-owned showrooms that relocated from the inner city.

When many of the *kothis* at Fateh Kadal were burned in a severe fire during Maharaja Hari Singh's (r. 1925–49) reign,[81] the owners were then provided land by the Maharaja near Bund, to set up their showroom. This relocation marked the end of Fateh Kadal as the nucleus of showroom trade related to what is described as the "Arts of Kashmir."

Most of the travelogues written between the 1870s and 1940s[82] portray the Kashmiri showroom owners as a group of incessant peddlers, competing among themselves, using guile and flattery to obtain a sale from the colonial visitor. The showroom owner or his agent is a charming and at times irritating figure who is always lurking in his boat, waiting the moment to seize upon the unwary

European.[83] In his description of the New Bazar, Oscar Eckenstein, an explorer who arrived in the city in 1885 gives full vent to the colonials' derision of the natives in his impression of the city's traders:

> As soon as I set foot on the lowest step in getting out of my boat, I was surrounded by a yelling crowd of native shopmen, each of them shouting out that he was the only honest man there—that he sold cheaper and better things than anybody else—that all the others were thieves and rogues, and such-like.[84]

One of the establishments that would gradually challenge this perception was that of *Suffering Moses*, which would over the years also emerge as one of the main Shiʿi-owned business enterprises. The firm was started by papier-mâché artist, Ḥājjī Ṣafdar Wanī (d. around 1950s) and his brother Ghulām Ḥusayn Wanī[85] in the 1880s, initially dealing only in papier-mâché before expanding into other crafts. Somewhere later in the twentieth century, Ṣafdar would shift his showroom to a *kothi* at Fateh Kadal.[86] Ṣafdar also worked as a successful government contractor on major infrastructure works that commenced during the reign of Maharaja Hari Singh (r. 1925–47). Writing in 1900, Isabel Savory captures both the fame of the showroom and the persona of the man who was responsible for establishing one of the most recognized and trusted firms dealing with the Arts of Kashmir:

> we went to the shop of Suffering Moses, well known to every visitor in Srinagar. [. . .]. He had already visited our camp that morning and had left his card [. . .] Suffering Moses, as he is always called, and now calls himself, no sooner caught sight of us on the river, than he was into *kishty* and after us. At last, personally conducted to his own bazzar, we were invited to sit down and given tea, [. . .], while the Sufferer, an old bearded man, who, after the manner of the East, had dyed his beard bright red, and wore a skull-cap and a long garment trimmed with fur, displayed his *papier mâché* and ornamental woodwork, his carved wood and copper tables, and his silver and silver-gilt bowls, goblets, candlesticks, photo frames, boxes, and what not from a vast selection we made various choices, to be packed then and there and sent direct to England. This he fulfilled to the letter.[87]

While Ṣafdar's dealing with the Europeans resembled that of his contemporaries, it was his nephew, Ḥājjī Mohyi-al Dīn (1912–2001), who would transform the functioning of the firm, and in the process the trade. Mohyi-al Dīn represented the second generation of Kashmiri showroom owners, and the deference that had marked the earlier exchange between the Kashmir traders and the colonial *sahibs* and *memsahibs*, had matured into a more balanced relation of almost equals. Numerous anecdotes have been recorded about Mohyi-al Dīn refusing to sell his products to buyers, whom he thought to be less discerning of the craftsmanship involved. This would have been an unheard sacrilege in the earlier generation of his father and uncle.[88]

Along with the *Suffering Moses*, the other Shiʿi-run showroom set up along the riverfront was owned by members of the Bānkā family. In the *Handbook to*

Kashmir, written in 1933 for the benefit of European visitors to the region, only two Shiʿi-owned showrooms find a mention in the list of thirty-three showrooms in the city selling objects and curios related to Kashmiri crafts; *AA Bānkā & Sons* at Bund and *Suffering Moses* at Fateh Kadal.[89] The firm *AA Bānkā & Sons* was also established by a papier-mâché artist, Akbar ʿAli Bānkā in 1892, and had their first major break in 1928, when they got a commission from Viscount Goshen, the Governor of Madras. In 1930, after doing the furniture for Viceregal Lodge at Shimla, the firm was given a Warrant of Appointment by the Viceroy, Lord Irwin (1926–31). This was followed by a commission for the new Viceroy House at Delhi (Rashtrapati Bhawan), executed under the supervision of the architect, Sir Edward Lutyen.[90] Somewhere in the 1920s, the firm shifted from Fateh Kadal to the Bund, the only papier-mâché showroom on the Bund in the pre-partition days.[91]

Another Shiʿi family to participate exclusively in the papier-mâché, was the firm of the Bābā family of Hasanabad, which was set up in 1920s. During the nineteenth century, an ancestor of the family Asad-al lah Bābā took to the art of papier-mâché, learning from one of the leading masters of the craft in Hassanabad. Asad-al Lah's five sons were also trained in the craft and would initially sell their products, in a *kothi* located near Fateh Kadal, owned by a Sunni merchant, operating under the name *Ganymede*. Soon, one of Asad-al Lah's sons, Ḥājjī Muhammad Qāsim Bābā, started traveling to the garrison town of Rawalpindi, selling his products directly to Europeans stationed in the town. Rawalpindi had emerged as a major center for trade between Punjab and Kashmir, eclipsing a similar role that had been played by Peshawar during the late eighteenth and early nineteenth century, the extent of which can be also understood from contemporary official records; the *Gazetteer of 1895*:

> A considerable portion of the trade of the Province with Kashmir passes through the city, a portion which, in 1885, amounted to 27 percent. Of the imports and 14 percent. Of the exports [. . .] Some of the commercial houses have very extensive dealing.[92]

Back in Srinagar, the Bābās continued their association with the *Ganymedes*. It was only in 1925 that they set up their own business establishment, and in the 1930s their own showroom in Srinagar, focusing exclusively on papier-mâché.[93] Writing in the 1970s, Ṣafdar mentions the pioneering role these Shiʿi artisan-traders performed in the survival and expansion of papier-mâché:

> During Dogra rule, the government did not pay any special attention to the development of this craft. This craft was in its last moments and had almost died down when from the Shiʿi (community) some hardworking, young and enterprising traders spread its appeal to Europe and America, due to which this craft prospered greatly, new designs and methods were invented. In this regard *Muhammad Qāsim* (Dalgate), *Suffering Moses* (Bund), *Ṣādiq ʿAli & Brothers* (Fateh Kadal) *Asia Crafts* (Bund), *Kashmir Papier Mâché Union* (Dalgate),

> *Messrs Jʿafar ʿAli* (Hassanabad) are worth mentioning. In addition to them there are other traders who work in papier-mâché.[94]

Challenges of Modernity: Missionaries and Education

Maharaja Pratap Singh's long reign of forty years[95] would see a gradual transformation of many aspects of Kashmir's public and civic infrastructure and an ever-increasing expansion of colonial imprint on the legal, education, and health system. Before his powers were fully restored in 1921, it was the British Resident through the State Council who would maintain a watchful eye on the administration, pushing the *darbār* toward administrative and infrastructural reforms.[96] In this British-owned scheme for an aggressively formulated reform, fiscal control, revision of taxation system, improvement of judicial, administrative systems, improvements of road, and a railway connection between Kashmir and British India formed the areas of concern.[97] Parallel to the maneuverings of the colonial administration, the Church Missionary Society (CMS) which had in 1852 established a mission in Lahore, started its operation in Kashmir in 1865, on the arrival of Dr William Jackson Elmslie (d. 1872).[98] Earlier in 1854 during, Gulab Singh's reign, Rev R Clark and Colonel Martin had arrived in the city to see possibility of missionary activities in the region.[99] Emslie's own visit was preceded by two missionaries, "Rev. W. Smith of Benares, and the Rev. R. Clark of Peshawar, reached Kashmir in the spring of 1863."[100] These early missionaries faced opposition from the *darbār* and on one occasion, Clark was set upon by an engaged mob, partly incited by the officials of the *darbār.*[101] Similarly, Rev W. Handcock who was also in Kashmir was prohibited by the *diwān* to openly preach in the city.[102] Similarly, the Muslim clergy of the city protested against Elmslie's preaching at one of the most revered Muslim sacred sites in Kashmir, *Dargah-i Hazratbal.*[103] The Chief Sunni Qāzi of the city, Moulvi Nāṣir issued a decree that a visit to the dispensary of the Mission would invalidate the marriage contract.[104] The Shiʿi attitude toward the missionaries seems to have been more ambivalent. Dr. Ernst F. Neve[105] (d. 1946) who would succeed Elmslie at the CMS dispensary in 1886 writes in his memoirs:

> About five percent, of the Mohammedans are Shiahs. Although a highly respectable community, these are looked upon by the orthodox Mussulmans as outcasts. Curiously enough, although the Sunnis are friendly with the Hindus, the Shiahs abhor them. The Shiahs are more friendly to Christians than ordinary Mohammedans.[106]

Yet, an incident in the Shiʿi majority village of Yechgam[107] resulted in a strain in this relation, when the son of the village *lambardar* (head man), whose mother had been treated by mission doctors converted to Christianity. Following the treatment, the appreciative *lambardar* family strikes a friendly acquaintance with the Mission doctors, and more visits follow. These visits are accompanied by subtle missionary endeavors, reciting Christian-themed stories, and gifting the family with books about Christianity. In a bibliography dedicated to the memory of another Christian missionary in Kashmir, Irene Petrie (d. 1897) the author touches upon the details of the episode, which highlight both the importance that the Mission doctors associated with contacts with the *lambaradar* family and the ensuing community backlash:

> In August, 1889, two fully qualified medical women [. . .] came to Yetchgam. The doctors operated successfully on the wife of the lumbardar that is, the hereditary tax-gatherer, the headman of the village, on whose character and influence its prosperity largely depends [. . .]. An influential maulvi had visited the village, and the people took the opportunity to lodge a complaint against the young man on account of non-attendance at the mosque and reading pernicious that is, Christian books given him in 1889. A great disturbance ensued, and he was threatened with excommunication.[108]

Elmslie's own biography, written posthumously by his wife shows how the missionary found better acceptance both among the native population and with the *darbār*, in their work as health workers.[109] Working as doctors and nurses, the missionaries found an organizational strategy in which to operate and more importantly influence upon the population an appreciation for Christianity.[110] The Bishop of Calcutta, during his visit to Kashmir, appreciated the practicality of the methods adopted by the missionaries in these words:

> He (Dr. Emslie) presents Christianity to the people in its most obviously beneficent aspect; and for this union of care for men's souls with the healing of their bodies the gospel narrative furnishes us with the very highest justification and precedent.[111]

The other significant area of operation of the missionaries was education. A semi-organized school had been set up by Clark in 1864 but it was only in 1881, that Rev J. H. Knowles established a school within the precinct of the Mission's hospital on the outskirts of the city at Drugjan. Nine years later the *darbār* gave permission to Knowles to shift the school to Fateh Kadal in the heart of the city. The work of Knowles was further strengthened with the arrival of Rev. Cecil Tyndale Biscoe in 1891.[112]

The response of a Kashmiri Sunni cleric, Moulvi Nāṣir to the Mission Hospital is also emblematic of initial Sunni reception to the introduction of Western education in the region. By equating the education in the missionary schools with "*nasarah ilm*" (Christian knowledge), the Sunni clergy class effectively foreclosed the participation of the community in the Mission's school. Within the Shiʿi society, while the *Firqa-i Jadid* would maintain a similar negative attitude toward missionaries and their work, proscribing attendance in the mission schools, the *Firqa-i Jadid* was more open to influences originating from the missionary-run institutions. One of Moulvi Ḥaidar's son, Moulvi Muhammad ʿAbbas adopted a Western way of dressing including sporting a necktie, which was mostly viewed as an anathema by Muslim community at large, both Shi'i and Sunnis. 'Abbas also picked up the English language from the missionaries in turn imparting lessons in Persian and Arabic to the missionaries.[113] When the *darbār* opened State School at Bagh-i Dilawar Khān, Ḥaidar enrolled two of his sons in the school.[114] In the 1880s two Kashmiri Shi'is, Āgā Sayyid Ḥusayn and Ḥakim Muhammad 'Ali (d.1933) enrolled in the Mission School, the first from Shi'i community. In 1894, Āgā Sayyid Ḥusayn would proceed to Lahore for completing his matriculation, the first among Kashmiri Muslims to do.[115] Yet the overall participation of Kashmri Shi'i in either the missionary schools or the State School remained limited to a few families in the city. While the engagement of Kashmiri Muslim society with the missionary schools would be a long-drawn process, changes affected in the administration made traditional *maktab*-based learning obsolete, especially for those pursuing a career in the state administration. The replacement of Persian with Urdu as the official language in 1889, adversely affected Persian-knowing individuals and families, who for most of the nineteenth century had functioned as educators and munshis working in various administrative departments. Similarly, the opening of missionary hospitals in the region also resulted in a gradual shift away from native practices of medicine; the Greco-Arab system of knowledge, known as *unanī* in Kashmir and most of Muslim South Asia.

In 1890, Moulvi Muhammad Yaḥya passed away to be succeeded by his son, Moulvi Rasūl Shāh as the mīrwa'iẕ. Rasūl Shāh, who had been barred from preaching in Srinagar after the 1872 riots, on his accession to the post of mīrwa'iẕ, emerged as a visionary who sought to effectively engage and manage aspects of the Sunni Muslims in both religious and secular realms. In 1899 he established the *Anjuman-i Nusrat-al Islam*, modelling it on the reform-oriented *Anjuman-i Himayat-al Islam*, which had been established in Lahore in 1884.[116] Conscious of the challenges of the missionary schools, and the lack of an organized competence in the traditional *madrasas* operated by clerical families, Rasūl Shāh sought to fashion a response which while rooted in the traditional system could also compete with the missionaries. Simultaneously with the establishment of the *Anjuman-i Nusrat-al Islam,* Rasūl Shāh, opened a *madrassa* which took shape of a Islamia High School in 1905, and was also provided with financial grants, albeit limited from the *darbār.*[117]

As opposed to the Sunni, the Shi'i lacked an organized answer to the changes in the region. After the death of Āgā Sayyid Mahdi in 1890, he was succeeded by his son, Āgā Sayyid Muhammad (d. 1931) as the religious head of the *Firqa-i Jadid.* One of the first major works that occupied Sayyid Muhammad was the construction of an *imāmbāda* at Budgam, the native village of the Āgā family. Completed in 1315 AH/1897 CE it would serve as the seat of his preaching and activities. Nevertheless, the construction of a new *imāmbāda* did not remove the bitterness and the ongoing dispute between the *Firqa-i Qadim* and *Firqa-i Jadid* for control of religious sites and Muharram ceremonies.[118] It was widely rumored among his supporters that Sayyid Muhammad was poisoned, though he survived the attempt at his life (Figure 5.5). Aside from the internal bickering between the two *firqa*'s, it was in 1324 AH/1906CE that the first Shi'i association,

Figure 5.5 Āgā Sayyid Muhammad, early twentieth-century Budgam (courtesy: Zulfikar Ali).

Anjuman-i Imāmmia was established, marking a tentative step toward reform and reorganization of the community life.

The Anjuman, *A Murder Case and Call to Reform*

On Saffar 9 1324 AH (1906 CE), Moulvi Ḥaidar ʿAli Ansarī presided over a special session of Kashmiri Shiʿi, attended by four hundred invited guests both from Srinagar city and the Shiʿi dominated villages. During the meet, Ḥaidar ʿAli laid the proposal for establishing an organization, *Anjuman-i Imāmmia* to look after the affairs of the Kashmiri Shiʿi, which was unanimously approved. In a tract which was distributed sometime after the inaugural session, the organizers explained how *anjumans* had been established in different cities of India with an aim to reform, impart education, religious training, culture, virtue, and good behavior to the community, a feat that the *Anjuman-i Imāmmia* sought to replicate in Kashmir.[119] While the tract makes no mention of the *Anjuman-i Nusrat-al Islam* which had been established seven years prior by the Rasūl Shāh, the Shiʿi under the leadership of Ḥaidar ʿAli were clearly seeking to emulate his success. The *Anjuman-i Imāmmia* which was financially supported through public contributions aimed at an ambitious program involving:

Improve the process of secular and religious education through the establishment of *madrassas* and by sermonizing,

> To root out customs which were cause of ruin for the community
> Improve the external conditions of community through a series of sermons
> Aid the destitute and poor, and
> To provide aid to orphans and assist in the funeral arrangements for those without any descendants.[120]

Yet the actual objectives achieved by the *Anjuman-i Imāmmia* were rather limited. In its annual report for the succeeding year the organizers were still looking to establish seventeen madrassas in various locations in both the city and villages which would provide religious education.[121] The lack of financial resources, as well as the required staff, greatly hampered the working of the organization.[122] Still, the work of the *Anjuman-i Imāmmia* was greatly facilitated by the presence of Munshi Ḥasan ʿAli of Nowpora who functioned as its treasurer. Though Ḥasan ʿAli's father had been a firm backer of Āgā Sayyid Mahdi, the son instead came to associate with Ḥaidar ʿAli because of his acceptance of Western education. Ḥasan ʿAli had been taught English by the missionary doctors and had served as a teacher in the school set up by Christian Mission Society at Fatah Kadal. While he would author a manuscript in refutation of Christianity, Ḥasan was nevertheless impressed by the missionary system of education. In one of his unpublished manuscripts, he goes to great lengths to describe the technological advances made by European nations, something he sought to imitate among Kashmiri Shiʿi.[123] The organizers of the *Anjuman* might have seemed hopeful of fulfilling their mission, yet their efforts were overtaken by a totally unrelated development in Zadibal. In his personal dairy, Ḥakim Ghulām Ṣafdar Hamdanī, details the incident which led to the closure of the *Anjuman-i Imāmmia* in these words:

> Sometime after the inaugural session of *Anjuman-i Imāmmia* (August,1907) there was an incident at Zadibal. A Pandit had opened a shop of pashmina wool there. This shop was the property of a Sunni who used to live in the upper floor (of the shop) along with his brother. The Pandit developed illicit relation with a girl in their family. One night both the brothers were out for a dinner invitation and this girl was alone in the house. The said Pandit also remained in the house. Destinies doing, late in the night one of the brothers returned home and saw the Pandit. He beat the Pandit to death. In the morning the other brother returned, and during the succeeding night both the brothers hid the corpse in the field of Shiʿi. Meanwhile police started searching and investigation. Finally, the body was discovered, and an innocent Shiʿi family was arrested. As a result, all the Sunnis and the Pandits turned against the Shiʿi and started harassing them. The Shiʿi's contacted Nawab Fateh ʿAli Qizalbash of Lahore. He sent a barrister from Lahore. All the accused were released, but the police had tortured them so badly that they passed away soon. All the money that had been collected by *Anjuman-i Imāmmia* was spent on the case. As the circumstances were unfavorable the *Anujman* soon stopped functioning.[124]

In the city, the consequence of court cases not only impacted the energy, time, and money spent on the *Anjuman-i Imāmmia* but also upset the delicate balance of quiet in the relation between the two Muslim communities. In the aftermath of the 1872 riot, the peace in the city could be best classified as a managed peace, enforced through the community elders and the *darbār*, in the succeeding years the city had witnessed a genuine coming together in pursuit of common commercial interest. This can be seen in the way Shiʿi *kār-khāna* owners operated with Sunni traders who owned a majority of the showrooms along the riverfront. Similarly, in the court disputes between the *Firqa-i Qadim* and *Firqa-i Jadid* regarding ownership of *Mʿārak*, representatives of the Sunni community also participated as facilitators, including Khwāja Mohyi-al Dīn Gandrū, the Sunni merchant who had been convicted for his role in the riot of 1872.

This gradual shift toward re-establishment of the cosmopolitan character of the city, last witnessed during the heydays of Mughal rule, can also be seen in the program for decoration and illumination of the main Sunni religious site, located in the heart of the city: *Khānaqāh-i Mʿaulā*. The initial *khatamband* work for the building interior had been undertaken under the Afghans- the papier-mâché work on the ceiling of the main shrine chamber took place during the closing years of the nineteenth and first quarter of twentieth century. In the absence of any court patronage, the work was commissioned by the Sunni elders of the city, the merchants and the traders, and the employment of Shiʿi papier-mâché artists on one of the most revered Sunni shrines of Kashmir is indicative of the toning down of sectarian prejudices within the city. This Shiʿi involvement is again reflective of the mediatory presence of the community elders, Shiʿi as well as Sunnis who in all probability oversee this program of artistic exchange, a project which highlights the transformative nature of the sectarian relations within the city during the closing years of the nineteenth century. This engagement of the two sects and the interdenominational dialogue within the Kashmiri Muslim community can also be mapped in other connected spheres of religious life in the city. In the first quarter of the twentieth century, the pioneering, Sunni owned publishing house of Kashmir: Ghūlam Muhammad Nūr Muhammad Tājiran-i Kutb, published a small tract, *Marṣiya Shahadat-i Ḥasanain* focusing on elegies written on the martyrdom of the imāms, Ḥasan and Ḥusayn. In addition to Persian *marṣiya* written by the famous Iranian poet, Muḥtasham- i Kashanī (d. 1578-8), the tract also included bilingual compositions on the subject by contemporary Kashmiri Sunni poets including Khwāja Muhammad Asʿad, Asʿad al-Lah Kalashpurī, Mir Shams -al Dīn Pandanī, and Pīr Qādir Shāh Malaratī. Though reverence for the two imāms can also be seen in earlier Sunni compositions in Kashmir, also mapped in the tract, in the work of Shaykh Yʿaqūb Ṣarfī and Bābā Dāwūd Khākī, the publication assumes a greater significance given the popularity of rituals linked to the martyrdom of the two, especially Imām Ḥusayn in contemporary Shiʿi society. The adoption of the print media, which could be widely circulated, can certainly be seen as an attempt to create and propagate a Sunni cult of the imāms. But in including work of a revered Shiʿi figure such as Muḥtasham, the publishers strove to establish an larger overarching theme of commemoration linked with the memory of Ḥusayn rather than represent competing iconographies. Also, from the eighteenth century we find that some Kashmiri Sunni poets using the format of the Mulla Ḥusayn Wāʿiẓ Kashifi's (d.15044) *Rawḍat al-Shuhadā*ʾ (The Garden of the Martyrs) to compose lengthy elegies in Persian, on the martyrdom and sufferings of Ḥusayn. Another popular Sunni ritual connected to the event of Ḥusayn's martyrdom was preserving a portion of the *qurban* (ritual meat slaughtered on ʿĪd), for consumption on Ashura. While I have not been able to date the origin of this ritual, but the tradition was well established in certain Sunni families of the city (also in rural Kashmir) as we come close to the twentieth century. Parallel to the engagement in the Muharram ceremonies, we find that in *Malud* ceremonies among Kashmiri Sunni community, along with verses of Sunni poets, *naats* of two Shiʿi poets, Ḥājjī Jān Muhammad Qudsī and Sayyid Muhammad Fakhir also formed a part of the performance, a practice which continues in contemporary Kashmir. While this progress toward a sectarian accommodation in the city might seem too slow or minimal, contrast this with the manner in which a Sunni elder of the city, ʿAli Khān was castigated half a century earlier, simply for marrying his daughters into Shiʿi families[125].

The peace in the city following the riots also resulted in a widespread program of mosque construction and repair in Shiʿi moḥala of the cities. Of these, the most significant was the completion of the *Masjid-i Ḥājjī ʿAidī* at Zadibal by Ḥājjī Ṣafdar in a distinct non-Kashmiri architectural style comprising domes and minarets (Figure 5.6). The largest mosque for the Shiʿi community till recent past, this building owed its origin to the patronage of Ṣafdar's father, the Peshawar-based merchant, Ḥājjī ʿAidī who as I have shown earlier was a benefactor of the Kashmiri Shiʿi. Significantly, within the city, the first recorded instance of the ʿĪd congregational prayer is said to have taken place in this mosque which also

Figure 5.6 Masjid-i Ḥājjī ʿAidī at Zadibal (courtesy: Zulfikar Ali).

included a separate *hammam* building and a wide-open forecourt.[126] Some of the other mosques which also included a *hammam*, whose construction can be traced to this period in the city include those at Babapora, Shamswari, and Nawa Kadal as well as some of the mosques in Zadibal area. During the first quarter of twentieth century, Malik Asad-al Lah, a wealthy shawl merchant based in Zadibal was responsible for financing hammams for many mosques in the city. Aside from philanthropic initiatives of wealthy community elders, most of this architectural proclivity was based on community funding, sourced from residents living in a particular area. Even in the case of the imāmbāda at Hasanbad which was constructed by Mīrzā Muhammad ʿAli, the initial construction in 1283 AH/1866 CE was begun by residents of Ashraf Moḥala (Nandpora) under the supervision of a local, Raḥman Ashraf.[127] Parallel to events in the city, the Āgā family of Budgam also oversaw construction of small mosques across the rural landscape of Kashmir.

But sometimes, stray incidents did manage to unravel any progress toward a Muslim ecumenicism, as can be seen in the entry for Muharram, 1317 AH/1899 CE, in Munshi Ḥasan ʿAli's *Tārīkh-i Kashmir*:

> This month the *Ahl-i Sunnat* people gave rise to another rumor, that the Shiʿi have killed a Sunni, as they had done earlier in the year 1305 AH (1887 CE). The foundation (of the rumor) was laid in this manner, that in the locality of Chattergam most of whose inhabitants are Shiʿi, one month back a man was found dead and the Sunnis from the surrounding areas made it known that the Shiʿis must have killed him. And this news, *payy-i ba payyi* (slowly) reached the city, and the general population of the city who have no temperament for (differentiating between) black and white, made this a proof in the lanes and bazars of the city [. . .] they don't have this realization that a religion which holds upholds the killing of a human is a false religion. Anyway, the investigating in the deceased commenced [. . .] It came out in the open that the deceased belonged to Shiʿi religion. Still these people were not ashamed, but the novelty that was introduced was, these people to remove the stain of reproach spread another news that in the city, there was a woman who had appeared in the clothes of a dervish whose name was Mukhta. *Ahl-i Sunnat* see her with great reverence and these days she was not in the city. Alas! Who did Satan inspire and under Satan's influence he said that Mukhta Sahiba has been killed by Shiʿi. Now what was to say, men and women started an uproar, and the affair reached such a turn that Shiʿi were openly cursed and at places they were attacked on road and looted [. . .]. If there was no fear of the *Sarkar-i Angrez* (British Government), these people would have attacked the Shiʿi without constraint. Finally, some respected Shiʿi personalities approached Bakshi Parmanand and he told Mīrzā Mustafa, who was a Sunni elder. And ordered him to make the people stop immediately. Consequently he (Mustafa) threatened people and made the *vaiz's* (preachers) understand, and to preach to the people till the time they, willingly or unwillingly, became silent. After a few days a strange spectacle took place, that *darvish* women arrived in the city, and people became extremely dishonored.[128]

While the failure of the *Anjuman-i Imāmmia* highlights the constraints in which the Shi'i community operated, Moulvi Ḥaidar 'Ali Ansarī made concentrated efforts at forging good terms with the Sunni religious establishment in the city. In an attempt toward mutual acceptability, Ḥaidar 'Ali sought to establish personal relations with two leading representatives of the Sunni community, the family of Qāzī Qawam-al Dīn who officiated as the Head Mufti, and the *Mīrwa'iẕ-i Kalan* family headed by Moulvi Rasūl Shāh.[129] Though Rasūl Shāh would be accused by his opponents for introducing the Wahhabism in the Kashmir, his interactions with the Ḥaidar 'Ali did manage to tone down the anti-Shi'i rhetoric in the city.[130] Simultaneously, interactions between Shi'i-Sunni courtiers and the merchants helped in rebuilding lines of communication between the elders of the community, which had come undone in the aftermath of the riot of 1872. This newfound *bonhomie* between the two communities is also reflected in a tract published by *Anjuman-i Nusrat-al Islam* to mark its annual conference:

> On the occasion of the congregation, at many places in the city, the residents of the city had made arrangements for welcome gateways etcetera, on a scale exceeding last year's preparations. Regarding decoration, what was new this year, which is worth mentioning is that the *Ahl-i Tashī* (Shi'i) also seeing the work as *qaūmī kām* (community work) participated in the event and the residents of Kamangarpora, in which most of the residents are *Ahl-i Tashī* erected a magnificent gateway.

This brief passage in a tract authored by the leading Sunni religious organization in Kashmir reflects a paradigm shift in the way those who spoke for the Kashmiri Sunni community viewed the Shi'i—the transformation of a community that had been considered as an outsider for most of the previous century was now seen as being a part of the same *qaūm*, same community. Unlike earlier references to Shi'i as *rāfizī*, that are to be found in eighteenth and nineteenth-century Sunni-authored texts, we find that in this particular instance, the use of the respectful term *Ahl-i Tashī*, showing a marked degree of accommodation of Shi'i sensibilities.[131]

Meanwhile, the *Firqa-i Jadid* continued its rigid stance on the issue of Western education, forbidding its members to interact with the missionaries. Though by the early twentieth century, the popular support *Firqa-i Jadid* enjoyed among Kashmiri Shi'i outstripped the influence of *Firqa-i Qadim*, under Āgā Sayyid Muhammad the group lost most of its revolutionary enthusiasm that had marked Āgā Sayyid Mahdi's career. During most of the twentieth century, the relations between the two Shi'i groups were marked by extreme rivalries, many a times personal between the two leading ulemas heading the contending factions. After the formation of *Anjuman-i Imāmmia*, Sayyid Muhammad established a rival organization, *Hami-al Islam*,[132] which also started a series of *maktabs* in the Shi'i-dominated area of Kashmir. Yet the focus of these *maktabs* remained limited to religious teaching, and the *firqa* as an institution remained impervious to the political and social challenges taking place in the region. Sayyid Muhammad also undertook the Kashmiri translation of *'Urwa al-Wuthqā*, the book on legal rulings of Grand Ayatollah Sayyid Muhammad Kāẓim Yazdī (d. 1919).[133] Popularly known as *Kāshir Kitāb,* this translation was widely studied in the network of *maktabs* operated by the *Firqa-i Jadid* under Sayyid Muhammad.

Aside from the two rival factions which came increasingly under the control of the clerical families, Ansarīs and the Āgā, we find that in the 1930s the first Shiʿi society without any clerical background, *Shiʿi Upliftment Association* was founded in the city by Shiʿi youth The founding president of the society was a wealthy philanthropist, Mīrzā Muhammad Taqī.[134] Grounded in a reformist agenda, the outlook for modernizing the Shiʿi society was primarily perceived as a goal that could be achieved through widespread acceptance of Western-style education.

The society functioned without any official recognition for some time before being dissolved, whereafter most of the members reorganized themselves in 1932–4 under the banner of *Anjuman-i Bahbūdī Shiyan-i Kashmir.* This nonpolitical organization was registered with the government as a society for social and religious reform and published its objectives, "to awaken the sleeping Shiʿi *qaum* (community)."[135]

Very early on the society was able to successfully petition the government for inclusion of *Nauroz,* as a state holiday.[136] Nevertheless, much of the society's time was spent in trying to get financial support from the government for the destitute, orphans, and widows. Given its success with the *darbār* on these issues, the *Anjuman-i Bahbūdī* expanded into a field which was the privilege of the ulema linked with *Firqa-i Qadim* and *Firqa-i Jadid.*[137] Somewhere in the 1930s, the *Anjuman-i Bahbūdī* decided to organize *nimaz-i juma* (Friday congregation prayer) in the city, after seeking guidance on the issue from Grand Ayatollah Abu'l Ḥasan Isfahanī (d. 1946), Grand Ayatollah Shaykh Muhammad-Ḥusayn Nainī Gharavī (d. 1936), Grand Ayatollah Shirazī,[138] and Allama Sayyid ʿAli Haʿirī (d. 1941), a respected alim of Kashmiri origin based in Lahore.[139] In *Masl'ia Nimaz-i Juma,* a tract published by the *Anjuman-i Bahbūdī,* the performance of the Friday congregation prayer is projected as a collective act which will help the community and the individual in receiving the blessings of Allah.[140] Additionally, in their question to Ayatollah Nainī, the *Anjuman-i Bahbūdī* makes the point that as a minority within Muslim society, Kashmiri Shiʿi are censured by the Sunnis for not offering the *juma*- facing their '*ṭʿan va malāmat*' (taunt and rebuke).[141] In popular Sunni traditions, Muslim men who willfully choose to refrain from offering *nimaz-i juma* for three consecutive Friday, are believed to have relapsed into a state of disbelief.[142] The criticism that the Shiʿi of Kashmir faced is similar to what had happened much earlier in Awadh, where one of the charges for Shiʿi departure from the Muslim body was linked to their non-performance of the *nimaz-i juma.* Where the issue of the *nimaz-i juma* championed by the *Anjuman-i Bahbūdī* was seen as an affirmative act in community participation, the *Masl'ia Nimaz-i Juma* did also seek to challenge the position of the ulema linked with the Ansarī and Āgā family, referring to them as "artificial leaders,"[143] unmindful of the consequences as the Shiʿi society stares into the abyss of oblivion.[144] The reaction as could be expected, given the circumstances, was swift from the two existing groupings. The elders in the *Firqa-i Jadid,* questioned the performance on basis of tradition arguing that "our forefathers did not observe." The response from *Firqa-i Qadim* was more nuanced. Taking a recourse to Shi'i religious writings, they argued that the performance of *nimaz-i juma* was not an obligatory act and as a proof pointed to *Javahir- al Kalām* (*c.* 1846) of the Iranian scholar, Shaykh Muhammad Ḥasan, a popular nineteenth-century work on Shi'i jurisprudence. In seeking a recourse to a theological understanding, the Ansarī ulema were not only defending their opposition to the establishing of the *nimaz-i juma*, but also attempting to open a line of communication with the educated youth running the *Anjuman-i Bahbūdī*. A majority of the members in the *Anjuman-i Bahbūdī* hailed from families who were traditionally supporters of the *Firqa-i Qadim*,[145] members that *Firqa-i Qadim* did not want to alienate any further.

Notwithstanding the pressure exerted by their opponents, the *Anjuman-i Bahbūdī* was able to organize the first *nimaz-i juma*, in the city at Dalgate; the date is not recorded but this must have been around the early 1930s. The congregation was led by Shaykh 'Abdul 'Ali (d. 1953), a respected religious scholar from the famed dynasty of Mullā Muqim. 'Abdul 'Ali had studied under Ayatollah Isfahanī, and in a letter written to his father, Shaykh Muhammad Ḥusayn (d. 1922) the Iraqi *mujtahid* fondly remembers 'Abdul 'Ali.[146] In the dispute between the *Firqa-i Qadim* and *Firqa-i Jadid*, the ulema from Muqim's family had largely remained detached, supporting neither of the competing parties. By the time we come to the close of the nineteenth century, we find that though respected, the family was nevertheless eclipsed even in their hereditary moḥala, Nabdipora, by newcomers: the Rizvī family linked to Ḥājjī Sayyid Ḥasan Rizvī, author of *Majālis-al Abrar*. Significantly, 'Abdul 'Ali's uncle, Shaykh Muhammad Mahdi (d. 1911), himself a reputed scholar trained in the seminaries of Najaf and Karbala, had on his return to Kashmir authored a work, *Khaṣāil-al Shi'i* (*c.* 1328 AH/1910 CE), to defend the Shi'i from "the disregard and ridicule of the local Sunnis who were ignorant and unaware about the Shi'i beliefs."[147] This is a major indicator that the desire, as a minority to make itself understood, was not limited to the youth trained in the system of modern education alone, but also shared by some of the traditional Shi'i scholarly families. One can argue that in the first half of the twentieth century, reform was the *mizaj*—the zeitgeist of Kashmiri society—both among Shi'i and Sunni, in Hindus[148] as well as Muslims.

After the success of the first congregation prayers in the city, the *Anjuman-i Bahbūdī* repeated the *nimaz-i juma* at Chinkral Moḥala, and then at Chattabal, before moving to Zadibal to offer the prayers at *Masjid-i Ḥājjī 'Aidī*. Where the earlier prayers had been held in the heart of the city, in mixed neighborhoods with a significantly larger Sunni population, moving the prayers to Zadibal was seen by the supporters of the two *firqa* as an outrage and assault on their territory. On the appointed Friday, as the worshippers proceeded to the mosque, the congregation faced physical assault, many were injured and in the disturbances the prayers were disrupted. In attacking the congregation, the followers of the two rival *firqa* forgot their mutual animosity, in defending what they believed to be their shared territory. Following the unsavory episode at *Masjid-i Ḥājjī 'Aidī*, Shaykh 'Abdul 'Ali dissociated from the *Anjuman-i Bahbūdī* and remained a recluse for the rest of his life. Somewhere later, the leader of *Firqa-i Jadid* issued a ruling declaring participation in any "*anjuman*" as un-Islamic.[149] Faced with internal dissension, the president of the *Anjuman-i Bahbūdī*, Ḥakim Ghulām Ṣafdar also resigned, and in less than a year the organization ceased to exist. The demise of the *anjuman* highlights how at the start of the twentieth century the two religious families: the Āgā (*Firqa-i Jadid*) and the Ansarī (*Firqa-i Qadim*) had emerged as the main centers of leadership within the Shiʿi society, effectively controlling both the religious and the secular aspects of life. Disillusionment with the two was mostly articulated by the emerging educated youth, who perceived the two *firqa's* as the cause of Shiʿi backwardness and disunity.

Following the disbandment of the *anjuman*, Munshi Muhammad Isḥāq (d. 1969) financed a newspaper, *Zulfikar*, which before its closure by the Dogra *darbār* in 1937 included hard-hitting editorials[150] and articles against what was termed as the self-serving, self-perpetuating, and hereditary mullās. Without naming the Āgā and the Ansarī family, articles in *Zulfikar*, would portray the two as the main reason for the *pastī* (downfall) of the Shiʿi society in Kashmir. The narrative of Shiʿi *pastī* itself was an imported imagination, drawing from the larger narrative of Muslim loss in South Asia following the failure of the Great Rebellion of 1857. As I have shown, the nineteenth century marks a period of incremental gain for Kashmiri Shiʿi, yet these zealous youth perceived only decay and decline. But this emerging intellectual discourse was not only limited to questioning the role of the ulema linked with the two *firqas* as the sole interpreters of religiosity in the Shiʿi society of Kashmir. Aside from the narrative of a divided house and the lack of modern education within the Shiʿi society, these writings are also vociferous in their denunciation of what is presented as un-Islamic and superstitious practices: the *wahm-o tawahhumāt* (false ideas and belief in fantasies). The widespread belief in talismanic and divination practices; in the efficacy of augury (*fāl*), amulets (*tāwīz*), astrology, and geomancy (*ramal*) in the Shiʿi society are marked for special rebuke and censure.[151] Though these practices are based within traditional Islamic knowledge system, the reformers of the twentieth century presented them as systematic of the malaise which affected the body of Kashmiri Shiʿi society, hindering it from "harnessing the full benefits of modernity, and in doing so also reclaiming the image of a pure and reformed Islam."[152] We also see in this modernizing reform-oriented critique, how the legitimacy of these practices is often questioned by not only linking it to the world of fantastical, but also in arguing for an assumed Hindu influence or source of these practices.[153] As the first generation of Kashmiri Shiʿi trained in the colonial system of education, the reform-oriented youth in their critique internalized many of the colonial narratives of the "natives" as backward and superstitious people.

Zulfikar's publisher, Isḥāq, had served as the founding president of *Shiʿi Upliftment Association,* and then as a key organizer of the *Anjuman-i Bahbūdī*, before joining popular politics in the 1930s as an associate of Shaykh Muhammad Abdullah. While, Isḥāq would embody a reformist agenda, seeking remedy to societal issues through a recourse to Islam freed from the hereditary religious classes-the moulvis, Ḥakim Ṣafdar in his *Shiʿi Mūsālmān aūr unkey Jamūd key*

Asbāb;[154] sought for a religious reformation, questioning the basis of such Shiʿi religious practices as *tabara* and *taqiya*, and the purposiveness of engaging in polemical debates surrounding the formative period of Muslim history. For Isḥāq, the desire for change and modernity within the contemporary Kashmiri Shiʿi society meant liberation from the traditional hereditary moulvis, while Ṣafdar's writing articulate for not only change in direction but also reworking of the inherited religious discourse. The reform-driven agenda articulated in the writings of Isḥāq and Ṣafdar would resonate and be elaborated upon in the works of two prolific columnist, Ḥakim Ghulām Ḥusayn Makhmūr (d. 2007) and Engineer Ghulām ʿAli Gulzar. In their writings, Makhmūr and Gulzar would represent a continuing desire to accommodate and assuage Sunni feelings in a desire for broader Muslim unity. Interestingly, neither Isḥāq nor Ṣafdar articulate a similar demand from the Sunnis for accommodating Shiʿi sensibilities. Despite their varying approaches, both reflect a deep impact of the teachings of the South Asian reformer and educationist, Sir Sayyid Aḥmad Khān (d. 1898), his rationalistic interpretation of Islam, as well as a desire to limit the Shiʿi-Sunni differences in the hope of securing a broader Muslim unity or as Ayesha Jalal terms it "Islamic universalism."[155]

Despite their vociferous zealousness, we find that these reforming dissenters failed to make any headway within the Shiʿi society at large, at least in the first half of the twentieth century. The paradigm of a reformed society, free of *tawahhumāt*, failed to appeal to a people for whom these very practices served as essentials of their existence as a pious community. The failure also needs to be seen against the privileged background of the reformers, the benefits of whose message was limited to a well to do sections of the society and continued to ignore the experience and expectations of those marginalized; the women, weavers, artisans, laborers, and peasants as well as the caste-based discriminations of those designated as low caste—*bey khāndani*.[156]

Aside from the reforming agenda of youth educated in western system, we find the continued participation of Kashmiri scholars in the *hazwas* of Iraq; embarking on a long journey to study under leading *mujtahids* of the shrine cities. This was not only limited to clerical families such as the Ansarīs and the Rizvīs of the *Firqa-i Qadim* or the descendants of Mullā Muqims alone, but also included members of the Āgā Sayyid Mahdi's dynasty, the Mūsāvīs, as well as many newcomers. Earlier somewhere around the late nineteenth century, Shaykh ʿAli Asghar (d. 1934), a near contemporary of Moulvi Ḥaidar ʿAli Ansarī completed his seminary training in Iraq, before returning to Kashmir in his old age. Hailing from a poor farmers' family, he was one of the first major nineteenth-century ʿ*alim* not belonging to any traditional scholarly family of Kashmir.[157] Given the fluctuating fortunes of the *hawza* in Iraq during this period, we find repeated instances of at least one mujtahid, Grand Ayatollah Isfahanī,[158] impressing upon his Kashmiri students their duty toward the *hawza*. In two separate letters written to Kashmiri ulema, Shaykh Muhammad Ḥusayn in 1343 AH/1924 CE and to Sayyid ʿAbdul Rasūl Rizvī in 1356 AH/1937 CE, Isfahanī apprises them about the precarious situation of the *hawza*, and the need to collect and transmit due share from the *khums* money to Iraq for the maintenance of this center of Shiʿi learning. The letter to ʿAbdul Rasūl, especially highlights both Isfahanī's concern for the well-being of the *hawza* and the importance of *vakīls*, such as Rasūl working in distant geographies like Kashmir for maintaining not only the scholarly but also a financial link between the *hawza* and Shiʿi communities:

> As of now the defense of *hawza ilmiyah* Najaf is the most pressing concern. Evidently, the preservation of this *hawza* is dependent on its financial aid. Because, if the financial support is stopped, then in these circumstances there is danger of its disintegration. Since last two–three years due to some national laws, the transmission of *shariah raqumat* (*khums* monies) to this place is difficult.
>
> Presently, the arrival of even a single rupee from there (Iran) is impossible [. . .]. Therefore, in any manner possible, through draft or *havala*, try to send the *sharih raqumat* to Najaf.[159]

Memorandum of the Kashmiri Mussalmans *and a Muslim Ashura*

In 1907, a petition from Kashmir arrived at the desk of Lord Minto (1905–10), Viceroy and Governor-General of India, whose office then forwarded it to Sir Louis Dane, the Secretary in the Foreign Department. The petition was signed by a group of twenty-seven individuals, who claimed to be the "*Representatives of Kashmiri Mussalmans.*" The memorandum begins with an acknowledgment of the role that Britain as the paramount power had played for the equitable welfare of the Kashmiri Muslims, recalling the hardships of older days, when:

> Azan (call to prayers) was prohibited; the zamindars of the valley who were unfortunately all Moslems, were treated as laden beasts with human faces; [. . .]. The horrible atrocities [. . .] still within living memory.[160]

The petitioners, without laying any blame on the Maharaja, go on to detail how the *darbār* functions in an anti-Muslim bias, with "Ministers who are all Hindus and are alert to let any opportunity to further the Hindu Cause slip by. As a result of this policy the Moslem interest are not only utterly ignored but their legitimate aspirations are cruelly suppressed."[161] The memorandum lists the discriminations and under-representation faced by the Kashmiri Muslims and suggests measures that the Kashmir *darbār* needs to take to remove this sense of discrimination. Though the memorandum was rejected by the British, it marks the first instance when the elders of Kashmiri Muslim society articulated a demand for their rights as subjects, subjects who they were keen to point out constituted an overwhelming majority, in the words of the petitioners, "95% of the total population [. . .] loyal and law abiding."[162] In the chequered history of Shiʿi-Sunni relations in Kashmir, the memorandum also marks the first instance in the history of modern Kashmir when the elites representing the two communities, signed themselves as comprising a united Muslim community. In addition to leading Sunni figure of the city, Khwāja Mohyi-al Dīn, Khwāja Sana-al Lah Shawl, Khwāja Mukhtar Shāh Ashai, and Sana-la lah Qadrī, the signatories also included two Shiʿi: Āgā Sayyid Ḥusayn Shāh Jalālī and Ḥājjī Jʿafar Khān.

The next engagement of the Kashmiri Muslim society with the British colonial authority came during the summer of 1924, when the news of the Governor-General, Lord Readings' visit to Kashmir spread in Srinagar. Earlier in the July of the same year, an agitation by the Muslim workers in the Silk Factory against their Pandit officers and lack of proper wages had been put down brutally with a bayonet charge, overseen by the heir-apparent, Raja Hari Singh.[163] With tempers rising high, the city presented a somber if not entirely grim spectacle. The brutal suppression of the workers was immediately followed by the arrival of the Shiʿi month of mourning, Muharram and the Ashura procession passing through the heart of the city.

Reminiscing about his college days, Ṣafdar writes about the nature of the Ashura procession in the city, and a singular event related with it which took place during the Muharram of 1923:[164]

> On the night of ninth Muharram (*shab-i Ashura*), a majlis would be held at his (Mīrzā Muhammad ʿAli) house. Around 3 am in the morning the procession of Zuljinnah would commence. It would be accompanied by ten or twelve men, reciting *la ilahailla-llah* (there is no god but Allah) slowly, slowly. A few torches would also accompany the procession for providing the light. In this small procession neither was *marṣiya* recited nor would people beat their chest. On reaching Kamangarpora, the Zuljinnah would be taken to the haveli of late Sayyid Aṣghar Shāh Jalālī, where people would pay their respect. From here the Zuljinnah would proceed to Imāmbāda at Zadibal (*Ma'rak*) where this brief procession would culminate in the darkness of night.

The entire journey from Namchibal to *Ma'rak* spread over a distance of two–three miles would be completed in a few hours of complete darkness. The Ashura of 1923 nevertheless marked a significant departure; two young mourners in the procession, Miyān Ghūlam Muhammad Khān and Yūsuf ʿAli Khān started to beat chest and recite *nūḥa* as soon as the mourners reached the main road. This innovation attracted a large number of mourners, and as more people started assembling, the procession made its way slowly to *Ma'rak*, reaching the end of destination around dusk. This is the first known instance when the Ashura' procession commenced during daytime in Kashmir. Happy with the turn of events, the organizers decided that to follow a similar pattern in the following year by talking out a daytime procession.

Next Muharram, the *darbār* passed an *hukum nama* (order), demanding of the organizer of the procession, Sayyid Ḥusayn Shāh Jalālī should follow established tradition, effectively forbidding a daytime procession. With feelings still running high against them, the *darbār* thought it best to avoid any large-scale gathering of their Muslim subjects during the daytime, hence the enforcement of the ban.

Also, with an impending visit of the Viceroy, it is possible that the Maharaja's government wanted to avoid any possible incident which could lead to further disturbances in the city.

The *darbār*'s order for an early morning procession was defied by the Jalālī who was supported by Khwāja Saʿad-al Din Shawl, one of the leading Sunni of the city. An attempt by the mourners to proceed to the main road was thwarted by the police when Ram Singh the Superintendent of Police confiscated the *tʿazia*(Quran carried in a small casket).[165] The mourners meanwhile refused to back down, and defying the police marched on to the main road with the active backing of the Sunni community. In the absence of the *tʿazia*, the procession was accompanied by two *alams* (religious flags), from the highly revered Sunni shrine of *Asar-i Sharif Shahrī*, Kalashpora.[166] Members of both the communities participated in this unique celebration of Ḥusayn's martyrdom which also became associated with an evolving discourse on the future of Kashmiri community in a post-maharaja, postcolonial world.

Thus, a procession that had started as a manifestation of Shiʿi community's desire for visibility in the public space and demonstrate their identity became associated with narrative of the Muslim identity of Kashmir. Representing a rare case of Shiʿi-Sunni ecumenism in Kashmir, it set the stage for future cooperation between the two communities in their struggle against the Hindu ruler. This integration of the Shiʿi and Sunni community in a quest for freedom would continue to be checked by sectarian tensions, tensions that originated at local level, in the moḥala, along the route of a procession, or in the utterance of an individual. But the political and increasingly the religious leaders of both the communities sought to minimize these irritants, to portray an image of Muslim unity.

Immediately following the Ashura, Khwāja Saʿad-al Dīn Shawl held a meeting of members of the Muslim community at his home. In the meet, it was decided that during Lord Reading's upcoming visit, a memorandum would again be submitted to the Viceroy, highlighting the continued discrimination faced by Kashmiri Muslims. Āgā Sayyid Ḥusayn, the first Muslim matriculate, working as *Wazir-i Wazarat* (administrator) for the district of Anantnag, had come into contact with a Shiʿi barrister from Lucknow, Āgā Ḥaidar, who was on a vacation in the city. With the memory of the rejected memorandum of 1907 fresh in the mind of the assembly, many of whom had signed it, Ḥusayn suggested to Shawl that they should request Āgā Ḥaidar to draft the memorandum. In the meantime, the *darbār* also came to know about the meeting and even raided the houseboat in which Āgā Ḥaidar was residing.[167] The events regarding the actual presentation of the draft are a bit murky, it was either submitted to the viceroy at *Khānaqāh-i Mʿaulā* during his boat procession in the city or when he was shopping along the Bund.[168] The Pandit newspaper, *Bahār-i Kashmir*, published from Lahore with its pronounced anti-Muslim stance describes the event in these words:

> Lord Reading and the rest of the party arrived in Srinagar on 14th October [. . .] After partaking lunch, the entire party embarked on steamboats and left for the Srinagar Residency, where arrangements for the Lord's disembarking had

> been made. [. . .] but when the procession passed near Shāh Hamdan, it [Shāh Hamadan] is the same place where a riot had taken place some days back, on Viceroy Ṣāhab's arrival thousands of Muslim who had assembled their earlier and were waiting for the arrival of Viceroy Ṣāhab, those boards which they had made earlier and on which the letter *zulum-o sitam* (oppression and tyranny), presented them before the Viceroy Ṣāhab.[169]

The memorandum submitted to Lord Reading echoed the earlier petition of 1907, yet the new petition included a longer list of demands worded more forcefully. It sought restoration of seized religious sites and lands, and inquiries into "Muslim grievances regarding the Zuljinnah procession, the incident at *Khanqah-e-Shāh-i-Hamdan* and those relating to Islamabad and Baramula,"[170] under an impartial European officer. The list of demands was no longer limited to a fair representation of Muslims in the administration but demanded an overhaul of the functioning of the government. Without voicing it openly, the text of the demand made it clear that the Muslim draftees of the memorandum saw the Maharaja's rule as a Hindu rule, and only the British paramount power could undo the institutional bias that lay at the heart of the Dogra regime. Crucially, the memorandum made a demand for, "An elected Legislative Assembly which should also work as a Constituent Assembly for the drafting of a Constitution for the State, [. . .] Muslim population must be kept in view while granting representation to the various communities."[171] Rather than seeking an accommodation with his Muslim subjects, the Maharaja sought to punish the principal movers behind the memorandum, Sa'ad-al Dīn Shawl was banished from the state and Ḥusayn Shāh Jalālī dismissed from his post as a *zailadar*. The *jāgīrs* of another prominent signatory to the memorandum, Khwāja Ḥasan Shāh Naqshbandī were confiscated, while his son Khwāja Nūr Shāh Naqshbandī was dismissed from the state services.[172] With the state in a flux, and the resentment against the maharaja growing, Pratap Singh, the longest-serving ruler of the Dogra dynasty, died on December 23, 1925.

Under the guidance of the community elite, the narrative of a discriminated Kashmiri Muslim began to dominate the collective Muslim idea about the rule of the Hindu maharaja. The Muslim identity served as a tool for promoting collective group interests as well as mobilizing an opinion against the Hindu rulers both in Kashmir and outside, especially among Punjabi Muslims. In articulating a Muslim identity, the Kashmiri Muslim community also came into conflict with the Pandit minority, whose domination in the administration was bound to lose in case of a proportional representation, as demanded by Muslim representatives. This fear of the numbers, also weighed heavily in some of the more rancorous articles published in *Gulzar-i Kashmir*, which served as one of the mouthpieces for Kashmiri Pandits.[173]

Following Pratap Singh's death, Sa'ad-al Dīn Shawl was allowed to return to Kashmir in 1926.[174] During his exile in Lahore, Shawl had been able to mobilize additional support for Kashmiri Muslims among the Muslims of Punjab. The All-India Muslim Kashmir Conference, which had been founded earlier in 1911 by Punjabi Muslims had made conscious efforts to highlight the plight of the Kashmiri

Figure 5.7 A meeting of *Anjuman-i Imāmmia* presided by Nawab Fateh ʿAli Khān, Srinagar, 1922 (courtesy: Hakim Shaukat Ali Hamdani).

Muslims. This was reinforced by holding conferences outside Kashmir as well as a visit of members to Srinagar.[175] Meanwhile, building upon the reproachment between the Shiʿi and Sunni, Ḥusayn Shāh Jalālī was able to revive the *Anjuman-i Imāmmia*, and laid the foundation of the first Shiʿi school, *Imāmmia School* at Zadibal in 1910. Under Jalālī, while working toward the upliftment of the Shiʿis, the *Anjuman* would actively support the demands voiced by the Sunnis as representing the collective Muslim body of Kashmir (Figure 5.7). The elite of the two communities, Shiʿi and Sunni, who during the nineteenth century had served as leaders of two competing communities would now work to secure the interest of a unified Muslim society.

In the early 1930s, three brothers from a Shiʿi family, Ḥakim ʿAli (d. 1975), Ḥakim Ghulām Ṣafdar (d. 1974), and Ḥakim Ghulām Murtaza (d. 1957) would constitute a group of educated Muslim youth who began to deliberate upon the state of Kashmiri Muslims and ways of empowering the Muslim community. The initial group was headed by Khwāja Ghulām Aḥmad ʿAshai (d. 1964), who had been prematurely retired by the government in the same year. Focusing on the discrimination faced by Kashmiri Muslims under the government, they started a campaign to publicize these grievances through Lahore-based newspapers. The group would later take the shape of Reading Room, which became actively involved in the political uprising against the Hindu Dogra rule under the leadership of Shaykh Muhammad ʿAbdullah (d. 1982). The Muslim struggle against the Hindu ruler helped create a network of personal relations between the Shiʿi and Sunni community both among the elders of the two groups and the educated youth. A particular case of co-operation between the two communities which helped in bridging the sectarian fault lines was the commemoration of Imām ʿAli's birthday on Rajab 13 as "Ali Day." The first such celebration was held in 1940 at Zadibal and presided over by Justice Sir ʿAbdu'l Qadir of Lahore the founding President of *Anjuman-i Himayat-al Islam*. Held in a Shi'i space of the city in close vicinity of *M'ārak*, the Ali Day became part of an annual celebration in the city's life with active participation of the Sunni elite.

The formulation of a Muslim identity came increasingly in conflict with a similar religious identity-based politics of the Kashmiri Pandit community. On July 13, 1931, a mass killing of twenty-two demonstrators by the Maharaja's troops, catapulted the simmering discontent against the Dogra rule into open rebellion, marking it as the foundational day in the narrative of freedom struggle of the Kashmiri Muslim society. Simultaneously Kashmiris would get drawn into the nationalist debates originating from the Indian mainland. A vast majority of Kashmiri Shi'i would politically and emotionally associate with the politics of Muslim League and the Pakistan movement, many participating in the rigors of freedom struggle and jail life, including the octogenarian, Āgā Sayyid Ḥusayn Shāh Jalālī. In the months leading up to the partition of British India, Pakistan Day would be observed by the Shi'i openly at Zadibal, marking the community's allegiance to the idea of Pakistan.[176] The label of being pro-Pakistani would remain with the Shi'i after Kashmir's accession to India in 1947, an accession which was followed by Abdullah's appointment as the Prime Minister of the state of Jammu and Kashmir.[177] In his autobiography, Isḥāq records the desperate situation faced by the Shi'i of Budgam following the tribal invasion of 1947, including a threat to arrest Āgā Sayyid Yūsuf (d. 1982), the revered religious leader of *Firqa-i Jadid*. Yūsuf who was based in Budgam had maintained an apolitical stand in the lead-up to the partition, but was accused by Shaykh 'Abdullah's supporters of having colluded with the tribal militia who entered Kashmir to secure its accession to Pakistan. A crucial element of Isḥāq's account of the events surrounding 1947 is his description of a massacre of several Kashmiri Muslims, predominantly Shi'i at Yechgam by Indian army,[178] the first recorded case of civilian killing in what would eventually enfold as the "Kashmir dispute."[179]

Kashmiri Shi'i and the Recent Past: Overview

Under the government of Shaykh 'Abdullah (1948–53, 1975–77),[180] not a single Shi'i would be inducted in his ministry and this pattern would continue way up till 1987, when Moulvi Iftikhar Ansarī (d. 2014), a Shi'i mid-level cleric, would be inducted as a cabinet minister under, Abdullah's son and successor, Farooq Abdullah. Meanwhile, in 1979, the Islamic Revolution in Iran would capture the imagination of many in the Kashmiri Shi'i society. Ayatollah Khomeni's Kashmiri roots would remain a source of pride for the community, a majority of whom completely aligned with the aspirations of the distant Islamic Republic. Visits to Kashmir of high-profile functionaries in the newly established Islamic Republic, including, Ayatollah Sayyid Ali Khamenei, Ayatollah Mehdavi Kani and Ayatollah Ali Gulzadeh Gafuri in the years following the revolution, also helped in popularizing the idea of religio-political authority of Khomeni among the Kashmiri Shi'i. To a large extent, this resulted in gradual displacement of Najaf based scholars who had traditionally served as the source of religious emulation for the Shiʿi of Kashmir. The Iran-Iraq war, the Baathist targeting of the *Ḥawzah* in Najaf, also resulted in a rupture in scholarly links connecting Kashmiri scholars to seminaries in Iraq, consequently we find a gradual movement away from Najaf toward Qum in Iran. The execution of a young Kashmiri seminarian in Najaf, Shaykh Nisar Ḥusayn (d. 1986)[181] by the regime of Saddam Ḥusayn, also brought to fore the risks of proceeding with religious studies in the Najaf *Ḥawzah*. While expanding their presence in Kashmir within the Shiʿi society, the Iranian establishment sought to promote an image of Shiʿi-Sunni unity, and during his visit to Srinagar, Khamenei would offer prayer in the main Jamia Masjid to showcase this spirit. Popular slogans, originating from Kashmiri Shiʿi sections such as, "news from Iran has arrived, Shiʿi-Sunni are brothers alike" sought to promote this spirit of Muslim ecumenicalism, while also linking it to the revolutionary regime in Tehran. The response from the Kashmiri Sunni religious leadership and elite to this development, and the Iranian regime at large, would be ambivalent at best. While some would welcome it, some choose to see the Iranian revolution as a sectarian threat to the Sunnis as a confessional community; and a challenge to their religious beliefs.[182]

Simultaneously, the execution in Pakistan of Zulfikar Ali Bhutto (d. 1979), the charismatic premier who was deposed by the Army Chief, General Zia-ul Haq (d. 1988) in a military *coup d'etat* marked a watershed movement in how Kashmiri Shiʿi viewed Pakistan. Many in the Kashmiri Shiʿi community thought of Bhutto as a Shiʿi—a belief that continues to resonate among sections of Kashmiri Muslim society even today, Shiʿi and Sunni alike. The Islamization campaign in Pakistan launched by Zia-ul Haq, and what was perceived as institutionally supported sectarian strife would contribute to a gradual disillusionment among the Kashmiri Shiʿi, from events and happening in that country.[183]

In 1983, the maverick Shiʿi leader, Moulvi Iftikhar Ansarī[184] contested and won an assembly election outside Srinagar, against a candidate from National Conference, the party founded by Shaykh Muhammad ʿAbdullah. While Ansarī's win was conditioned by a degree of Sunni support, nevertheless his victory was perceived as that of a Shiʿi religious leader against a Sunni candidate from the Sunni party. Shiʿi celebration in the city, after the delayed results were finally declared added to the sense of Sunni unease over what was in the end an inconsequential electoral victory.[185] This, in turn, resulted in the first major Shiʿi-Sunni riot of the twentieth century. Besides Zadibal, Shiʿi populated *moḥala* in mixed neighborhood of the old city were targeted by mobs, mostly workers and supporters of the National Conference. The riots occurred at a time, when the process of migration from the dense and congested neighborhoods of the old city had started. For Shiʿi living in these old neighborhoods, aside from the challenges of living in a decaying urban landscape of the downtown, the disturbances added another reason for leaving: insecurity.

Consequent to the riots, we find that Shiʿi living in the mixed moḥalas of Kamangarpora, Namchibal, Babapora, Fateh Kadal, Nawa Kadal, Nawpora, and Daulatabad in the old city relocated to areas with substantial Shiʿi population, such as Zadibal, Baghwanpora, Shalimar, or Bemina. Over the decades this resulted not only in thinning out Shiʿi presence in the historic city, but also in setting up of Shiʿi enclaves, spatially and socially disconnected from a wider, predominantly Sunni morphology of the city. Further exacerbating this broadening sectarianism of the physical landscape is the gradual ideological shift within the native Ḥanafī community toward a more sectarian brand of Sunni Islam; the *Ahl-i Ḥadīth*[186] and the *Salafī*. To a large extent, this trend is continuing and gets replicated in towns and villages outside of Srinagar. It was in the 1970s that a Sunni preacher based in the city and linked with the *Ahl-i Ḥadīth,* Moulvi Ghulam Nabi Mubarki (d. 1978) or as he was popularly known based on his oratorical skills, *Nʿabih Kumir*,[187] publicly denounced the Shiʿi mourning ceremonies and the Ashura procession. Within the city, Mubarki was responsible for popularizing an urban legend,[188] which warned the believing Sunni about the dangers of witnessing the Ashura procession, an act which Mubarki preached would invalidate the marriage contract of the observer.[189] While countless Sunnis would ignore his rhetoric, a limited few even participating in the procession, given the implication, Nabi's denunciations did manage to influence many in the Sunni society. In my interview with Ḥakim Imtiyaz, who has documented the Shiʿi sociopolitical history of modern Kashmir, he dwelled upon how some Sunni families with houses on the procession route would close their windows during the passage of the mourners.[190] Yet, he and many others in the Shiʿi community narrate countless anecdotes of not only Sunnis but also Kashmiri Pandits, honoring the procession with *niyāz* (offerings) to mark the fulfillment of a vow.[191]

While Mubarki's sermons did manage a degree of alienation among the Sunnis from the Ashura ritual and generate sectarian disquiet in the city especially among the mourning Shiʿi, this tribulation in the city's urban and religious life had a short trajectory. In the end, Mubarki's rhetoric was limited to the period of mourning season of Muharram,[192] and marked a brief interlude in his primary and sustained polemical discourse against his fellow Sunnis, the Ḥanafīs. The immediate cause for Mubarki's public outcry was the rising popularity of the Ashura procession among the Sunni youth, who would come onto the streets to witness this ritual passage through the heart of the city.[193] Though the interactions between the Shiʿi performance and the Sunni observers, took place mostly along the edges of the procession, such public spectacles in the city did help in familiarizing the Sunni audience with a Shiʿi ritual, in turn leading to acceptance of such practices and eventually more tolerance.[194] In condemning the Muharram mourning ceremonies, Mubarki was echoing the archetypal *Ahl-i Ḥadīth* narrative that sought to proscribe rituals and practices rooted in popular culture as representing *bʿidah* (innovation) and *shirk* (polytheism). Additionally, in targeting the Ashura, Mubarki sought to represent himself as the lone speaker for the Sunni collective willing to take upon the deviant nature of the Shiʿi performances. While censure of the Shiʿi as a sect, or of the Shiʿi practices, was also prevalent among the Ḥanafī religious classes, this critique had not manifested itself in the public spaces. Mubarki's rhetoric was the first public break from the tradition of Muslim ecumenicalism that had marked Shiʿi-Sunni relations in the twentieth century. His play on the acceptability of Shiʿi practices and performances can also be read as a propaganda tool to attract Sunni audiences to the *Ahl-i Ḥadīth* cause, in a city which was (and possibly remains) predominantly Ḥanafī.

Outside Srinagar, within the Shiʿi settlements, the period leading from the 1970s into the 1980s marked a flourishing of the Muharram ceremonies and processions. Within the city, the two Shiʿi factions, organized separate Ashura processions, one on the old route from Namchibal to *Mʿārak* organized by *Firqa-i Qadim* and a rival one proceeding from *Rūżā-i Mīr Shams-al Dīn ʿIraki to Imāmbāda Hasanabad* under the patronage of *Firqa-i Jadid*. The two processions were coordinated in a manner to avoid an overlap along the procession route, but many mourners would participate in both the processions. In 1978, due to political pressure from the chief minister of the state, Shaykh Muhammad ʿAbdullah, the two groups finally agreed to participate in a single Ashura procession commencing from Abi Guzar, with the responsibility of managing the event undertaken by the factions on a rotational basis. An earlier attempt, to organize a united, single Ashura procession in the 1950s by Munshi Muhammad Isḥāq under the banner of *Shiʿi Federation* had come unstuck with the removal of ʿAbdullah as Prime Minister of the state in 1953.[195] Till 1989, when the procession was banned by the state government, the Ashura march from Abi Guzar in the commercial heart of the city, to Zadibal in the cities Shiʿi dominated suburbs, covering a distance of five miles, spread over an entire day, would mark the most elaborate and imposing liturgical event in the city life.

Across Kashmir itself, following Zia-ul Haq's death in 1988,[196] popular protests, followed by an armed rebellion against the Indian state backed by Pakistan, increasingly took a communal coloring. The large-scale migration of Pandits from Kashmir made the rebellion a Muslim alone affair, in which the military and administrative power of Hindu majority Indian state was arranged against the sole Muslim-dominated region of India. The quest for '*Āzadī*' (freedom) from India remained the hope for a majority of Kashmiri Muslims, Shiʿi and Sunni alike. While the overwhelming participants in the armed rebellion were and remain Sunnis, some Shiʿis also took up arms against the Indian state.[197]

The fall of Saddam Hussain, and the sectarian killings in Iraq along with the desecration of a revered Shiʿi shrine at Samarra, rekindled sectarian disquiet in Kashmir, which had largely been overshadowed by political turmoil related to Kashmir's own insurgency. The rise of the Islamic State in Iraq was initially welcomed by some in the Kashmiri Sunni community, who saw it as the face of a Sunni resurgence in post-Saddam Iraq. The failure of the Arab Spring, events in Syria, the role of Iran, and the armed opposition, further split the opinion among Kashmiri Muslims on the sectarian ground. For a significant majority of Kashmiri Shiʿi, supporting Iran and the religious leadership in Iran is often conflated with a correctness of religious belief. It can be argued that in the 1980s following the Iranian revolution, and more specifically following the Ḥājj incident in 1987 resulting in the death of many Iranian pilgrims, Saudi Arabia did enjoy a similar paradigm of loyalty among Kashmiri Sunnis. This support has gradually dissipated to small core group of idealogues among the *Deobandī*,[198] *Ahl-i Ḥadīth*, and *Salafī's*.

The fluid nature of public opinion within the Kashmiri Sunni society on the political confabulations across the Muslim nations; the emerging disillusionment with not only the Saudi state but also the religious establishment, contrasts with the near universal and uncritical identification of the Kashmiri Shiʿi with the Iranian establishment and the office of the *Rehbar* (Supreme Leader). Within the Kashmiri Sunni society this at times generates a charge of sectarian politics against the Shiʿi.

Nevertheless, in the public spaces tensions due to these transnational events feature mostly on social media debates and conversations that have so far not resulted in an event of physical violence. Despite the ever-increasing number of these conflicts that are widespread across the sectarian fault-line in the Islamic world, the particulars of political uncertainty facing Kashmiri Muslims, the aspirations of freedom from India, and the ensuing struggle against the Indian state continue to define the Sunni-Shiʿi relation in the region. Though a section of the Shiʿi society remains apprehensive of a possible future outside the Indian state, an overwhelming majority of the Kashmiri Shiʿi still ascribe to the narrative of "*Āzadī*." The dismemberment of the state of Jammu and Kashmir in August 2019 and the withdrawal of the special constitutional status that had at least in theory governed Kashmir's relation with the Delhi, by the right-wing Bharatiya Janta Party (BJP) government is an undeniable inflection point in Kashmir's politics.[199] Many among the Kashmiri Muslim society, Shiʿi and Sunni alike, perceive this change as a threat to their Muslim existence.

As an argument, even in these changing and testing times, the case for boundaries defining Shiʿi-ness or Sunni-ness in contemporary Kashmir does exist- boundaries that have shown a marked resilience in their continued presence. Yet, these boundaries are not exclusionary to the extent they were at the start of the nineteenth century. The process of sectarian coexistence, an inspiration for Kashmiri Muslim collective identity that was first proposed in the early twentieth century holds true even today, after the passing away of a tumultuous century. Seemingly, despite the frayed edges, the core of this Muslim ecumenicalism in Kashmir holds. The Muslim society of Kashmir does exhibit and operate at multiple levels of societal exchanges, making these boundaries permissive to both change and newer meanings and interpretations. Each and every individual interaction is adding and changing the nature of what being a Shiʿi or Sunni means. Do then, our inherited identities still characterize how we identify as individuals, as people? The answers may be too varied and diverse to reach a conclusion. But, if events in India and across the world are an indicator, it seems so. How the future may translate, is, and remains an open question. In a world of increasing polarization and politicised identities, can we in Kashmir, foreground our future on the footsteps of this initial narrative of coexistence. May we as people be able to build upon it and cross the other divides in our societies, is a hope for Kashmir as for the rest of South Asia.

APPENDIX I

LETTER OF ḤAKIM ʿAẒIM, WRITTEN TO MOULVI SAYYID RAJAB ʿALI SHĀH

(Translation: Stephan Popp)

To the Greatly generous, Abundant in blessing Honourable servants[1] of His Prosperous, entirely splendid Excellency, the illustrious Jenab Maulvi Ṣāhab, the father of virtues, of enduring rankings, the barrier to incidents, Naṣr ud-dunyā vad-dīn, the morning of the weak and oppressed, our greatest master (*maulānā*) and generous refuge, may his (lit. *Their*) honour be increased!

After explaining the wish to achieve the joy of being close to (you) the shop brimming with grace, I notify you that the rays of the Glosses to Elegant Wishes (*taʿlīqa bi-munya*) and the lightning of the exalted letters in which the sun rises shone in the corners of the dark realm of the habitually foul heart. Its bright sun-blazing splendor has made the nest of the sad mind, which had become a den for the bats of sorrow, the horizon where the lights of joy rise. The advice and counsel that you have demonstrated in Indian language from the words of thanks and patience of those dependent on the times and preferences about being silent about outright praise and slander of oneself and the others have planted advice in the soil of the earth behind the Nawab and beyond merit of the fine cracks of the government.[2]

A half-verse came to my mind,[3] which has sweetened the sweet brain of That pen gourmet very much: "The bitterness of envy has not made the pen desirous of sugarcane." Silence has a delight that does not come up in talk.

Earlier, for this pen-tongued (person) could not control the two languages. He brought part of the miracle of the time to the exhibition of speech, but it has become stammering now by the advisable hint of the cupbearer (= the pir). He has recorded all of it, which had been before a joke before (*perhaps: most [beshtar] of which had been a joke before [peshtar]*), in the volume of silence according to the righteous guidance enveloped in the pages of forgetting, turned the reins of (his) determination quickly toward writing a complaint, and hurried on the way to the aim of displaying it.

You gave the illustrious book "The Uncovering of the Veil" to each one of the friends in India by excessive generosity and munificence, and one copy of it to this abecedarian in the school of ignorance, in utmost kindness and goodness. Therefore your gift, like a spring cloud, is universal like a skilled secret carrier whom they have sent to approve their mistress.

To the aims of some faulty, defiant people, I have stayed sometime in the pericardium of concealment, divided that bride into seven each, and hid the visible face in the veil of seclusion from the high-rising slander of the rivals from the relatives of corruption for some weeks. When it had not come on the bridal thrones of high and low for several times, I gave it a shining appearance like a ray. Its publishing came out like that one famous in the horizons, and its perfection seemed utterly impossible. So after a long while, it reached me with the knowledge of Muhammad Hasan Turk. From the testimony of the issues of expression and the flashes of meanings, the outward eyes of the far-sighted became blind, and the eyes of the black-bodied behaving like bats became dark.[4] During the investigation, a half-verse indicating the date of completion came to my mind, with some rhyming phrases that contain the conclusion, which I have named "The anklets of the charming brides of thought." I have written a supplement to the above-mentioned book and summed them up, so that their crowns do not make those delicate (brides) born from (my) personality heavy and slow.

Some judicious people have suggested that these sentences needed to be put in the corrective view of the scholars of the time. Although I have said that this means harvesting fruit from the forefathers who offer a potshard in the opinion (that it is) a jewel for the gemmologist, my friends have not accepted my word for their babies (?) and have answered: Has this shining jewel not been an eardrop for the ear of your reason (= *have you not understood*), which they have said and truly pierced a pearl (*Arabic*):

Sending the slanderer (*nammāl*)/the ants (*nimāl*) is perfect friendship; by [. . .][5] half the men are locusts. Which means, my effort continues to the utmost; the gifts correspond to him who gives.

I had requested a proof for this word because I offer(ed) my service in the same days. A respectable man whom I trusted did not meet (him), and my heart did not give in to the messengers of the traders. Having sent that for such a long time at an adverse fate, I necessarily intended to bring out the shining pearls of its sad contents, which I had spun together in new ways, and arrange it on the lines of a Kashmiri marthiya, so that your Lordship's beautiful (?) grace receives a jewel tear, the price of which gives plenty of recompense to each of those who ask for help. With this precious pearl in the crown, (your) glorious crest will be remembered in the plain of the Last Judgment. But they have given priority to a group (that is) all faults (*baġy*), the disciples of Sayyid Ibrahim, who hides in confusion about religion, over all adversaries. They have taken the ball of precedence from Āzar the Idol-maker. They have made the market of remembering His Excellence the Lord of Martyrs, may he be lauded and praised, a dead market for *marṣiyas*, and spoiled the belief of the people by listening to one marthiya after the other, so that mentioning it again would be excessive for the discerning mind.

In short, the marthiya of that group, which consists of most writers, have all the words of the *marṣiya* as a wish (*munya*) in the ear, and they try to dishonor and reproach those who commemorate. But they know that their sad predominance deserves an enormous price for their above-mentioned piety. In the era of *Sardār* ʿAbdullah Khān Afghan, who had sparked a fire in Zadibal from utmost hatred, fanatism, and enmity for keeping up the anger, which ruined the believers daily in the publication from the mourning rites. They altered them every night clandestinely. And more so in the era of ʿAbdullah Khān Afghan, in which ʿAbdullah's mouth said more and more that in his days the remembrance of the Lord of Martyrs, peace be upon him, and the faith of the mourners, should be canceled from the minds. Strangers prohibited crying when remembering Husain PBUH. It has gone so far now that we have to cry very much.

May God the Exalted, the lord of power and wealth, and the friend of success and bravery, inspire you[6] that you become a champion in this important affair in the region of Kashmir! More than this would be outside of good manners, which forbid verboseness. Best wishes, the pauper (*fuqarā*).

APPENDIX II

GROANS OF THE MUSLIMS OF KASHMIR

Petition To His Highness the Maharaja Saheb Bhadur- in- Council, Srinagar

May it please Your Highness,

The humble petition of the Muslims of all the sects of Kashmir respectfully showeth:-

That the Muharram procession all over the World starts early morning and ends by after-noon according to the timing of the original event. Unfortunately, an ex-parte despotic order based on false report, was issued last year requiring the Shias to perform this ceremony by night on the plea that lest the Sunnis be offended. The falsity of the plea is evident from the fact that the Sunnis & the Shias have been jointly performing this ceremony by day time several years since. Last year being forced on this very occasion no ceremony could be discharged, but at the same time we were told that permission would be given next year on the receipt of representation. The representation was duly submitted to Your Highness through proper channel; which has not so far been favoured with any reply. Some days before the last ceremony the Sunni raises, on being summoned before the Superintendent Police, told him plainly that there was no objection from the Sunnis. When preparations were being made for the procession, the Supdt. Police arrived 2 A.M. on the spot, where from the procession starts, attended with 20 Sorwars, armed with swords, & 60 constables armed with bludgeons, prepared especially to terrorise and keep us back from discharging religious obligations. He ordered those who were near the Zuljanah (Imam Hosains' Horse) to start at 3.30 A.M which was agreed to be carried out; but then raised another obstruction by demanding those present to furnish security, binding to run Zuljanah so fast as to reach Imambara before sun-rise. There were about a Lac of people, the Muslims of all sects, gathered together to perform the sacred ceremony. On being told that carrying out the order of reaching the Imambara before sun-rise with so large a crowd was impracticable, The Supt. Police, under instructions from the District Magistrate (both unsympathetic,) restored to tyrany [*sic*]so far unheard of and unknown, that the Zuljanah with all decorations was taken away in sheer contempt to the Thana & thens to the Hindu Supdt's house; and so defiling the Zuljanah & all his accessories. After the time of ceremony was over, i.e. by about 1P.M., the horse was returned to the Muawalli [*sic*] without any decorations. This outrage was more than enough to create an uncontrollable situation all over the city; had not religious feelings intervened and dictate to the congregation to proceed on with the procession carrying a Holy Quran and leaving the Zuljanah, the Supdt. Police ran away leaving the procession, consisting of all sects of the Muslim numbering about a Lakh, to itself proceed on its way unguarded; and yet the procession reached its destination (Imambara Zadibal) and thens to Alam Saheb's Ziarat peacefully and tranquilly. This fact alone falsifies the assumption that the Muslim sects were not united in desire of performing the ceremony during the day time. In short the joint complaints of the Shias & the Sunnis are:-

(1) That the Sunnis are unjustly stigmatized of being hostile to the ceremony, while they have been performing it jointly with the Shias in Srinagar years since and while their brotheren [*sic*] all over India do perform it yearly with no less zeal than Shias.
(2) That security was demanded for performance of a purely religious, mourning ceremony, while every facility is always afforded with open hearts to other communities viz Aryas, Sikhs, Sanatanists & Pundits etc.; and in some cases State assistance in the shape of sites, furniture and guards, is also given to them in spite of the fact that their processions are usually political and joyously boistrous [*sic*].
(3) The Zuljanah was grossly insulted as stated above a contempt to our religious, sacred symbols, which can be better be imagined than described. The shocking tyranny and sacrilege were committed while even the intolerable had not been infringed in any way. The Zuljanah on account of veneration is kept aloof from being used for full 40 days after the ceremony; and what a heart rending disgrace it was that the same Zuljanah, with decorations was driven forcibly away and locked contemptuously by non-Muslims.
(4) That the decorations, as reported by the Mutawali are still missing, which proved beyond doubt that the Zuljanah was disrespectfully handled without the least regard to our religious susceptibilities.
(5) That our religious liberty has been not only singularly interfered high-handedly, but grossly outraged.

The united appeal of the whole Muslim community with bleeding hearts is that a special committee, properly constituted be appointed to investigate into this unprecedented case, or as an alternative we may be allowed to institute formal judicial proceedings against the officers concerned.

In conclusion we beg to submit that we have numerous other serious grievances to ventilate, which will form the subject of a subsequent petition.

Dated Srinagar
the 18th September, 1924.
We beg to remain
Your Highness' most obedient subjects,

Muslims
Through the President & Raises,
Signatories:
Mirwaiz Moulvi Ahmadullah Hamdani, President Anjuman i Khankah Mualla, Srinagar (Kashmir).
Khawja Hassan Shah Nakashbandi, Raise & Jāgīrdār, Srinagar.
Moulvi Sharifud Din, Mufti Azam Kashmir, Srinagar.
Sheikh Mohammad Ishaq, Vice-President Anjumani Hamdard Kashmir, Srinagar.
Moulvi Mohammad Jawad, Shia Mufti, Srinagar.
Mir Syed Hosain Jalali, President Anjuman i Imamia Kashmir, Srinagar.
Aga Abdullah, Merchant, Srinagar
Syed Said Shah Jalali, Vice President Anjuman i Imamia Kashmir, Srinagar.
Khawja Sadudin Shawl, Raise, Srinagar.
Khawja Ghulam Mahyudin, Raise, Srinagar.
Mir Maqbool Shah Saheb, Sajada Nisheen Ziyarati Dastgir Saheb, Srinagar.

NOTES

Introduction

1 The spindle is an important part of the *yandir* (spinning wheel), used in spinning of pashmina, the fine wollen fabric used to make the much-famed Kashmiri shawls. Given the large-scale prevalence of shawl weaving in Kashmiri society, it was an essential household item in a majority of Kashmiri homes during the nineteenth century.

2 G. T. Vigne, *Travels in Kashmir, Ladak, Iskardo, the Countries Adjoining the Mountain-Course of the Indus, and the Himalaya, North of the Panjab*, vol. i (London: H. Colburn, 1842), 84.

3 Also referred to as *Tārīkh-i Kashmir ʿAẕamī*, see Khwāja ʿAẕam Dedhmarī, *Tārīkh -i Kashmir/Vāqiʿāt-i Kashmīr* (Srinagar: Research Library, MS. 1836). For an Urdu translation of the original Persian work, see Khwāja ʿAẕam Dedhmarī, transl. (urdu) Z. S. Azhar, *Vāqiʿāt-i Kashmīr* (Srinagar: Gulshan Publishers, 2003).

4 As an established Sufi order operating from a *khānaqāh*, *Naqshbandīs* were late entrants to the religious landscape of Kashmir and the *Kubrawī* and the *Suhrawardī* had provided religious leadership among the Sunni society since the late fourteenth century. For a general study, see Dedhmarī, *Vāqiʿāt-i Kashmīr*.

5 ʿAẕam said of his year of passing.
The light of faith upon Sāṭiḥ's grave.

6 Kalhānā transl. M. A. Stein, *Rajatarangini* (Srinagar: Gulshan Books, 2007), 353, 357.

7 See Abū'l Rahim al Beruni, transl. W. C. Sachan, *Alberuni's India*, vol. ii (Delhi: S. Chand & Co., 1964), 206.

8 Muhammad ibn Yʿaqūb al-Kulaynī, transl. Sayyid Ḥasan, *Usūl-i Kāfī* (Lucknow: Nizami Press Book Depot, 2001), 141–74.a.

9 See Suhanna Shafiq, *The Maritime Culture in Kitāb Ajaib al Hind (the Book of the Marvels of India) by Buzurg Ibn Shahriyar* (unpublished M.Phil thesis, 2011), University of Exeter.

10 Ibid., 69.

11 Finbarr Barry Flood, *Objects of Translation: Material Culture and Medieval "Hindu-Muslim" Encounter* (Princeton: Princeton University Press, 2018), 65–9.

12 Similarly Aslam uses *Ahl-i Tashayyuʿ* for the Shiʿi community, see, Abu'l Qāsim Muhammad Aslam, *Gowhar-i ʿĀlam* (Bodleian Library, Oxford University MS. S. Digby Or. 133).

13 Ibid., ff. 176.

14 In his mention of Aslam, the twentieth century historian, Sufi, mistakenly refers to him as the son of Khwāja Muhammad Aʿẕam Dīdahmarī, see, G. M. D. Sufi, *Kashir*, vol. i (Lahore: University of Punjab, 1949), xii.

15 This could be seen as popular reinterpretation of Shiʿi worldview, in which "the Shīʿites are 'brothers', the other Muslims merely 'people' (nās)." Josef van Ess, transl. John O' Kane, *Theology and Society in the Second and Third Centuries of the Hijra*, vol. i (Leiden: Brill, 2017), 319.

16 For a critique of what is understood by sectarianism in the Muslim world and a reading of the different layers and meanings it has assumed in contemporary writings

on Muslim world, see Fanar Haddad, *Understanding "Sectarianism": Sunni-Shi'a Relations in the Modern Arab World* (London: C. Hurst & Co Publishers Ltd, 2019).

We find the use of *'Ahl al-Ahwā'* by early Sunni theologians for those "followers of Islām, whose religious tenets in certain details deviate from the general ordinances of the Sunnite confession," which is often translated into sectarian, though Goldziher argues against it. See I. Goldziher, "Ahl al-Ahwā'," in *Encyclopaedia of Islam, Second Edition*, edited by P. Bearman, Th Bianquis, C. E. Bosworth, E. van Donzel, W. P. Heinrichs, last visited online on April 7, 2022, http://dx.doi.org/10.1163/1573-3912_islam_SIM_0377. The term *'Ahl al Firaq'* traditionally and more commonly used for a sect also forms part of the title of two works on sects and schisms in Islam, that of the Sunni scholar Abū Manṣūr al Baghdadī (d. 1037 CE) and the Shiʿi, Abū Muhammad al-Nawbakhtī (d. 912–22 approx.).

17 For an overview of the operation of orthodoxy and heresy in turn leading to formations of sects, see John B. Henderson, *The Construction of Orthodoxy and Heresy: Neo-Confucian, Islamic, Jewish, and Early Christian Pattern* (Albany: State University of New York, Press, 1998).

18 Writing in the seventeenth century, the fourth Mughal emperor, Jahangir (r. 1569–1627) in his autobiography speaks about the existence of two distinct Shiʿi communities in Kashmir:

The military are Imami Shiites, and some belong to the Nurbakhsh sect.

Wheeler M. Thackston (transl. and ed.), *The Jahangirnama: Memoirs of Jahangir, Emperor of India* (Oxford: Oxford University Press, 1999), 334.

19 See Charles Ellison Bates, *Gazetteer of Kashmir and the Adjacent Districts* (Calcutta: Office of the Superintendent of Government Printing, 1873), 30.

20 See Chitralekha Zutshi, *Languages of Belonging: Islam, Regional Identity, and the Making of Kashmir* (Delhi: Permanent Black, 2004), and Mridu Rai, *Hindu Rulers, Muslim Subjects, Islam, Rights and the History of Kashmir* (Princeton: Princeton University Press, 2004).

21 Simon Wolfgang Fuchs, *In a Pure Muslim Land, Shiʿism Between Pakistan and the Middle East* (Chapel Hill, NC: The University of North Carolina Press, 2019), 1. In addition to Fuchs, Juan Coles's book looks into the role of Shiʿism in the formation of Awadh state, while Andreas Rieck's study provides a much-needed insight on the Shiʿi of Pakistan and sectarianism. For details, see J. R. I. Cole, *Roots of North Indian Shi'ism in Iran and Iraq, Religion and State in Awadh, 1722-1859* (Berkley: University of California Press, 1989) and Andreas Rieck, *The Shias of Pakistan, An Assertive and Beleaguered Minority* (Oxford: Oxford University Press, 2015).

22 In two letters written in 1969 to a senior Kashmiri cleric, Āgā Sayyid Yūsuf al Mūsāvī, Khomeini writes about his family link to Kashmir. For a reproduction of the letter and a generic discussion on Khomeini's Kashmiri roots, see Justice Hakim Imtiyaz Hussain, *The Shiʿas of Jammu & Kashmir: An Analytical Study of the Shiʿa Community in the State of Jammu & Kashmir from 1324 to 1947 AD*, vol. i (Srinagar: Srinagar Publishing House, 2017), 603–5.

Chapter 1

1 Born in 1882, Ṣughrā Mīrzā was an advocate of Hindu-Muslim unity, a poet whose writing are replete with concerns for women upliftment, as well as a philanthropist. See K. Lalita and Susie J. Tharu (ed.), *Women Writing in India: 600 BC to the Early*

Twentieth Century (New York: Feminist Press), also Sajjad Shahid, "Strange Turns in the Fight for Equality," *The Times of India*, March 16, 2014.

2 The travel to Kashmir was advised by Col. Anderson, the surgeon at British Residency in Hyderabad, and in their journey the Mīrzās were also joined by Lt Ḥaidar Mīrzā, Ṣughrā's younger brother, see Ṣughrā Hemayun Mīrzā, *Rahbar-i Kashmir* (Hyderabad: Azam State Press, 1930), 17.

3 From the first quarter of the nineteenth century till the early part of the twentieth century, more than fifty travelogues were composed by European visitors to Kashmir.

4 At one place Ṣughrā, after visiting a *kārkhāna* (workshop), refers to the artisans working there with a certain sense of pride as "our *desī* (native) artisans." Mīrzā, *Rahbar-i Kashmir*, 40.

5 Hājjī Jaʿfar Khān was a prominent Afghan trader, who arrived and settled down in Srinagar, somewhere in the late nineteenth century. His daughter was married to Sayyid Ḥusayn's eldest son, Sayyid Mustafa. For details, see Justice Hakim Imtiyaz Hussain, *The Shi'as of Jammu & Kashmir (1324-1947)*, 2 vols.

6 Mīrzā, *Rahbar-i Kashmir*, 78–9.

7 Similarly, Mīrzā records in some details about the *urs* of the Sunni saint Sayyid Qamr-al Dīn held at Ganderbal, especially the riverine procession leading from Srinagar to the shrine of Qamar-al Dīn, ibid., 73–5.

8 The main *khānaqāh* in Kashmir, *Khānaqāh-i Mʿaulā* at Srinagar which was reconstructed in 1733, had a basic plan measuring 22 m x 22 m.

9 The etymological origin of *Mʿārak* is derived from the Arabic word *Mʿārikā* (battleground). The event of Karbala that is commemorated by Shiʿi Muslims is also sometimes referred to as *mʿārikā-i Karbala* (The Battle of Karbala). The Mughal historian Badayunī in his history refers to mourning assemblies that were held in Delhi to commemorate the martyrdom of Imām Husayn, which were known as *Mʿārikā*. See Hakim Sameer Hamdani, "The Maarak and the Tradition of Imambadas in Kashmir," in *Marg*, September-December (Mumbai: The Marg foundation, 2015).

10 This happened on *Rajab* 12 (seventh month of Muslim calendar), 1289 AH (1872 CE), see Peer Hassan Shah, transl. Shafi Shauq, *Tareikh-e Hassan: A History of Kashmir*, vol. i (Srinagar: Jammu & Kashmir Academy of Art, Culture & Languages, 2016), 417 and Ḥakim Ghulām Ṣafdar Hamdanī, ed. Ḥakim Sameer Ḥamdanī and Maqbūl Sājid, *Tārīkh -i Shiyan-i Kashmir* (Srinagar: Imam Hussein Research & Publishing Centre, 2014), 213–16.

11 Mīr Muqim was appointed to the office of *naīb subedarī* (deputy governorship) of Kashmir by the Mughal *subedar*. Yet in the difficult and often turbulent times related to the post-Aurangzeb rule in Kashmir, the office of *naīb* was always up for grabs. Muqim lost his office to a rebel force led by Abu'l Qāsim Khān. Unable to restore his position, Muqim along with Khwāja Zahir, proceeded to Lahore and invited Aḥmad Shāh to annex Kashmir. For detail of the events, see Pīr Ḥasan Shāh Kuihāmī, transl. Shams-ud Dīn Aḥmad, *Tārīkh-i Ḥasan*, vol. i (Srinagar: Jammu & Kashmir Academy of Art, Culture & Languages, 1998).

12 George Forster, *A Journey from Bengal to England through the Northern Part of India, Kashmire, Afghanistan, and Persia, and into Russia by the Caspian Sea*, vol. ii (London: R. Faulder, 1798), 36.

13 Ibid., 29. Of the revenue generated seven lakh rupees were remitted to the treasury at Kabul.

14 Ibid., 24.

15 Ibid.
16 Interestingly, the work does not account for the rule of Sūkh Jiwan Mal (1753–62), a Punjabi Hindu who after assuming the *subedarī* of Kashmir made an attempt to stand independent of the Kabul court. Ram Joo is also silent about hardships faced by Kashmiri Muslims under the Dogra rule, see Pandit Ram Joo Dhar, *Kafiyat-i Intizām -i Mūlk-i Kashmir* (Srinagar: Research Library, Accession no: 1913), 3.
17 A tax based on shariah, levied on non-Muslims living under the jurisdiction of Muslim rulers.
18 Dhar, *Kafiyat-i Intizām -i Mūlk-i Kashmir*, 3.
19 Kuihāmī, *Tārīkh-i Ḥasan* (1999), vol. ii, 753, also, see Hamdani, *Shiyan-i Kashmir.*
20 Hamdanī, *Tārīkh-i Shiyan-i Kashmir*, 198–9. Also see Kuihāmī, *Tārīkh-i Ḥasan* (1999), vol. i and ii. For details on the working of Khawand Maḥmūd, see Itzchak Weisman, *The Naqshbandiyya; Orthodoxy and Activism in a Worldwide Sufi Tradition* (New York: Routledge, 2007).
21 Kuihāmī, *Tārīkh-i Ḥasan* (1999), vol. ii, 785.
22 The nature of the "truth" remains unsaid, also, the wording of the phrase would indicate that for the Shiʿi, Ḥāfiz Kamāl was essentially seen as a Sunni. See Hamdanī, *Tārīkh-i Shiyan-i Kashmir.*
23 Kuihāmī, *Tārīkh-i Ḥasan* (1999), vol. ii, 750.
24 Forster, *A Journey from Bengal to England*, vol. ii, 14–15.
25 Kuihāmī, *Tārīkh-i Ḥasan* (1999), vol. ii, 763–5. Amīr Khān had executed Khwāja Kamal-al Dīn Naqshbandī in retribution for his murder of Ḥāfiz ʿAbdullah. Given the hold of Naqshbandī's on the religious circle of Srinagar, this would have antagonized them greatly, hence the delegation to Kabul seeking the *ṣubedar*'s dismissal.
26 Anonymous, *Bahāristān-i Shāhī*, transl. K. N. Pandit (Srinagar: Gulshan Books, 2013), 19.
27 See Sayyid ʿAli, *Tārīkh-i Kashmir* (Chronicle of Kashmir), transl. Ghulām Rasūl Bhat (Srinagar: Center of Central Asian Studies, 1994).
28 Dedhmarī, *Vāqiʿāt-i Kashmīr*, 77.
29 Ibid., 76.
30 ʿIrakī's year of passing is mentioned on the margins of manuscript of Malik's *Tārīkh-i Kashmir*, kept at Research Library, Srinagar. See Ḥaidar Malik, *Tārīkh -i Kashmir* (Research Library, Srinagar, MS. 1856).
31 In its native land of origin, Iran, the importance of the order lay, "in exemplifying the messianic-tinged Ṣūfī-Shīʿī ferment that preceded and, in some measure, prepared the way for the establishment of the Ṣafawid state." Hamid Algar, "Nūrbakhshiyya," in *Encyclopaedia of Islam, Second Edition*, edited by P. Bearman, Th Bianquis, C. E. Bosworth, E. van Donzel, W. P. Heinrichs, Available online: http://dx.doi.org/10.1163/1573-3912_islam_SIM_5992, last accessed 2021.
32 ʿAli, *Tārīkh-i Kashmir*, 3.
33 Ibid.
34 Mostly ʿIrakī is referred to as Mīr Shamas ʿIrakī or alternatively as Mīr Shamas or Shamas ʿIrakī, see Dedhmarī, *Vāqiʿāt-i Kashmīr.*
35 Ibid., 173–5, 177.
36 The only notable exception to this is Ḥaidar Malik, who started his life as a courtier in the court of Chak sultans before becoming a part of Mughal administration of Kashmir. Nevertheless, both Malik and his ancestors were supporters of the *Nūrbakhshī* order, and it is possible given the time that he may have been initiated in the order, though he makes no such mention in his work. See Malik, *Tārīkh-i Kashmir.*

37 In 'Ali's account we find an isolated report about a *reshī*, *Bābā Lustī*, who was targeted by the Shi'i. See 'Ali, *Tārīkh-i Kashmir*, 62–3. The Shi'i historian Malik is highly reverential in his description of the founder of *Reshī* order, see Malik, *Tārīkh-i Kashmir*, 101–2.
38 Interview with Sayed Mujtaba Jilani, Srinagar, 2021.
39 For a study of the *Nūrbakhshī* order, see Shahzad Bashir, *Messianic Hopes and Mystical Visions: The Nūrbakhshīya between Medieval and Modern Islam* (Columbia: University of South Carolina Press, 2003).
40 While most Sunni writers refer to Bābā 'Ali as a simpleton who was caught in the guise of 'Irakī, Malik refers to him as one "who possessed the purest of conscience," see Malik, *Tārīkh-i Kashmir*, 103.
41 Dedhmarī refers to Shaykh Ismā'īl as the Shaykh-al Islam of Kashmir, see Dedhmarī, *Vāqi'āt-i Kashmīr*, 171. 'Irakī's biographer writes in detail about Ismā'īl's defection of the *Nūrbakhshī* cause and reports that he died from leprosy. For details, see Mullā Muhammad 'Ali, transl. Ghulām Rasūl Jān, *Tuḥfatūl Aḥbāb* (Srinagar: Jan Publications, 2006).
42 The author of *Bahāristān* records the event in these words:

> he (Mīrzā Haidar) decided to put an end to his (Dāniyāl's life). He summoned Shaykh Fatah-ul Lah to his presence and told him to fabricate false witnesses and the proof against Shaykh Dāniyāl. That ungodly (*khudā nā tars*) fellow made strenuous efforts and bribed for this purpose some corrupt and wicked people, whose decrees in matter of religion were hardly tenable and whose moral dispensations were hardly popular.

Anonymous, *Bahāristān-i Shāhī*, 115.
43 About Malik Mūsā, the historian Malik writes:

> During his reign, he devoted himself to the obliteration of the infidels and busied himself with the spread of the religion of prophet. He made desolate most of the temples [. . .]., Malik, *Tārīkh-i Kashmir*, 61.

44 'Ali, *Tārīkh-i Kashmir*, 29–30.
45 *Tuḥfatūl Aḥbāb: A Muslim Missionary in Medieval Kashmir: Being English Translation of Tuḥfatūl Aḥbāb*, transl. K. N. Pandita (New Delhi: Eurasian Human Rights Forum, 2009), 118–19
46 Pandita, *Tuḥfatūl Aḥbāb*, 116–17.
47 Jonarāja Kalhānā, Shuka Shrivara et al., transl. J. C. Dutt, *Rajatarangini: Kings of Kashmira*, a translation of Sanskrit work, 3 vols. (Srinagar: Gulshan Books, 2009), 408.
48 For a telling instance of this behaviour, see Pandita, *Tuḥfatūl Aḥbāb*, 121–3.
49 The *masnavi* forms the first volume of a seven-volume collection, *Haft Awrang*.
50 Pandita, *Tuḥfatūl Aḥbāb*, 153–6.
51 In South Asia, biographical notices of prominent Sufis broadly fall under two distant categories *malfuzāt* and *tazkiras*. Where *malfuzāt* text are dedicated to the memory of a single saintly figure and serve as dedicated biographies, *tazkira* are envisioned as general biographical works and are not limited to a specific individual, order or time frame. In Kashmir the genre of *malfuzāt* does not exist as a separate category.
52 Bābā Dawud Khākī, transl. Makhdūm Muhammad Khalil Qureshī, *Dastur-al Salikin sharah Virad-al Muridīn* (Srinagar: Sheikh Muhammad Usman & sons, 2001), 402–3.

For the polemical nature of such encounter, in addition to Khākī's, *Dastur-al Salikin* and *Virad-al Muridīn,* also, see Bābā Ḥaidar Tūlmūlī, transl. Ghūlam Rasūl Faruqī, *Hidayet-al Mukhlisin (Taj-al Āshiqin)* (Srinagar: Bait-al Ḥilal Alim-o Adab, 2004).

53 Tūlmūlī was a non-native from Gujrat in mainland India, who arrived in Kashmir in 906 AH/1500 CE, in his teenage years, see Tūlmūlī, *Hidayet-al Mukhlisin*, 9–12, 83–4.

54 Ibid., 95–6.

55 These include:

Dastur-al Salikin and *Virid-al Muridīn* written by Bābā Dawud Khākī', *Hidayet-al Mukhlisin* of Bābā Ḥaidar Tūlmūlī, *Majmu'a Mukhbir-al Israr wa Sultaniya* of Shaykh Aḥmad Chaglī, *Chilchilat -al Arifin* of Khwāja Isḥāq Qārī and *Sey Ghazal-i Miram* of Khwāja Miram Bazaz.

56 See the account of Mullā Yūsuf and Khwāja Mūsā in *Chilchilat -al Arifin.* Qārī argues that those who deny Makhdūm's spiritual status are grave sinners, while also acknowledging the existence of these deniers, for details see, Qārī, *Chilchilat -al Arifin.*

57 See Tūlmūlī, *Hidayet-al Mukhlisin*, 178, 179.

58 Bābā Dawud Khākī, transl. Qārī Saif al Dīn, *Dastur-al Sīlikin* (Srinagar: Ashraf Book Centre, 1971), 53, 65.

59 In contemporary Kashmir, among devotees the shaykh is often invoked as "Sultanā."

60 A similar report can also be seen in Qārī's work, for details, see Khwāja Ishāq Qārī, *Chilchilat-al Arifin,* (Srinagar: Research Library, MS. 500), ff. 27.

61 While mentioning their names, Qārī curses both Ghāzī Chak and ʿIrakī, see, Qārī, *Chilchilat-al Arifin,* ff. 27 and 29.

62 For an understanding of how pivotal ʿIrakī and Makhdūm remains in modern historiography, see the editorial notes by Shams-ud Dīn Aḥmad to Kuihāmī's *Tārīkh-i Ḥasan* which highlights the binary approach of contemporary academics in dealing with the past.

63 See Mīr Saʿad ul-Lah Shāhabādī, *Bagh-i Suleimān* (Srinagar: Research Library, MS.1194). The translation of the original Persian is by Mehran Qureshi, Srinagar, 2021.

64 In Tūlmūlī's account, all the Prophets, saints, and the combined angels descended over the grave to pray over the dead saint for a period of 40 days, a practice that he argues would continue till the Day of Judgement, see, Tūlmūlī, *Hidayet-al Mukhlisin,*167.

65 Some reports also speak about the ruling Chak sultan praying over the deceased shaykh.

66 Ḥabib outlived his uncle, the new sultan, dying in 1573, see Mohibbul Hasan, *Kashmir under the Sultans* (Srinagar: Ali Mohammad & Sons, 1974), 151.

67 The chronology related to this event is not clear. 'Ali mentions it as 967 AH/1559–60 CE, the author of *Bahāristān-i Shāhī* mentions 1554 as the year when Ghāzī Chak became ruler of Kashmir. The rulership here marks Ghāzī assuming the position of vizier and not kingship. After ruling as a sultan for three years he abdicated the throne in favor of his brother Ḥusayn Shāh, passing away in 1567 at the age of fifty-eight, see *Bahāristān-i Shāhī*, 127, 'Ali, *Tārīkh-i Kashmir,* 34 and Hasan, *Kashmir under the Sultans*, 152.

68 The Chaks were divided into two branches, one based in Kupwara which retained its Sunni belief and the principal branch originally from Dardistan in the Nelum valley, who converted to Shiʿism and they rose to power as sultans of Kashmir. For details, see G. M. D. Sufi, *Kashir*, vol. i (Lahore: University of Punjab, 1949).

69 ʻAli, *Tārīkh-i Kashmir*, 34.
70 Dedhmarī, *Vāqi ʻāt-i Kashmīr*, 198.
71 Including Malik Regi Dār the brother of the *vazīr* Malik Saif Dār. After an incident involving Shaykh Sihab-al Dīn, it seems both brothers changed their perspective regarding ʻIrakī. For details, see Pandita *Tuḥfatūl Aḥbāb*, 106, 110.
72 Some months after ʻIrakī's arrival, the reigning sultan, Ḥasan Shāh, passed away. After his funeral, ʻIrakī expressed his apprehension of possible opposition from the *mullās* in these words:

> Owing to the demise of the king, my mission is disrupted, and my return (to Khurasan) hindered. I do not know how the mullahs are going to interfere in my affairs.

Pandita, *Tuḥfatūl Aḥbāb*, 94.
73 Ibid., 253.
74 Raina bestowed his own land at Zadibal to ʻIrakī, who then constructed a *khānaqāh* at the site. On his death, ʻIrakī was buried within the precinct of the *khānaqāh* which continued to serve as the principal seat of the order in Kashmir, see Pandita, *Tuḥfatūl Aḥbāb*, 184–6.
75 Pandita, *Tuḥfatūl Aḥbāb*, 184.
76 The fights between Ḥasan Shāh's son Muhammad Shāh and his cousin Fateh Shāh for the throne can be seen as beginning of the ascendancy of Kashmiri nobles at the cost of the authority of the Shāhmirī sultans. For details, see Hasan, *Kashmir under the Sultans*.
77 One of the four legal schools among Sunnis, the Ḥanfī's trace their origin to the Iraqi scholar, Abū Ḥanīfa (d. 767). Historically the Ḥanfī school remained the predominant school of jurisprudence among Sunnis of South Asia, including Kashmir.
78 Mīrzā Ḥaidar Dughlat, transl. E. D. Ross, *Tārīkh-i Rashidī: A History of the Moghuls of Central Asia* (Srinagar: Gulshan Books, 2012), 118–19.
79 ʻAli, *Tārīkh-i Kashmir*, 32
80 Dedhmarī, *Vāqi ʻāt-i Kashmīr*, 185.
81 Ghulām Rasūl Jān, *Jāmia-al Kamālat Ḥazrat Ishān Shaykh Yʻaqūb Sarfī* (Srinagar: Indian Printing Press, 1995), 127. Also see Dedhmarī, *Vāqi ʻāt-i Kashmīr.*
82 Dedhmarī, *Vāqi ʻāt-i Kashmīr*, 185.
83 See Anonymous, *Bahāristān-i Shāhī* and Hasan, *Kashmir under the Sultans.*
84 For details, see Qārī, *Chikhilat-al ʻArifin.*
85 Malik, *Tārīkh-i Kashmir*, 73.
86 Shuka 124–5.
87 *Khusraw-i ʻAādil* is a reference to the Sasanian emperor, Khosrow I. (d. 579), who on account of his knowledge, virtues, and reforms is remembered as the epitome of just ruler in Persianate cultures.
88 A disciple of Shaykh Ḥamza, Khwāja Tahir Rafiq (d.1596) is seen as the prime mover behind the appeal of Kashmiri Sunni ulema to Akbar. See Jan, *Jāmia-al Kamālat*, 128, also, see Sufi, *Kashir.*
89 *Ḳiṣāṣ* in Muslim law is the principle of retaliation applied in case of killings (*ḳiṣāṣ fi ʻl-nafs)* or non-fatal wounding (*ḳiṣāṣ fi-mā dūn al-nafs*). See J. Schacht, "Ḳiṣāṣ," in *Encyclopaedia of Islam*, Second Edition, edited by P. Bearman, Th Bianquis, C. E. Bosworth, E. van Donzel and W. P. Heinrichs, Last visited online 2021, http://dx.doi.org/10.1163/1573-3912_islam_SIM_4400.
90 Anonymous, *Bahāristān-i Shāhī*, 132.

91 Mīrzā Muqim's Shi'i origin was used as an excuse by the Sunni ulema at Akbar's court against him, and consequently he along with Mīr Y'aqūb, the emissary of the sultan of Kashmir, were executed for their role in the trial of the Sunni qāzī's at Srinagar. The conspiracy against Mūqīm was orchestrated by two leading Sunni religious figures at the Mughal court, the *ṣadr* Shaykh 'Abd-al Nabī (d. 1583) and Makdūm-al Mūlk 'Abdullah Sulṭānpūrī. For details, see Maulana Muhammad Ḥusayn Azad, *Darbar-i Akbarī* (Delhi: National Council for Promotion of Urdu Language, undated), 316–27.

92 Ibid., 133–43.

93 Ibid., 135.

94 Ibid., 134.

95 For details, see Hakim Sameer Hamdani, *The Syncretic Traditions of Islamic Religious Architecture of Kashmir* (*Early 14th-18th Century*) (New York: Routledge, 2021), 71–4.

96 Bābā Dawud Khākī, *Qasideh-i Ghusuliya Yūsuf Shāh*, transl. Mehran Qureshi (Srinagar: Research Library, Ms. 1914), ff. 5.

97 For details, see Anonymous, *Bahāristān-i Shāhī* and Dedhmarī, *Vāqi'āt-i Kashmīr.*

98 For an official Mughal account of the conquest of Kashmir, see Shaykh Abū'l Fażl, transl. H. Beveridge, *Akbar Nāmā*, 2 vols. (Calcutta: The Asiatic Society, 2000).

99 Dedhmarī, *Vāqi'āt-i Kashmīr*, 85.

Chapter 2

1 Hamdanī, *Tārīkh-i Shiyan-i Kashmir*, 424.

2 Ḥakim Mullā 'Azim, *Maktūb Ḥakim 'Azim baray-i Moulvi Rajab 'Ali Shāh*, transl. Stephen Poop, Personal collection, Hakim Shaukat Ali Hamdani, Srinagar.

3 The ḥakim on account of his learning was styled as the second Bū 'Ali Sina (Avicenna) among the local Shi'i community. In addition to his principal task of being the Maharaja's chief physician he was also responsible for reorganizing the sericulture industry in Kashmir. Aside from his Kashmiri *marthiyas*, not much survives of his works. A manuscript of *Risala-i Faizha*' a Persian composition on poetry copied by the Ḥakim in 1248 AH/1832 CE with his notes on the margin survives with his descendants. Hamdanī, *Tārīkh-i Shiyan-i Kashmir*, 311–15, 347; Zutshi, *Languages of Belonging*, 72 and Sufi, *Kashir*, vol. ii, 575. Also, see Maqbūl Sājid, *Kuliyāt-i Ḥakim 'Azim wa Munshi Muhammad Yūsuf* (Srinagar: Imam Hussein Research & Publishing Centre, 2000) and Shahid Badgami, *Kashir-i-Marsyuk Tawarīkh* (Delhi: Taj Printing Services, rpt.2014).

4 One of 'Abdullah's predecessors, *ṣubedar* Mīr Hazar, was in the habit of gathering Shi'i men, tying them in jute sacks and then drowning in Dal Lake. The rule of the pleasure-loving Shi'i *subadar* Amīr Khān proved some relief to the Shi'i of Kashmir. See Kuihāmī, *Tārīkh-i Ḥasan* (1999) vol. ii, 750, 790.

5 Ibid., 806–7. Also, see Hamdanī, *Tārīkh-i Shiyan-i Kashmir*, 343–6.

6 Hamdanī, *Tārīkh-i Shiyan-i Kashmir,* 209–10.

7 Kuihāmī, *Tārīkh-i Ḥasan* (1998), vol. i, 592.

8 Kuihāmī would add to this the provocation of taking out a *shabih* (coffin) and more importantly cursing of the *shabah*.

9 Shauq, *Tareikh-e Hassan*, 416.

10 Ibid., 409.

11 Mullā Khalil Marjānpūrī, *Tārīkh-i Kashmir* (Srinagar: Research Library, Mss. 1074), ff. 161.

12 Kuihāmī, *Tārīkh-i Ḥasan* (1999), vol. ii, 787. According to the Shiʿi author ibn Reza, the residents of Hasanabad under the guidance of Sayyid Hadi constructed an *imāmbāda*, which was then destroyed by the Afghans. The work of ibn Razā suffers from a weak chronology and many of the events related by him are confused and unreliable. Most probably based on Kuihāmī account it seems that the construction of an *imāmbāda* at Hasanabad been started, when the Afghans came to know about it and destroyed it. For details, see Sayyid ʿAli ibn Razā, transl. Sayyid Muhsin Kashmirī, *Kuhl-al Jawahir* (Lahore: MAAB, 2013), 47, 76.
13 For an account of both, see Marjānpūrī, *Tārīk -i Kashmir*, ff. 161–3.
14 For details, see Marjānpūrī, *Tārīkh-i Kashmir* and Kuihāmī, *Tārīkh-i Ḥasan* (1999), vol. ii.
15 For a Shiʿi account of the *ṣubedar*, see Hamdanī, *Tārīkh-i Shiyan-i Kashmir* and ibn Razā, *Kuhl-al Jawahir.*
16 Ḥakim Ghulām Ṣafdar Hamdanī, *Aūsh ti Āab* (Delhi: Skyline Publishers, 2009), 90; translation author.
17 Ibid., 91; translation author.
18 Ibid., 92.
19 Ibid., 89; translation author.
20 Maqbūl Sājid, *Kaeshri Marsiyuk Safar* (Srinagar: Jammu & Kashmir Academy of Art, Culture & Languages, 2013), 289.
21 Ibid., 319.
22 Marjānpūrī, *Tārīkh-i Kashmir*, ff. 161.
23 George Forster, *A Journey from Bengal to England through the Northern Part of India, Kashmire, Afghanistan, and Persia, and into Russia by the Caspian Sea*, vol. ii (London: R. Faulder, 1798), 20.
24 Janet Rizvi and Monisha Ahmed, *Pashmina: The Kashmir Shawl and Beyond* (Mumbai: Marg Publications, 2009), 208–9.
25 Ibid.
26 Vigne, *Travels in Kashmir, Ladak, Iskardo,* vol. ii, 84–5.
27 Kuihāmī, *Tārīkh-i Ḥasan* (1999), vol ii. 790, Marjānpūrī, *Tārīkh-i Kashmir*, ff. 159.
28 Marjānpūrī, *Tārīk-i Kashmir.* Also see Hamdanī, *Tārīkh-i Shiyan-i Kashmir*, 208.
29 Kuihāmī, *Tārīkh-i Ḥasan* (1999), vol ii, 790. The *ṣubedar* was also responsible for imposing *jiziya* tax on Kashmiri Hindus.
30 Ibid., 800.
31 Kuihāmī, *Tārīkh-i Ḥasan* (1999), vol. ii, 800–1, 890. For a Shiʿi version of the event, see Hamdanī, *Tārīkh-i Shiyan-i Kashmir*, 208–9.
32 Hamdanī, *Tārīkh-i Shiyan-i Kashmir*, 208.
33 Marjānpūrī, *Tārīkh-i Kashmir*, ff. 160.
34 On possible movement of Iranians within the territory of the Dūranīs, see Sajjad Nejatie, "Iranian Migrations in the Durrani Empire, 1747-1793," *Comparative Studies of South Asia, Africa and the Middle East* 37, no. 3 (2017), 494–509.
35 This is how modern Shiʿi historian would interpret Āqā Rahīm intentions, see Hamdani, *Tārīkh-i Shiyan-i Kashmir*, 208.
36 Importantly, the incident occurred during the rule of Kifayat Khān, who is considered by the Shiʿi historians as a Shiʿi. Āqā Rahīm's action against the Khwāja was also conditioned by a desire to seek retribution from Khwāja ʿĪsā for his murder of Muhammad Taqi, a close associate of Rahim, see Kuihāmī, *Tārīkh-i Ḥasan* (1999), vol. ii, 800 and Hamdanī, *Tārīkh-i Shiyan-i Kashmir*, 208–9, 299.

37 B. Hopkins, *The Making of Modern Afghanistan* (New York: Palgrave Macmillan, 2012), 132.
38 See Forster, *A Journey from Bengal to England through the Northern Part of India.*
39 B Hopkins, *The Making of Modern Afghanistan* (New York: Palgrave Macmillan, 2012), 132.
40 Forster, *A Journey from Bengal to England through the Northern Part of India*, vol ii, 36.
41 Victor Jacquemont, *Letters from India; describing a Journey in the British Dominions of India, Tibet, Lahore and Cashmere during the years 1828, 1829, 1830, 1831*, vol. i (London: Edward Churton, 1834), 155.
42 Ibid.
43 William Moorcroft and George Trebeck, *Travels in the Himalayan Provinces of Hindustan and the Panjab; in Ladakh and Kashmir; in Peshawar, Kabul, Kunduz, and Bokhara*, vol. ii (London: J Murray, 1841), 194.
44 Willem Floor, *The Persian Textile Industry in Historical Perspective 1500-1922* (Paris: L'Harmattan, 1999), 309. Also, see Charles Issawi (ed.), *The Economic History of Iran 1800-1914* (Chicago: University of Chicago Press, 1971).
45 Floor, *The Persian Textile Industry in Historical Perspective 1500-1922*, 309.
46 Mughal moḥala is located in Lal Bazaar area of the city and was traditionally populated by members of the Mughal family.
47 See Jacquemont, *Letters from India.*
48 W. H. Floor, The Merchants (tujjār) in Qājār Iran in *Zeitschrift der Deutschen Morgenländischen Gesellschaft* (Wiesbaden: Harrassowitz Verlag, 1976), 103.
49 Maryam Ekhtiar Sheila R. Canby, Navina Haidar, and Priscilla P. Soucek (ed.), *Masterpieces from the Department of Islamic Art in the Metropolitan Museum of Art* (New York: The Metropolitan Museum of Art, 2011), no. 283, 342, 398–9, ill. 398.
50 Ibid.
51 For a detailed analysis of the Qizalbash in nineteenth-century Afghanistan, see Solaiman M. Fazel, *Ethnohistory of the Qizalbash in Kabul: Migration, State and a Shi'a Minority*, PhD thesis (Department of Anthropology, Indiana University, 2017).
52 Bihbahānī traced his descent from the famous Safavid ulema, Mullā Muhammad Ṣaleh Mazandaranī, the brother-in-law of Isfahan's Shaykh al Islam, Mullā Muhammad Bāqir Majālisī (d. 1699).
53 Ahmad Behbahani, *Mir'atul-Ahwal–i Jahan Numa*, transl. A. F. Haider, *India in the Early 19th century* (Patna: KhudaBaksh Oriental Public Library, 1996), 172.
54 There is much confusion about Mullā Muqims' year of death with three different dates recorded, 1195 AH/1780 CE, 1274 AH/1857 CE, and 1235 AH/1819 CE.
55 Hamdanī, *Tārīkh-i Shiyan-i Kashmir*, 276–7, also, see Sayyid Muḥsin Kashmirī, *Danishnama Shiyan-i Kashmir* (Lahore: MAB, 2011), 184.
56 Behbahani, *Mir'atul-Ahwal–i Jahan Numa*, 172.
57 For Sayyid Dildar, see Jaun Cole, *Sacred Space and Holy War: The Politics, Culture and History of Shi'ite Islam* (London: I.B. Tauris, 2005).
58 The possession of miraculous power would be associated with both Mullā Muhammad Muqim and a younger contemporary Akhūnd Mullā Muhammad Razā Kashmirī, who flourished during the time of Nawab Sa ʿadat ʿAli Khān (r. 1798–1814), for details, see Sayyid Muhammad Ḥusayn, *Taẕkira-i Beybaha* (Delhi: Dayiratul al-Muraif Iran va Hind), 325–6.
59 Behbahani, *Mir'atul-Ahwal-i Jahan Numa*, 160.
60 Jadunath Sarkar, *Fall of the Mughal Empire*, vol. i (Delhi: Orient Longman, 1971), 15.

61 See Sayyid Ghulām ʿAli Khan, *ʿImād-al Sadāt.*

62 After initially opposing the idea, Nasirābadī finally offered the first Friday congregational prayer on Rajab 13, 1200 AH (1786 CE). For the controversy around the issue and Badshāh's role in it, see J. Cole, *Roots of North Indian Shi'ism in Iraq and Iran*, 127–30.

63 Hamdanī, *Tārīkh-i Shiyan-i Kashmir.*

64 Nasirābadī would in time would assume the position of Lucknow's chief *mujtahid*, see Cole, *Roots of North Indian Shi'ism in Iraq and Iran*, 104.

65 Syed Athar Abbas Rizvi, *A Socio Intellectual History of the Isna Ashari Shi'i in India*, vol. ii (Canberra: Ma'rifat Publishing House, 1986), 92–3.

66 For details on the life of these Kashmiri scholars, see Mīrzā Muhammad ʿAli Kashmirī, *Najum-al Sama fi Tarajim al Ulema*, ed. Mīr Hāshim Muḥadīth (Tehran: Sazman Tableghat Islami, 1967).

67 Rizvi, *A Socio Intellectual History of the Isna Ashari Shi'i in India*, vol. ii, 96–7.

68 See Cole, *Roots of North Indian Shi'ism in Iraq and Iran.*

69 See Justin Jones, *Khandan-i-Ijtihad: Genealogy, History, and Authority in a Household of ʿulama in Modern South Asia* (Cambridge: Cambridge University Press, 2019).

70 Muhammad Najmul Ghanī, *Tārīkh-i Awadh*, vol. iv (Lucknow: Munshi Nawal Kishore, 1919), 17–18, 252, 267, 268.

71 Ibid., 309.

72 Ibid., 268.

73 Reginald Heber, *Narrative of a Journey through the Upper Provinces of India from Calcutta to Bombay, 1824–1825*, vol. i (Philadelphia: Carey, Lea & Carey, 1829), 341.

74 Ghanī, *Tārīkh-i Awadh*, vol. iv, 6.

75 See Rizvi, *A Socio Intellectual History of The Isna Ashari Shi'i In India*, vol. ii, 227–30.

76 Nawab Saʿadat ʿAli Khān II.

77 Behbahani, *Mir'atul-Ahwal-i Jahan Numa*, 197.

78 Jabbār Khān belonged to the Afghan royalty and was the eldest among the competing sibling for the throne of Kabul. The British diplomat Burnes, who met in Kabul sometime after the Sikh conquest of Kashmir, writes about him:

> We had previously heard about the amicable character of our host, Nawab Jubbar Khan [. . .]: himself the eldest of his family, he has no ambitious views, though he once held the government of Cashmeer [. . .]. Never was a man more modest or more beloved [. . .]. His manners are remarkably mild and pleasing [. . .]. It is delightful to be in his society.

Sir Alexander Burnes, *Travels into Bokhara; being the Account of a Journey from India to Cabool, Tartary, and Persia; also, Narrative of a Voyage on the Indus, from the sea to Lahore, with Presents from the king of Great Britain; Performed under the Orders of the Supreme Government of India, in the Years 1831, 1832, and 1833* (London: John Murray, 1834), 134–5.

Jabbar Khān's rule of six months in Kashmir also finds a positive mention in the history of a Kashmiri Pandit writer Birbal Kachru, who remarks on his just and impartial rule. See Bashar Bashir, *A Kashmiri version of Majmu al Tawarikh of Birbal Kachru with Commentary and Notes* (PhD. Thesis: University of Kashmir, 1997), 520.

79 Mohan Lal, *Travels in the Panjab, Afghanistan & Turkistan to Balkh, Bokhara and Herat; and a Visit to Great Britain and Germany* (London: WH Allen & Co., 1856), xv, xvi.

80 Lal, *Travels in the Panjab, Afghanistan & Turkistan to Balkh, Bokhara and Herat*, xv.

81 Sir Alexander Burnes, *Travels into Bokhara*, 22.
82 Louis E. French, Ranjit Singh, *The Shawl, and the Kaukab-i Iqbal-i Punjab* in *Sikh Formation: Religion, Culture, Theory*, April–August, 2015, vol. ii, Issue 1/2 (London: Taylor and Francis), 83–107.
83 Ibid.
84 For a discussion of the Sikh Empire, see Priya Atwal, *Royals and Rebels: The Rise and Fall of the Sikh Empire* (London: Oxford University Press, 202).
85 Bashir, *A Kashmiri version of Majmu al Tawarikh of Birbal Kachru*, 504.
86 Ibid., 539–40.
87 Sufi, *Kashir*, vol. ii, 724.
88 See P. N. K. Bamzai, *Culture and Political History of Kashmir*, vol. iii (New Delhi: MD Publications Pvt Ltd: 1994), 623–4.
89 See Marjānpūrī, *Tārīkh-i Kashmir.*
90 The killed included Khwāja Muʿīn-al Dīn Kawūsa and his son-in-law, Mīrzā Kallū. See Sufi, *Kashir*, vol. ii, 730.
91 Two earlier attempts by Ranjit Singh to annex Kashmir in 1813 and 1814 had ended in a failure. See Sufi, *Kashir*, vol. ii, i.

Chapter 3

1 Author's interview, Maqbool Sajid, Srinagar, 2021. Sajid has documented more than 500 *marṣiya* from the nineteenth century.
2 For details, see *Biyāz*, unpublished manuscript (Research Library, Srinagar, MS. 1657), and *Biyāz*, unpublished manuscript (Research Library, Srinagar, MS. 1658).
3 See *Biyāz*, unpublished manuscript (Research Library, Srinagar, MS. 1656), ff. 105, 123.
4 *Biyāz*, Private collection, Sayyid Ḥabib-ul Lah, Reshipora.
5 Qāsim Kalim, *Kuliyat-i Khwāja Ḥasan Mir* (Srinagar: Imam Hussein Research & Publishing Centre, 2001), 345.
6 During my study, I came across some other limited instances of conversion into Shiʿism during the nineteenth century, but these events were not part of an organized campaign but seem to have been dictated by the particular circumstances surrounding individual spiritual quest.
7 Maqbūl Sajid, *Naqūsh-i Khwāja Dāim* (Srinagar: Imam Hussein Research & Publishing Centre, 2006), 12. Later in his life, Dāim went on a pilgrimage to Iraq, where he is reported to have died and buried in Karbala.
8 The earliest example of a *manqabat* in Kashmiri can be traced to sixteenth-century *Kubrawī* Sufi, Khwāja Ḥabib-al lah Ḥūbbī.
9 Sajid, *Naqūsh-i Khwāja Dāim*, 210
10 The tree of blessedness which grows in heaven.
11 The reference here is to the Twelve Imāms.
12 In popular Shiʿi culture of Kashmir, Imām ʿAli is often invoked by the title of Shāh (king).
13 The *nashid* then goes on to seek the intercession of the rest of the eleven imām.
14 "This cannot be a human composition but is divinely inspired" is a common *ẕākir* trope frequently voiced in defining this literary genre during public performance.
15 Marjānpūrī, *Tārīkh -i Kashmir* (MS. 2259), ff. 10.

16 See Hamdanī, *Tārīkh-i Shiyan-i Kashmir*, also, see Budgami, *Kāshir-i Marsyuk Tawarīkh*.
17 See Marjānpūrī, *Tārīkh -i Kashmir* (MS. 2259).
18 Vigne, *Travels in Kashmir, Ladak, Iskardo*, vol. ii, 84–5.
19 Following the riots, most of these Iranian merchants withdrew from the city, never to return. In *Umdat Ut-tawarikh*, the merchants are described as Mughal, and on being informed about the riot, Maharaja Ranjit Singh orders the *ṣubedar* to make all efforts to draw them back to Srinagar, for details, see, Sohan Lal Suri, transl. V. S. Suri *Umdat Ut-tawarikh*, Daftar III (Amritsar: Guru Nanak Dev University, 2001,2002), 17.
20 The procession would halt at Khairpur for the night, before proceeding the next morning toward Char.
21 *Yā Shāh* (O Master), they cry for help is to Imām ʿAli.
22 For details, see, Ḥakim ʿAẕim, 'Qafas (Cage)' in Sajid, *Kuliyāt-i Ḥakim ʿAẕim wa Munshi Muhammad Yūsuf*, 121–31.
23 We have no way of understanding, whether the call for prayers was even sounded in Shiʿi mosques in this period. Given that such a call would include the typical Shiʿi invocation, "I bear witness that 'Ali is the friend of Allah," it seems highly improbable that this would happen at least in the mixed neighborhoods of the city.
24 Marjānpūrī, *Tārīkh -i Kashmir* (MS. 2259), ff. 8, 9.
25 Ibid., ff. 7.
26 See Marjānpūrī, *Tārīkh -i Kashmir* (MS. 2259).
27 See J. Keay, *China: A History* (UK: Hachette, 2009).
28 Waleed Ziad, *Hidden Caliphate: Sufi Saints Beyond the Oxus and Indus* (Cambridge, MA: Harvard University Press, 2021), 166.
29 See Itzchak Weismann, *The Naqshbandiya, Orthodoxy and Activism in a Worldwide in Sufi Tradition* (London: Routledge, 2007).
30 Moorcroft leaves us with the following observation on his meeting with Shāh Niyaz:

> I was much pleased with the earnestness with which our new friend recapitulated the heads of this discussion, and with the apparent frankness and cordiality of his manners. After a short time I took leave of our host.

Willim Moorcraft and George Trebeck, *Travels in the Himalayan Provinces of Hindustan and the Panjab; in Ladakh and Kashmir; in Peshawar, Kabul, Kunduz, and Bokhara*, vol. i (London: John Murray, 1837), 244.
31 Ziad, *Hidden Caliphate*, 166.
32 One of the earliest examples of a Persian *shahar-ashūb* (or *shahar-angiz*) in the ghazal form is to be found in the compilation of Sayfī Bukharī (d. 909). See *Encyclopedia of Islam*, vol. ix (Leiden: Brill, 1997), 212.
33 Hammad Rind, reply to tweet on https://twitter.com/HammadHRind/status/1398936016837394432, accessed on May 30, 2021.
34 Sufi mentions that Mujrim was a frequent visitor to the shrine of Shaykh Ḥazma Makhdūm at Srinagar. In his *diwān* Mujrim has written a poem in praise of another prominent Sunni Sufi, Shaykh ʿAbdu'l Qādir Gilānī (d. 1166 CE), the founder of the Qādrī Sufi *silsala*. Though relatively obscure during the Sultanate period, the Qādrī order resurfaced as a major Sufi *silsala* in Srinagar during the Afghan rule. For details, see Mīrzā Mahdi Murjim, *Diwān* (Srinagar: Research Library, MS. 350). Also see Sufi, *Kashir*, vol. ii and Hamdanī, *Tārīkh-i Shiyan-i Kashmir*, 235.

35 See Murjim, *Diwān*, ff. 160–4, translation: Mehran Qureshi, Srinagar, 2021.

36 Somewhere in the 1860's, Mahdah Shāh Deykah (d. 1895) wrote a satire on the elders of the city, celebrating some and lampooning others. In addition to Sunni and Pandits, Deykah also mentions some Shiʿi ulema and merchants including Moulvi Jawad (Ansarī), Moulvi Ṣafdar, (Ḥakim) Baqir, Ḥājjī ʿAbid, Mīrzā Rasūl, Mīrzā Muhammad ʿAli, Sayyid Shāh (Jalali?), and Ḥājjī Ṣafdar (Baba), see, Mahdah Shāh Deykah, *Raʿyis Nāma-i Kashmir* (Srinagar: Research Library, Srinagar, MS. 664).

37 For a study of patronage of Muslim places of worship in the eighteenth century, see Hamdanī, *The Syncretic Traditions of Islamic Religious Architecture of Kashmir.*

38 Traditionally, it is believed that the mosque was partially opened for prayers in 1843 by Shaykh Ghūlam Mohyi-al Dīn, who served the Lahore *darbār* as *ṣubedar* of Kashmir from 1841 to 1845. See Sufi, *Kashir*, vol. ii, 745.

39 Hamdanī, *Tārīkh-i Shiyan-i Kashmir*, 212.

40 Sufi, *Kashir*, vol. ii, 732–3.

41 Hamdanī, *Tārīkh-i Shiyan-i Kashmir*, 212.

42 Mīrzā Najaf ʿAli, *Ṣurat-i jamʿ wa-kharj-i māliyāt-i Qandahār* (Bodleian Library, Oxford University, MS. S Digby Or. 173), ff. 41.

43 Even today mourners in Muharram *majalis* and procession in Kashmiri Moḥala (Lucknow) and Moḥala-i Shiyan-i Kashmir (Lahore) recite Kashmiri verses in their gatherings keeping alive a cherished memory linking them to the land of their forefathers. Author's interview, Mehmood Mehdi Abdi, Mumbai, 2021.

44 Most Kashmiri Shiʿi who arrived in Lucknow after the riots of 1830 settled down in Golaganj and Wazirganj. Additionally, we find the presence of Kashmiri Sunni in the city at Katra Abu Turab Khan. The most famous of the Kashmiri Sunni families in Lucknow was that of the Khwājas who were famous ḥakim of Lucknow. Author's interview, Mehmood Mehdi Abdi, Mumbai, 2021.

45 Rubāb bint Imra' al-Qays in Arabic.

46 Author's interview, Vaibhav Koul, Delhi, 2021. According to Vaibhav, the last member from the Kashmiri Hindu (Pandit) community to recite *nūḥa* was Pandit Brij Mohan Nath Kacher of Kashmiri Moḥala, who was active till the 1960s.

47 Shāh Niyaẕ was also a poet, whose *Chāi Nāma* (Book of Tea) is part of a literary genre celebrating the culture of tea, a genre that seems to have achieved a level of fame in the nineteenth century. See Khwāja Shāh Niyaẕ Naqshbandī, *Chāi Nāma* (Lahore, *Matbah-i mujdadi*, undated).

48 Najaf introduces himself as Ḥājjī Sayyid Najaf ʿAli son of Sayyid Malik Muhammad Khān of Lahore. See ʿAli, *Ṣurat-i jamʿ wa-kharj-i māliyāt-i Qandahār*, ff. 70.

49 Pashmina, the raw goat wool used in the making of Kashmiri shawls, was and is still sourced from Ladakh, in a region closer to Tibet, known as Changthan.

50 Moorcroft briefly stayed in Muhsin ʿAli's house, whom he describes as "a wholesale dealer in tea to a large extent," during his stay at Leh, about which he writes, "We encamped at the house of Mohsin Ali, a Kashmiri merchant, whom I had appointed British facter at Lē {Leh}." See Moorcroft and Trebeck, *Travels in the Himalayan Provinces of Hindustan and the Panjab*, vol. i, 354 and 423.

51 ʿAli, *Ṣurat-i jamʿ wa-kharj-i māliyāt-i Qandahār*, ff. 70. Also see Simon Digby, "From Ladakh to Lahore in 1820-1821: The Account of a Kashmiri Traveler," *Journal of Central Asian Studies*, vol'iii, no:1 (Srinagar: Kashmir University, 1997), 8.

52 It was on July 31, 1823, that Moorcroft started his journey from Srinagar. See Moorcraft and Trebeck, *Travels in the Himalayan Provinces of Hindustan and the Panjab*, vol. i.

53 Moorcraft and Trebeck, *Travels in the Himalayan Provinces of Hindustan and the Panjab*, vol. ii, 275.
54 Ibid., 252.
55 Ibid., 243.
56 The first major Shiʿi-Sunni riot in 1635 involved the Naqshbandī shaykh, Khwāja Khawand Maḥmūd Naqshbandī. Similarly, Khwāja Muhammad Āftāb Naqshbandī and Khwāja Padhshāh Naqshbandī played a significant role in instigating and sustaining the mobs targeting Shiʿis during the riots of 1719. In the riots of 1776, the body of a Shiʿi, Anwar Malik, was quartered from the gates of the *Khānaqāh-i Naqshbandīyā* in Srinagar. See Hamdanī, *Tārīkh-i Shiyan-i Kashmir*, 198–208. Also see Marjānpūrī, *Tārīkh -i Kashmir* and Khuihāmī, *Tārīkh-i Ḥasan* (1999).
57 For details, see the descriptions provided by Kuihāmī, *Tārīkh-i Ḥasan* (1999). Also see Pīrzada Abdul Khaliq Tahirī, *Awliyā-i Kashmir* (Srinagar: Gulshan Publications, 2003). For an understanding of the prominence of the order in eighteenth-century Srinagar, see Dedhmarī, *Vāqiʿāt-i Kashmīr.*
58 Shāh Niyaz's understanding of Moorcroft's mission is reflected in his advice to the *khalun* about how to treat the Britisher:

> but to treat us civilly and that the minister might feel assured we were what we professed to be, inoffensive travellers and merchants

Moorcroft and Trebeck, *Travels in the Himalayan Provinces of Hindustan and the Panjab,* vol. i, 244.
59 Mīr Iʿzzat al-Lah (d. 1825) was the principal *munshi* of Moorcroft, who also left his impression of his travel with Moorcroft. See Digby, *From Ladakh to Lahore in 1820-1821.*
60 Moorcroft and Trebeck, *Travels in the Himalayan Provinces of Hindustan and the Panjab,* vol. i, 247.
61 Simon Digby based on the account of Najaf 'Ali's also points to this understanding of the Kashmiri merchants and their information gathering capacity:

> One may note also the informative role of educated and travelled Muslims, mainly Kashmiri, in the last days of Ladakhi independence under its ancient native dynasty. Najaf 'Ali's narrative illustrates the process of transmission, by Persian-speaking, travelled Indian and Kashmiri Muslims, of information about the changing state of European and global politics and technology, to this remote and threatened Tibetan Buddhist kingdom in the decades before it lost its independence.

Simon Digby, *From Ladakh to Lahore in 1820-1821: The Account of a Kashmiri Traveler.*
62 Moorcroft refers to him as Nakaju, "a Kashmirian, who was our chief opponent." Moorcroft and Trebeck, *Travels in the Himalayan Provinces of Hindustan and the Panjab*, vol. i, 452.
63 Moorcroft and Trebeck, *Travels in the Himalayan Provinces of Hindustan and the Panjab*, vol. i, 452, 453.
64 Stein describes the *Aksakal* as "headman, literally 'white beard.'" See M. Aurel Stein, *Sand-Buried Ruins of Khotan* (Cambridge: Cambridge University Press, 2014), 169. In official British documents from the later part of the nineteenth century, *Aksakal* is sometimes defined "as an informal post, acting as agent or attorney for a trader,"

rather than the trader himself. See Government of India, Foreign and Political Department, Series E, Proceedings, August 1916, Nos. 63–68, National Archives, New Delhi.

65 See Henry Landsell, *Chinese Central Asia, A Ride to Little Tibet*, vol. i. (London: Sampson Low, 1893). The position of *Aksakal* became a part of the British colonial set-up and the appointment of the *Aksakal* was done after considerable consideration. See File No. 1–11, Foreign, Frontier-A, 1899, National Archives of India, New Delhi. For a general understanding of British interest in Chinese Turkistan, see details of Douglas Forsyth's mission to Yarkand, Government of India, Foreign and Political Department, No. 6 0f 1871, National Archives of India, New Delhi. Details of Forsyth's mission are also recorded in Gordon's account of the embassy, which speaks about the presence of Kashmiri soldiers in the army of the Amīr of Kasghar. See Sir Edward Thomas Gordon, *The Roof of the World: Being a Narrative of a Journey over the High Plateau of Tibet to the Russian Frontier and the Oxus Sources on Pamir* (Edinburgh: Edmonston & Douglas, 1876), 94.

66 During his travels, Stein managed to "obtain" a large collection of manuscripts from both Kashmir and the Grotto of the Thousand Buddhas at Tun-huang, which was celebrated as "harvest of ancient manuscripts and records comprises some 11,000 documents, in about a dozen scripts and languages. [. . .]. These include the oldest existing specimens of Chinese Buddhist pictorial art; block-printed texts dating from the ninth century; a Sanscrit MS. on palm leaves of the fourth century." See Vincent A. Smith, The Work of Sir M. Aurel Stein K.C.I.E. in *The Journal of the Royal Asiatic Society of Great Britain and Ireland*, Jan. 1919, Cambridge University Press, 56.

67 Stein, *Sand-Buried Ruins of Khotan*, 163, 165. Additionally, Stein's enquiries into the artefacts and antiques of Khotan were responded to only by Kashmiris living in Yarkand. According to Stein, Kashmiris were innate peddlers and their connections and knowledge of arts and crafts were impressive.

68 *Naqal as Asal Hukumnama Maharaj zair tanazay-i Ahl-i Tashayyu'*, MS. Personal Collection, Hakim Shaukat Ali Hamdani, Srinagar.

69 Ibid. Also see Hamdanī, *Tārīkh-i Shiyan-i Kashmir.*

70 In a letter written by Mullā Ṣadiq Ansarī to Sayyid Ḥusayn, son of Sayyid Dildār ʿAli Shāh, Ṣadiq makes a reference to money remitted by Ḥakim Mahdi to Kashmir. See Sayyid Muhamad ʿAbbas, *Auraq al-Zahab* (Qum: Kitabshinasi-i Shiʿi, 1974), 984.

71 For an understanding of the architecture of the Mʿārak, see Hakim Sameer Hamdani, *The Maarak and Tradition of Imambadas in Kashmir, Marg* (Mumbai: Marg Publication, 2015), 56–69. For a historical account, see Hamdanī, *Tārīkh-i Shiyan-i Kashmir.*

72 Hamdanī, *Tārīkh-i Shiyan-i Kashmir, 289.*

73 In some traditions the date is mentioned as 868 CE.

74 Among the Sayyid families based in Srinagar, a branch which was initially based in Chinkral Mohala is famous by the surname "*waʿiẕ*" (preacher). During the second half of the nineteenth century the family produced many reputed religious scholars. Based on the unique surname, it is possible to posit that some scholars in the family also started preaching publicly, but in the absence of any textual, oral, or even family tradition this is difficult to establish when and at which platform.

75 ibn Razā, *Kūhal-al Jawahir*, 78. Though the writer of *Kūhal-al Jawahir* has provided many details linked with the role his family (Mousavī-Ardabelī) played in Kashmir,

the work suffers from discrepancies both in its chronology and in the event description. Importantly, the details which ibn Razā provides us about members of his family and their role in nineteenth-century Kashmir are not supported by another other work originating in this time period from Shiʿi circles linked to Kashmir.

76 For details on the Shaykh Mohyi-al Dīn, see Bashir, *A Kashmiri Version of Majmu al Tawarikh of Birbal Kachru* and Sufi, *Kashir*, vol. ii.

77 The *Ākhbārāt's* are a series of monthly reports written from 1846 to 1853, by Saif-al Dīn primarily for Sir Henry Lawrence, the British governor of Punjab, apprising the latter about developments in the court of Kashmir. Serving as the official news writer for the British, Saif-al Dīn's twelve-volume *Ākhbār* provides an interesting overview on the functioning of the court and British involvement in the state. For details, see Mirza Saif-al Dīn, *Ākhbārāt* wa *Murasala Jāt Siyāsī wa Mūlkī dar 'Ahdi Maharaja Gulab Singh* (Srinagar: Research Library, MS.1420–1427, 1429–1430, 1433, 1434–1436).

78 Earlier on Saif-al Dīn writes that Gulab Singh had taken ill since a few days back and a team of royal physicians comprising Ḥakim ʿAẕim, Ḥakim Ata-al Lah and Ḥakim Ghafar were called to the court for treating him. The maharaja later on caught cold and in the end was cured by the medication prescribed by Ḥakim ʿAẕim. During his illness, ʿAẕim would regularly visit the Maharaja and give his opinions on different subjects. Saif-al Dīn ends the report on a rather cryptic note, saying that the maharaja was very respectful and kind to the ḥakim. On the side margins, Saif-al Dīn lists the entry under the heading "the reality of Maharaja Ṣāhab's kindness (*maharbānī*) to Ḥakim ʿAẕim." See Saif-al Dīn, *Ākhbārāt*, MS.1421, ff. 19.

79 Ibid., ff. 33.

80 Saif-al Dīn, *Ākhbārāt*, MS. 1420, ff. 87. Gilgit was conquered by the Sikh army under Zorawar Singh in 1840, but the area also known as Gilgit-Baltistan proved difficult to hold on. During Mohyi-al Dīn's rule, the area was reoccupied by the Sikh army under Vazir Lakhpat Rai in 1842.

81 Saif-al Dīn also refers to ḥakim as *dārōghah -i kiram kashān* (in charge of sericulture). See Saif-al Dīn, *Ākhbārāt*, MS. 1423, ff. 43.

82 Saif-al Dīn, *Ākhbārāt*, MS. 1421, ff. 33.

83 Ibid., 1421 ff. 45.

84 Saif-al Dīn provides a detailed description on how Gulab Singh disposed of the *jāgīrs* on assuming control of Kashmir as ruler. Ibid., ff. 4–7.

85 Also see Sajid, *Kuliyāt-i Ḥakim ʿAẕim wa Munshi Muhammad Yūsuf*.

86 For details, see Saif-al Dīn, *Ākhbārāt*, MS. 1421.

87 The manuscript of *Risāla–i Faizha'*, a Persian composition on poetry, was copied by the ʿAẕim in Lahore, the capital city of Sikh Empire. See Saifi Bukharīi *Risāla–i Faizha'*, MS. Personal Collection, Justice Ḥakim Imtiyaz Hussain, Srinagar.

88 Based on family traditions, Ṣafdar states that ʿAẕim joined the Lahore court following Ranjit Singh's conquest of Kashmir. See Hamdanī, *Tārīkh-i Shiyan-i Kashmir*, 312.

89 ʿAẕim, *Maktub Ḥakim ʿAẕim baray-i Moulvi Rajab ʿAli Shāh*.

90 Munshi Muhammad Yūsuf Bābā would also proceed to Skardu after the conquest of Gilgit as special representative of his cousin, ʿAẕim. Later he would be appointed by the *darbār* as the physician for Sakrdu. While Yūsuf would return to Srinagar after some time, his son Munshi Muhammad ʿAli would also be appointed as the physician for Sakrdu. See Saif-al Dīn, *Ākhbārāt,* MS. 1420, ff. 87.

91 See Kalim, *Kuliyat-i Khwāja Ḥasan Mir.*
92 See Budgamī, *Kāshir-e-Marsyuk Tawarīkh*.
93 See Hamdanī, *Aūsh ti Āab.*
94 The Ansarī's trace their descent from a Mullā ʿAlam Ansarī, a fifteenth-century scholar who arrived in Kashmir as an associate of Sayyid Ḥusayn Qūmmī, the progenitor of the main branch of Rizvī Sayyids in Kashmir. For details, see Sayyid Muḥsin Kashmiri, *Danishnama-i Shiyān-i Kashmir* (Karachi: MAAB, 2011) and Hamdanī, *Tārīkh-i Shiyan-i Kashmir.*
95 For Mullā Fazl ʿAli Ansari, see Hamdanī, *Tārīkh-i Shiyan-i Kashmir*, Kashmiri, *Danishnama-i Shiyān-i Kashmir* and Sajid, *Kuliyāt-i Ḥakim ʿAẕim wa Munshi Muhammad Yūsuf.*
96 Traces of this scholarship can be seen both in religious studies and in the field of *marṣiya* writing.
97 Thus, while Mullā ʿAbd al-Ghanī, the author of *Jāmi al Rizvī*, was a respected *a'lim*, the fame of his cousin, Mullā Abu al-Ḥakim Sāṭiḥ (d. 1143 AH/1730 CE), rested on his poetical composition, emerging as the favored court poet of the Mughal emperor Fa'rukh Siyar (r. 1713–19). In Sāṭiḥ's Persian *diwān* only a few isolated verses in praise of the Shiʿite Imāms can be found. The same holds true of many other Kashmiri Shiʿi poets who lived under the Mughals, including Maulana Auj'ī Kashmirī, Ḥājjī Ḥaidar, Muhammad Rizā Mushtaq, Muhammad Rafī, and so on. The work of these Mughal era poets are mostly secular in nature, devoid of any reference to their Shiʿi identity, or any *marṣiya* eulogizing the memory of the most popular Shiʿi imām, Ḥusayn. See Mīrzā Muhammad ʿAli Kashmirī, *Tazkira-i Zafran Zar*, ed. Dr. Karim Najafi Barzegar (Tehran: Society for the Appreciation of Cultural Works and Dignitaries, 2009), 50–2. Also see Ḥājjī Muhammad Aslam Khān Aslaḥ, *Tazkira-i-Shoura-i Kashmir* (Lahore: Iqbal Academy, 1983).
98 The family of Sayyid Ṣalih Rizvī, the *marṣiya* writer, played a major role in this, especially his son, Sayyid Ṣafdar Shāh (d. 1255 AH/1839CE).
99 Muqim is generally said to have passed away in 1195 AH/1750 CE, but Mahdi Khatāʿi in his note on the sole surviving manuscript of *Kashkūl*, Muqim's compendium of Shiʿi prayers and supplications, mentions the year of his teacher's death around 1235 AH/1819 CE. For details, see Kashmiri, *Danishnama-i Shiyān-i Kashmir*, 185.
100 Sayyid Murtazā Ḥusayn, *Matlaʿ-i Anwār* (Karachi: Khorasan Islamic Research Center, 1981), 234.
101 Personal collection, Āgā Sayyid ʿAbd al-Baqi Rizvī, Srinagar.
102 Ḥusayn, *Matlaʿ-i Anwār*, 234.
103 The Treaty of Amritsar (*bai nāma-i Amritsar)* signed on March 16, 1846, between Gulab Singh and officials of the East India Company represented by F. Currie and Henry Lawrence resulted in the sale of Kashmir to Gulab Singh for one crore rupees. For details, see Diwān Kripa Ram, transl. Kirpa Ram, Sukh Dev Singh Charak and Anita K. Billawaria, *Gulab Nama: A History of Maharaja Gulab Singh of Jammu and* Kashmir (Srinagar: Gulshan Books, 2005).
104 Ibid. Also see Rizvi, *A Socio Intellectual History of the Isna Ashari Shi'i in India*, vol. ii, 103–5.
105 Rizvi, *A Socio Intellectual History of the Isna Ashari Shi'i in India*, vol. ii, 333. Also see Mushirul Hasan, "Traditional Rites and Contested Meanings: Sectarian Strife in Colonial Lucknow," *Economic and Political Weekly* 31, no. 9 (March 2, 1996), 548.
106 The Muharram ceremonies, processions, and assemblies take place in a part of old Lahore which still retains its association with Kashmir, *Moḥala Shi'iyan-i Kashmir.*

107 Hamdanī, *Tārīkh-i Shiyan-i Kashmir*, 263.

108 Ḥusayn, *Matla'-i Anwār*, 47–9, 336–8. Also see Rizvi, *A Socio Intellectual History of the Isna Ashari Shi'i In India*, vol. ii, 155.

109 *Maktūb Mullā Ḥakim 'Aẕim baray-i Mullā Ṣādiq 'Ali Ansarī*, personal collection, Zakir Sayyid Yūnis Hamdanī, Labartal, Budgam. The text of the letter copied by a renowned scholar from the late nineteenth century, Sayyid Ḥusayn of Labartal, exists as marginalia in a lithographic edition of *Nukhbah*. The copied text also includes a diverse assortment of Persian and Arabic verses ranging from the *divān* of Imām 'Ali to those written on the merits of good penmanship. Given the diffused nature in which the letter has been copied, it is difficult to establish with certainty the sections which are authored by 'Aẕim, apart from the reference to the ḥadīth.

110 He also authored a work on the subject. See Mullā Ṣādiq 'Ali Ansarī, *Al-Saif al Muntaqī 'Ali M'iānadī al Murtaza* (Srinagar: Research Library, MS. 1441).

111 The ḥadīth which is characterized as weak forms a part of debates related to methodology in theology classes within Shi'i seminaries. Author's interview, Sayyid Muhsin Kashmirī, Florida, 2022.

112 Author's interview, Sayyid Muhsin Kashmirī, Florida, 2022.

113 Personal collection, Hakim Shaukat Ali Hamdani, Srinagar.

114 Hamdanī, *Tārīkh-i Shiyan-i Kashmir*, 289.

115 Mrs. Harvey, *The Adventures of a Lady in Tibet, China and Kashmir* (London: Hope & Co., 1853), 248, 261–2.

116 Harvey, *The Adventures of a Lady*, 249.

117 See Saif-al Dīn, *Ākhbārāt*.

118 In a rather lengthy description, Deykah portrays the merchant as an effeminate who lost his wealth due to his debauchery and then fled to Tibet during the reign of Maharaja Ranbir Singh, see, Deykah, *Ra'yis Nāma-i Kashmir*, ff. 24–5. The work is generally derogatory in its description of the Shi'i.

119 Saif-al Dīn, *Ākhbārāt*, MS. 1429, ff. 103.

120 Deykah praises both the father and the son for their wealth and philanthropy in the city, see, Deykah, *Ra'yis Nāma-i Kashmir*, ff. 32, also, see, Hamdanī, *Tārīkh-i Shiyan-i Kashmir*, 397–8.

121 *Naqal as Asal Hukumnama Maharaj zair tanazay-i Ahl-i Tashi*, MS. Personal Collection, Hakim Shaukat Ali Hamdani, Srinagar.

122 See Saif-al Dīn, *Ākhbārāt*.

123 "Āukūt, or harvest-home festival, which takes place on the second day of the Diwali, when the city people are fed at the expense of the State on the first fruits of the autumn harvest.[. . .] Huge feasts [. . .] are prepared at six appointed places—for the better class Pandits, the common Pandits, the better class Mūsālmans, the common Mūsālmans, the Shi'is and the Dogras." Walter R. Lawrence, *The Valley of Kashmir* (London: H. Frowde, 1895), 271.

124 See Saif-al Dīn, *Ākhbārāt*, MS. 1423, ff. 110, 142.

125 Ibid.

126 Saif-al Dīn, *Ākhbārāt*, MS. 1421, 71.

127 Lawrence, *The Valley of Kashmir*, 271.

128 In his letter Ṭālib 'Ali mentions how he came to know of the sad news through a letter (from the nawab?) provided by Muhammad 'Ali. Further down in his condolence Ṭālib writes if destiny prevails, he will personally visit Murad 'Ali to offer his condolences. See *Maktūb Munshi Ṭālib 'Ali baray-i Nawab Murad 'Ali Khān, Khairpur*, personal collection, Hakim Shaukat Ali Hamdani, Srinagar.

129 Mīrzā Muhammad Mujrim Kashmirī, *M'ayār Lughāt Qūyim: Firhangh Shāhnama*, ed. Murtaza 'Imranī (Tehran: Intishārat Sukhan, 1978), 22.
130 Saif-al Dīn, *Ākhbārāt*, MS. 1422, ff. 146.
131 Deykah, *Ra'yis Nāma-i Kashmir*, ff. 32.
132 Saif-al Dīn, *Ākhbārāt*, MS. 1427, ff. 101.
133 Hamdanī, *Tārīkh-i Shiyan-i Kashmir*, 397–8.
134 Both the Jamia Masjid and *M'ārak* are based on the Iranian four *iwan* mosque plan, with the central open courtyard of the mosque transformed into the roofed *pukhir* of *M'ārak*. For details, see Hamdanī, *The Syncretic Traditions of Islamic Religious Architecture of Kashmir.*
135 Mīrzā Muhammad 'Ali is specially remembered for arranging for the wedding expenses of girls belonging to impoverished families in the city. For details, see Hamdanī, *Tārīkh-i Shiyan-i Kashmir*, 289. Deykah also lauds the merchants unlimited philanthropy, see, Deykah, *Ra'yis Nāma-i Kashmir*, ff. 32.
136 Literally lover, *muḥib* is used here to signify a friend of the Prophet's family. *Muḥib*, *dost* (friend), along with *mūmin* are some of the terms employed by Kashmiri *marṣiya* writers for addressing the congregation of mourners.
137 The Kufis betrayed Ḥusayn at Karbala and played a leading role in imprisoning surviving members of his family, publicly parading them in the streets of Kufa. The phrase "like a Kufi" has become synonymous among Kashmiri Shi'i for someone who betrays with no shame. Often, it is used as a slight against the Sunnis, though the use is not limited to such a meaning alone.

Chapter 4

1 The *nisba* Qazvinī is probably based on Sayyid Ibrahim's association with the ulema of Qazvinī family who operated their school in the shrine city of Karbala, Iraq. The family had migrated from Qazvin, Iran to Iraq in the late eighteenth century under the brothers, Sayyid Muhammad Bāqir al Qazvinī and Sayyid Muhammad 'Ali al-Qazvinī. The leading 'alim of the family in nineteenth century Iraq included Sayyid Ibrahim al Qazvinī (1799–1848). Sayyid Ibrahim's *nisba* would be based on his associations with the school of Qazvinī's in Iraq rather than the toponym Qazvin.
2 See Saif-al Dīn, *Ākhbārāt*, MS.1422.
3 For Mullā Ashraf, see Stephen Frederic Dale, "A Safavid Poet in the Heart of Darkness: The Indian Poems of Ashraf Mazandarani," *Iranian Studies* 36, no. 2 (June 2003): 197–212. In Kashmir, Ashraf is also said to have composed a *marṣiya* for the *Nūrbakhshī* shaykh, Mīr Shams-al Dīn 'Iraki. See Kashmiri, *Danishnama-i Shiyān-i Kashmir*.
4 While we find greater reliance on Iranian munshis in the first half of nineteenth century, the same were increasingly replaced by men of Indian origin after 1857. For an account of Iranian munshis, see the account of early European victors to Kashmir, especially, Moorcroft and Trebeck, *Travels in the Himalayan provinces of Hindustan and the Panjab*, 2 vols.
5 For Shi'i mujtahids in the nineteenth century, see Meir Litvak, *Shi 'i Scholars of Nineteenth-century Iraq: The 'Ulama' of Najaf and Karbala'* (Cambridge: Cambridge University Press, 1998).

6 The issue is believed to have first risen during the rule of the Shi'i Mughal subedar of Kashmir, Ibrahim Khān (d.1709), son of the famous Mughal governor, 'Ali Mardan Khān (d. 1657). For details, see Sayyid Abū'l Qāsim Rizvī, *Al S'ādah fi Sayādat al S'ādāt* (Lahore, 1890).
7 Saif-al Dīn, *Ākhbārāt*, MS.1422, ff. 110.
8 Ibid.
9 Ibid.
10 Hamdanī, *Tārīkh-i Shiyan-i Kashmir*, 265.
11 See Mullā Muhammad Bāqir, *Risālah i Hidāyat al Dhalīl ilā Siwā' al Sabīl* (Lahore: Ṣahab Saqib, 1308 AH/1890 CE).
12 Ḥakim 'Aẓim, *Maktub Ḥakim 'Aẓim baray-i Moulvi Rajab 'Ali Shāh*.
13 Hamdanī, *Tārīkh-i Shiyan-i Kashmir*, 265, and Sajid, *Kuliyāt-i Ḥakim 'Aẓim wa Munshi Muhammad Yūsuf*, 24.
14 The only historical document relating to the functioning of M'ārak and the role of the M'ārakdars as its *mutwalī* is to be found in an official decree from the Mughals in eighteenth century. This legal document is preserved with the M'ārakdar family. See Personal collection, Sayyid Jalāl-al Dīn M'ārakdar, Zadibal, Srinagar. For the role of *mutwalī* as administrator of an endowed property (wakf) especially in nineteenth-century colonial South Asia, see Eric Lewis Beverley, "Property, Authority and Personal Law, Waqf" in Colonial South Asia," *South Asia Research* 31, no. 2: 155–82 (New Delhi: Sage Publications, 2011).
15 Āgā Sayyid Ḥasan M'ārakdar, *Irshād ul Jāhilīn wa Tanbīh ul Ghāfilīn* (Srinagar: Bardkar Press, undated), 4–5. Also see Sajid, *Kuliyāt-i Ḥakim 'Aẓim wa Munshi Muhammad Yūsuf*, 27.
16 The text of 'Aẓim's verdict does not even indicate if in their role of M'ārakdari, the family of M'ārakdars are allowed to collect the donations made to the *Imāmbāda*.
17 This would be the main argument used against the M'ārakdars, when the issue finally landed in the court, for details see *Rūbakār az Adalat-i Sadr-i Srinagar az misl-177, Faisla* 13 Poh, 1925 Bikrami, Personal collection, Hakim Shaukat Ali Hamdani, Srinagar.
18 Tracing their descent in Kashmir through the *Kubrawī* shaykh, Sayyid Taj-al Dīn Hamdanī, buried at Shahmpora, Nowhatta in Srinagar.
19 The Madnī sayyids trace their decent from Sayyid Muhammad Madnī, a fifteenth-century missionary who is associated with the court of Zain-al Ābidīn and is buried near Nowshera.
20 Sayyid 'Ali b. Ṣafdar is considered among the *mujtahids* of Lucknow. For details, see Kashmiri, *Danishnama-i Shiyān-i Kashmir*.
21 Cole, *Roots of North Indian Shi'ism in Iran*, 80.
22 Hamid Algar's introduces the term in describing how many Shi'i religious families produced successive generation of eminent scholars. See Hamid Algar, "Allama Sayyid Muhammad Husayn Tabatabai: Philosopher, Exegete and Gnostic," *Journal of Islamic Studies* (Oxford: Oxford University Press, 2006).
23 Mullā Muhammed predeceased Akhūnd Mullā Javad. See Kashmiri, *Danishnama-i Shiyān-i Kashmir*.
24 In addition to Akhūnd Javad, Mullā Fazal 'Ali had three other sons, Mullā 'Abdullah (d.1296 AH/1878 CE), Mullā 'Abbas and Mullā Muhammad Ḥusayn. The family continued through the line of Mullā 'Abbas. Akhūnd Javad had a son who predeceased his father, passing away in 1264 AH/1847 CE. For details, see Munshi

J'afar, *Tanbīh ul ibād fī ahwāl-i Moulvi Muhammad Javad* (Srinagar: All Jammu & Kashmir Shi'i Association, 1377 AH/1957).

25 Sayyid Bāqir addresses Mullā Javad with the honorific title of *Hūjjat-al Islam* (Proof of Islam). In nineteenth century Shi'i'a world the title was rarely used, though during the reign of the Fatah Ali Shah (r. 1797–1834) of Iran it was at times used for leading *mujtahids*. The large-scale use of the term for mid-level clerics is a contemporary phenomenon, see Sayyid Bāqir, *Risāla-i Sayf al Sāram* (Lahore: Sahafi, undated), 22.

26 Hamdanī, *Tārīkh-i Shiyan-i Kashmir*, 253.

27 Ann Willner and Dorothy Willner, "The Rise and Role of Charismatic Leaders," in *The Annals of the American Academy of Political and Social Science*, Vol. 358 (New Nations: The Problem of Political Development, March 1965), 79.

28 Ḥasan A. Mīrzādeh, Asnadazkamkhai Mali bazairan-imuslamanshabiqario hind darmashaddarduran-i Qajjar, in vol. 4, no: 16–17, 1391, http://shamseh.aqr-libjournal.ir/issue_4930_4946.html.

29 Hamdani, *Tārīkh-i Shiyan-i Kashmir*, 255.

30 Bāqir, *Risāla-i Sayf al Sāram*, 23. Bāqir also claims that many individuals whose ancestors were known by the surname of Dar, Joo, Mīr and Bhat have recently started claiming to be Sayyids, ibid.

31 Author's interview, Mohammad Huzaifa Nizam, Peshawar, 2021. According to the Census of 1911, out of a total population of 3,577 Shi'i living in Peshawar, a majority traced their roots to Kashmiri. See C. Latimer, *Census of India, 1911, vol xiii, North-West frontier Province* (Peshawar: Commercial Press, 1912), 72.

32 Ibid. For a description of the bazar of Peshawar in the early twentieth century, see E. G. G. Hasting, *Report of the Regular Settlement of the Peshawar District of the Punjab* (Lahore: Central jail Press, 1878). Hasting's reports about how, 'The trades of working in leather and copper, silver wire making, dyeing, cleaning and winding silk, and the preparation of snuff, are carried on by Cashmiris, Peshdwaris and Cabulis', Ibid., 19.

33 Bāqir, *Risāla-i Sayf al Sāram*, 23.

34 According to Muhsin Kashmirī, the total amount due to sayyids from Ṣafdar's *khums* amounted to ten thousand rupees, of which half the money had been distributed by the merchant himself, while the rest of five thousand rupees were sent to Akhūnd Mullā Javad for distribution, Mohsin also asserts that in his distribution Jawad followed in the footsteps of his father, ensuring that all those who claimed to be sayyid received a share from the *khums* money. for detail, see Sayyid Mūhsin Kashmirī, *Groh bandi dar Kashmir*, unpublished paper, 2021.

35 Anonymous, *Risāla-i 'Igala* (Lucknow: Maṭbah-i Islam, 1890).

36 For an understanding of how the Rebellion was seen in British imagination as a product of Muslim religiosity, see Ilyse R. Morgenstein Fuerst, *Indian Muslim Minorities and the 1857 Rebellion; Religion, Rebels and Jihad* (London: I.B. Tauris, 2017). Also check, S.R. Wasti, "British Policy towards the Indian Muslims Immediately after 1857," in *Muslim Struggle for Freedom in India* (Delhi: Renaissance Publishing House, 1993).

37 For an understanding of this early migration to Punjab, see Victoria Schofield, *Kashmir in Conflict: India, Pakistan and the Unending War* (London: I.B. Tauris, 2010) and Zutshi, *Languages of Belonging*.

38 Ranjit Singh also encouraged the settling of Kashmiri shawl weavers in Punjab, to cater to the court demand for the shawl cloth, which was then used ' to pay allowances to his followers, to grant robes of honor, and to send gifts to the other

rulers, including officials of the British East India Company', Michelle Maskiell, "Consuming Kashmir: Shawls and Empire, 1500-2000," *Journal of World History* 13, no. 1 (Spring, 2002): 35.

39 Frederic Drew, *The Jummoo and Kashmir Territories: A Geographical Account* (London: E. Stanford, 1876), 179.

40 Maskiell, *Consuming Kashmir: Shawls and Empire*, 39.

41 Ibid., 51.

42 See Saif-al Dīn, *Ākhbārāt*, MS. 1424.

43 The pitiful condition of the shawl weavers is described by Temple, who visited Kashmir twice (1859, 1871) during Ranbir Singh's reign in these words:

> The shawl-weavers, too are Muhammadans, and form a numerous and withal a miserable class, badly paid, badly nourished and badly housed, and therefore physically and morally wretched.

Richard Temple, *Journals Kept in Hyderabad, Kashmir, Sikkim And Nepal*, vol. i (London: WH Allen & Co., 1887), 276.

44 Ibid., vol. ii, 144.

45 See Zutshi, *Languages of Belonging*.

46 Khwāja Mohyi-al Dīn Gandrū also owned a house at Zaina Kadal near the bridge. This house which still exits was later bought by a Shiʿi trader, Ḥājjī Jaʿfar Khān and is still remembered as *Jaʿfar Khan sinz koothi*.

47 Temple, *Journals Kept in Hyderabad, Kashmir, Sikkim And Nepal*, vol. ii, 60.

48 Temple refers to him as Mukhta Shāh. Khwāja Mukhtār also authored a manual of Kashmiri crafts, see Temple, *Journals Kept in Hyderabad, Kashmir, Sikkim And Nepal*, vol. ii.

49 Temple speaks about Ghafar Shāh is his second visit of 1871, though it is possible that he met him earlier too. In his journal of 1859, he speaks of meeting an unnamed Naqshbandī Sayyid. Fauq on the other hand names him as Gafūr, son of Aḥmad Shāh, son of Shāh Niyaẓ. For details, see Temple, *Journals Kept in Hyderabad, Kashmir, Sikkim and Nepal*, vol. ii. and Mohammad Dīn Fauq, *Tārīkh Aqwam Kashmir* (Srinagar: Gulshan Publishers, 1996), 156.

50 Mohammad Dīn Fauq, *Mashahir-i Kashmir* (Lahore: Zafar Brothers, 1930), 20–3, also, see Fauq, *Tārīkh-i Aqwam Kashmir*, 292.

51 Ibid., 300.

52 The Jalālī's were a Sayyid family hailing from Iran, whose ancestor had arrived in Kashmir during the late Mughal period. For details, see Kashmiri, *Danishnama-i Shiyān-i Kashmir.*

53 Bates, *Gazetteer of Kashmir*, 30.

54 Ibid.

55 Ibid., 31.

56 Muzaffar Khan, *Kashmiri Muslims: An Historical Outline*, vol. ii (Srinagar: Humanizer Publications, 2012), 280–1.

57 For the architecture of the mosque, see Hamdani, *The Syncretic Traditions of Islamic Relegious Architecture of Kashmir.*

58 Deykah, *Raʿyis Nāma-i Kashmir*, ff. 24–5.

59 Hamdani, *Tārīkh-i Shiyan-i Kashmir*, 290–1.

60 Not much has been written on the origin of the institution of Mīrwaʿiẓ and Kashmir. For details, see Sheikh Showkat Hussain, *Kashmir Profiles* (Beirut: Dar-al Kutub al ʿIlmiyah, 1971), 30–4.

61 Moulvi Muhammad Shāh S'aādat, *Tārīkh-i Kashmir ki roznama dairy* (Srinagar: Ghūlam Muhammad Nūr Muhmmad Tajiran-i Kutb, 1947). Also see Fauq, *Mashahir-i Kashmir*, 120–24.

62 Munshi Ḥasan 'Ali was a teacher, who helped the Christian missionaries in setting up a school in Srinagar. Ḥasan 'Ali's *Vaq'āt -i Kashmir* is based on journal that the author composed during the reign of Maharaja Pratap Singh in late nineteenth century. Of the original five volumes, only three remained with his descendants. In his autobiography, Munshi Isḥāq borrows liberally from the journal while detailing out some of the events in nineteenth century. Unfortunately, the manuscripts of the journal written in Persian and Urdu, were forwarded to a publisher in Lal Bazar but have neither been published nor the original manuscripts returned to the owners. Some of the events in the book have been published in the revised edition of Hamdani, *Tārīkh-i Shiyan Kashmir*, Munshi Muhammad Isḥāq, *Nida-i Ḥaq* (Srinagar: Markaz-i Ishayat, 2014), and *Jamia Masjid Heritage Corridor: Conservation and Revitalization Plan* (INATCH: 2009, unpublished report).

63 Nowpora is a mixed neighborhood in Srinagar city with a small but relatively well-off Shi'i population.

64 Should be 1872.

65 Isḥāq, *Nida-i Ḥaq*, 31–2.

66 Bates, *Gazetteer of Kashmir*, 32.

67 Kuihāmī, *Tārīkh-i Ḥasan* (199), 594–96.

68 For details see Khuihāmī, *Tārīkh-i Ḥasan* (1999), 593–96, Hamdanī, *Tārīkh-i Shiyan-i Kashmir*, 215–16. For a copy of the verdict of Maharaja Ranbir Singh on the riots, which includes the testimony of Aziz Khān, a Sunni *karkhandar* from Malik Ṣāhab in Srinagar, see *Hawal-i Sarkar-i Wala Madar Maharaja Ranbir Singh dar Maramlah Gharat-i Ahl—i Tashi,* Personal collection, Hakim Shaukat Ali Hamdani, Srinagar.

69 See Isḥāq, *Nida-i Ḥaq*,

70 In another instance Gandrū asks the Sunnis of Malik Ṣāhab locality to desist from building a bathing house and *hammam* in the neighborhood, as it faced the shrine of Shaykh Ḥamza and would be disrespectful to the saint's memory. On the merchant's advice, the residents then decide to build a mosque instead. See *Hawal-i Sarkar-i Wala Madar Maharaja Ranbir Singh dar Maramlah Gharat-i Ahl—i Tashi.*

71 *Hawal-i Sarkar-i Wala Madar Maharaja Ranbir Singh dar Maramlah Gharat-i Ahl—i Tashi.*

72 For the Kashmiri text of the *marṣiya*, see Maqbūl Sājid, *Kuliyat-i Munshi Muhammad Mustafa wa Munshi Muhammed Yūsuf* (Srinagar: Imam Hussein Research & Publishing Centre, 2002).

73 See Hamdanī, *Tārīkh-i Shiyan-i Kashmir*, 292; regarding the *bagh* of Muhammad 'Ali of which no trace or description survives, Gates provides us with this brief description:

> The Mar or snake canal maybe held to flow from the Naopoura Kadal on the south-west margin of the Dal; it passes successively the Mīrzā Muhammad Ally {Ali} Bagh on the right bank, the Mīrzā Raza Bagh on the left bank.

Bates, *Gazetteer of Kashmir*, 359.

74 *Hawal-i Sarkar-i Wala Madar Maharaja Ranbir Singh dar Maramlah Gharat-i Ahl—i Tashi.*

75 Hamdanī, *Tārīkh-i Shiyan-i Kashmir*, 215–16.

76 Bates, *Gazetteer of Kashmir*, 32.

77 *Riot between Sheas and Soonees in Cashmere*, Foreign Department, Political B, progs. March 1873, nos. 75–79. National Archives, Delhi.

78 Mukerjee was also responsible for reviving the sericulture industry in the state. During Maharaja Pratap Singh's time he served as minister of the state before finally leaving Kashmir for his native Calcutta, where he died in 1920 as vice-chairman of Calcutta Corporation. See *The Pioneer Mail and Indian Weekly News, Volume 47, 1920.*

79 *Riot between Sheas and Soonees in Cashmere*, Foreign Department.

80 Ibid.

81 Pandit Hargopal Kaul Khasta, *Gūldastā-i Kashmir* (Srinagar: Sheikh Ghūlam Muhammad & Sons, 1956), 211. Also see Bates, *Gazetteer of Kashmir.*

82 Khwāja Sa'ad al-Dīn, 'Shi'i Nāma' in *Asun ti Gindun*, vol. i (Sringar: Ghūlam Muhammad wa Nūr Muhammad, 1903), 19–21.

83 Hamdanī, *Tārīkh-i Shiyan-i Kashmir*, 290.

84 Sayyid Sajād (transl.), *Dastāvizat T'amir-i Imāmbāda Hassanabad*, Personal collection, Mirza Muhammad Reza, Srinagar.

85 The building was demolished in the 1990s and a new expanded structure created in its place. For details, see Hamdani, "The Maarak and the Tradition of Imambadas in Kashmir."

86 *Biyāz*, Private collection. Munshi Nazir Aḥmad, Srinagar.

87 The brothers, Bābū Rishambar and Nilambar were Bengali civil servants whose services was retained by the Kashmir darbār. In addition to their work in the judiciary, the two were also involved in reviving the sericulture industry in Kashmir. For details, see Lawrence, *The Valley of Kashmir.*

88 Isḥāq, *Nida-i Ḥaq*, 76.

89 'Ali Malik was brother-in-law of Ḥājjī Ṣafdar Bābā and a *kar khandar* himself.

90 In their deposition in the court the Jalālī's maintained that the transfer took place through the agency of the Mīr family, who were projected by the Jalālī's as the real custodians of the *imāmbāda* as opposed to the M'ārakdars. Accordingly, the Jalālī's maintained the transfer happed through Khalil Mīr, son of Hatim Mīr who was the custodian at the time of *imāmbāda's* reconstruction in 1831. For details, see *Rūbakār az Adalat-i Sadr-i Srinagar.*

91 In the Sunni too, a similar caste-based division "*aseil*" for the upper caste and "*kaminah*" for those termed as lower caste existed.

92 Acquisition of wealth was a possible mean for circumventing the disadvantage of caste. There are instances, especially from the twentieth century when improvised upper class families married their daughters into economically well-off families of lower social standing, such a union proving beneficial to both the parties. Nevertheless, such instances are far limited in nineteenth century Kashmir.

93 For the events that took place during this time, see Hamdanī, *Tārīkh-i Shiyan-i Kashmir.*

94 Following, 'Abdullah's early death in 1891 during a cholera pandemic, Ṣafdar effectively took over the management of the *imāmbāda*. This, and the leading role he played in the legal entanglements related to the custodianship of the *M'ārak* and the *Rūżā-i- Mīr Shams-al Dīn 'Iraki* at Zadibal, would result in popularizing the *Firqa-i Qadim* as *Firqa-i Ṣafdar Shāh.* In contemporary Kashmir the party is simply known as *Moulvi Ṣāhabī* as opposed to members of the *Firqa-i Jadid* who are represented as *Āgā Ṣāhabī.*

95 The issue of the custodianship of ʿIraki shrine was finally resolved in a court case decided in 1944. See Hamdanī, *Tārīkh-i Shiyan-i Kashmir*, 281.
96 Hamdanī, *Tārīkh-i Shiyan-i Kashmir*, 267.
97 See Maqbūl Sājid, *Ḥakim Ḥasan ʿAli: Shaksiyat ti Fann* (Srinagar: Imam Hussein Research & Publishing Centre, 2002).
98 A particularly divisive question which gave rise to public passions was the issue of companionship of Mʿammūr-i Ḥabshī. See Bashir Ahmad Khan, "The Ahl-i-Ḥādith: A Socio-Religious Reform Movement in Kashmir," *The Muslim World* 90 (Spring 2000): 143.
99 Lawrence, *The Valley of Kashmir*, 285.
100 See Āgā Bākir al-Mūsāvī al-Najafī, *Nafḥtah al-Najaf* (Srinagar: TFC Center, 2018).
101 In addition, Ḥaidar ʿAli studied under Mullā Ḥusayn Fazil-i Irdkanī, Mīrzā Abū'l Qāsim Ṭabāṭabāʾī, and Shaykh Zain-al ʿĀbidīn Mazandaranī. For details, see Kashmiri, *Danishnama-i Shiyān-i Kashmir.*
102 In his writings Ḥaidar addresses Mahdi as Ḥājj Mahdi Shāh. See Mullā Ḥaidar ʿAli Kashmirī, *Risāla-i Fasl al Khitāb* (Lahore: Matbah-i Islamī, 1888).
103 See Sayyid Ḥasan Rizvī, *Majālis-al Abrar* (Srinagar: Research Library, MS. 3075), Bāqir, *Risāla-i Sayf al Sāram* and Bāqir, *Risālah i Hidāyat al Dhalīl ilā Siwā' al Sabīl.*
104 The wearing of a turban was a normative practice among adult Muslims within Kashmir but assumed a special significance among the ulema classes. Rizvī's critique of Mahdi is for attiring himself in a turban which because of its distinctive shape and color was the privilege of the ulema.
105 Rizvī, *Majālis-al Abrar*, ff. 12.
106 Mīrzā Ḥusayn Nūrī Tabrisī, *Badr Mushʿashʿa* (Bombay, 1890).
107 Ḥaidar ʿAli performed his Ḥājj in 1331 AH/1912 CE. Author's interview, Dr. Amjad Ansari, Srinagar, 2021.
108 "very few Kashmiris make the pilgrimage to Mecca, though the journey is now easy, and does not cost more than Rs. 340. In 1892 twenty-one Kashmiris went to Mecca, and this was an unusually large number," Lawrence, *The Valley of Kashmir*, 285.
109 Unfortunately, we do not have the names of Mahdi's companions on this pilgrimage.
110 Ibid. Rizvī's text clearly indicates the growing popularity of Sayyid Mahdi's among the masses.
111 Hamdanī, *Tārīkh-i Shiyan-i Kashmir*, 228.
112 See Ḥakim Ghulām Ṣafdar Hamdanī, "Yad-i Ruftagan," in *al-Irshad* (Budgam: Anjuman-i Sharie Shiyan, 1381AH/1961CE), Ramzan and Shawwal issue.
113 Munshi Muhammad Jaʿfar, *Shajrah-Mullā khāndan,* Personal collection, Dr. Amjad Ansarī, Srinagar.
114 Author's interview with Zakir Sayyid Sami-al Lah Jalālī, Srinagar, Kashmir, 2021.
115 Author's interview, Munshi Ghulam Hassan, Srinagar, 2017 and Mīrzā Muhammad Raza, Srinagar, 2020.
116 Hakim ʿAli Raza, *Dairy*, Personal collection, Hakim Bashir Ahmad, Srinagar.
117 Ḥakim Ghulām Ṣafdar Hamdanī, *Dairy*, Personal collection, Hakim Shaukat Ali Hamdani, Srinagar.
118 Author's interview with Aga Faisal Qizalbash, Srinagar, 2021.
119 See Saif-al Dīn, *Ākhbārāt*, MS. 1424.
120 Popularly known as the nawabs of Nawab Gunj, Lahore, the Qizalbash nawabs would maintain a sustained interest in affairs of Kashmiri Shiʿis. For Nawazish ʿAli Khān, see Sir Roper Lethbridge, *The Golden Book of India, a Genealogical and*

Biographical Dictionary of the Ruling Princes, Chiefs, Nobles, and Other Personages, Titled or Decorated, of the Indian Empire (London: Sampson Low, Marston & company, 1900), 221.

121 Author's interview with Āgā Faisal Qizalbash, Srinagar, 2021.

122 Moulvi Iftikhar Ansarī, *Maktub wa Shajrah-i varisan-i Moulvi Ḥaidar ʿAli Ansarī*, Personal collection, Hakim Shaukat Ali Hamdani, Srinagar.

123 Author's interview with Āgā Pervaiz Safvī, Srinagar, 2021.

124 Author's interview with Āgā Sayyid Bāqir Mūsāvī, Srinagar, 2021.

125 See Yaqoob Laway and others versus Gulla and others, 2004 (III), SLJ 761, High Court, Srinagar.

Chapter 5

1 Lawrence, *The Valley of Kashmir*, 285.

2 See Saif-al Dīn, *Ākhbārāt*, MS. 1424, 1425, 1426.

3 See Sufi, Kashir, vol ii, 483. An incomplete *biyaz* of Mahdi in his own hand is to be found in the private library of Justice Hakim Imtiyaz Ḥusayn, Srinagar.

4 After graduating from the University of Calcutta, Mukerjee joined the bar in Lahore in 1867. See William Digby, *Condemned Unheard: the Government of India and HH the Maharaja of Kashmir* (London: Indian Political Agency, 1890), 58.

5 Hamdanī, *Aūsh ti Āab.*

6 Also known as Baghwanpora, the ḥakims trace their decent from Ḥakim Hemayun who is said to have arrived in Kashmir as a part of the Mughal emperor, Akbar's entourage in the sixteenth century. Unlike, the ḥakims from the Mullā and Qizalbash family, those of Baghwanpora remained uninvolved in community matters and dissensions. For details on the family, see Hamdanī, *Tārīkh-i Shiyan-i Kashmir*, 339–42.

7 On Naqī, see Hamdanī, *Tārīkh-i Shiyan-i Kashmir*, 356. The ḥakim collapsed in open court, and the maharaja is said to have cried out, '*Naqī da putur koun hai*' (who is Naqī's son). Author's interview with Aga Faisal Qizalbash, Srinagar, 2021.

8 See Maqbūl Sājid, *Ḥakim Ḥasan ʿAli: Shaksiyat ti Fann* (Srinagar: Imam Hussein Research & Publishing Centre, 2002).

9 Amar Singh would serve as the vice president of the Administrative Council as well as the Commander-in-Chief of the state's army. His son, Hari Singh, would succeed his uncle to the throne in 1925. For details, see Sufi, Kashir, vol. ii.

10 For an analysis of the British encroachment on Pratap Singh's authority, see Robert A. Huttenback, "The Emasculation of a Princely State: The Case of Kashmir," *Journal of Asian History* 7, no. 1 (1973): 1–29.

11 See Razā, *Dairy.*

12 Ibid.

13 On the other hand, in his memoirs ʿAli Razā related an incident where Pratap Singh solicited the aid of Ḥakim Mahdi to have his father, Maharaja Ranbir Singh poisoned. Though the claim of parricide is unsubstantiated, Ranbir was open about his preference for Amar Singh to succeed him.

14 Bāqir, *Risāla-i Sayf al Ṣāram*, 18.

15 MS. W.636, Walter Art Museum, Maryland. Those who worked on the paintings in the album are not named.

16 Bāqir, *Risāla-i Sayf al Ṣāram*, 21.

17 See Maqbūl Sājid, *Kuliyat-i Munshi Mustafa ʿAli and Munshi Muhammad Yūsuf*, vol. i (Srinagar: Imam Hussein Research & Publishing Centre, 2000).
18 The school was set up in in 1874 and would later be renamed as MP School.
19 In the Munshi family archives (at Srinagar), there is a letter from the British Resident at Kashmir, conveying the Viceroy's appreciation for the Ḥasan, Personal collection, Munshi Altaf, Srinagar.
20 The second Delhi Darbār was held in 1903, to mark the succession of Edward VII as the Emperor of India.
21 Hamdanī, *Tārīkh-i Shiyan-i Kashmir,* 337.
22 Ibid., 338.
23 These include works on both religious as well as secular subjects printed by Mirzā Muhammad of Shiraz in Bombay and more significantly the publishing house of Munshi Nawal Kishore, set up at Lucknow in in 1858. For an overview of lithographic production in nineteenth century India, see Lithography ii. In India, entry in *Encyclopedia Iranica*, available online: https://iranicaonline.org/articles/lithography-ii-in-india, last accessed December 30, 2021.
24 Personal collection, Yasmin ʿAli, Srinagar.
25 See Hamdani, *Tārīkh-i Shiyan-i Kashmir,* 338.
26 Mīrzā Abu'l Qāsim would remain the most prolific Kashmiri *marṣiya* writer, whose poetical composition has achieved a popular acclaim among the audience that remains unsurpassed to this day. For more on his life and works and details on his forced migration, see Maqbūl Sājid, *Mīrzā Abu'l Qāsim: Maqām ti Kalām*, vol. 3 (Srinagar: Imam Hussein Research & Publishing Centre, 2003).
27 Biharī was a Ḥanafī scholar who served in the Mughal court under Emperor Aurangzeb (r. 1658–1707) and Shāh ʿĀlam (r. 1707–1712) as a qazi, tutor to the Imperial family and as a minister. For details, see Asad Q. Ahmed, "The Sullam al-ʿulūm of (d. 1707) Muḥibb Allāh al-Bihārī," in *The Oxford Handbook of Islamic Philosophy,* ed. Khaled El-Rouayheb and Sabine Schmidtke (Oxford: Oxford University Press, 2016).
28 For details, see Kashmiri, *Danishnama-i Shiyān-i Kashmir.*
29 *Maktūb Ḥakim Ḥasan ʿAli baray-i Nawab Fateh ʿAli Khan Qizalbash*, Personal collection, Hakim Bashir Aḥmad, Srinagar.
30 For Tonkī, see Abū Majid Muhammad, *Tazkira Maulana Mufti Muhammad ʿAbdullah Tonkī*, 2021, available online: www.dawateislami.net, last accessed December 30, 2021.
31 This includes Pandit Salgiram Kaul Sālik, whose *qasida* (panegyric) on the accession of George V. (r. 1910–36) as Emperor of India, was corrected by Ḥasan ʿAli, Personal Collection, Munshi Ashraf, Srinagar.
32 Author's interview, Bismillah Rizvī, Srinagar, 2019.
33 See Mīrzā, *Rahbar-i Kashmir.*
34 Personal collection, Shaykh Muhammad Shafʿi, Srinagar.
35 Author's interview, Āgā Sayyid Mudasir Rizvī, Srinagar, 2021.
36 Author's interview, Bismillah Rizvī, Srinagar, 2021.
37 The first organized religious school for women within Kashmiri Shiʿi society was started by Sayedah Nisar Fatima (d. 1999), daughter and wife of renowned ʿ*alims*. Her school, *Maktab-i Tʿalim Quran wa Ḥadīth* was started in 1979 at Khandah in South Kashmir and trained women form both Shiʿi as well as Sunni background, author's interview, Sibti Hasaan, Srinagar, 2022.

38 The Gazetteer of 1873 is the only official document with figures based on sectarian lines. Of the total estimated Shiʿi population of Kashmir (15,000), 8,000 was based in Srinagar. As against this the Sunni population of the city stood at one-thirds of the total population of the community in Kashmir. See Bates, *Gazetteer of Kashmir*, 30.
39 Ṣafdar argues that the Shiʿi avoided jobs which had a public dealing and while it may seem as a probable reason given the strain in sectarian relations in the city, it would be difficult to accept this as sole reason. Ṣafdar goes on to list some major occupations that were not represented in Shiʿi society of Kashmir till mid-twentieth century. For details, see Hamdani, *Tārīkh-i Shiyan-i Kashmir*, 160.
40 The Sunni *shawlbafs* accounted for 16 percent of the total Sunni population. See Bates, *Gazetteer of Kashmir*, 30.
41 For details see Rai, *Hindu Rulers, Muslim Subjects*.
42 Andrew Wilson, *The Abode of the Snow* (London: Willam Beackwood & Sons, 1875), 366.
43 The date of construction of the house was found carved on a wooden beam, during the dismantling of the building. Author's interview, Sayyid Danish Rizvī, Srinagar, 2021.
44 A case would be *Khānaqāh-i Sokhta*, Nawa Kadal, the seat of the powerful family of Pandit courtiers: Dhars, which also became the chosen area of residence for the Ansarī's on their arrival in Srinagar.
45 Celebrated on March 21, Navrouz represents a pre-Islamic, Iranian festival celebrating the New Year which was incorporated in Muslim societies imbibed with Persianate cultural influences. Among the Shiʿis the festival was reinvented as the day on which the first Shiʿi imām, ʿAli succeeded to the office of Caliphate.
46 Author's interview, Prof. Sayyid Vilayat Rizvī, Srinagar, 2021.
47 The family of Ḥājjī Asghar Mīr.
48 Ṣafdar Bābā was originally from Babapora but settled down in Nowpora where he had relations with the Sayyids of Madnī family. In Calcutta he operated a business house dealing with Kashmiri crafts under the name "Liberty Arts & Crafts." Author's interview with Āgā Faisal Qizalbash, Srinagar, 2021.
49 The expensive Kashmiri shawl, make a brief appearance in one of Tagore's stories, *The Son of Rashmani*.
50 Author's interview, Sayyid Mohsin Kashmiri, Florida, 2021.
51 Author's interview, Sayyid Zahoor Rizvī, Srinagar, 2021.
52 File Foreign Department, General A, Proceedings, January 1911, nos. 1–2, Government of India, National Archives, Delhi.
53 *Shajray-i Tayibiya Sayyid Ṣāliḥ Rizvī madafun Haigam*, 2001, bearing the stamp of Āgā Sayyid ʿAbdu'l Baqī Rizvī of Nabdipora, Personal collection of Sayyid Akhter Rizvī, Narbal, Srinagar.
54 For details on Chinese government in the region, see J. Dowson, "Route from Kashmír, viâ Ladakh, to Yarkand, by Ahmed Shāh Nakshahbandi," *The Journal of the Royal Asiatic Society of Great Britain and Ireland* 12 (1850): 372–85.
55 File Foreign and Political Department, Secret E, proceedings August 1916, nos. 63–68, Government of India, National Archives, Delhi.
56 For Trans-Himalayan trade in the region, see Janet Rizvi, *Trans-Himalayan Caravans: Merchant Princes and Peasant Traders in Ladakh* (Delhi: Oxford University Press, 2004).
57 Baqir, *Risāla-i Sayf al Ṣāram*, 21.

58 *Gazetteer of Kashmir and Ladak Together with Routes in the Territories of the Maharaja of Jammu and Kashmir* (Calcutta: Superintendent Government Printing Press, 1890), 496.
59 Author's interview Shaykh Muhammad Shafʿi, Srinagar, 2021.
60 The work was completed in Srinagar in 1264 AH/1847 CE, with the initial sections composed at Skardu, Personal collection, Munshi Altaf, Srinagar.
61 See Muhammad Ḥasan Ḥasrat, *Tārīkh-i Adbiyat-i Baltistan* (Rawalpindi: T.S. Printer, 1992), 159.
62 Author's interview, Ḥasan Ḥasrat, Skardu, 2021.
63 The name of the ʿalim is not mentioned in the report. See *Revised List of Ruling Princes Chiefs and Leading Personages of Jammu and Kashmir State and Gilgit Agency* (New Delhi: Government of India Press), 20–1.
64 Lawrence, *The Valley of Kashmir*, 378.
65 Sufi, *Kashir*, vol. ii, 578.
66 Bāqir, *Risāla-i Sayf al Ṣāram*, 16.
67 Author's interview, Munshi Ghulām Hasan, Srinagar, 2017.
68 J. Duguid, Letters from India and Kashmir: Written 1870; Illustrated and Annotated 1873 (London: George Bells and Sons, 1874), 203–6. We find a similar description in Marion Doughty's account about a visit to the *kothi* of a leading silversmith in the city. For details, see Marion Doughty, *Afoot through the Kashmir Valleys* (London: Sands & Company, 1901), 159–65.
69 This was followed by an informal visit in October 1924, for details see Yvonne Fitzroy, *Courts and Camps in India: Impressions of a Viceregal Tours, 1921-1924* (London: Methuen, 1926), 217.
70 Fitzroy, *Courts and camps in India*, 222.
71 "the Maharajah, who every evening steamed up and down the watery highway of the city, [. . .] much to the delight of his faithful subjects, who clustered like bees on every commanding point that afforded a view of the royal progress." W. Wakefield, *The Happy Valley Sketches of the Kashmir and the Kashmiris* (London: Sampson Low, Marston, Searle, & Rivington, 1879), 168.
72 Ibid., 115.
73 Along the Jhelum riverfront, the showroom of H.R. Jailal the silversmith, and Tarachand-Arjandev silversmith and banker were the only two major, non-Muslim establishments, both at Fateh Kadal.
74 Petrocokino mentions Bahar Khān (*sic*. Shāh) and Samad Shāh as renowned establishments for not only acquiring shawls but also acted as providers of boats, tents, furniture, and bankers, see Ambrose Petrocokino *Cashmere, Three Weeks in a Houseboat* (New York: Longmans, Green, 1920), 67.
75 J.L.K. Jalālī, *Handbook to Kashmir* (Srinagar, 1933), 161–2.
76 See Syed Ali Nadeem Rezavi, "Bazars and Markets in Medieval India," *Studies in People's History* 2, no.1 (2015): 61–70.
77 W. Burns Thomson, *Seedtime in Kashmir* (London: James Nisbet & Co', 1875), 78.
78 See F. Ward Denys, *Our Summer in the Vale of Kashmir* (Washington: James William Bryan Press, 1915).
79 This bazar which still exists as one of the major wholesale markets of the city is today remembered as Maharaj Gunj, its original name all but forgotten. In subsequent decades, especially in the first half of twentieth century, after the introduction of motorized transportation, many residents living along major roads, opened shops on the ground floor of their homes, given rise to a new urban

morphology in which continuous linear lines of shops opening onto major roads define the market in major town and cities of Kashmir

80 Oscar Eckenstein, *The Karakorams and Kashmir; An Account of a Journey* (London: T.F. Unwin, 1896), 19.

81 In the aftermath of Kashmir's accession to India in 1947, Hari Singh was forced to appoint his son, Karan Singh as the Prince Regent. He continued in his titular post of Maharaja till 1952 when the title was abolished.

82 More than fifty European travelogues written during this period also touch upon Kashmir.

83 'I found the native dealer very objectionable. He is difficult to avoid.', Eckenstein, *The Karakorams and Kashmir*, 17. For a similar account, see Walter Del Mar, *The Romantic East, Burma, Assam, & Kashmir* (London: Adam and Charles black, 1906) and T. R. Swinburne, *A Holiday in the Happy Valley, with Pen and Pencil* (London: Smith, Elder & Co., 1907).

84 Eckenstein, *The Karakorams and Kashmir*, 19–20.

85 In a visiting card of the firm reproduced in 1900, the name is mentioned as M. H. Suffdur Mogol, it is possible that the MH in card referred to another of the Wani brothers, Muhammad Ḥaidar. Both Muhammad Ḥaidar and Ṣafdar ʿAli died childless, the firm being inherited by Ghulām Ḥusayn's children. The use of Mogol rather than the family surname Wani, might have been done to attract European fascination with the Mughals. For details, see Isabel Savory, *A Sportswoman in India* (London: Hutchinson & Co., 1900), 193.

86 In the 1950s the firm would re-establish itself at the *Bund*, operating from a houseboat moored on the river, Author's interview, Muzaffar Wānī, Srinagar, 2021.

87 Savory, *A Sportswoman in India*, 193–4.

88 See Brigid Keenan, *Travels in Kashmir* (Delhi: Oxford University Press, 1989).

89 Jalālī, *Handbook to Kashmir* (Srinagar, 1933), 157–64.

90 The city would be officially opened by the Viceroy, Lord Irwin, as the new capital of British Raj on 10th October 1931.

91 Jalālī, *Handbook to Kashmir*, 161–2.

92 *Gazetteer of the Rawalpindi District, 1893-1894* (Lahore: Civil and Military Gazette, 1895), 257.

93 According to Qāsim Bābā's son, Zulfikar Bābā this happened in late 1930s, thought according to Malik Mahdi grandson of Qāsim's brother, Mustafa Bābā, the first establishment was set up in 1925 by Mustafa Bābā. Author's interview, Zulfikar Bābā, Washington, 2021 and Malik Mahdi, Srinagar, 2021.

94 Hamdanī, *Tārīkh-i Shiyan-i Kashmir*, 360–1.

95 It was on account of his long reign, that Pratap was also referred to as "*Budhi Raza*," the Old King.

96 For a narrative sympathetic to Pratap, see Madhvi Yasin, *British Paramountcy in Kashmir, 1876–1894* (New Delhi: Atlantic Publishers, 1984).

97 Yasin, *British Paramountcy in Kashmir*, 33, 39.

98 It was on May 9, 1865, that Elmslie opened the first dispensary for Kashmir Medical Mission, at Srinagar. See Thomson, *Seedtime in Kashmir*, 96.

99 Ashley Carus-Wilson, *Irene Petrie, Missionary to Kashmir* (London: Hodder& Stoughton, 1903), 118.

100 Thomson, *Seedtime in Kashmir*, 81.

101 "In the month of April 1864, Mr. Clark, accompanied by Mrs. Clark, and having with him some reliable native assistants, re-entered the valley [. . .]. On their arrival

at Srinagar, they were at once mobbed by a crowd of a thousand people, who threatened to set the house on fire, some of them coming within the compound and throwing stones.", Thomson, *Seedtime in Kashmir*, 81.

102 Ibid., 97.

103 Ibid., 100–1.

104 Ibid., 212.

105 Neve would set up the Kashmir Mission Hospital in 1880, and this was followed by the Kashmir State Leper hospital in 1891. For details, see Ernst F. Neve, *The Pir Panjal: Life and Missionary Enterprise in Kashmir* (London: Church Missionary Society 1915).

106 Neve, *The Pir Panjal: Life and Missionary Enterprise in Kashmir*, 30.

107 Also written as Itchgham, the village is located in the district of Budgam in Central Kashmir.

108 Ashley Carus-Wilson, *Irene Petrie, a Biography* (New York: Fleming H. Revell Company, 1901), 285.

109 See Thomson, *Seedtime in Kashmir.*

110 Also see *The Ministry of Healing in India: Handbook of Christian Medical Association of India* (Weselyan Mission Press, 1932).

111 Thomson, *Seedtime in Kashmir*, 114.

112 For details, see C. E. Tyndale Biscoe, *Kashmir in Sunlight & Shade* (London: Seeley, Service & Co., 1922).

113 Hamdanī, *Tārīkh-i Shiyan-i Kashmir*, 30.

114 Ibid., 259.

115 Author's interview, Aga Faisal Qizalbash, Srinagar, 2021.

116 On *Anjuman-i Ḥimayat-al Islam*, see S. M. Ikram, *Indian Muslims and Partition of India* (Delhi: Atlantic Publishers, 1992), 207.

117 See Rai, *Hindu Rulers, Muslim Subjects.*

118 See Isḥāq, *Nida-i Ḥaq*. Also see, *Dastāvizat* (Srinagar: Research Library, MS. 3049).

119 For details, see Munshi Ḥasan ʿAli, *Anjuman-i Imamia Srinagar* (Srinagar: 1324 AH/1906 CE).

120 Ali, *Anjuman-i Imamia*, 4, 5.

121 See Munshi Ḥasan, ʿAli, *Anjuman-i Imamia Srinagar* (Srinagar: 1325 AH/1907 CE).

122 Still, the *Anjuman* did operate seventeen madrasas, including one at Maharaj Gunj the main commercial heart of the city with a negligible Shiʿi presence. However, most of these madrasas were short-lived.

123 Private Collection, Dr Ifthikhar Munshi, Srinagar, 2020.

124 Hamdanī, *Tārīkh-i Shiyan-i Kashmir*, 262.

125 Deykah, *Raʿyis Nāma-i Kashmir*, ff. 33.

126 Hamdanī, *Tārīkh-i Shiyan-i Kashmir*, 287.

127 The inhabitants of Ashraf Moḥala commenced work at the site by clearing the debris of the previous building which had been burned by the Afghans. They donated some of their own land for the expansion of the building and also contributed 1400 work days of labor. For details, see Sajād, *Dastāvizat Tʿamir-i Imāmbāda Hassanabad.*

128 Munshi Ḥasan ʿAli, *Tārīkh-i Kashmir*, reproduced in Hamdani, *Tārīkh-i Shiyan-i Kashmir*, 207.

129 Isḥāq, *Nida-i Ḥaq*, 72.

130 According to Isḥāq, Rasūl Shāh's opponents used to refer to him as Rasūl *Rāfiz*. See Isḥāq, *Nida-i Ḥaq*.

131 Similarly, from the first quarter of twentieth century we find in the vernacular, Kashmiri Sunni referring to the Shiʿi as "*khudhi*" a somewhat neutral counterpart to the derogatory slur, *rāfizī*.
132 Hamdanī, *Tārīkh-i Shiyan-i Kashmir*, 269.
133 The book is titled *Miraj-al Falah Minhaj-al Salah*, though it became more popular under the name *Kāshir Kitāb* (The Kashmiri Book). It is considered among the first work of prose undertaken in Kashmiri. Author's interview, Maqbool Sajjid, Srinagar, 2021.
134 Isḥāq, *Nida-i Ḥaq*, 47.
135 *Anjuman-i Bahbūdī Shiyan-i Kashmir, Agraz-o Makasid* (Srinagar: KPCM, 1351 AH/1932 CE), 3.
136 File Records, *Anjuman-i Bahbūdī Shiyan-i Kashmir*, Personal collection, Hakim Shaukat Ali Hamdani, Srinagar.
137 *Masl'ia Nimaz-i Juma* (Srinagar: Kashmir Printing Press, undated). The tract was published by *Anjuman-i Bahbūdī Shiyan-i Kashmir*, though the name of the organization does not appear in the publication. Author's interview, Munshi Ghulām Hassan, Srinagar, 2018.
138 It is not clear whether this is Grand Ayatollah Mīrzā Mahdi al-Shirazī (d. 1961) or his contemporary and cousin, Grand Ayatollah Mīrzā 'Abd al -Hadī Shirazī (d. 1962). See *Masl'ia Nimaz-i Juma*.
139 Born in Lahore in 1288 AH/1871 CE to a respected scholar Sayyid Abū'l Qāsim, Haʿirī completed his learning in Iraq and like his father maintained great interest in the affairs of Kashmiri Shiʿi. He also wrote his support for the organizers of the Kashmir Conference held in Gujranwala, Punjab in 1929, which provided an opportunity to voice support for the freedom of Kashmiri Muslims against the Dogra rule. For details, see Kashmiri, *Danishnama-i Shiyān-i Kashmir*, 294.
140 *Masl'ia Nimaz-i Juma*, 3.
141 Ibid., 6.
142 This is based on popular interpretation of a ḥadīth found in traditional Sunni collection in which the Prophet is reported to have said: Whoever leaves *Juma* three times without a valid necessity, then a seal is placed on his heart.
143 Ibid., 2.
144 Ibid., 3.
145 The stepmother of Ḥakim Ghulām Ṣafdar, *Anjumans'* first president, was the eldest daughter of Moulvi Ḥaidar ʿAli Ansarī, while his brother was married to another of Ḥaidar's daughter.
146 *Maktūb Ayatollah Abū'l Hasan Isfahanī baray-i Shaykh Muhammad Ḥusayn*, Personal collection, Prof. Shaykh Shafʿi, Srinagar.
147 Shaykh Muhammad Mahdi Kashmirī, *Khaṣāil-al Shiʿi* (Lahore: Fʿaiz Aam Press, 1910), 2.
148 In the Kashmiri Hindu society, a key reforming agenda was the issue of widow remarriage.
149 File Records, *Anjuman-i Bahbūdī Shiyan-i Kashmir*, Personal collection, Hakim Shaukat Ali Hamdani, Srinagar.
150 The editor of the newspaper, Ḥakim Ghulām Ḥusayn Makhmur, had recently completed his graduation and would also follow Isḥāq in his political career.
151 The belief in the efficacy of Shiʿi pirs engaged in these practices resonates in contemporary Sunni society, where some still seek them for achieving their

beloved, or educational, matrimonial, or financial success or health benefit. Author's interview, Sayed Mujtaba Gilani, Srinagar, 2021.

152 See Ḥakim Ghulām Ṣafdar Hamdanī, *Shiʿi Mūsālmān aūr unkey Jamūd key Asbāb* (Srinagar: Gulshan Press, undated).

153 See Hamdanī, *Shiʿi Mūsālmān aūr unkey Jamūd key Asbāb* and *Zulfikar.*

154 Hamdanī, *Shiʿi Mūsālmān aūr unkey Jamūd key Asbāb.*

155 Ayesha Jalal, "Negotiating Colonial Modernity and Cultural Difference: Indian Muslims' Conceptions of Community, 1878-1914," in *Modernity and Culture: from the Mediterranean to the Indian Ocean*, ed. Leila Tarazi Fawaz and C. A. Bayly (New York: Columbia University Press, 2002), 230.

156 None of the reformers in their writings addressed the issue of caste-based structure of the Shiʿi society, unlike their limited focus on the need to educate women.

157 For a detailed description of Shiʿi scholars of Kashmir, see Kashmiri, *Danishnama-i Shiyān-i Kashmir.*

158 Isfahanī assumed the position sole *marjaʿ-i taqlid* of the Shiʿi world around 1935 and continued in this role till his death.

159 Based on the Urdu translation of Isfahanī's letter, see Kashmiri, *Danishnama-i Shiyān-i Kashmir*, 321.

160 Foreign Department, General-B, Progs. January 1909, Nos. 15/16, National Archives, New Delhi.

161 Ibid.

162 Ibid.

163 See Yousf Saraf, *Kashmiris Fight for Freedom (1819-1946)*, vol. i (Lahore: Ferozsons, 1977), 333–34.

164 Though Hamdanī mentions the date as 1921, this seems to be wrong and given the chronology of the events he has listed, it should be 1923. See Hamdanī, *Tārīkh-i Shiyan-i Kashmir*, 398.

165 Saraf, *Kashmiris Fight for Freedom*, 334.

166 Hamdanī, *Tārīkh-i Shiyan-i Kashmir*, 399. Isḥāq on the other hand maintains that the *alams* were from the Khānaqāh-i Mʿaulā. See Isḥāq, *Nida-i Ḥaq.*

167 Saraf, *Kashmiris Fight for Freedom*, 335–9.

168 Ibid., 336.

169 Bishambar Nath Zutshi (ed.), *Bahar-i Kashmir*, October, 1924, 31 (Lahore: National Art Press), 31.

170 Saraf, *Kashmiris Fight for Freedom*, 336.

171 Ibid., 336.

172 Ibid., 338. Also see Hamdanī, *Tārīkh-i Shiyan-i Kashmir.*

173 See Bishambar Nath Zutshi (ed.), *Bahār-i Kashmir*, October 1924.

174 Muhammad Dīn Fauq, *Masheir Kashmir* (Lahore: Zafar Brothers, 1930), 23.

175 See Ayesha Jalal, *Self and Sovereignty, Individual and Community in South Asian Islam since 1850* (London: Routledge, 2000).

176 Another similar event took place at Jamia Masjid, Srinagar under the leadership of Mīrwaʿiẕ Yosuf Shāh (d. 1968), who was the political and ideological rival of Shaykh Muhammad ʿAbdullah. For an understanding of the bitter rivalry between the two, and the ensuing disturbances in the city, see Sʿaādat, *Tārīkh-i Kashmir ki roznama Dairy.*

177 During the tumultuous days of partition and an invasion of Kashmir by members of the frontier tribes seeking Kashmir's accession to Pakistan, Munshi Muhammad

Isḥāq, a Shiʿi leader close to Shaykh Abdullah was appointed as Emergency Officer for Budgam. This district still retains a substantial Shiʿi population. See Isḥāq, *Nida-i Ḥaq*.

178 For a contemporary account of these events, see Isḥāq, *Nida-i Ḥaq*.

179 For more on the tribal invasion, see Alastair Lamb, *Incomplete Partition: The Genesis of the Kashmir Dispute, 1947–1948* (Oxford: Oxford University Press, 2002).

180 After Kashmir's accession to India following the partition of South Asia in 1947, Shaykh ʿAbdullah governed the state of Jammu & Kashmir as Emergency Administrator from August 1947–March 1948, as Prime Minister from 1948–53 and as Chief Minister from 1975–82, when he died in office.

181 Nisar left for Najaf in 1964, where he studied under Grand Ayatollah Sayyid Abū'l Qāsim Khoei (d. 1992). Author's interview, Shaykh Muhammad Shafʿi, Srinagar, 2021.

182 Some of the articles published in an Urdu language Iranian periodical, *Rah-i Islam*, which gave a Shiʿi interpretation of pivotal moments in the formative period of Muslim history, gave rise to this Sunni disquiet.

183 See Rieck, *The Shias of Pakistan, An Assertive and Beleaguered Minority.*

184 Ifthikhar, a mid-level cleric, was the head of the *Firqa-i Qadim*, who dabbled in politics from early in his life. Over the years he would be associated with different political parties, with competing political ideologies, including the National Conference.

185 In the State Assembly, National Conference secured a comfortable majority, winning forty-six of the seventy-five seats. The main opposition, Indian National Congress, of which Ifthikar was the successful candidate managed to secure a mere twenty-six seats.

186 Often misrepresented as Wahabi's, the *Ahl-i Ḥadīth* emerged in the nineteenth century colonial India, with a *Salafi* background, ideologically linked to the reformist traditions of Shāh Walīullāh Dehlavī (d. 1762).

187 *Kumir* is the Kashmiri word for dove, and would signify sweet, melodious oration.

188 This legend was the most common Sunni trope signifying the deviant nature of the Ashura ceremonies. Among the Ḥanafī's this narrative was also propagated by Kazim Shāh Bukharī of the Ḥanafī Arabic College, Noor Bagh. Author's interview, Moulvi Ghulām ʿAli Gulzar, Srinagar, 2021.

189 Author's interview, Justice Hakim Imtiyaz Hussain, Srinagar, 2021.

190 Ibid.

191 As a participant in the Ashura procession, I have similar personal recollections dating back to the late 1930s.

192 These sermons were generally limited to the initial ten days of the Muharram, sometimes culminating in the Friday sermon preceding the Ashura. The main seat of operation of Mubārkī was the Bazar Masjid at Zaina Kadal, but some of the sermons were also delivered in the mosques at Barbar Shah and Gaw Kadal.

193 The anti-Ashura rhetoric of Mubārkī, nevertheless, was limited to questioning of the material manifestation of the Shiʿi ceremonies. It did not seek to question the Shiʿi historiography of the events leading to up to Karbala or to absolve the Umayyads. Author's interview, Moulvi Ghulām ʿAli Gulzar, Srinagar, 2021. For an overview of the Ahl-i-Ḥadīth in Kashmir and Mubārkī's role in it, see Khan, *The Ahl-i-Ḥādith: A Socio-Religious Reform Movement in Kashmir*.

194 In the 1980s, many of the public buses operating in the city would during the ten days of Muharram leading up to Ashura bear small black pieces of cloth to mark the

event. A vast majority of these buses would be operated by Sunni drivers. Similarly, from seventh to tenth Muharram the state television would refrain from playing any music on its broadcasts.

195 For details, see Hussain, *The Shiʿas of Jammu & Kashmir*, 427–28.

196 The death of Zia marked another episode of anti- Shiʿi riot in the city, after the Shiʿi were accused of celebrating his death. The incident happened during the month of Muharram, and one of the most vivid moments was the attack on Shiʿi mourners near Jamia Masjid, Srinagar. Given the disturbances, the Ashura procession could not be taken out on its traditional route in the city. Since 1989, the main Ashura procession from Abi Guzar culminating at Zadibal has been banned by the state government.

197 The militant organization, *Hizb-al Muminin* is the only Shiʿi armed group, but most of its attacks were limited against those Shiʿi who were perceived as being close to the Indian state.

198 A reformist movement that originated in nineteenth century colonial India, the Deobandi's operate within the Hanafī school, and have a strong predisposition to textual interpretations and condemning cultural practices linked with Sufi shrines of South Asia. In their public outrances, some preachers associated with the Deobandī's have openly censured Shiʿi as unbelievers, including in Kashmir where the sermons of young preachers such as Muhammad Nuʿmān Bhat (*Nowsherī*) represent this pattern of polemical condemnation.

199 See "From Domicile to Dominion: India's Settler Colonial Agenda in Kashmir," May 10, 2021, 134 *Harvard Law Review*, 2530.

Appendix I

1 It was common to address the servants of an important person instead of himself, supposing the matter was not important enough that he dealt with it in person.

2 Traditional introduction after the titles, beginning with "after." It usually goes along the lines of "After offering thanks to the <*compliments*> lord . . ." But the author feels familiar enough to skip this formality for the next, that is, "yearning for a meeting." This is mere courtesy, of course. The rest of the paragraph thanks for the previous letter, which must be praised according to the position of its sender.

3 Putting it this way, and especially with "my," indicates a certain familiarity between sender and addressee. A formal letter would have "Half-verse": and then the relevance, if necessary. Verses often close a paragraph but not here.

4 I suppose this is because the testimony was so brilliantly clear.

5 Unclear.

6 Here the writer assumes the informal *tu* = Urdu *tum*, indicating the addressee is a close friend.

BIBLIOGRAPHY

Manuscripts

Al-Biyāz Ibrahimī, Personal collection, Hakim Shaukat Ali Hamdani, Srinagar.

Abu'l Qāsim Muhammad Aslam, *Gowhar-i 'Ālam*, Bodleian Library, Oxford University MS. S. Digby Or. 133.

Bābā Dawud Khākī, *Qasideh-i Ghusuliya Yūsuf Shāh*, Srinagar: Research Library, MS. 1914.

Bābā Dawud Mishkwatī, *Israr-al Abrar*, Srinagar: Research Library, MS. 755.

Biyāz, Srinagar: Research Library, MS. 1656.

Biyāz, Srinagar: Research Library, MS. 1657.

Biyāz, Srinagar: Research Library, MS. 1658.

Biyāz, Private collection, Munshi Nazir Aḥmad, Srinagar.

Biyāz, Private collection, Sayyid Ḥabib-ul Lah, Reshipora.

Dastāvizat, Srinagar: Research Library, MS. 2492.

Dastāvizat, Srinagar: Research Library, MS. 3049.

Ḥaidar Malik, *Tārīkh -i Kashmir*, Srinagar: Research Library, Srinagar, MS. 39, 1856.

Ḥājjī Ghulām Mohyi-al Dīn Miskin, *Tārīkh –i Kabir*, Srinagar: Research Library, MS. 2044, 2045, 2046, 2048, 2074.

Ḥakim 'Ali Raza, *Dairy*, Personal collection, Hakim Bashir Ahmad, Srinagar.

Hawal-i Sarkar-i Wala Madar Maharaja Ranbir Singh dar Maamlah Gharat-i Ahl—i Tashi, Personal collection, Hakim Shaukat Ali Hamdani, Srinagar.

Jamia Masjid Heritage Corridor Conservation and Revitalization Plan, INATCH, 2009, unpublished report.

Khwāja 'Azam Dedhmārī, *Tārīkh –i Kashmir/Vaq'āt-i Kashmir*, Srinagar: Research Library, MS. 1836.

Khwāja Ishāq Qārī, *Chilchilat-ul 'Arifin*, Srinagar: Research Library, MS. 500.

Mahdah Shāh Deykah, *Ra'yis Nāma-i Kashmir*, Srinagar: Research Library, MS. 664.

Maktūb Ayatollah Abū'l Ḥasan Isfahanī baray-i Shaykh Muhammad Ḥusayn, Personal collection, Prof. Shaykh Shaf'i, Srinagar.

Maktūb Ḥakim 'Azim baray-i Moulvi Rajab 'Ali Shāh, Personal collection, Hakim Shaukat Ali Hamdani, Srinagar.

Maktūb Ḥakim Ḥasan 'Ali baray-i Nawab Fateh 'Ali Khan Qizalbash, Personal collection, Hakim Bashir Aḥmad, Srinagar.

Maktūb Mullā Ḥakim 'Azim baray-i Mullā Ṣādiq 'Ali Ansarī, Personal collection, Zakir Sayyid Younis Hamdani, Labertal, Budgam.

Maktūb Munshi Tālib 'Ali baray-i Nawab Murad 'Ali Khan, Khairpur, Personal collection, Hakim Shaukat Ali Hamdani, Srinagar.

Mīr Sa'ad ul-Lah Shāhabādī, *Bagh-i Suleimān*, Srinagar: Research Library, MS. 1194.

Mīrzā Mahdi Mujrim, *Dīvān-i Mujrim*, Srinagar, Research Library, MS. 350.

Mīrzā Muhammad Mujrim Kashmiri, *M'ayār Lughāt Qūyim: Firhangh Shāhnama*, ed. Murtaza 'Imranī, Tehran: Intishārat Sukhan, 1978.

Mīrzā Najaf ʿAli, *Ṣurat-i jamʿ wa-kharj-i māliyāt-i Qandahār*, Bodleian Library, Oxford University, MS. S. Digby Or. 173.

Mīrzā Saif-al Dīn, *Ākhbārāt wa Murasala Jāt Siyāsī wa Mulkī dar 'Ahdi Maharaja Gulab Singh*, Srinagar: Research Library, MS. 1420–27, 1429–30, 1433, 1434–36.

Moulvi Iftikhar Ansarī, *Maktub wa Shajrah-i varisan-i Moulvi Ḥaidar ʿAli Ansarī*, Personal collection, Hakim Shaukat Ali Hamdani, Srinagar.

Mullā 'Abd al- Ghanī b. Abī Ṭālib, *Jāmi al Rizvī*, Srinagar: Research Library, MS. 1225, 1228.

Mullā 'Abd al- Ḥakim Sāṭiḥ, *Kuliyāt-i Mullā Sāṭiḥ*, Srinagar: Research Library, MS. 535.

Mullā Abdul Nabī, *Wajiz-ut Tārīkh*, Srinagar: Research Library, MS. 1048.

Mullā Ḥakim Ḥabib -ul Lah, *Biyāz –i Ḥabib*, Personal collection, Hakim Bashir Ahmad, Srinagar.

Mullā Khalil Marjānpūrī, *Tārīkh –i Kashmir*, Srinagar: Research Library, MS. 800, 1074.

Mullā Mahdi, *Biyāz –i Mahdi*, Personal collection, Justice Hakim Imtiyaz Hussain, Srinagar.

Mullā Muhammad Amin Ghanī K ashmirī, *Manẓūm Manāẓirah Shiʿi va Sunni*, Srinagar: Research Library, MS. 1227.

Mullā Muhammad Muqim, *Kashkūl*, Personal collection, Āgā Sayyid 'Abd al- Baqi Rizvī, Srinagar.

Mullā Ṣādiq ʿAli Ansarī, *Al-Saif al Muntaqī ʿAli Mʿiānadī al Murtaza*, Srinagar: Research Library, MS. 1441.

Munshi Muhammad Jaʿfar, *Shajrah-Mullā khāndan*, Personal collection, Dr. Amjad Ansarī, Srinagar.

Munshi Muhammad Jaʿfar, *Shajrah-Mullā wa Munshi wa Jalālī khāndan*, Personal collection, Hakim Shaukat Ali Hamdani, Srinagar.

Naqal as Asal Hukumnama Maharaj zair tanazay-i Ahl-i Tʿashi, Personal Collection, Hakim Shaukat Ali Hamdani, Srinagar.

Pandit Birbal Kāchru, *Majmat-al Tārīkh*, Srinagar: Research Library, MS. 130.

Pandit Narayan Koul Aʿijaz, *Tārīkh -i Kashmir*, Srinagar: Research Library, MS. 1485, 1842, 2360.

Pandit Ram Joo Dhar, *Kafiyat-i Intizām –i Mulk-i Kashmir*, Srinagar: Research Library, M.S. 1913.

Pandit Salgiram Kaul Salik, *Qasida-i George Panjum*, Personal Collection, Munshi Ashraf, Srinagar.

Qāzī Mūsā Shahid, *Risāla dar Taṣawwuf*, Srinagar: Research Library, M.S. 1644.

Revised List of Ruling Princes Chiefs and Leading Personages of Jammu and Kashmir State and Gilgit Agency, New Delhi: Government of India Press.

Rūbakār az ʿAdalat -i Sadr-i Srinagar az misl-177, Faisla 13 Poh, 1925 Bikrami, Personal collection, Hakim Shaukat Ali Hamdani, Srinagar.

Ṣayfī Bukharī, *Risāla-i Faizha*, Personal collection, Justice Hakim Imtiyaz Hussain, Srinagar.

Sayyid Ḥasan Rizvī, *Majālis-al Abrar*, Srinagar, Research Library, MS. 3075.

Sayyid Muhsin Hamdani, *Groh bandi dar Kashmir*, unpublished paper, Florida, 2021.

Sayyid Sajād (transl.), *Dastāvizat Tʿamir-i Imāmbāda Hassanabad*, Personal collection, Mirza Muhammad Reza, Srinagar.

Sayyid Samʿi-al Lah Jalālī, *Shajrah Jalālī khāndan*, unpublished paper, Srinagar, 2021.

Shajray-i Tayibiya Sayyid Ṣāliḥ Rizvī madafun Haigam, Personal collection, Sayyid Akhter Rizvī, Srinagar.

Shaykh Muhammad Hadi, *Aḥwal-i khāndan-i Mullā Muqim*, Personal collection, Hakim Shaukat Ali Hamdani, Srinagar.
Vāthiqa-nāma, Srinagar, Research Library, MS. 574.
Yaqoob Laway and others vs. Gulla and others, 2004 (III), SLJ 761, High Court, Srinagar.

Official reports & Correspondence (Sources)

India Office Records and Library, London.
Jammu and Kashmir State Archives, Jammu & Srinagar Repository.
National Archives of India, New Delhi.

Unpublished Thesis

Bashar Bashir, *A Kashmiri version of Majmu al Tawarikh of Birbal Kachru with Commentary and Notes*, PhD. Thesis, University of Kashmir, 1997.
Solaiman M Fazel, *Ethnohistory of the Qizalbash in Kabul: Migration, State and a Shi'a Minority*, PhD. Thesis, Indiana University, 2017.
Suhanna Shafiq, *The Maritime Culture in Kitāb Ajaib al Hind (the Book of the Marvels of India) by Buzurg Ibn Shahriyar*, M.Phil Thesis, University of Exeter, 2011.

Books and Journals

Kashmiri, Persian and Urdu

Āgā Bākir al-Musavī al-Najafi, *Nafḥtah al-Najaf*, Srinagar: TFC Center, 2018.
Āgā Sayyid Ḥasan Mʿārakdar, *Irshād ul Jāhilīn wa Tanbīh ul Ghāfilīn*, Srinagar: Bardkar Press, undated.
Allama Sayyid ʿAli ibn Razā, transl. Sayyid Mohsin Kashmiri, *Kūhal-al Jawahir*, Karachi: MAAB, 2013.
Anis Kazmi, *Mīrzā Abu'l Qāsim: Maqām ti Kalām*, vol. i, Srinagar: Imam Hussein Research & Publishing Centre, 2002.
Anis Kazmi, *Mīrzā Abu'l Qāsim: Maqām ti Kalām*, vol. v, Srinagar: Imam Hussein Research & Publishing Centre, 2010.
Anjuman-i Bahbūdī Shiyan-i Kashmir, *Agraz-o Makasid*, Srinagar: KPCM, 1351 AH/1932 CE.
Anjuman-i Bahbūdī Shiyan-i Kashmir, *Masl'ia Nimaz-i Juma*, Srinagar: Kashmir Printing Press, undated.
Anonymous, *Risāla-i ʿIgala*, Lucknow: Maṭbah-i Islam, 1890.
Asun ti Gindun, vol. i, Srinagar: Ghūlam Muhammad wa Nūr Muhammad, 1903.
Bābā Dawud Khākī, transl. Qārī Saif-al Dīn, *Dastur-al Salikin*, Srinagar: Ashraf Book Centre, 1971.
Bābā Dawud Khākī, transl. Makhdūm Muhammad Khalil Qureshī, *Dastur-al Salikin sharah Virad-al Muridīn*, Srinagar: Sheikh Muhammad Usman & Sons, 2001.

Bābā Dawud Khākī, transl. S.M. Ḥabib, *Virid-al Muridīn*, Srinagar: Sultaniya Book Depot, 2012.
Bābā Ḥaidar Tūlmūlī, transl. Ghūlam Rasūl Faruqī, *Hidayet-al Mukhlisin (Taj-al Āshiqin)*, Srinagar: Bait-al Ḥilal Alim-o Adab, 2004.
Bishambar Nath Zutshi (ed.), *Bahar-i Kashmir*, October 1924, Lahore.
Ghulām Muhammad Mattū, *Tārīkh –i Shiyan-i Kashmir*, Shalina: Idarah Imām Zamān, 2010.
Ghulām Rasul Jān, *Jāmia-al Kamālat Ḥazrat Ishān Shaykh Y'aqūb Sarfī*, Srinagar: Indian Printing Press, 1995.
Ḥājjī Muhammad Aslam Khān Aslah, *Tazkira-i- Shoura-i Kashmir*, Lahore: Iqbal Academy, 1983.
Ḥakim Ghulām Ṣafdar Hamdanī, *Aūsh ti Āab*, Srinagar: Maktab-i Lalla Rukh, 1958.
Ḥakim Ghulām Ṣafdar Hamdanī, *Aūsh ti Āab*, ed. Hakim Sameer Hamdani, Delhi: Skyline Publishers, 2009.
Ḥakim Ghulām Ṣafdar Hamdanī, *Shi'i Musalmān aūr Unkey Jamūd key Asbāb*, Srinagar: Gulshan Press, undated.
Ḥakim Ghulām Ṣafdar Hamdanī, "Yad-i Ruftagan," in *al-Irshad*, Budgam: Anjuman-i Sharie Shiyan, 1381 AH/1961 CE, Shawwal issue.
Ḥakim Ghulām Ṣafdar Hamdanī, ed. Ḥakim Sameer Ḥamdanī and Maqbūl Sājid, *Tārīkh –i Shiyan-i Kashmir*, Srinagar: Imam Hussein Research & Publishing Centre, 2014.
Khwāja 'Azam Dedhmārī, transl. (urdu) Z.S. Azhar, *Vaq'āt-i Kashmir*, Srinagar: Gulshan Publishers, 2003.
Khwāja Shāh Niyaẕ Naqshbandī, *Chāi Nāma*, Lahore: Maṭbah-i Mujdadi, undated.
Maqbūl Sājid, *Ḥakim Ḥasan 'Ali: Shaksiyat ti Fann*, Srinagar: Imam Hussein Research & Publishing Centre, 2002.
Maqbūl Sājid, *Kaeshri Marsiyuk Safar*, Srinagar: Jammu & Kashmir Academy of Art, Culture & Languages, 2013.
Maqbūl Sājid, *Kuliyāt-i Ḥakim 'Aẕim wa Munshi Muhammad Yūsuf*, Srinagar: Imam Hussein Research & Publishing Centre, 2000.
Maqbūl Sājid, *Kuliyat-i Munshi Muhammad Mustafa wa Munshi Muhammad Yusuf*, vol. i, Srinagar: Imam Hussein Research & Publishing Centre, 2002.
Maqbūl Sājid, *Mīrzā Abu'l Qāsim: Maqām ti Kalām*, vol ii., Srinagar: Imam Hussein Research & Publishing Centre, 2003.
Maqbūl Sājid, *Mīrzā Abu'l Qāsim: Maqām ti Kalām*, vol. iii, Srinagar: Imam Hussein Research & Publishing Centre, 2011.
Maqbūl Sājid, *Mīrzā Abu'l Qāsim: Maqām ti Kalām*, vol. iv, Srinagar: Imam Hussein Research & Publishing Centre, 2010.
Maqbūl Sājid, *Naqūsh-i Khwāja Dāim*, Srinagar: Imam Hussein Research & Publishing Centre, 2006.
Maulana Muhammad Ḥusayn Azad, *Darbar-i Akbarī*, Delhi: National Council for Promotion of Urdu Language, undated.
Mazoor Hashemi, *Ḥusayniyāt*, Srinagar, 1996.
Mīrzā Ḥusayn Nūrī Tabrisī, *Badr Mush'ash'a*, Bombay, 1890.
Mīrzā Muhammad, "Ali Kashmiri," in *Tazkira-i Zafran Zar*, ed. Dr. Karim Najafi Barzegar, Tehran: Society for the Appreciation of Cultural Works and Dignitaries, 2009.
Mīrzā Muhammad 'Ali Kashmiri, *Nujum-al Sama fi Tarajim al Ulema*, ed. Mīr Hashim Muḥadith, Tehran: Sazman Tableghat Islami, 1967.
Moulvi Muhammad Shāh S'aādat, *Tārīkh-i Kashmir ki roznama Dairy*, Srinagar: Ghūlam Muhammad Nūr Muhmmad Tajiran-i Kutb, 1947.

Muhammad Dīn Fauq, *Masheir Kashmir*, Lahore: Zafar Brothers, 1930.
Muhammad Dīn Fauq, *Tārīkh Aqwam Kashmir*, Srinagar: Gulshan Publishers, 1996.
Muhammad Ḥasan Ḥasrat, *Tārīkh-i Adbiyat-i Baltistan*, Rawalpindi: T.S. Printer, 1992.
Muhammad ibn Y'aqūb al-Kulaynī, transl. Sayyid Ḥasan, *Usūl-i Kāfī*, Lucknow: Nizami Press Book Depot, 2001.
Mullā Ḥaidar 'Ali Kashmirī, *Risāla-i Fasl al Khitāb*, Lahore: Maṭbah-i Islamī, 1888.
Mullā Muhammad 'Ali, transl. Ghulām Rasūl Jān, *Tuḥfatūl Aḥbāb*, Srinagar: Jan Publications, 2006.
Mullā Muhammad Bāqir, *Risālah i Hidāyat al Dhalīl ilā Siwā' al Sabīl*, Lahore: Sahab Saqib, 1308 AH/1890 CE.
Munshi Ḥasan Ali, *Anjuman-i Imamia Srinagar*, Srinagar, 1324 AH/1906 CE.
Munshi Ḥasan Ali, *Anjuman-i Imamia Srinagar*, Srinagar, 1325 AH/1907 CE.
Munshi Ja'far, *Tanbīh ul ibād fī ahwāl-i Moulvi Muhammad Javad*, Srinagar: All Jammu & Kashmir Shi'i Association, 1377AH/1957.
Munshi Muhammad Isḥāq, ed. Munshi Ghulam Ḥasan, *Nida-i Ḥaq*, Srinagar: Markaz-i Ishayat, 2014.
Munshi Muhammad Ṣadiq, *Kāshir-e-Marsy*, 2 vols., Srinagar, 1968–9.
Pandit Hargopal Kaul Khasta, *Gūldastā-i Kashmir*, Srinagar: Sheikh Ghulam Muhammad & Sons, 1986.
Pīr Ḥasan Shāh Kuihāmī, transl. Shams-al Din Ahmad, *Tārīkh-i Ḥasan*, vol. i, Srinagar: Jammu & Kashmir Academy of Art, Culture & Languages, 1998.
Pīr Ḥasan Shāh Kuihāmī, transl. Shams-al Din Ahmad, *Tārīkh-i Ḥasan*, vol. ii, Srinagar: Jammu & Kashmir Academy of Art, Culture & Languages, 1999.
Pīrzada Abdul Khaliq Tahiri, *Awliyā-i Kashmir*, Srinagar: Gulshan Publications, 2003.
Pīrzadah 'Abdul Khāliq Ṭāhirī, *Muḥsin-i Kashmir ya'nī Ḥazrat Makhdūm Ḥamzah raḥmatullah 'alaihi kī sīrat mubārakah, ḥālāt-i zindagī aur karāmāt vaghairah kā tazkira*, Srinagar: City Book Centre, 2008.
Qasim Kalim, *Kuliyāt-i Khwāja Ḥasan Mir*, Srinagar: Imam Hussein Research & Publishing Centre, 2001.
Sayyid Abū'l Qāsim Rizvī, *Al Sādah fi Sayādat al S'ādāt*, Lahore, 1890.
Sayyid 'Ali, *Tārīkh-i Kashmir* (Chronicle of Kashmir), transl. Ghulām Rasūl Bhat, Srinagar: Center of Central Asian Studies, 1994.
Sayyid Anis Kazamī, *Kāshir-e-Marsy Hinz Tārīkh*, Budgam: Gulshan Adab, 1976.
Sayyid Bāqir Rizvī, *Risāla-i Sayf al Ṣāram*, Lahore: Sahafi, undated.
Sayyid Farzand 'Ali Khan, *Riyaz al Jinān*, Ludhiana: Maṭbah Majm'a al Bahrein, 1870.
Sayyid Ghulam 'Ali Khan, *'Imād-al Sa'adat*, Lucknow: Munshi Nawal Kishore, 1897.
Sayyid Muhamad 'Abbas, *Auraq al- Zahab*, Qum: Kitabshinasi-i Shi'i, 1974.
Sayyid Muhammad Ḥusayn, *Tazkira-i Beybaha*, Delhi: Dayiratul al-Muraif Iran va Hind.
Sayyid Muḥsin Hamdani Kashmiri, *Danishnama-i Shiyān-i Kashmir*, Karachi: MAAB, 2011.
Sayyid Murtaza Ḥusayn, *Maṭla'i Anwar*, Karachi: Khurasan Islamic Research Center, 1981.
Sayyid 'Ali Naqī Rizvī, *Daf'a al Mughālṭah*, Bombay: Maṭbah-i Muhammdi, 1889.
Shahid Budgami, *Kāshir-e-Marsyuk Tawarīkh*, Delhi: Taj Printing Services, 2014.
Shaykh Muhammad Mahdi Kashmirī, *Khaṣāil-al Shi'i*, Lahore: F'aiz Aam Press, 1910.
Ṣughrā Hemayun Mīrzā, *Rahbar-i Kashmir*, Hyderabad: Azam State Press,1930.

English

Abū'l Rahim al Berunī, transl. W.C. Sachan, *Alberuni's India*, vol. ii, Delhi: S. Chand & Co., 1964.

Ahmad Behbahani, *Mir'atul-Ahwal–i Jahan Numa*, transl. A.F. Haider, *India in the Early 19th Century*, Patna: Khuda Baksh Oriental Public Library, 1996.

Alastair Lamb, *Incomplete Partition: The Genesis of the Kashmir Dispute, 1947-1948*, Oxford: Oxford University Press, 2002.

Alex Shams, "From Guests of the Imam to Unwanted Foreigners: The Politics of South Asian Pilgrimage to Iran in the Twentieth Century," *Middle Eastern Studies* 57 (2021): 581–605.

Ambrose Petrocokino, *Cashmere, Three Weeks in a Houseboat*, New York: Longmans, Green, 1920.

Andreas Rieck, *The Shias of Pakistan, An Assertive and Beleaguered Minority*, Oxford: Oxford University Press, 2015.

Andrew Wilson, *The Abode of the Snow*, London: Willam Beackwood & Sons, 1875.

Ann Willner and Dorothy Willner, "The Rise and Role of Charismatic Leaders," in *The Annals of the American Academy of Political and Social Science*, Vol. 358, New Nations: The Problem of Political Development, March 1965.

Anonymous, *Bahāristān-i Shāhī*, transl. K.N. Pandit, Srinagar: Gulshan Books, 2013.

Ashley Carus-Wilson, *Irene Petrie, a Biography*, New York: Fleming H. Revell Company, 1901

Ashley Carus-Wilson, *Irene Petrie, Missionary to Kashmir*, London: Hodder& Stoughton, 1903.

Ayesha Jalal, "Negotiating Colonial Modernity and Cultural Difference: Indian Muslims' Conceptions of Community, 1878-1914," in *Modernity and Culture: From the Mediterranean to the Indian Ocean*, ed. Leila Tarazi Fawaz and C.A. Bayly, New York: Columbia University Press, 2002, 230–60.

Ayesha Jalal, *Self and Sovereignty, Individual and Community in South Asian Islam since 1850*, London: Routledge, 2000.

B. Hopkins, *The Making of Modern Afghanistan*, New York: Palgrave Macmillan, 2012.

Bashir Ahmad Khan, "The Ahl-i-Ḥādith: A Socio-Religious Reform Movement in Kashmir," *The Muslim World* 90 (Spring 2000): 133–57.

C. Latimer, *Census of India, 1911, vol xiii, North-West Frontier Province*, Peshawar: Commercial Press, 1912.

C.E. Tyndale Biscoe, *Kashmir in Sunlight & Shade*, London: Seeley, Service & Co., 1922.

Charles Ellison Bates, *Gazetteer of Kashmir and the Adjacent Districts*, Calcutta: Office of the Superintendent of Government Printing, 1873.

Chitralekha Zutshi, *Languages of Belonging: Islam, Regional Identity, and the Making of Kashmir*, Delhi: Permanent Black, 2004.

Diwan Kripa Ram, transl., Kirpa Ram, Sukh Dev Singh Charak and Anita K Billawaria, *Gulab Nama: A History of Maharaja Gulab Singh of Jammu and Kashmir*, Srinagar: Gulshan Books, 2005.

E.G. Hasting, *Report of the Regular Settlement of the Peshawar District of the Punjab*, Lahore: Central Jail Press, 1878.

Eric Lewis Beverley, "Property, Authority and Personal Law, Waqf in Colonial South Asia," in *South Asia Research*, Vol. 31(2), New Delhi: Sage Publications, 2011, 155–82.

Ernst F. Neve, *The Pir Panjal: Life and Missionary Enterprise in Kashmir*, London: Church Missionary Society, 1915.

F. Ward Denys, *Our Summer in the Vale of Kashmir*, Washington: James William Bryan Press, 1915.

Fanar Haddad, *Understanding 'Sectarianism': Sunni-Shi'a Relations in the Modern Arab World*, London: C. Hurst & Co Publishers Ltd, 2019.
Finbarr Barry Flood, *Objects of Translation: Material Culture and Medieval "Hindu-Muslim" Encounter*, Princeton: Princeton University Press, 2018.
Frederic Drew, *The Jummoo and Kashmir Territories: A Geographical Account*, London: E. Stanford, 1876.
Geneive Abdo, *The New Sectarianism: The Arab Uprising and the Rebirth of the Shi'a-Sunni Divide*, Oxford: Oxford University Press, 2017.
George Forster, *A Journey from Bengal to England through the Northern Part of India, Kashmire, Afghanistan, and Persia, and into Russia by the Caspian Sea*, 2 vols, London: R. Faulder, 1798.
G.M.D. Sufi, *Kashir*, 2 vols., Lahore: University of Punjab, 1949.
G.T. Vigne, *Travels in Kashmir, Ladak, Iskardo, the Countries Adjoining the Mountain-Course of the Indus, and the Himalaya, North of the Panjab*, vol. i, London: H Colburn, 1842.
Hakim Sameer Hamdani, "The Maarak and the Tradition of Imambadas in Kashmir," in *Marg*, September–December, Mumbai: The Marg Foundation, 2015.
Hakim Sameer Hamdani, *The Syncretic Traditions of Islamic Religious Architecture of Kashmir, (early 14th–18th Century)*, New York: Routledge, 2021.
Hamid Algar, "Allama Sayyid Muhammad Husayn Tabatabai: Philosopher, Exegete and Gnostic," in *Journal of Islamic Studies*, Oxford: Oxford University Press, 2006, 326–51.
Henry Landsell, *Chinese Central Asia, A Ride to Little Tibet*, vol. i., London: Sampson Low, 1893.
Ilyse R. Morgenstein Fuerst, *Indian Muslim Minorities and the 1857 Rebellion; Religion, Rebels and Jihad*, London: I.B. Tauris, 2017.
Isabel Savory, *A Sportswoman in India*, London: Hutchinson & Co., 1900.
Itzchak Weisman, *The Naqshbandiyya; Orthodoxy and Activism in a Worldwide Sufi Tradition*, New York: Routledge, 2007.
J. Dowson, "Route from Kashmir, viâ Ladakh, to Yarkand, by Ahmed Shāh Nakshahbandi," *The Journal of the Royal Asiatic Society of Great Britain and Ireland*, 12 (1850).
J. Duguid, *Letters from India and Kashmir: Written 1870; Illustrated and Annotated 1873*, London: George Bells and Sons, 1874.
J. Keay, *China: A History*, London: Hachette, 2009.
Jadunath Sarkar, *Fall of the Mughal Empire*, vol. i, Delhi: Orient Longman, 1971.
Janet Rizvi, *Trans-Himalayan Caravans: Merchant Princes and Peasant Traders in Ladakh*, Delhi: Oxford University Press, 2004.
J. R. I. Cole, *Roots of North Indian Shi'ism in Iran and Iraq, Religion and State in Awadh, 1722-1859*, Berkley: University of California Press, 1989.
J. R. I. Cole, *Sacred Space and Holy War: The Politics, Culture and History of Shi'ite Islam*, London: I.B. Tauris, 2005.
J.L.K. Jalālī, *Handbook to Kashmir*, Srinagar, 1933.
John B. Henderson, *The Construction of Orthodoxy and Heresy: Neo-Confucian, Islamic, Jewish, and Early Christian Pattern*, Albany: State University of New York, Press, 1998.
Josef van Ess, transl. John O' Kane, *Theology and Society in the Second and Third Centuries of the Hijra*, vol. i, Leiden: Brill, 2017.
Justice Hakim Imtiyaz Hussain, *The Shi'as of Jammu & Kashmir: An Analytical Study of the Shi'a Community in the State of Jammu & Kashmir from 1324 to 1947AD*, 2 vols., Srinagar: Srinagar Publishing House.

Justin Jones, *Khandan-i-Ijtihad: Genealogy, History, and Authority in a Household of 'ulama in Modern South Asia*, Cambridge University Press: 2019.

K. Lalita and Susie J. Tharu (eds.) *Women Writing in India: 600 BC to the Early Twentieth Century*, New York: Feminist Press.

K.N. Pandita (transl.), *Tuḥfatūl Aḥbāb: A Muslim Missionary in Medieval Kashmir: Being English Translation of Tuḥfatūl Aḥbāb*, New Delhi: Eurasian Human Rights Forum, 2009, 118–19.

Kalhānā, transl. M.A. Stein, *Rajatarangini*, Srinagar: Gulshan Books, 2007.

Kalhānā Jonarāja, Shuka Shrivara, et al., transl. J.C. Dutt, *Rajatarangini: Kings of Kashmira, a Translation of Sanskrit Work*, 3 vols., Srinagar: Gulshan Books, 2009.

Lloyd Ridgeon (ed.), *Shi'i Islam and Identity: Religion, Politics and Change in the Global Muslim Community*, London: I.B. Tauris, 2012.

Louis E. French and Ranjit Singh, *The Shawl, and the Kaukab-i Iqbal-i Punjab in Sikh Formation: Religion, Culture, Theory*, vol. ii, Issue 1/2, London: Taylor and Francis, April-August, 2015.

M. Aurel Stein, *Sand-Buried Ruins of Khotan*, Cambridge: Cambridge University Press, 2014.

Madhvi Yasin, *British Paramountcy in Kashmir, 1876-1894*, New Delhi: Atlantic Publishers, 1984.

Marion Doughty, *Afoot through the Kashmir Valleys*, London: Sands & Company, 1901.

Maryam Ekhtiar, Sheila R. Canby, Navina Haidar, and Priscilla P. Soucek (eds.), *Masterpieces from the Department of Islamic Art in The Metropolitan Museum of Art*, New York: The Metropolitan Museum of Art, 2011.

Meir Litvak, *Shi 'i Scholars of Nineteenth-century Iraq: The 'Ulama' of Najaf and Karbala'*, Cambridge: Cambridge University Press, 1998.

Michelle Maskiell, "Consuming Kashmir: Shawls and Empire, 1500-2000," *Journal of World History* 13, no. 1 (Spring 2002): 27–65.

Mīrzā Ḥaidar Dughlat, transl. E.D. Ross Tārīkh-i, *Rashidī: A History of the Moghuls of Central Asia*, Srinagar: Gulshan Books, 2012.

Mohan Lal, *Travels in The Panjab, Afghanistan & Turkistan to Balkh, Bokhara and Herat; and a Visit to Great Britain and Germany*, London: W.H. Allen & Co., 1856.

Mohibbul Hasan, *Kashmir under the Sultans*, Srinagar: Ali Mohammad & Sons, 1974.

Mridu Rai, *Hindu Rulers, Muslim Subjects, Islam, Rights and the History of Kashmir*, Princeton: Princeton University Press, 2004.

Mrs. Harvey, *The Adventures of a Lady in Thibet, China and Kashmir*, London: Hope & Co., 1853.

Mushirul Hasan, "Traditional Rites and Contested Meanings: Sectarian Strife in Colonial Lucknow," *Economic and Political Weekly* 31, no. 9 (March 2, 1996): 548.

Muzaffar Khan, *Kashmiri Muslims: An Historical Outline*, 2 vols., Srinagar: Humanizer Publications, 2012.

Nader Hashemi and Danny Postel (eds.), *Sectarianization: Mapping the New Politics of the Middle East*, Oxford: Oxford University Press, 2017.

Oscar Eckenstein, *The Karakorams and Kashmir; an Account of a Journey*, London, T.F. Unwin, 1896.

Peer Hassan Shah, transl. Shafi Shauq, *Tareikh-e Hassan: A History of Kashmir*, vol. i, Srinagar: Jammu & Kashmir Academy of Art, Culture & Languages, 2016.

P.N.K. Bamzai, *Culture and Political History of Kashmir*, vol. iii, New Delhi: MD Publications Pvt Ltd, 1994.

Priya Atwal, *Royals and Rebels: The Rise and Fall of the Sikh Empire*, London: Oxford University Press, 2020.
Reginald Heber, *Narrative of a Journey through the Upper Provinces of India from Calcutta to Bombay, 1824-1825*, vol. I, Philadelphia: Carey, Lea & Carey, 1829.
Richard Temple, *Journals Kept in Hyderabad, Kashmir, Sikkim And Nepal*, vol. i, London: WH Allen & Co.,1887.
Robert A. Huttenback, "The Emasculation of a Princely State: The Case of Kashmir," *Journal of Asian History* 7, no. 1 (1973): 1–29.
Sajjad Shahid, "Strange Turns in the Fight for Equality," *The Times of India*, March 16, 2014.
Sayid Athar Abbas Rizvi, *A Socio Intellectual History of the Isna 'Asharī Shī'is in India (7th to 16th Century AD)*, 2 vols, Canberra: Ma'rifat Publishing House, 1986.
Shahzad Bashir, *Messianic Hopes and Mystical Visions: The Nūrbakhshīya between Medieval and Modern Islam*, Columbia: University of South Carolina Press, 2003.
Shaykh Abū'l Fażl, transl. H. Beveridge, *Akbar Nāmā*, 2 vols., Calcutta: The Asiatic Society, 2000.
Simon Digby, "From Ladakh to Lahore in 1820-1821: The Account of a Kashmiri Traveler," in *Journal of Central Asian Studies*, vol. iii, no. 1, Srinagar: Kashmir University, 1997.
Simon Wolfgang Fuchs, *In a Pure Muslim Land, Shi'ism Between Pakistan and the Middle East*, Chapel Hill, NC: The University of North Carolina Press, 2019.
Sir Alexander Burnes, *Travels into Bokhara; Being the Account of a Journey from India to Cabool, Tartary, and Persia; also, Narrative of a Voyage on the Indus, from the Sea to Lahore, with Presents from the King of Great Britain; Performed under the Orders of the Supreme Government of India, in the Years 1831, 1832, and 1833*, London: John Murray, 1834.
Sir Edward Thomas Gordon, *The Roof of the World: Being a Narrative of a Journey over the High Plateau of Tibet to the Russian Frontier and the Oxus Sources on Pamir*, Edinburgh: Edmonston & Douglas, 1876.
Sir Roper Lethbridge, *The Golden Book of India, a Genealogical and Biographical Dictionary of the Ruling Princes, Chiefs, Nobles, and other Personages, Titled or Decorated, of the Indian Empire*, London: Sampson Low, Marston & Company, 1900.
S.M. Ikram, *Indian Muslims and Partition of India*, Delhi: Atlantic Publishers, 1992.
Sohan Lal Suri, transl. V. S . Suri, *Umdat Ut-tawarikh*, 6 vols., Amritsar: Guru Nanak Dev University, 2001, 2002.
S.R. Wasti, "British Policy Towards the Indian Muslims Immediately after 1857," in *Muslim Struggle for Freedom in India*, ed. S. R. Waste, Delhi: Renaissance Publishing House, 1993, 1–24.
Stephen Frederic Dale, "A Safavid Poet in the Heart of Darkness: The Indian Poems of Ashraf Mazandarani," *Iranian Studies* 36, no. 2 (June 2003): 197–212.
Syed Ali Nadeem Rezavi, "Bazars and Markets in Medieval India," *Studies in People's History* 2, no. 1 (2015): 61–70.
The Ministry of Healing in India: Handbook of Christian Medical Association of India, Weselyan Mission Press, 1932.
The Pioneer Mail and Indian Weekly News, Volume 47, 1920.
T.R. Swinburne, *A Holiday in the Happy Valley, with Pen and Pencil*, London: Smith, Elder & Co., 1907.
Victoria Schofield, *Kashmir in Conflict: India, Pakistan and the Unending War*, London: I.B. Tauris, 2010.

Vincent A. Smith, "The Work of Sir M. Aurel Stein K.C.I.E.," in *The Journal of the Royal Asiatic Society of Great Britain and Ireland*, January 1919, Cambridge University Press, 49–61.

W. Burns Thomson, *Seedtime in Kashmir*, London: James Nisbet & Co', 1875.

W. Wakefield, *The Happy Valley Sketches of The Kashmir And The Kashmiris*, London: Sampson Low, Marston, Searle, & Rivington, 1879.

Waleed Ziad, *Hidden Caliphate: Sufi Saints Beyond the Oxus and Indus*, Cambridge, MA: Harvard University Press, 2021.

Walter Del Mar, *The Romantic East, Burma, Assam, & Kashmir*, London: Adam and Charles Black, 1906.

Walter R Lawrence, *The Valley of Kashmir*, London: H. Frowde, 1895.

W.H. Floor, "The Merchants (tujjār) in Qājār Iran," in *Zeitschrift der Deutschen Morgenländischen Gesellschaft*, Wiesbaden: Harrassowitz Verlag, 1976, 101–35.

Wheeler M. Thackston (transl. and ed.), *The Jahangirnama: Memoirs of Jahangir, Emperor of India*, Oxford: Oxford University Press, 1999.

Willem Floor, *The Persian Textile Industry in Historical Perspective 1500-1922*, Paris: L'Harmattan, 1999.

William Digby, *Condemned Unheard: the Government of India and HH the Maharaja of Kashmir*, London: Indian Political Agency, 1890.

Willim Moorcraft and George Trebeck, *Travels in the Himalayan provinces of Hindustan and the Panjab; in Ladakh and Kashmir; in Peshawar, Kabul, Kunduz, and Bokhara*, vol. i, London: John Murray, 1837.

Yousf Saraf, *Kashmiris Fight for Freedom (1819-1946)*, vol. i, Lahore: Ferozsons, 1977.

Yvonne Fitzroy, *Courts and Camps in India: Impressions of a Viceregal Tours, 1921-1924*, London: Methuen, 1926.

Zackery M. Heern, *The Emergence of Modern Shi'ism: Islamic Reform in Iraq and Iran*, London: Oneworld Publications, 2015.

Online Resources

Abu Majid Muhammad, *Tazkira Maulana Mufti Muhammad 'Abdullah Tonkī*, 2021, available online: www.dawateislami.net.

Encyclopaedia of Islam, Second Edition, ed. P. Bearman, Th Bianquis, C.E. Bosworth, E. van Donzel and W.P. Heinrichs, http://dx.doi.org/10.1163/1573-3912_islam_SIM_0377.

Encyclopedia Iranica, available online: https://iranicaonline.org/articles/lithography-ii-in-india.

INDEX

ʿAbbas Mīrzā 53
ʿAbdullah Khān 1, 37–9, 78, 162, 163
Abu'l Qāsim Muhammad Aslam 4
Āgā Ḥakim Baqir Qizalbash 116
Āgā Ḥasan Jān 53
(Āgā) Sayyid Ḥusayn Shāh Jalālī 11–13, 125, 152–6
Āgā Sayyid Mahdi (also, *Sarkar* Āgā Mahdi) 97, 107–14, 116, 117, 140, 142, 146
  leads ḥājj caravan 112
Āgā Sayyid Muhammad 140, 146, 147
  imāmbāda Budgam 140
  poisoned 140
Ahl-i Ḥadīth 158, 159
Aḥmad Shāh Abdalī 13
Akbar ʿAli Bānkā 137
Akhund Mullā Muhammad Jawad 49
Akhund Mullā Muhammad Jawad Ansarī 94–7, 107, 125
Alchi (temples) 3
ʿAli b. Abī Ṭālib (imām) 17, 18, 36, 46, 53, 62, 105, 129, 155
  Kashmiri *manqabat* 64, 65
ʿAli b. Mūsā Rāzā (imām) 93
  Rizvī Sayyids 93–7, 116, 124, 128, 129, 148, 150
ʿAli Shāh Chak 33, 34
Allama Sayyid ʿAli Haʿrī 147
al-Mahdi (imām) 3, 77
Amīr Khān Jawān Sher Qizalbash 16
Anjuman-i Bahbūdī Shiyan-i Kashmir 147–9
Anjuman-i Himayat-al Islam 156
Anjuman-i Imāmmia 141–3, 146, 155
Anjuman-i Nusrat-al Islam 140, 146
Āqā Aḥmad Bihbahānī 48–50, 52
Āqā Rahīm 41–4
Arab Spring 159
Aukut 83
Awadh 50–3, 73, 77, 80, 81, 93–8, 121, 124, 147
Ayatollah Abu'l Ḥasan Isfahanī 147, 150, 151
Ayatollah Ali Gulzadeh Gafuri 156
Ayatollah Mehdavi Kani 157
Ayatollah Mīrzā Ḥusayn Nūrī Tabrisī 112
Ayatollah Mīrzā Sayyid Muhammad al-Ḥasan Shirazī 111
Ayatollah Ruhallah Khomeini 8, 157
Ayatollah Sayyid Ali Khamenei 156
  office of *Rehbar* 160
Ayatollah Shaykh Muhammad Ḥusayn Nainī 147
ʿAzim Khān 46–7

Bābā ʿAli Najār 19, 21
Bābā Dāwūd Khākī 24–6, 34–6, 143
Bābā Ḥaidar Tūlmūlī 24–7
Bābū Nilambar Mukerjee 105, 120
Bābū Rishambar Mukerjee 107
Bagh-i Dilawar Khan 83, 121
  school at 140
Bahāristān-i Shāhī 17, 18, 30–3
Bulbul Shāh 17, 18
Bund 135, 137, 153
Buzurg b. Shahriyar 3

cast-system 108, 150
Christian missionary work 138–40, 142
  Dr. William Jackson Elmslie 138, 139
  muslim response 139, 140
cow-killing 55, 56

East India Company 54, 75, 97

Fateh Kadal (also, Third Bridge) 134–7, 139, 157
Fateh Shāh 19, 29

Firqa-i Qadim (also, *Firqa Ṣafdar Shāh*)-*Firqa-i Jadid* 107–9, 111–17, 139, 140, 143, 146–50, 156, 159
Franco-Prussian War of 1871 98

gendered spaces 125
Ghāzī Shāh 25, 27, 31–3
Gulab Singh 38, 78, 81–4, 97, 116, 120, 138
Gund Hassi Bhat 65

Ḥabib Shāh 27
Ḥadīth 45
  Ḥadīth Sa'ah 82
Ḥāfiz 'Abdullah 15
Ḥāfiz Kamāl 15, 16
Ḥājjī 'Abid 82, 83, 90, 92
Ḥājjī 'Aidī 97
  masjid at Zadibal 144, 148
Ḥājjī Baqir 77
Ḥājjī Khwāja Ṣafdar Bābā 90, 96, 99, 115, 129
Ḥājjī Sayyid Ḥasan Rizvī 112, 123
  wife 125
Ḥakim 'Abdullah 125
Ḥakim Ghulam Ṣafdar Hamdani 137, 138, 142, 149, 150, 152, 155
Ḥakim Ḥabib-al Lah 120, 121, 124
Ḥakim Mahdi 108, 109, 115, 116, 120
Ḥakim Mahdi Khān 52, 53, 73, 77, 93, 94
Ḥakim Naqī Qizalbash 120
Harsadeva 2, 3
Hasanabad 66, 103, 126, 129, 132, 137
  cemetery 44
  imāmbāda 101, 106, 145, 159
  mosque 41
  Mughal Mosque 55
  riots 38
Hindu-Muslim riot 154
Ḥusayn b. 'Ali (imām) 4, 9, 12, 38–40, 46, 47, 50, 59, 73, 80, 81, 92, 104, 107, 143, 144, 163–5
Ḥusayn Bayqara 18
Ḥusayn Shāh Chak 25, 32, 33

'Id 53, 144
'Īdgāh 31, 42, 55
ihtiyāt 82, 94
Isfahan 44, 45, 48, 122

Ja'far al Ṣādiq (imām) 45
Jalālī family 99, 104, 107, 114, 116, 124, 127
Jamia Masjid (Srinagar) 13, 15, 35, 36, 55, 66, 67, 70, 72, 85, 101, 157
Ju'ma Khān Alkozī 39

Kabul 6, 14, 16, 38, 43, 54, 57, 71, 94–6
Kamangarpora 84, 102, 107, 132, 146, 157
Karbala 9, 40, 46–8, 59, 73, 104, 148
Kasghar 43, 71, 105
Khālsa 54, 55
Khān Bahadur Moulvi Sayyid Rajab 'Ali Khān 37, 79–81
khums 10, 77, 89, 90, 93–7, 107, 108, 111, 112, 131, 151
Khwāja Ḥabib-al lah Nowsherī 16
Khwāja Ḥasan Mīr 80
Khwāja Ḥassī Bhat 39, 40, 62, 64, 86
Khwāja 'Īsā 14, 41–3
Khwāja Isḥāq Diwānī 71
Khwāja Isḥāq Qarī 25, 31
Khwāja Mohyi-al Dīn Gandrū 98–100, 132, 143
Khwāja Muhammad 'Azam Dedhmārī 2–4, 18, 19, 28, 30, 31, 36
Khwāja Muhammad Baqir Gundī 124
Khwāja Muhammad Dāim 64, 65
Khwāja Muhammad Fazil 40
Khwāja Sa'ad-al Dīn Shawl 153, 154, 166
Khwāja Sana-al Lah Shawl 103
Khwāja Shāh Niyaẕ Naqshbandī 71, 74–6, 99
Khwāja Zahir Dedhmārī 13
Kubrawī 3, 18, 19, 21, 28, 75

Leh 71–7, 130, 131

Mahanand Jeo Dhar 106
Majlis-i Chihlum 11–13
maktab (also, *madrassa*) 51, 80, 81, 123–5, 140–2, 146, 147
Malik Mūsā Raina 19, 22, 28, 29
M'ārakdar family 92–4, 108, 113, 116
marṣiya 62–6, 69, 70, 73, 77, 79, 80, 84–7, 90, 92, 93, 101, 103, 106, 119–22, 152, 162
  Sunni *marṣiya* writer 143

Mashad 44, 53, 82, 96
Maulanā ʿAbd al-Raḥmān Jāmī 23
Mecca 45, 46
memorandum to British colonial authority, in 1907 151, 152
in 1924 153, 154
merchants in the city 83, 99, 102, 108, 126–9, 132–8, 146
as *Aksakal* 76
decline of shawl merchants 98–100
depicted in *shahar-ashūb* 72
Iranian merchants in city 14, 41–6, 48, 59, 69, 82, 90, 95
Kashmiri merchants in Central Asia 71
at Leh 74, 75
Peshawar 96, 97
phyīr circuit 126–31
satire of Dekyah 101
at Yarkand 76
Mīr Hazār Khān 14
Mīr Muqim Kanth 13
Mīr Sayyid ʿAli Hamdanī 18
son Mīr Sayyid Muhammad Hamdanī 19
Mīr Shams-al Dīn ʿIraki 18–32, 36, 69, 93
shrine 92, 108, 159
Mīrwaʿiẕ Muhammad Yaḥya (also, Moulvi) 101, 102, 140
Mīrwaʿiẕ Rasūl Shāh 102, 104, 140, 141, 146
Mīrzā Abu'l Qāsim 124
Mīrzā Ḥaidar Dughlat 29–31
Mīrzā Lāmʿih 120
Mīrzā Muhammad ʿAli 83, 84, 86, 95, 96, 99–101, 103, 107, 115, 127, 129, 145, 152
family 116
son of Mīrzā Rasūl 83, 96, 97
Mīrzā Muhammad Kāmil Kashmirī 51
Mīrzā Muhammad Taqī 147
Mīrzā Muqim 33
Mīrzā Mustafa 145
Mīrzā Najaf ʿAli 74
Mīrzā Razā 39
Mīrzā Saif-al Dīn 78, 82–4, 90, 91
Moulvi ʿAbdullah II 125
Moulvi Ghulam Nabi Mubarki *Kumir* 158, 159
Moulvi Imdād ʿAli 12
Moulvi Nāṣir-al Dīn 104, 138
Mufti Muhammad Shāh Sʿaādat 101
Muʿammad ibn Yaʿqūb al-Kulaynī 3
mujtahid 48, 51, 52, 81, 90, 110–13, 148, 150
principle of *ijtihād* 82
Mullā ʿAbdu'l Ḥakim Sāṭiḥ 2, 51
Mullā ʿAbdullah Ansarī 81, 114
Mullā ʿAli Padshāh 49, 50
Mullā Fazl ʿAli Ansarī 80–2, 90, 94, 95
Mullā Ḥaidar ʿAli Ansarī (also, Moulvi Ḥaidar ʿAli) 110–12, 114, 116, 125, 128, 139–42, 146, 150
Mullā Ḥakim ʿAbdullah 86
Mullā Ḥakim Muhammad ʿAẕim 37, 38, 78–83, 86, 90–3, 120
letter to Moulvi Sayyid Rajab ʿAli Khān 161–3
succeeded by son Ḥakim ʿAbdul Raḥim 78, 120
Mullā Ḥakim Muhammad Javad 38, 39, 41
Mullā Khalil Marjānpūrī 38, 39, 41–3, 48, 66 67, 69–71, 74
Mullā Mahdi 120, 121
Mullā Mahdi Khatāʿi 80
Mullā Mahdi Mujrim 71, 74
Mullā Muhammad Muqim 48, 49, 51, 94
brother Mullā Mahdi 130, 131
daughter Fatima Begam 125
descendants shaykh family 124, 148, 150
school 80–1
Mullā Muhammad Qāsim Hamdanī 121
Mullā Ṣādiq ʿAli Ansarī 82, 95, 110, 125
Munshi Aḥmad ʿAli Ghazī 121, 122
Munshi Ḥasan ʿAli 102, 145
Munshi Muhammad Isḥāq 102, 107, 114, 149, 150, 156, 159
Munshi Mustafa ʿAli 106, 121, 124
Munshi Ṭālib ʿAli 84
Mūsā al Kazim (imām) 93
Mūsavī Sayyids 93, 94, 96, 97, 124, 131, 150

Najaf 46, 97, 110, 111, 131, 148, 151
Namchibal 116, 157
Ashura procession 84, 152, 159
Naqshbandī (order) 2, 3, 15, 23, 71, 75
family 99
Khānaqāh-i Naqshbandī 15
Khawājāghan-i Naqshbandī 78

Nawab ʿAli Rizā Qizalbash 81
Nawab Asaf-al Dawlah 49
Nawab Fateḥ ʿAli Qizalbash 124, 142
Nawab Ibrahim Khān 50
  compilation of *Biyāz Ibrahimī* 50
Nawab Nawazish ʿAli Qizalbash 81, 116
nimaz-i jamat 90, 92
  nimaz-i juma 147, 148
Nūrbakhshī 3, 5, 18, 20, 21, 23, 30

Pandit Birbal Kāchru 54, 55
Pandit Ram Joo Dhar 14
pīrs 120
  practices condemned 149
Pratap Singh 83, 115, 120, 138, 154

Qāzī Aḥmad ʿAli 62–5
Qāzī Aḥmad Dīn 64
Qāzī Ḥabib 32
Qāzī Ḥabib-al Lah 15
Qāzī Kadal 42
Qāzī Mūsā *Shahid* 32, 33, 35, 36
Qāzī Qawam-al Dīn 146
Qizalbash 47, 81, 116, 120

Rajā Birbal Dhar 57
Raj Kāk Dhar 78, 84, 91, 127
Ranbir Singh 97, 99, 108, 109, 113, 120, 131
Ranjit Singh 37, 46, 48, 53–5, 57, 79, 96, 120
Reshīs (native Sufi order) 3, 19, 20
  founded by Shaykh Nūr-al Dīn 20
Rīnchanā (also, Sultan Ṣadr al-Dīn) 17, 18

Saddam Hussain 157, 159
Sayyid ʿAbbas Shāh 61
Sayyid ʿAbdullah Shāh Jalālī 107, 108, 113–15
Sayyid ʿAli 17, 18, 22, 25, 27, 30, 31
Sayyid Dildār ʿAli 49, 50
Sayyid Ibrahim Qazvinī (also, Mullā Ibrahim) 89–93, 108, 162
Sayyid Muhammad Baqir 94, 132
Sayyid Muhammad Madnī 100
  shrine of 101
Sayyid Murtazā Ḥusayn 80
Sayyid Mustafa Shāh 60, 61
Sayyid Rasūl Rizvī 131, 150, 151
Sayyid Ṣafdar Shāh Jalālī 107, 108, 115, 116
Sayyid Ṣafdar Shāh Razvī 48, 81
  grandson Sayyid Abuʿl Ḥasan 81
  khums disposal 94
  son Sayyid ʿAli Shāh 48, 49, 81, 94
Sayyid Tūrab Shāh Madnī 129–31
Sayyid Zamān Shāh 103, 131
Shahmīrī 3, 17, 27–9
Shaykh ʿAbdul ʿAli 148, 149
Shaykh Ḥamza Makhdūm 2, 20, 21, 23–7, 31, 34, 35
  shrine of 34, 35, 67, 101
Shaykh Ismāʿīl 21
  son Bābā Fateh-ul Lah (also, Shaykh Fateh-ul Lah) 22
Shaykh Muhammad Abdullah 149, 155–7, 159
Shaykh Muhammad Mahdi 148
Shaykh Muhammad Mahdi Tabataba'i 48
Shaykh Muqim 103
Shaykh Yʿaqūb Ṣarfī 36, 143
Shiʿi Federation 159
Shiʿi scholarship in Kashmir 7, 48–52, 64, 77, 80, 82, 94, 112, 124, 150, 157
Shiʿi-Sunni riots 1, 7, 10, 13, 49, 59, 84, 157
  in 1762 16, 17, 21
  in 1788 39
  in 1793 42, 43, 47
  in 1801 38–41, 47, 48
  in 1830 66–73, 77–9, 81, 82, 98, 126, 130
  in 1872 89, 97–107, 109, 116, 127, 140, 143, 144
  in 1983 157
  first riot 36
  Naqshbandī involvement 75
Sir Henry Lawrence 81
Skardu (also, Iskardu) 71, 129, 133
  Mullā ʿAziz-al Lah copying *Zad-al Mad* 131
  Munshi Muhammad ʿAli at dispensary 131
  Rajā Aḥmad Shāh 84
  Rajā ʿAli Shāh 84
  Sayyid Fazal Shāh poet 131
  Sayyid Muhammad Taqi 131
Suffering Moses (also, Ḥājjī Ṣafdar Wani) 136, 137
Ṣughra Hemayun Mīrzā 11–13, 125
Suhrawardī 3, 75

Ustād Muhammad Ja'far 39, 86

Vazir Pannu 102

Walter R. Lawrence 83, 109, 120, 132

Yarkand 43, 71, 76, 82, 105, 129, 130
Yechgam 138, 139, 156

Zadibal 11, 27, 37, 38, 40, 42, 49, 50, 66, 80, 86, 91, 92, 94-6, 99, 100, 107, 112, 121, 125, 126, 128, 129, 132, 142, 144, 145, 158, 159, 162
celebrating Ali Day 155
cemetery of Baba Mazar 44
imāmbāda at (also, *M'ārak*) 7, 11–13, 39, 66, 67, 69, 73, 77, 78, 84, 90, 106, 152, 165
khānaqāh at 22, 30
murder at 142, 143
nimaz-i Juma 148
Pakistan Day 156
riots 16, 102
Zain-al Ābidīn (imam) 93
Zia-ul Haq 157
Zulfikar Ali Bhutto 157
Zuljinnah 152, 154, 164, 165

www.ingramcontent.com/pod-product-compliance
Lightning Source LLC
Chambersburg PA
CBHW062220300426
44115CB00012BA/2153
9780755643943